MW01620487

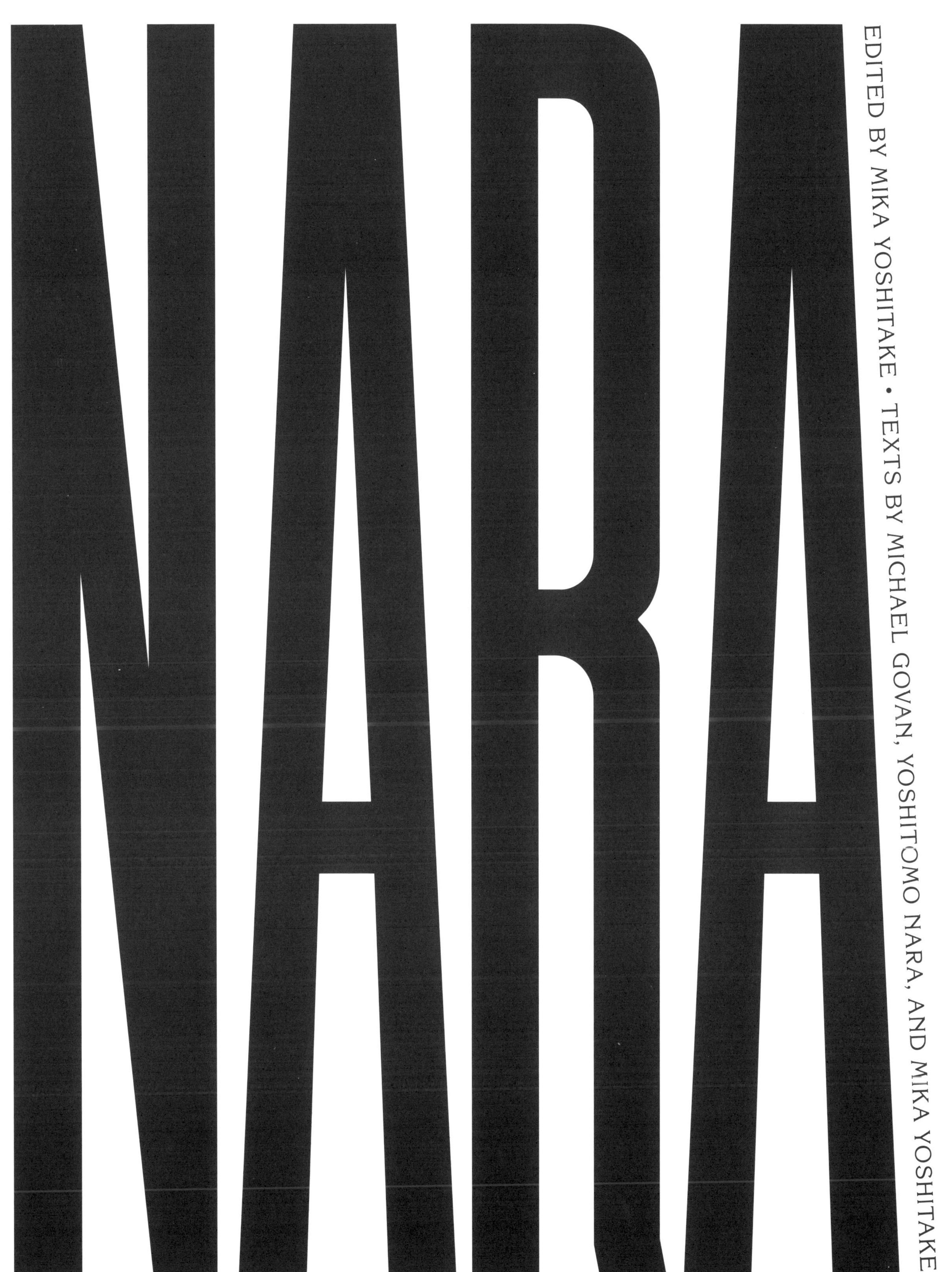
NARA
EDITED BY MIKA YOSHITAKE • TEXTS BY MICHAEL GOVAN, YOSHITOMO NARA, AND MIKA YOSHITAKE

LOS ANGELES COUNTY MUSEUM OF ART

YOSHITOMO NARA

FOREWORD

Yoshitomo Nara's art is known around the world but has not been the subject of a major museum exhibition on the West Coast of the U.S. This was the impetus for *Yoshitomo Nara*, a large survey of painting, sculpture, drawing, and installation intended to convey the breadth of Nara's work made over more than three decades.

In 2017 LACMA was able to acquire a large, beautiful painting titled *Girl from North Country*, thanks to support from Sally and Ralph Tawil. In a meeting in which the work was presented to our Board of Trustees, I saw one of our most senior board members—a former chairman who is an expert in nineteenth- and early twentieth-century European and American painting but not always receptive to contemporary art—staring intently at the work, which is a monumental, generalized portrait of a young girl. A little worried about his reaction, I stood next to him to hear what he might say. "Now, that's a painting!" he exclaimed, and proceeded to remark on the layers of subtle color and the directness of the composition.

It shouldn't have surprised me that Nara's painting would appeal to such refined tastes. The more I studied Nara's work, the more I uncovered the variety of his art historical interests, including twelfth-century Japanese Buddhist sculptures and handscroll paintings, Spanish Romanesque devotional figures and frescoes, Italian early-Renaissance painters (including Giotto), and modern influences ranging from British painters like Stanley Spencer to the School of Paris. Our big, encyclopedic museum, encompassing so much art history, seemed a fitting venue for a Nara retrospective.

It was in visiting N's YARD, the artist's new gallery project outside Tokyo (he resists calling it a museum), that I could begin to feel how all that art history collided with Nara's connection to the images and music of the present. Appropriately, visitors to that gallery, and our exhibition, first encounter a wall of album covers the artist has collected. Nara has said he received his earliest visual education through album covers. They are important in terms of image construction, but also in terms of the music they represent, which is a transmitter of culture.

Nara took his interest in rock and roll, and his upbringing in Japan, with him when he went to art school in Düsseldorf, at the center of European high culture. As he traveled throughout Europe, Nara absorbed deep art historical traditions, including the work of old masters (of which I am often reminded when looking at his drawings). As a result, it seems to me, his work blends his early interest in popular music imagery with a fascination with European art. Between East and West, between pop culture and high culture, Nara has invented something new. Marrying the directness and accessibility of music and album cover art with the subtlety and complexity of Renaissance paintings, his work is rich and resonant. That he can do all these things is what makes him special.

The publication you hold in your hands is not the kind of traditional catalogue that museums typically produce. As Nara already has a vast bibliography of scholarly publications to his name, we seized on the opportunity to do something different—something that would address the musical foundations of his practice. At an early catalogue meeting, when it became clear that a large retrospective book wasn't necessary, I offhandedly suggested we produce a limited-edition vinyl record. Nara was immediately receptive and developed the idea for an album of songs drawn from his personal playlist of 1960s and 70s hits, with one original song written and performed by Yo La Tengo, with whom he has a friendship. To our good fortune, the band responded enthusiastically and agreed to record several cover songs in addition to an original composition.

Side A of the record, performed by Yo La Tengo, contains "Blues Stay Away from Me" (The Delmore Brothers), "Wasn't Born to Follow" (The Byrds), "Roll On Babe" (Ronnie Lane & the Band "Slim Chance"), "It Takes a Lot to Laugh, It Takes a Train to Cry" (Bob Dylan), "Bleeding" (a new song by Yo La Tengo), and "Smile a Little Smile for Me" (The Flying Machine). Side B contains Geoff & Maria Muldaur's "Trials, Troubles, Tribulations," Andwella's "Saint Bartholomew," Bobby Charles's "Street People," Karen Dalton's "Something on Your Mind," Larry McNeely's "Mississippi Water," and Donovan's "Universal Soldier."

This print publication—which features an insightful essay by exhibition curator Mika Yoshitake and columns by Nara, previously unpublished in English, about still more great music of the 1960s and 70s—was conceived as a companion to the album, but also as a standalone book. Taken together, the book and album testify to the formative influence of the music of this period on the works presented in the exhibition. (We encourage anyone who is not inclined to purchase the limited-edition vinyl to listen to these songs on your favorite digital music platform.)

One important source for this exhibition is a number of conversations I had in L.A. and Shanghai with renowned art collector Budi Tek, who is an ardent supporter of Nara's work and was especially excited for LACMA to develop an exhibition that might travel. Budi Tek and his Yuz Museum in Shanghai are in an ever-deepening collaboration with LACMA, and we are beginning to share a number of exhibitions. We are so pleased this show will tour to the Yuz Museum, in addition to the Guggenheim Museum Bilbao and Kunsthal Rotterdam.

I want to thank Tim Blum, of Blum & Poe gallery, who lived in Tokyo from 1989 to 1994, during which time he worked with many contemporary Japanese artists. He met Nara in 1995 just after establishing his gallery with Jeff Poe, gave him his first solo show in L.A. that same year, and went on to represent him for twenty-five years. Tim is responsible for Nara's presence and popularity in Los Angeles, and has been both personally and professionally supportive of the exhibition. I also extend my gratitude to Arne and Marc Glimcher at Pace Gallery, who were extremely enthusiastic about the show from the very beginning and who have generously supported it.

I wish to recognize curator Mika Yoshitake, who thoughtfully and conscientiously guided this exhibition to full fruition, bringing her vast knowledge of postwar Japanese art to bear on its organization. Lucky for LACMA, Mika had just moved back to Los Angeles after many years on the East Coast when the possibility of working on this exhibition first arose, and she has navigated its complexities with grace and aplomb. Mika's efforts were supported on the artist's side by Nara's indefatigable assistant, Satoko Hamada, to whom we are indebted.

I also acknowledge the many great talents of LACMA Publisher Lisa Gabrielle Mark, who oversaw the publication and also ventured into new territory to produce the album with musical collaborators Yo La Tengo. In addition to recording a number of exquisite covers and composing a new song for Side A, Ira Kaplan, Georgia Hubley, and James McNew of Yo La Tengo advised on the mastering of songs on Side B, with Greg Calbi of Sterling Sound mastering the entire album.

When I first arrived at LACMA in 2006, the museum was celebrating its fortieth anniversary. One of the gifts it received at that time that stood out for me was Nara's *Black Dog*, from Peter Norton and Eileen Harris Norton, which was included in the 2019 exhibition *The Life of Animals in Japanese Art*, organized by LACMA's Robert Singer for the National Gallery of Art in Washington, DC. And while *Black Dog* made a lasting impression on me, paving the way for the later acquisition of *Girl from North Country*, I am deeply grateful for the opportunity this exhibition has afforded me to learn more about this important artist and his singular contribution to global contemporary art.

MICHAEL GOVAN
CEO and Wallis Annenberg Director
Los Angeles County Museum of Art

UNIVERSAL SOLDIER MIKA YOSHITAKE

> I was forging my own mental connections between the music and visual art.... I would embark on a journey with the songs and the [record] jacket to an imaginary world. I'd create my own translations of the lyrics in a way that had nothing to do with the English language, while I transformed the jacket image in my mind, kind of like imagining a music video.
> —Yoshitomo Nara[1]

Yoshitomo Nara's instantly recognizable portraits of wide-eyed but vaguely menacing figures have permeated the global art world, and he has become one of the most beloved Japanese artists of our time. As a young artist in the late 1980s Nara gravitated toward the anti-establishment ethos of punk music, which he had been listening to since the 1970s: lyrics by bands including the Ramones, the Sex Pistols, and the Clash appeared in his artwork, and he often imbued his figures with a sense of immediacy and riotousness. Later, Nara's work from the mid-1990s came to international attention as part of the Japanese "Neo-Pop" movement, which many associate with a playful appropriation and simulation of a wide range of subcultures. Spanning street culture, manga, anime, and underground music and upending modernist hierarchies of high and low, the art of this generation was dubbed "Superflat" by artist Takashi Murakami.[2]

Nara's immense popularity within the Neo-Pop milieu as well as the association of his graffiti-like drawings and paintings with rebellious punk culture have dominated the critical global reception of his practice to this day. After spending formative years as a young artist in Germany, however, Nara began to see his work more in dialogue with artists like Raymond Pettibon, and with American and European subcultures. Punk and rock music were the major filters through which Nara's work was presented in a 2010 survey at New York's Asia Society, with sections devoted to "Music" and "Rebellion."[3] The 2013 exhibition *Damage Control: Art and Destruction Since 1950* included Nara's *In the Floating World* series (1999), in which the artist defaced Japanese woodblock prints, showing them alongside the Chapman

1 Yoshitomo Nara, "Jūdai no koro, boku wa rekōdo jaketto de bijutsu o mananda" [In My Teens, I Studied Art through Record Jackets], *BT*, June 2015, 167. Translation by Chisato Uno. Reprinted in this volume, pp. 114–15.

2 Nara was prominently featured in exhibitions organized by Murakami. See Takashi Murakami, *Superflat* (Tokyo: Madra Publishing, 2000), and *Little Boy: The Arts of Japan's Exploding Subculture* (New York: Japan Society, 2005). It is worth noting the observation of one critic in Japan who saw the nature of Superflat to be predicated on "Japanese identity as an 'Euro-American other.' It became an ideology that controlled the reality of an uneven society. The ideology of 'postwar Japan = Superflat' was the product of a Euro-American orientalism." Minoru Shimizu, "Sayonara PC, sayonara innosento: 'Nara jidai' no gensetsu o megutte" [Goodbye, PC, goodbye innocent: Following the story of the "Nara Era"], *BT*, December 2001, 95. Translation by author.

3 Music was central to Nara's 2010 survey at the Asia Society, but the show focused heavily on the influence of punk and rock music on his artistic practice. See Miwako Tezuka, "Music on My Mind: The Art and Phenomenon of Yoshitomo Nara," in *Yoshitomo Nara: Nobody's Fool*, ed. Melissa Chiu and Miwako Tezuka (New York: Asia Society, 2010).

Brothers' *Insult to Injury* (2003), a series of grotesque figures drawn directly over Francisco de Goya's *Disasters of War* (1810–20) etchings.[4] While American curators and critics have drawn parallels between Nara's practice and punk's anarchic attack on establishment culture, a closer look at his oeuvre reveals the influence of folk music, which he had begun listening to and collecting years before his discovery of punk. This exhibition aims to reset some of the dominant perceptions of Nara's work by shifting the focus from the harshness and intensity of his earlier practice to the self-critical introspection and individuality that have become more prevalent in the quiet, contemplative work he has made in the last decade, particularly since the great 2011 Tōhoku earthquake and tsunami.

Music has been a passion for Nara since he began to listen to folk songs at age nine, and his relationship with music manifests in several ways. The artist's vast record collection is a testament to his great admiration for album cover art; as he has said, "Album covers were the first things that spoke to me as works of visual art.... For me, having been brought up in a rural area where there were no museums, this was my very first art experience."[5] Nara's love of music ended up providing him with an unorthodox art education: the images on record covers not only became signifiers for music but also introduced him to a vast array of artistic genres, with covers and their corresponding music merging in his subconscious. Today, Nara's studio wall displays a vast array of records he has accumulated over the past forty years, including folk, rock, blues, soul, and punk albums. Following his well-known immersion in punk rock, Nara has recently gravitated back toward a roster of singer-songwriters and folk singers: recent images of his studio show John Hiatt's *Overcoats* (1975); Chris Smither's *Don't It Drag On* (1972); *Anthems in Eden* (1969), an anthology of British and Irish folk songs; and albums by female folk legends Karen Dalton (*In My Own Time*, 1971), Linda Perhacs (*Parallelograms*, 1970), and Vashti Bunyan (*Just Another Diamond Day*, 1970). The image on the cover of the Hiatt album, showing the singer half-submerged in water, wearing his overcoat, inspired a motif that recurs in many of Nara's works, including *In the Deepest Puddle II* (1995; p. 24), *Fountain of Life* (2001; p. 192), and *In the Milky Lake/Thinking One* (2011; p. 80).

These records speak to an empowerment of the individual rooted in the countercultural revolution of the 1960s. When Nara first listened to the anti-establishment songs of this era, he did not understand their lyrics, but found that the album covers communicated the value of an ecological consciousness, the importance of individual liberation and morality, and a drive to return to DIY aesthetics.[6] For the young Nara, growing up in Japan among the ruins of war, the records and their covers served as sources of escape and eventually as a valuable form of self-empowerment, allowing him to deal with the complexities of living with the remnants of Japan's imperial past and in close proximity to signs of ongoing conflict.

4 Russell Ferguson, "The Show Is Over," in *Damage Control: Art and Destruction Since 1950* (New York: DelMonico Prestel; Washington, DC: Hirshhorn Museum and Sculpture Garden, 2013).

5 Yoshitomo Nara, "Artist Statement for LACMA" (unpublished statement, 2018). Translation by author.

6 Devendra Banhart, conversation with author, May 29, 2019. Banhart pointed to the zeitgeist of the *Whole Earth Catalog* (published between 1968 and 1972). "At a time when the New Left was calling for grassroots political (i.e., referred) power, Whole Earth eschewed politics and pushed grassroots direct power—tools and skills. At a time when New Age hippies were deploring the intellectual world of arid abstractions, Whole Earth pushed science, intellectual endeavor, and new technology as well as old. As a result, when the most empowering tool of the century came along—personal computers (resisted by the New Left and despised by the New Age)—Whole Earth was in the thick of the development from the beginning." Stewart Brand, *Whole Earth Catalog* (1968), accessed June 25, 2019, http://www.wholeearth.com/history-whole-earth-catalog.php.

Music's ability to convey emotional depth and atmospheric power finds a parallel with Nara's artworks. His work, which combines visuality, emotion, and often text, has evolved dramatically over the last three decades, from his earliest allegorical paintings from 1987 to his more recent portraits. He is best known for his portraits of vaguely ominous-looking characters with penetrating gazes, who occasionally wield knives or cigarettes, as well as heads and figures that float in dreamy landscapes. Nara's paintings from the 1990s and 2000s, in particular, are marked by layered brushwork and a kaleidoscopic palette. They stand in contrast to both the rougher, DIY aesthetic of his earlier works on paper and the smooth, highly polished fiber-reinforced plastic used in his early sculpture. Recently, he has shifted to a much more contemplative mode, making ceramics and sculptures in cast bronze whose mottled surfaces evoke the artist's hand. Expressing a kinship with the rawness of folk music, Nara has said, "If viewers are able to see beyond the impulsive and surface-level impact of [my] work, and sense a moving quietude and depth, then, no doubt, these effects are influenced by such music."[7]

* * *

Nara was born in 1959 in the city of Hirosaki in Aomori Prefecture in the northernmost region of mainland Japan, near an area once occupied by the 8th Division of the Imperial Japanese Army; his elementary and junior high schools were former army barracks. A latchkey kid, Nara often played alone while his parents worked, with an abandoned ammunition depot serving as one of his first "playgrounds."[8]

During World War II, the U.S. Allied occupation had turned parts of the imperial army site into its Misawa Air Base, which throughout Nara's childhood supported American war efforts Vietnam. One of the artist's earliest, most visceral memories is tuning in to the midnight Far East Network (FEN) radio broadcast that served the base. Living among past and current symbols of warfare while listening to news of the Vietnam War broadcast in Japanese and to American rock and folk, Nara had the sensation that the "entire area was filled with debris and ghosts."[9]

As the political landscape of the world changed with the Vietnam War, and as Japanese protests against the Treaty of Mutual Cooperation and Security Between the United States and Japan increased, Nara was captivated by folk songs of the civil rights era and anti-war rock music, and he delved deeper into folk through Appalachian music and its various roots in African and British ballads.[10] The footage of the war that Nara saw on TV and in newspapers was burned deep into his mind as he listened to these songs, and he felt he was experiencing the war in real time.[11] Alongside these anti-war sentiments, through these songs of angered

7 Nara, "Artist Statement for LACMA."

8 Mika Kuraya, "Where the Wild Children Are," in *Once in a Life: Encounters with Nara*, ed. Dominique Chan and Fumio Nanjo (Hong Kong: Asia Society, 2016), 124.

9 Quoted in Kuraya, "Where the Wild Children Are," 124. Translation by author.

10 Yoshitomo Nara, "Looking Back, When I Was in High School, I Never Thought I Would Pursue a Path in Art," in *Yoshitomo Nara: For Better or Worse, Works 1987–2017* (Toyota: Toyota Municipal Museum of Art, 2017), 6.

11 The bands and artists Nara listened to in the 1970s include Bob Dylan, the Byrds, Country Joe McDonald, David Bowie, Roxy Music, Lou Reed, King Crimson, Fairport Convention, Townes van Zandt, Eric Anderson, Randy Newman, Neil Young, Don Nix, Jackson Browne, the Eagles, the New York Dolls, the Ramones, Bob Marley, Dr. Feelgood, Patti Smith, the Sex Pistols, the Clash, Happy End, and Morio Agata. Yoshitomo Nara, *The Little Star Dweller* (Tokyo: Rokkingu On, 2004), 17.

youth, Nara developed a strong ethical conviction to always pursue what felt "real" based on his lived experience.[12] This revelation recalls the lyrics of "Universal Soldier" (1964), one of Nara's favorite war-protest songs from the time, which calls on individuals to take responsibility for war, rather than blaming nations, race, religion, or ideologies: "He's the Universal Soldier and he really is to blame / His orders come from far away no more / They come from here and there and you and me / And brothers, can't you see / This is not the way we put an end to war."[13]

One of the first American musicians Nara saw play live was Neil Young in Tokyo in 1976. Nara began working part-time and DJing at rock cafes in Hirosaki while immersing himself in all kinds of books, including the late 1960s underground, experimental serial manga *Garo*, famous for its non-narrative format.[14] One of the first works that Nara bought, at age nineteen, was a woodblock print by *Garo* artist Seiichi Hayashi, who designed the cover for folk and rock musician Morio Agata's album *Otome no Roman* (1972).[15] Nara's experience working at rock cafes and learning about experimental artists and illustrators helped arm him with a sensibility for album covers, which he later designed for bands including the Birdy Num Nums, Shonen Knife, the Star Club, and R.E.M.[16] Through this cover artwork, the artist has built an audience beyond the art world.

Nara moved to Tokyo to pursue art in 1978, and began studying painting at Musashino Art University in 1979.[17] Bored by the academic curriculum, he spent most of his time at record shops and attending live concerts of bands such as Friction, Lizard, Millers, the Stalin, and the Star Club, who were at the center of the "Tokyo Rockers" (Japanese punk and New Wave) movement.[18] During his second year of college at age twenty, he took a leave of absence and used his tuition money to embark on a backpacking trip across Europe. In February 1980, he headed on a flight connecting through Dubai and Cairo to Paris, then spent three months traveling by train through Belgium, Holland, Germany, Austria, Switzerland, Italy, France, Spain, and Portugal before eventually flying back to Japan through Pakistan. For Nara, this trip was the first time he was made aware of what it felt like to be a "foreigner": he remembers that children "burnt a hole" into him with their stares.[19] Yet he also developed strong connections with people of his generation who, despite differences in geographic upbringing or language, shared his taste in music, film, and literature. He began sensing an urgency to capture these precious moments of interpersonal connection, which transcended language, through his art.

On his European tour, Nara frequented museums with art historical masterpieces but was also struck by early devotional sculptures, such as the twelfth-century Mother and Child from the Church of Santa Maria de Covet at Museu Nacional d'Art de Catalunya in Barcelona. Drawn to the Romanesque style in which accentuated facial features reflect strong devotion, he saw an affinity with Buddhist sculptures, where strength

12 Nara, *The Little Star Dweller*, 16.

13 Donavan, "Universal Soldier," lyrics by Buffy Sainte-Marie (New York: Vanguard, 1964).

14 Yoshitomo Nara, "Hansei (Kari)" [Half a life (draft)], *Eureka* 49, no. 13 (August 2017): 236.

15 Yoshitomo Nara, "Jūdai no koro," 164. Reprinted in this volume, pp. 126–27.

16 Nara also provided the cover artwork for Fantômas's *Suspended Animation* (2005); Bloodthirsty Butchers' *Bloodthirsty butchers vs +/- PLUS/MINUS* (2005/7); Tiki Tiki BAMBoooos' *Cloudy, Later Fine* (2005); Absynthe Minded's *There Is Nothing* (2007); Bloodthirsty Butchers' *Don't Shoot That Guitarist* (2007); Jim Black's AlasNoAxis's *Houseplant* (2009); Momokomotion's *Punk in a Coma* (2009); Mara & The Inner Strangeness's *In Dark Places* (2011); *Naninimo Makezu: Songs for Children from ARABAKI* (2011); and Morio Agata's *Gusuperi Yōnenki* (2012), among others.

17 Nara was admitted to the sculpture department in 1978 and moved to Tokyo, but decided not to enter the program because he wanted to pursue painting. He was accepted into the painting program in 1979.

18 See Gin Satoh, *Underground GIG: Tokyo 1978–1987* (Tokyo: Slogan, 2019).

19 Nara, *The Little Star Dweller*, 24. Translation by author.

of devotion is proportional to the amount of stylistic deformation and presence. These traditions would have a direct impact on the figuration in some of Nara's first wooden sculptures and paintings, characterized by disproportionately small arms and tapered feet on rounded surfaces, as in *Don't mind little Q* (1993) and *Light My Fire* (2001).[20] While Nara was not exposed to contemporary art on this trip, he also gravitated toward isolated instances of powerful expressive techniques by artists such as Vincent van Gogh. His encounters with these works of art encouraged him to develop his own artistic method; Nara realized that although his art school classmates back in Japan were far more technically gifted than him, he could make work that was incomparable to the work of others and not tied to art history or technical perfection.[21]

In 1981, Nara transferred to Aichi Prefectural University of the Arts, just east of Nagoya in central Japan, where he would earn his BA in 1985.[22] He rented a tiny prefabricated home built out of two conjoined six-tatami-mat rooms, which measured less than two hundred square feet. Working part-time at a record rental shop, Nara focused on his art at home rather than spending time at school. He went on a second journey to Europe in 1983, connecting through Karachi on Pakistan International Airlines. This time around, while he did not set out with a purpose, he was able to observe the "spirit" of contemporary artists who were making art that was alive in the present—work that was not an extension of art history, but that opened up contemporary society and subculture.[23]

Through his experiences with contemporary art, Nara realized that his work needed to focus on his thoughts and feelings at very particular moments in time. Around 1983 he began making daily drawings, or what he called "graffiti": diaristic works that provided a cathartic outlet, reflecting his mood each day, but had nothing to do with the curriculum at art school. He also began producing a series of drawings he would insert inside plastic bags, which were sealed and inscribed with texts he wrote. For his graduation piece, Nara submitted a collage work: Japanese paper on a plywood panel that he picked up off the street and drew on with a colored pencil; the piece took him one week to produce. Despite his unorthodox methods, Nara was accepted into Aichi Prefectural University of the Arts' master's program, from which he graduated in 1987. He also began teaching prep school art students.[24]

In 1987 Nara headed to Europe a third time to see Documenta 8 in Kassel, Germany, and stayed with a college friend who had moved to Düsseldorf to study. He visited the Kunstakademie Düsseldorf and noticed that the students were not technically advanced, but had heightened senses of individuality, something he also witnessed at Documenta. Wanting to pursue an equally idiosyncratic art practice, Nara became determined to study in Germany, and applied to the Kunstakademie. To his surprise, he was accepted into the art school—one of the world's most influential—and studied in Düsseldorf from

20 Yoshitomo Nara and Erimi Fujiwara, "Welcome to Nara ākaibu! Sōzō no gensen ni ukabu itsutsu no shima" [Welcome to the Nara archive! The origins of creation that float on five islands], *BT*, December 2001, 84.

21 Nara, *The Little Star Dweller*, 26–27.

22 The bands and artists Nara listened to from 1980 to 1983 include Talking Heads, the B-52's, Kraftwerk, the Pop Group, Bow Wow Wow, Pigbag, Tom Tom Club, Devo, Black Flag, Nick Lowe, Yazoo, the Go-Go's, Tom Verlaine, R.E.M., Soft Cell, Guernica, the Pale Fountains, Echo & the Bunnymen, Madonna, Metallica, Prince, Cabaret Voltaire, and Japanese bands including the Roosters, the Stalin, Inu, and the Star Club. Nara, *The Little Star Dweller*, 28.

23 Nara, *The Little Star Dweller*, 35.

24 The bands and artists Nara listened to between 1984 and 1988 include XTC, Nick Cave and the Bad Seeds, Aztec Camera, the Pogues, the Smiths, the Red Hot Chili Peppers, the Stone Roses, D.A.F., Der Plan, Cobra, the Hooters, the Feelies, the Gun Club, Pussy Galore, Yuchoten, the Blue Hearts, Shonen Knife, the Sugarcubes, the Cowboy Junkies, Love and Rockets, Cocteau Twins, the Cramps, Nirvana, Soundgarden, Green Day, Sonic Youth, Dinosaur Jr., and bands on the 4AD label. Nara, *The Little Star Dweller*, 48.

1988 to 1993. During this time, he began frequenting Ratinger Hof, a club famous for hosting *Neue Deutsche Welle* (German New Wave) bands such as D.A.F. (Deutsch Amerikanische Freundschaft) and Kraftwerk.

At the Kunstakademie, eighty students were divided into four studios. At the end of their first year, they took an exam to move forward into their desired genres. Though Nara's lack of command of German made it challenging for him to participate in discussions, he passed the exam. He was invited by German painter A. R. Penck to pursue his studies and was granted a *Meisterschüler* (master course) title in painting. This was a period of great isolation for Nara, during which he was reminded of his adolescent years in Aomori. The two psychologically coincided inside him; as he recalls, "The sky above winter in Germany was exactly like the sky in Aomori. It was an unexpected rediscovery of an almost forgotten value."[25] Many of Nara's friends were ethnic minorities who lived in a dormitory that integrated students from a variety of schools; the most memorable were Vietnamese students who would tell him about family members who had died from Napalm attacks during the Vietnam War. Nara learned that Phan Thị Kim Phúc, the girl who was famously photographed running naked in the street after being severely burned from a Napalm attack, had been transported to various hospitals in Germany to recover and had eventually studied medicine in order to become a physician.

In some of Nara's earliest works made in Düsseldorf, allegories of good and evil collapse, and innocence becomes one with destruction itself.[26] In these fresco-like paintings, the composition is divided in half or in quadrants, and outlined figures with elongated heads wear halos, with their hands transforming into flames or knives. In *Untitled (after overpainting)* (1987–97; p. 29), for example, two donkey-like heads, each with a candlelight flame, float on top of each another, while on the right panel, rain falls from a manhole-like halo over the head of a praying blond figure. The words "*unter himmel*" (under heaven) are written across the bottom half, connecting the vertical break between the two wooden panels and creating a symbolic tension between dark evil and innocent light. *People on the Cloud* (1989; p. 28) touches more explicitly on these themes. A horizon line divides the composition between patched areas of blue (skies) above and yellow (land) below, with animals, people, and hybrid figures crawling along the outer edges of the frame; Nara masterfully situates these forms between the symbolic and physical planes of the piece. The head of a solemn girl is separated from the bottom half of her body while an angel on a cloud looks on in lament, holding a halo in her hand, and a praying priestess clutches a cigar-shaped loaf of bread in her mouth. Each figure is surrounded by anxiety and sadness, with gazes that verge on imminent violence. Nara deliberately combines allegory with abstraction, including patchworked sections of reworked paint that allow us to read the multiple elements as signifiers for a fraught ideology and interiority.

25 Nara, *The Little Star Dweller*, 54. Translation by author.

26 Noi Sawaragi, "Kiga to katsubo no e Nara Yoshitomo to anniya no sekai" [Pictures of starvation and craving: Yoshitomo Nara and the world of pleasure], *Eureka* 49, no. 13 (August 2017): 236.

Critic Midori Matsui has drawn on psychoanalysis to comment on the way Nara's works from this period "juxtapose heterogeneous details to suggest emotional totality" and resemble "the two dominant methods of image formation in dreams, condensation and displacement, while capturing the undifferentiated state of a child's psyche," with figures co-existing in different moments in time.[27] While this literary reading accounts for the multiplicity of signifiers in Nara's early works, the artist's ability to combine allegory with abstraction seems to open up a more affective reading that recalls the psychologically arresting portraits by abstract modern artist Saburō Asō, one of Nara's first professors at Musashino Art University.

Up until this period, Nara had for the most part illustrated the backgrounds of his artworks, but he began to concentrate on the figures themselves, simultaneously simplifying and intensifying their gazes by experimenting with their sideways stances and slightly off-center placement, and bringing them into a bolder and fuller focus against monochromatic backgrounds. "These blank backgrounds reflected liberation from the places that I had become familiar with. These works were born not from confronting the other, but from confronting my own self," the artist has said.[28] *The Girl with the Knife in Her Hand* (1991; p. 22) is a quintessential portrait from this period, focusing on a single, ominous young figure with gazing eyes who floats in an empty atmosphere that oscillates between an innocent violence and violent innocence. The figures in other works from this period wield knives or cigarettes; some of these works are also emblazoned with exclamatory texts. These figures' upward gazes invite confrontation, suggesting that the artist himself has become the antagonist.

Before graduating from the Kunstakademie, Nara showed his work in Amsterdam at Galerie d'Eendt and in Cologne at Galerie Johnen + Schöttle. In 1994, Jorg Johnen, co-owner of Galerie Johnen + Schöttle, found Nara a large studio in Cologne. The space was divided into three and his studio neighbors were sculptor Charles Worthen, who had attended Tokyo University of the Arts and spoke Japanese, and Dan Asher, a New Yorker who worked in a variety of mediums including video, sculpture, drawing, and street photography, and had photographed rock, pop, reggae, and punk musicians such as Lou Reed, Patti Smith, David Byrne, and Bob Marley. Nara lived in Cologne until 2000 and was highly productive, showing not just in Japan and Germany but also in Los Angeles, New York, and London. He spent a lot of time traveling back and forth between Japan and Germany, focusing on the production of large-scale fiberglass dog sculptures with the help of his friends and former students. This series would capture the hearts of many fans, becoming larger-than-life symbols for loneliness and acceptance that are as iconic as Nara's portraits.

27 See Midori Matsui, "Art for Myself and Others: Yoshitomo Nara's Popular Imagination," in *Yoshitomo Nara: Nobody's Fool*, 16.

28 Nara, *The Little Star Dweller*, 60. Translation by author.

The year 1995 proved particularly important for Nara. He published his first book of paintings, *In the Deepest Puddle*, which included a quote on the cover from novelist Banana Yoshimoto, whose books Nara would later illustrate.[29] The cover work depicts a girl with her enlarged head wrapped in bandages and her body half-submerged in rippling water that echoes her bandages and haunting, bean-like eyes. In 1995, Nara also had his first show with then-small Los Angeles gallery Blum & Poe.[30] The exhibition, *Pacific Babies*, included a sailor dress–clad mannequin with a gray-blond wig lying face down in a bed of white and yellow daisies, as well as a vernacular painting of a girl with tapered legs and hands standing at the edge of a long path to a house. While the sculpture collapsed innocent youth and the grotesque, recalling a hilarious and potentially violent scene from a Paul McCarthy video or Mike Kelley installation, the painting conjured a nostalgia for the unknown.[31] The positive reaction to *Pacific Babies* and subsequent exhibitions at Blum & Poe in which Nara showed fiberglass masks, his *Cup Kids* sculptures (1995), and sculptures of dogs on stilts catapulted him to recognition, especially in popular culture.

In 1998, Nara was invited by Paul McCarthy to be a guest professor in the MFA department at the University of California, Los Angeles (UCLA), with fellow Japanese artist Takashi Murakami. Nara and Murakami lived as roommates from April to June 1998, and found that their working methods could not have been more different: while Nara worked alone, mostly inside their apartment, Murakami spent a majority of his time on the phone and sending faxes back and forth between L.A. and his studio in Japan. This was Nara's first time living in the U.S. and he was shocked by the relative ease of life in Los Angeles, with Japanese supermarkets and fast food restaurants that served Japanese food, including the UCLA cafeteria. By the time he published *Slash with a Knife*, a book comprising mostly his works on paper, in fall 1998, he had been invited to show his work at museums in Europe (*Somebody Whispers* at the Institut für moderne Kunst Nürnberg in 1999) and the U.S. (*Lullaby Supermarket* at the Santa Monica Museum of Art and *Walk On* at the Museum of Contemporary Art, Chicago, both in 2000). *Walk On* featured *The Little Pilgrims (Night Walking)* (1999), an installation comprising dozens of disorienting sculptures of "sleepwalkers" in colorful garb walking sideways on the walls.

During his stay in the U.S., Nara began experimenting with the techniques of Dadaism and détournement, in which existing artworks are defaced as anti-authoritarian attacks against the art establishment. Nara undertook subversive appropriations of Japanese woodblock prints, manipulating forms to distort the serenity of landscapes or figures and adding poetic phrases, often drawn from folk, rock, or punk lyrics, to recontextualize the works. Particularly poignant are the set of sixteen works on paper from his 1999 *In the Floating World* series. The

29 Nara illustrated the covers of Banana Yoshitomo's novels *Hinagiku no Jinsei* [Daisy's Life] (2000) and *Argentine Hag* (2002).

30 Full disclosure: the author has guest curated exhibitions for Blum & Poe.

31 See Blum & Poe, "*Pacific Babies*" (press release, 1995).

artist drew a ghastly, enlarged face in place of the moon in *Full Moon Night* (p. 141), while in *Slash with a Knife* (p. 131) he oriented Katsushika Hokusai's famous cresting *The Great Wave* (c. 1829–33) sideways, morphing it into the hair of a monstrous female figure.

Through his travels in Europe and the U.S., Nara had undoubtedly noticed the omnipresence of specific Japanese prints such as Hokusai's *The Great Wave*, perceiving that the image had become a form of Pop art. As Alexandra Munroe has argued, the familiarity of these prints, built up by late nineteenth-century Europeans, has been internalized and responded to by many Japanese artists, who "parody how Japan saw itself through orientalist projections by composing a portrait of Japan through distortions of Japonisme over a Westernized self-image."[32] However, while Tadanori Yokoo's psychedelic designs or Masami Teraoka's large-scale appropriations of Japan's woodblock prints employ slick, otherworldly visions, Nara's affect is quite distinct: in *No Nukes!* (p. 140), for example, he turns a dreamy Mt. Fuji-scape by Hokusai into a scene of impending disaster. As Russell Ferguson has noted, "The [*In the Floating World*] series as a whole expresses an insouciant disregard for the past, including the now-valued art of the past.... Nara's work has more in common with Marcel Duchamp's application of a moustache to a postcard of the Mona Lisa, *L.H.O.O.Q.*, 1919, in which the element of blithe disrespect is essential. Nara treats *ukiyo-e* [a seventeenth- to nineteenth-century artistic genre of woodblock prints that gave rise to the merchant class] not as emblems of a revered historical Japan, but as images no more important than those he wishes to make himself."[33]

After returning to Cologne in 2000, Nara experienced a series of events that made him feel unwelcome in Germany: he was interrogated by security at the Frankfurt airport and received a demolition notice on his studio building ordering him to move out within three months. He decided to return permanently to Japan and moved to Fussa, on the outskirts of Tokyo near the U.S. Yokota Air Base. There, he began to prepare for his first major survey exhibition, *I DON'T MIND, IF YOU FORGET ME.,* which would appear at the Yokohama Museum of Art in 2001 before traveling to Ashiya, Hiroshima, and Asahikawa, with a final stop in Nara's hometown of Hirosaki in fall 2002. Having amassed a large audience over the years, he decided to create a communal piece by asking his fans to make felt, knit, and stuffed toys using motifs from his works, which he would place in transparent acrylic boxes shaped like letters, spelling out the exhibition title. The exhibition also included *Fountain of Life*, a motorized sculptural installation of heads with closed eyelids that tower over one another inside an enormous cup with water that streams down the figures' cheeks, forming a fountain of tears. The melancholy of this work is palpable, and the figures' clean profiles evoke the abstract, richly outlined paintings of Japanese abstract painter Morikazu Kumagai.[34]

32 Alexandra Munroe, "Pulp Fiction and the Floating World," in *Paintings by Masami Teraoka* (Washington, DC: Arthur M. Sackler Gallery, 1996), 39.

33 Ferguson, "The Show Is Over," 113.

34 The bands and artists Nara listened to between 1988 and 2000 include Carter the Unstoppable Sex Machine, Superchunk, NOFX and the Fat Wreck Chords label bands, Bad Religion, the Offspring, Rancid, Alanis Morissette, Blur, Pearl Jam, Smashing Pumpkins, the Beastie Boys, Nenezu, PJ Harvey, Beck, Guitar Wolf, Oasis, the Chemical Brothers, Goldie, Puffy, the Flaming Lips, the Prodigy, Yo La Tengo, Radiohead, Tortoise, Stereolab, Kazuyoshi Nakamura, Thee Michelle Gun Elephant, Eastern Youth, Mayumi Kobayashi, and Eels. Nara, *The Little Star Dweller*, 92.

In 2001 Nara was invited to travel to Afghanistan with photographer Rinko Kawauchi for the inaugural issue of *FOIL*, a Japanese culture magazine. The visit swept him away: his encounters in Afghanistan were like none he had experienced before, and he sensed an enormous gap between the popular perception and real-life conditions of the Afghani people. "The young kids I met at an abandoned elementary school with walls sprayed with bullet holes like a starry night sky were smiling; even the people washing clothes by the river were smiling.... The old man who was watering a beautiful flowerbed in front of the collapsing school was also smiling," he recalls.[35] While Nara had been asked to submit paintings for the issue, whose theme was "No War," he was unable to consolidate his experiences on canvas and decided to publish a selection of his photographs instead. This discovery has led him to explore other political, colonial, and anthropological histories through subsequent travels, including residencies to work with communities in northern Japan, where he also traced his native roots; a trip to Sakhalin, a contested island between Russia and Japan, where his maternal grandfather had worked; and a recent visit to meet refugee families in Jordan.

Nara began creating portable installations of his paintings, drawings, and sculptures in collaboration with graf, a DIY creative design team, in 2003. The designers assisted Nara with a series of "drawing huts" that contain the artist's works and ephemera and play music; these range from the three-part installation *S.M.L.* (2003) to the epic twenty-six-installation exhibition *A to Z* (2006). These domestic environments culminated in *My Drawing Room* (2008; pp. 50–64), a painted wooden architectural structure that recreates Nara's studio space. A hand-painted billboard with the words "Place Like Home" hangs on the exterior, and the inside features piles of drawings on the floor and a desk with figurines, mix CDs that Nara curated, vernacular paintings, drawings, ephemera, and collectibles from vintage Americana shops that the artist has accumulated over the years.

In 2005 Nara moved into a beautiful studio that overlooks the green pastures in Nasushiobara, Tochigi Prefecture, where he would eventually open N's YARD, a space that houses his artwork and collection. The paintings he began making in this period are layered in a vast array of palettes that create a kaleidoscopic effect, with many works featuring different colored eyes. The backgrounds are often dark and thickly layered, with iridescent colors that float in and out of sight, evoking the existential effects of Mark Rothko's soft, saturated forms. The works depict single figures and resemble portrait paintings by modern European artists such as Amedeo Modigliani and Léonard Tsuguharu Foujita (a small Foujita work in Nara's collection is in fact included in *My Drawing Room*), yet their singularity and directness—seen especially in the recent works *Miss Margaret* (2016; p. 75) and *Midnight Truth*

35 Nara, "Kabul Diary," *The Little Star Dweller*, 109. Translation by author.

(2017; p. 100)—project a complex expression that combines sadness, anger, and serenity, which Nara achieves by reworking and repainting the faces multiple times. In *Missing in Action—Girl Meets Boy—* (2005; p. 68), fire from an atomic bomb explosion is reflected in the figure's right eye, representing a memory of Hiroshima, where this work is housed.

Nara's work took a dramatic shift following the March 2011 Tōhoku earthquake and tsunami and the Fukushima Daiichi nuclear disaster, which occurred only forty-three miles north of his studio. Emotionally affected by the aftermath, Nara painted *In the Milky Lake/Thinking One,* a portrait of a solemn-faced girl with closed eyelids who wears a green dress and is half-submerged in a barely visible pool of water; it was the only major painting he produced in 2011. He also began to work with his bare hands, making ceramics and casting bronze sculptures of large rotund or oblong heads in a Buddhist foundry in Toyama. The uneven surfaces on the faces of the sculpture reflect the tactile workings of the artist's hand, and their closed eyes and serene expressions are reminiscent of the cast impression of death masks, invoking the ghosts of the thousands who had died in these recent tragedies. In contrast to the process of making his portraits, which he describes as an "ascetic training...[in which] there is a kind of masochistic pleasure toward something sadistic, like for an ascetic monk,"[36] the heads have a profoundly intimate, earthly presence, as Nara lets himself "run wild while carving the piece, or clawing at it with my hands."[37] *In the Milky Lake* and the bronze head sculptures were exhibited in a major survey of Nara's work, *a bit like you and me...*, at the Yokohama Museum of Art in 2012.

While confronting the 2011 natural and nuclear disasters, Nara also made *Miss Spring* (2012; p. 139), a portrait of a wide-eyed girl with a high forehead who stands against a cherry blossom–pink background and stares straight at the viewer, with prism-like teardrops glistening in her eyes. A symbol of hope, this portrait served as the cover image for the guidebook that accompanied Ryuichi Sakamoto's No Nukes 2012 concert.[38] Nara had been aware of the existence of nearby nuclear plants (which provided electricity to major cities in Japan) since he was a child, and knew that nuclear waste was returned to Aomori. During high school, he did research into nuclear development in Japan and noticed a persistent effort to disassociate "the negativity linked to the atomic bomb from the use of nuclear power to rebuild and develop Japan after the war."[39] After the Three Mile Island accident occurred in Pennsylvania in 1979, Nara's interest in opposing nuclear energy deepened, and "No Nukes" activism began appearing in his work in the mid-1990s, many years before the Fukushima Daiichi nuclear disaster.[40]

In July 2012, another Nara figure, the "No Nukes Girl" from his 1998 work *No Nukes* (p. 138), became an unexpectedly powerful symbol when the artist temporarily allowed protesters to download a high-

36 Quoted in "Nara Yoshitomo rongu intabyū: 'E ni egakareru mono no tame ni' egaku" [Yoshitomo Nara long interview: paint for "what is being painted"], *Neppū*, October 2017, 15. Translation by Chisato Uno.

37 Quoted in "Nara Yoshitomo rongu intabyū," 15.

38 Edan Corkill, "Nara's 'No Nukes Girl' Joins the Protesters," *Japan Times*, July 20, 2012.

39 Yoshitomo Nara in conversation with Romina Provenzi, "Yoshitomo Nara's Lessons in Clay," *Elephant Magazine*, August 17, 2018, https://elephant.art/yoshitomo-naras-lessons-in-clay.

40 Nara in conversation with Provenzi, "Yoshitomo Nara's Lessons in Clay."

resolution image of the work to brandish during one of Japan's largest anti-nuclear protests.[41] As many as 100,000 people gathered to rail against the government's decision to restart two nuclear reactors in Fukui Prefecture, many with this image in hand.[42] *Miss Spring* was also used as a powerful backdrop banner by the protest organizers during the demonstrations.

Nara's work offers an inclusive new model for considering art's relationship to global culture. While Pop art and Neo-Pop prompted audiences to think about the immediacy, accessibility, and ubiquity of images, Nara's art rewards both the quick glance and the slow gaze. And while images like *No Nukes* lend themselves to reproduction and proliferation in the context of activism and social media, his solitary and singular portraits occupy the same museum walls as wide-ranging artistic influences like Léonard Tsuguharu Foujita, Amadeo Modigliani, and Henri Matisse. In short, Nara has created a body of work that can have the lasting social impact of a protest song, the timelessness of a classic rock melody, and the introspective tenderness of a great folk ballad.

41 Corkill, "Nara's 'No Nukes Girl.'"

42 Piers Williamson, "Largest Demonstrations in Half a Century Protest the Restart of Japanese Nuclear Power Plants," *Japan Focus* 10, no. 15, issue 27 (July 1, 2012).

II

THE GIRL WITH THE KNIFE IN HER HAND

Mumps, 1996
The Last Match, 1996
The Longest Night, 1995
Sleepless Night (Sitting), 1997
The Girl with the Knife in Her Hand, 1991
Walk On I, 1993
In the Deepest Puddle II, 1995
Abandoned Puppy, 1995
Give You the Flower, 1990
Make the Road, Follow the Road, 1990
People on the Cloud, 1989
Untitled [after overpainting], 1989–97
Emergency, 2013
Romantic Catastrophe, 1988

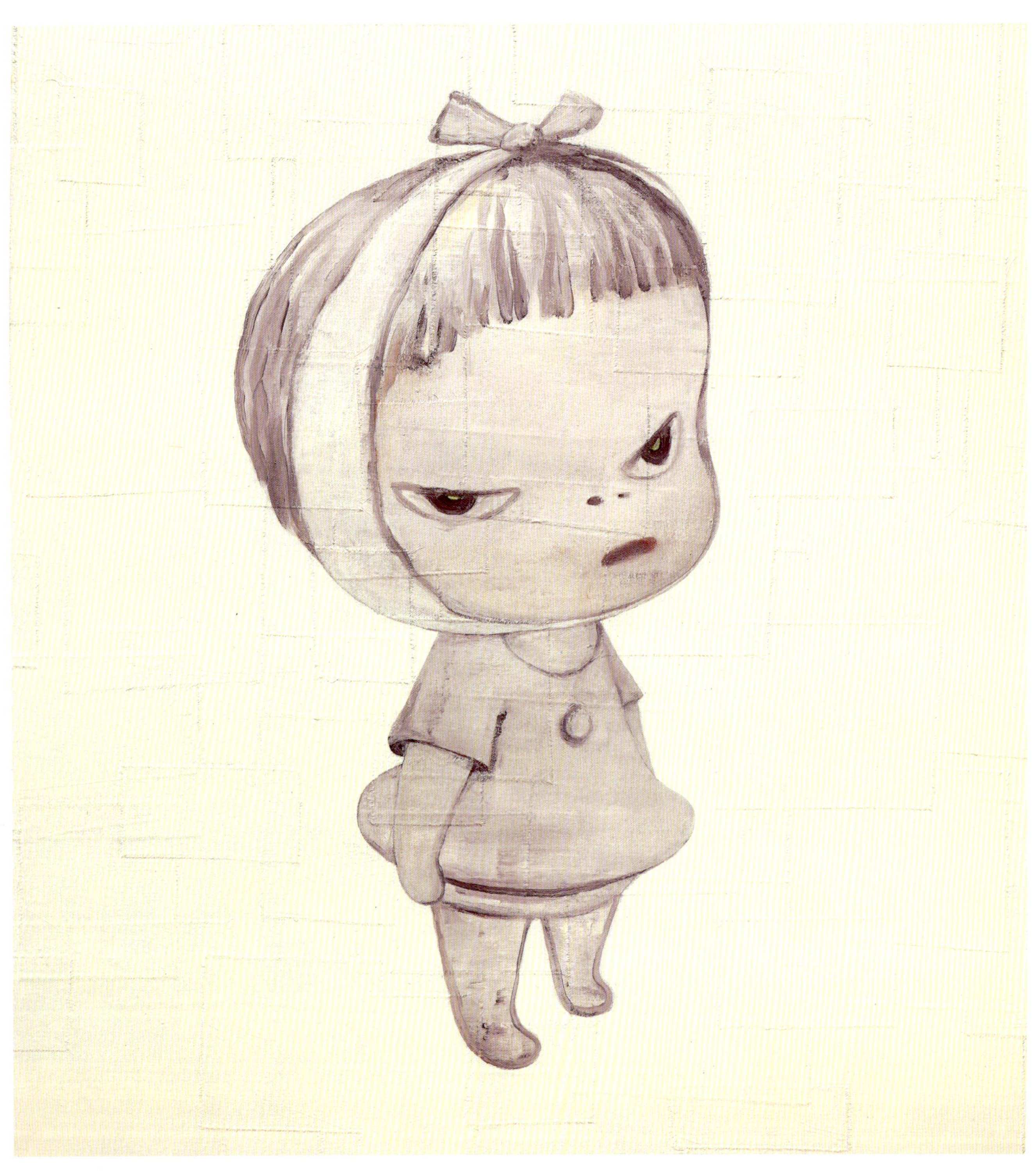

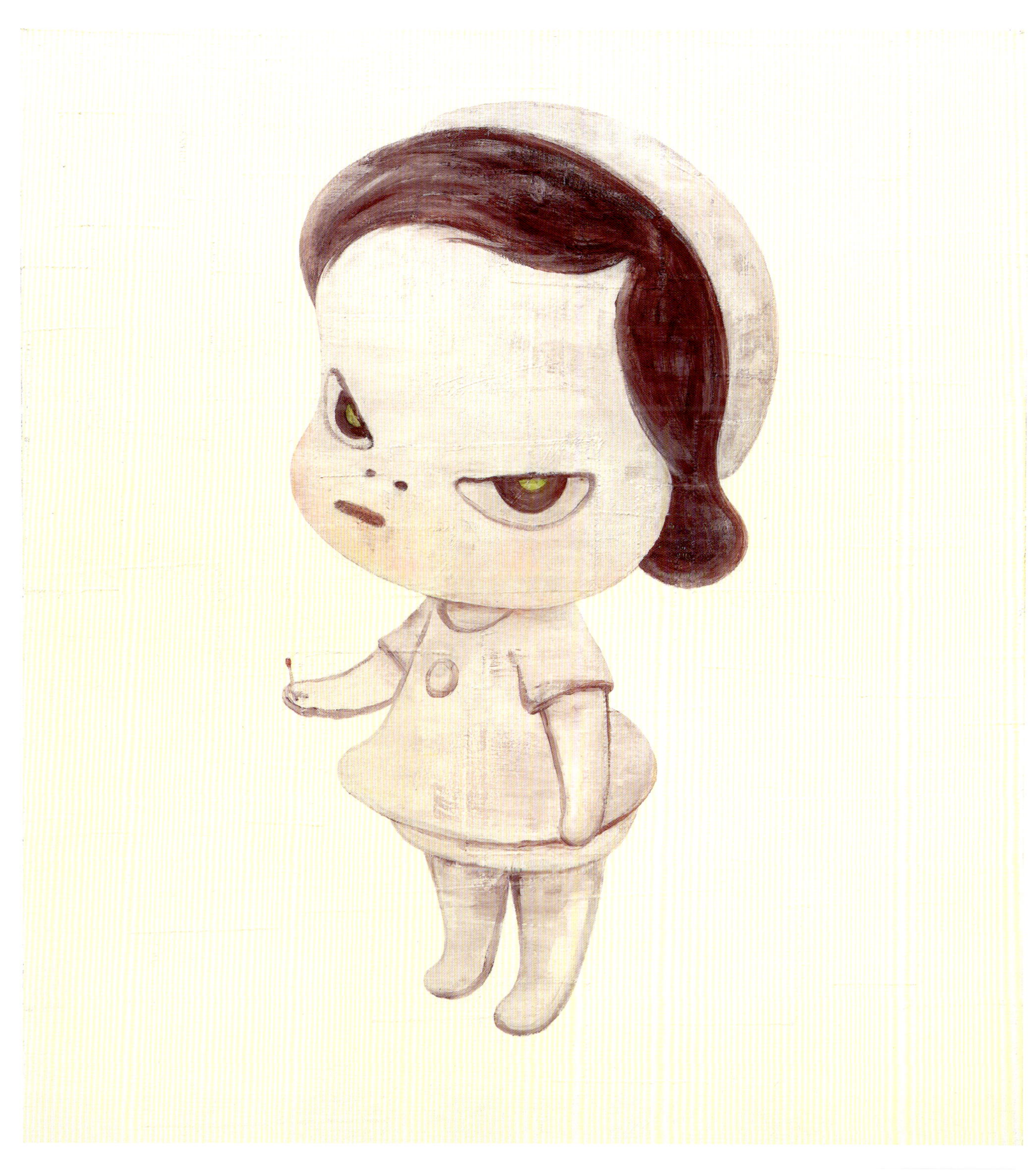

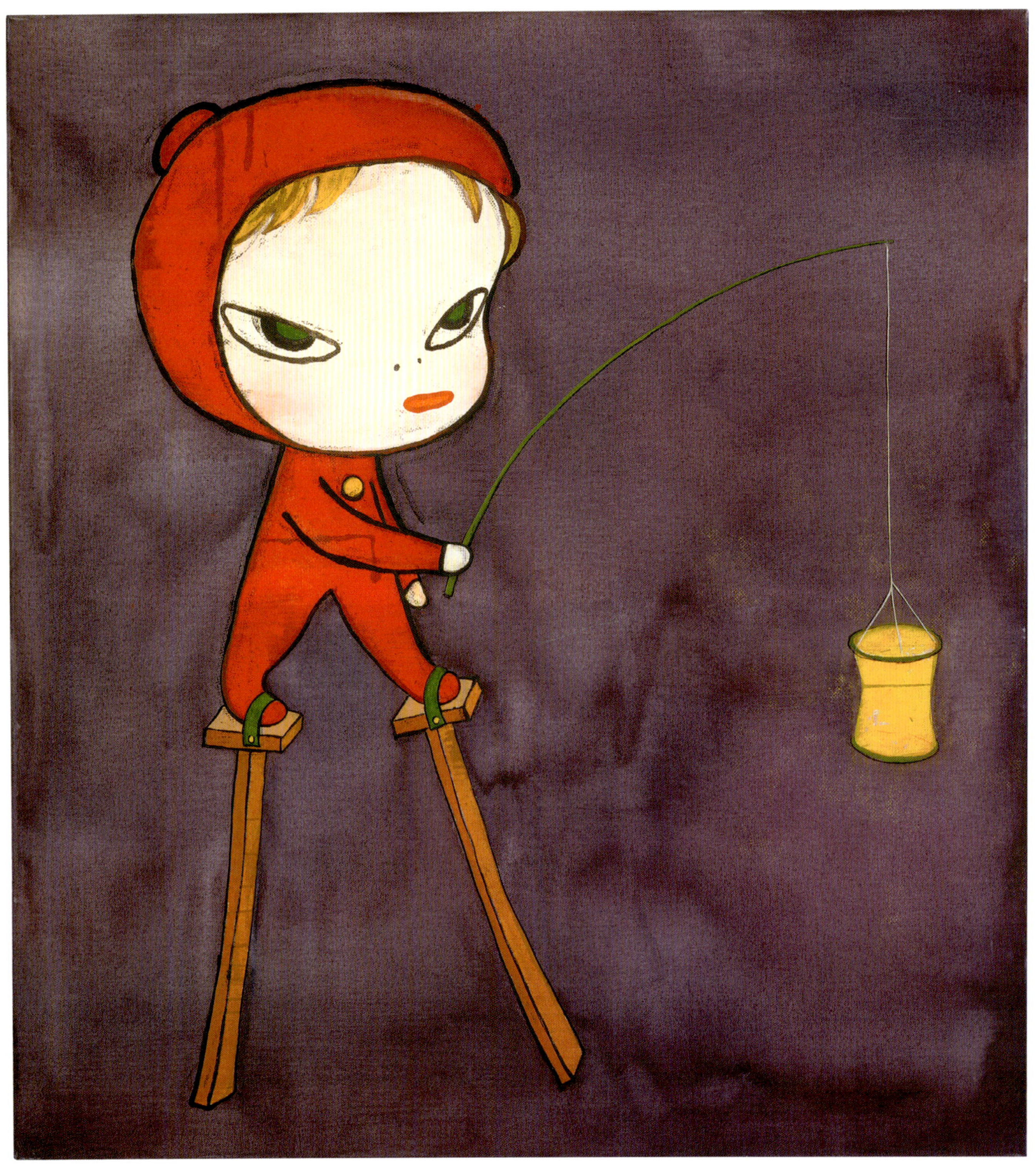

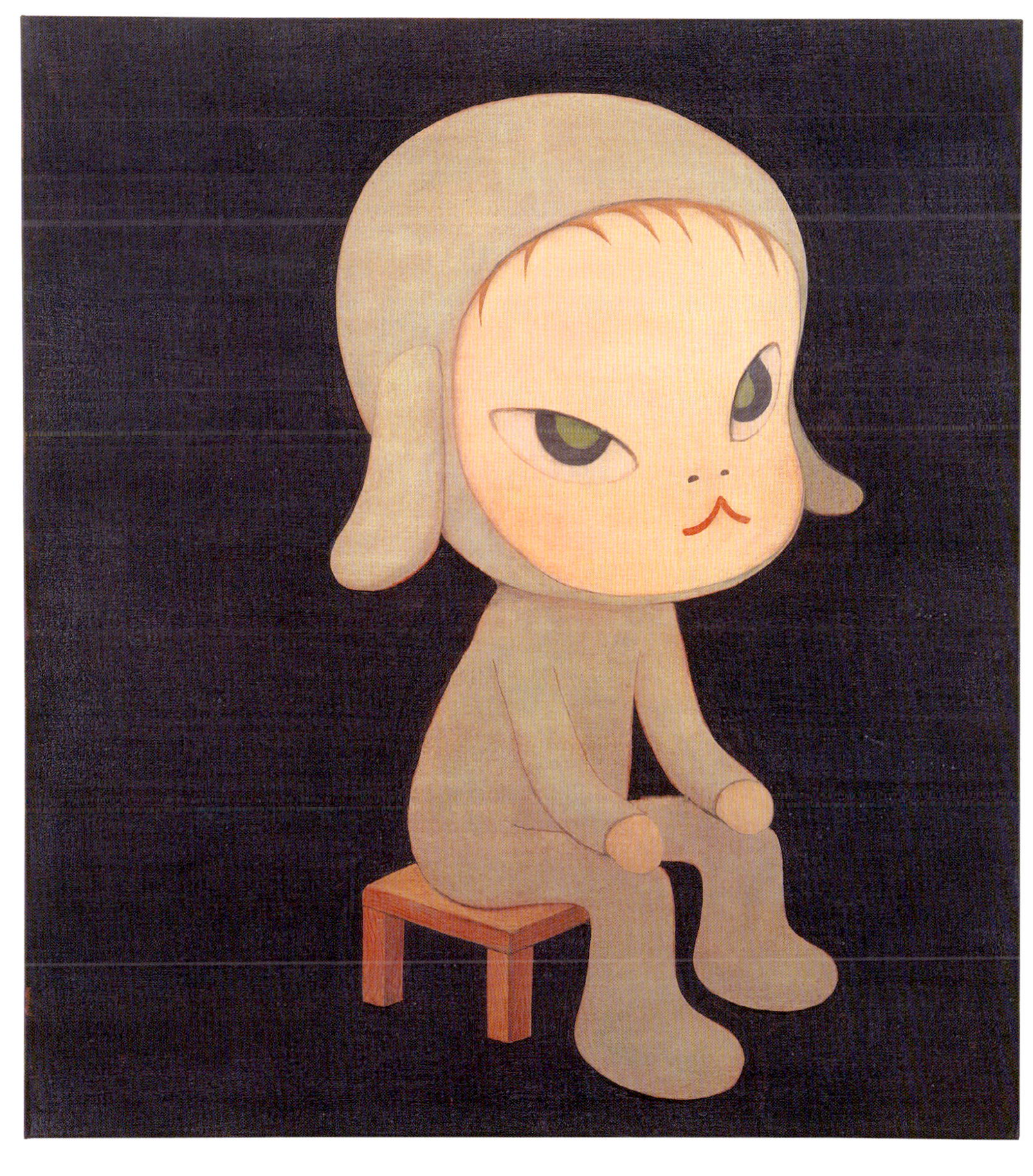

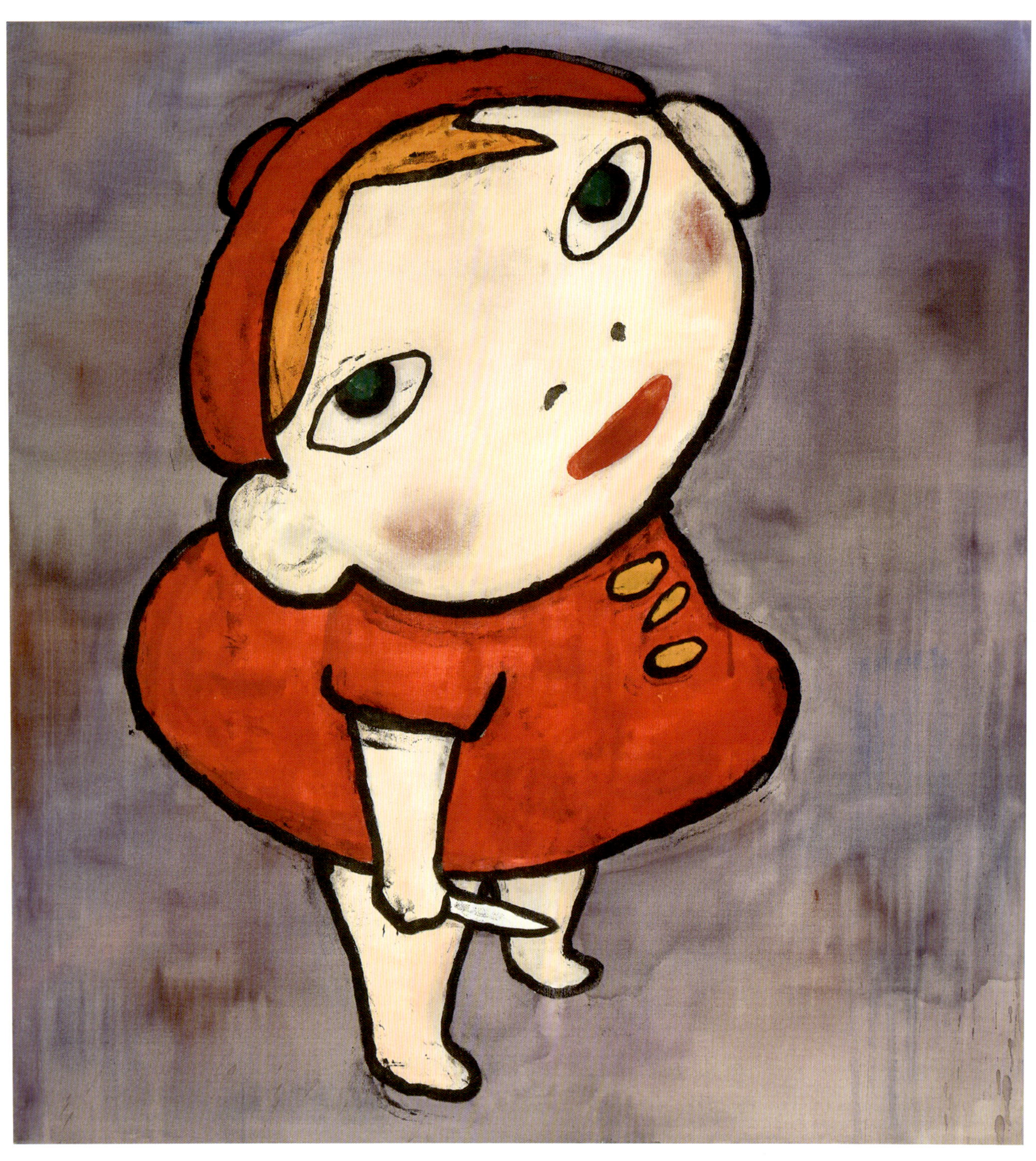

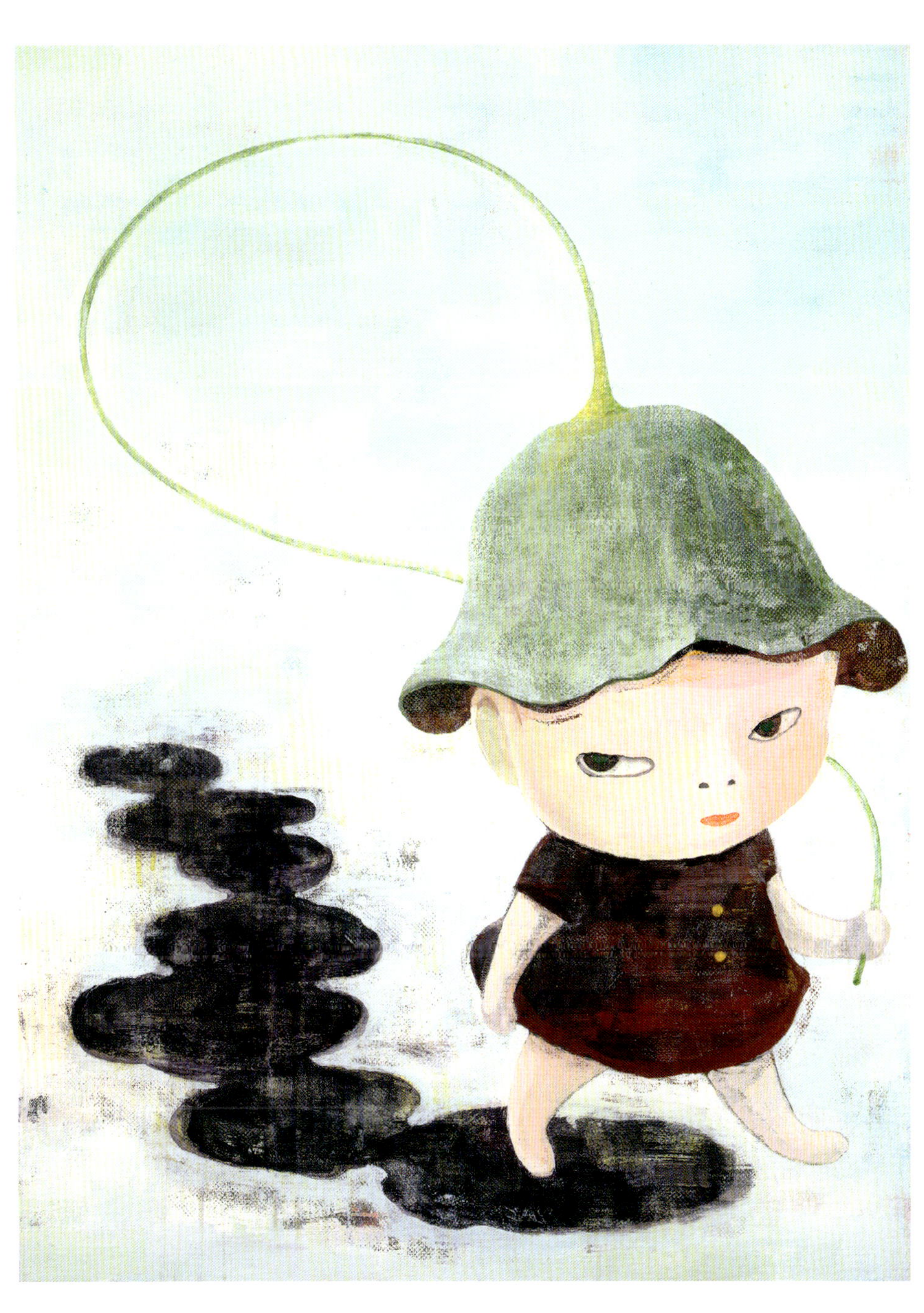

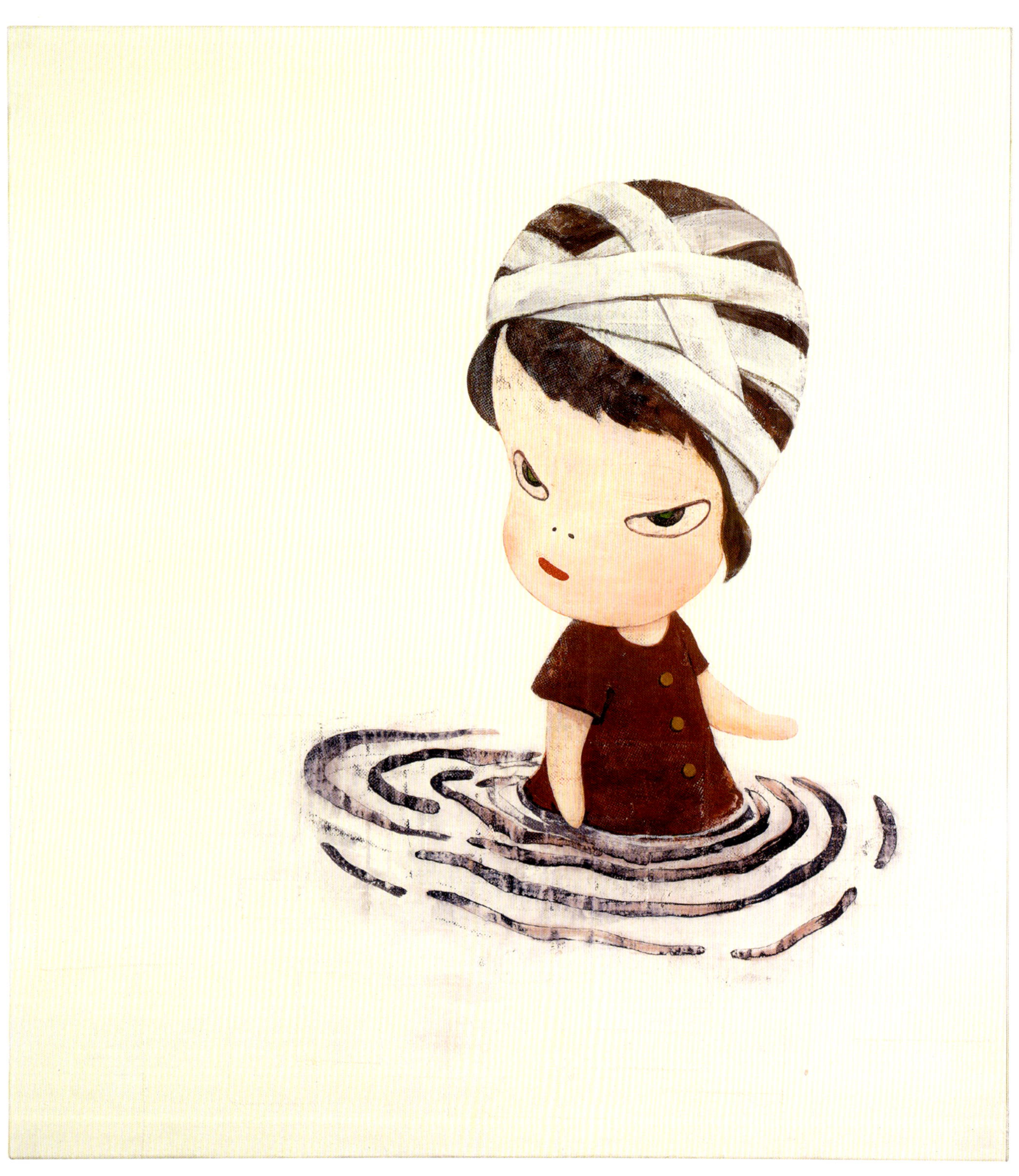

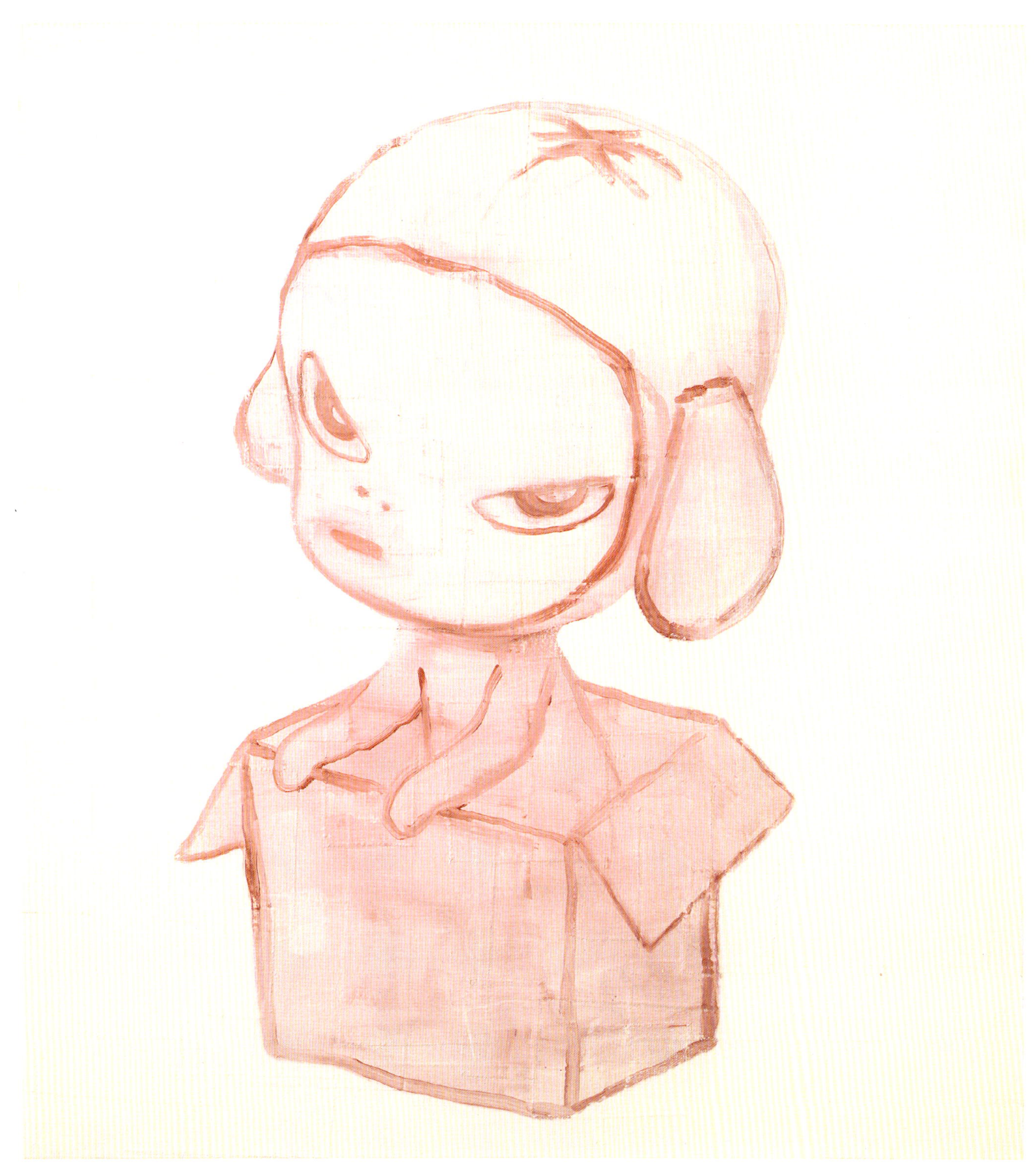

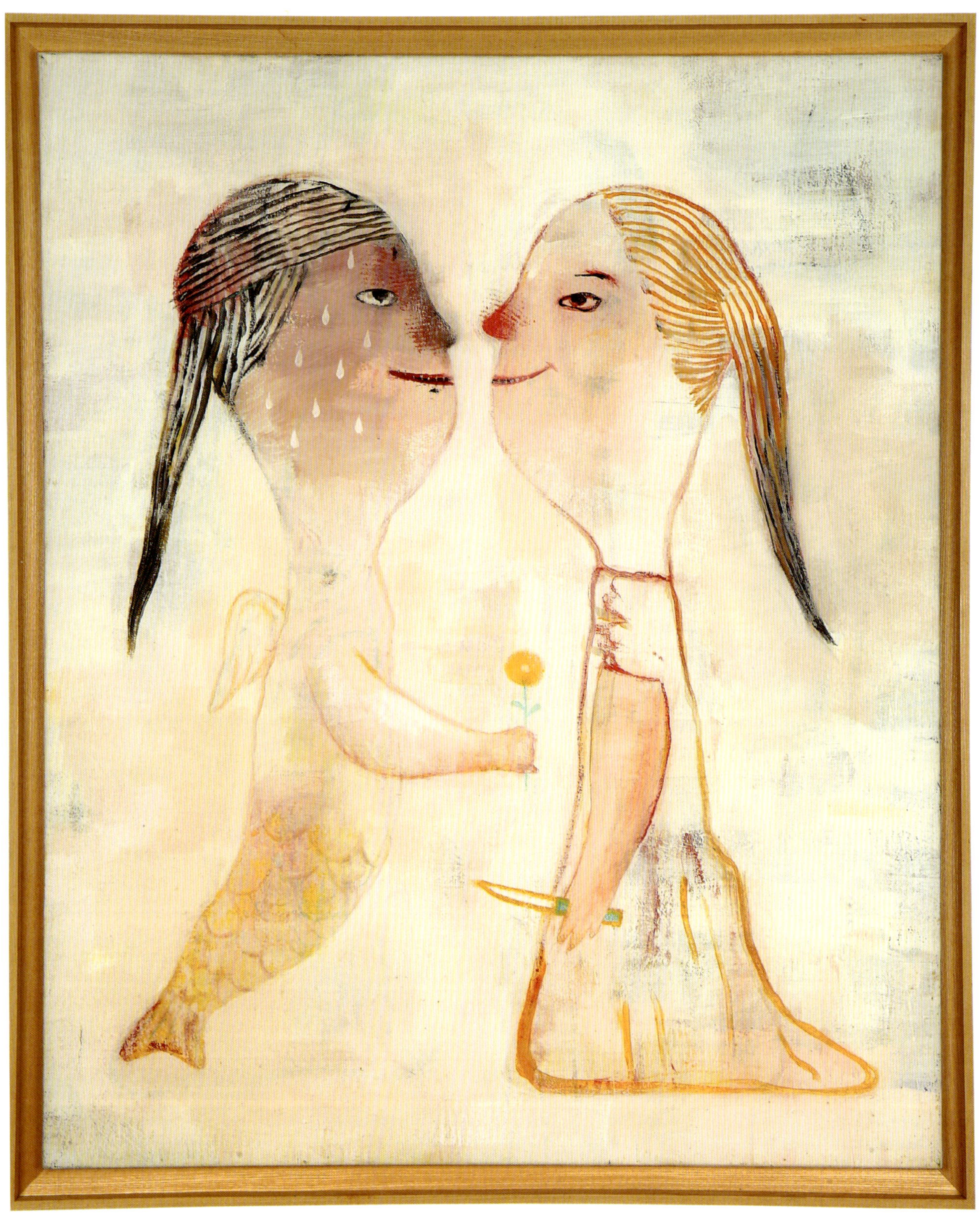

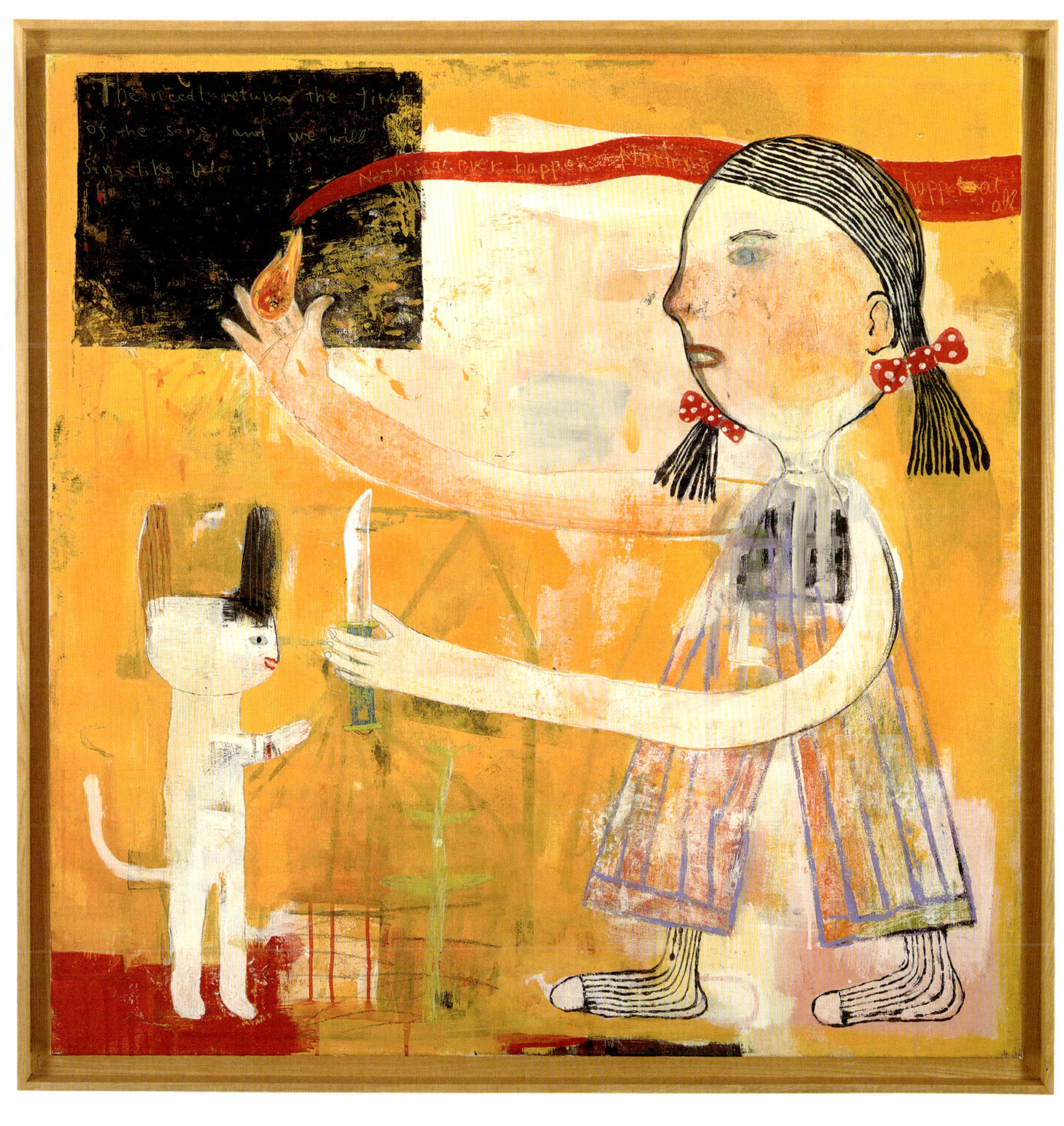
of the song and we will
Nothing ever happens Nothing
at all

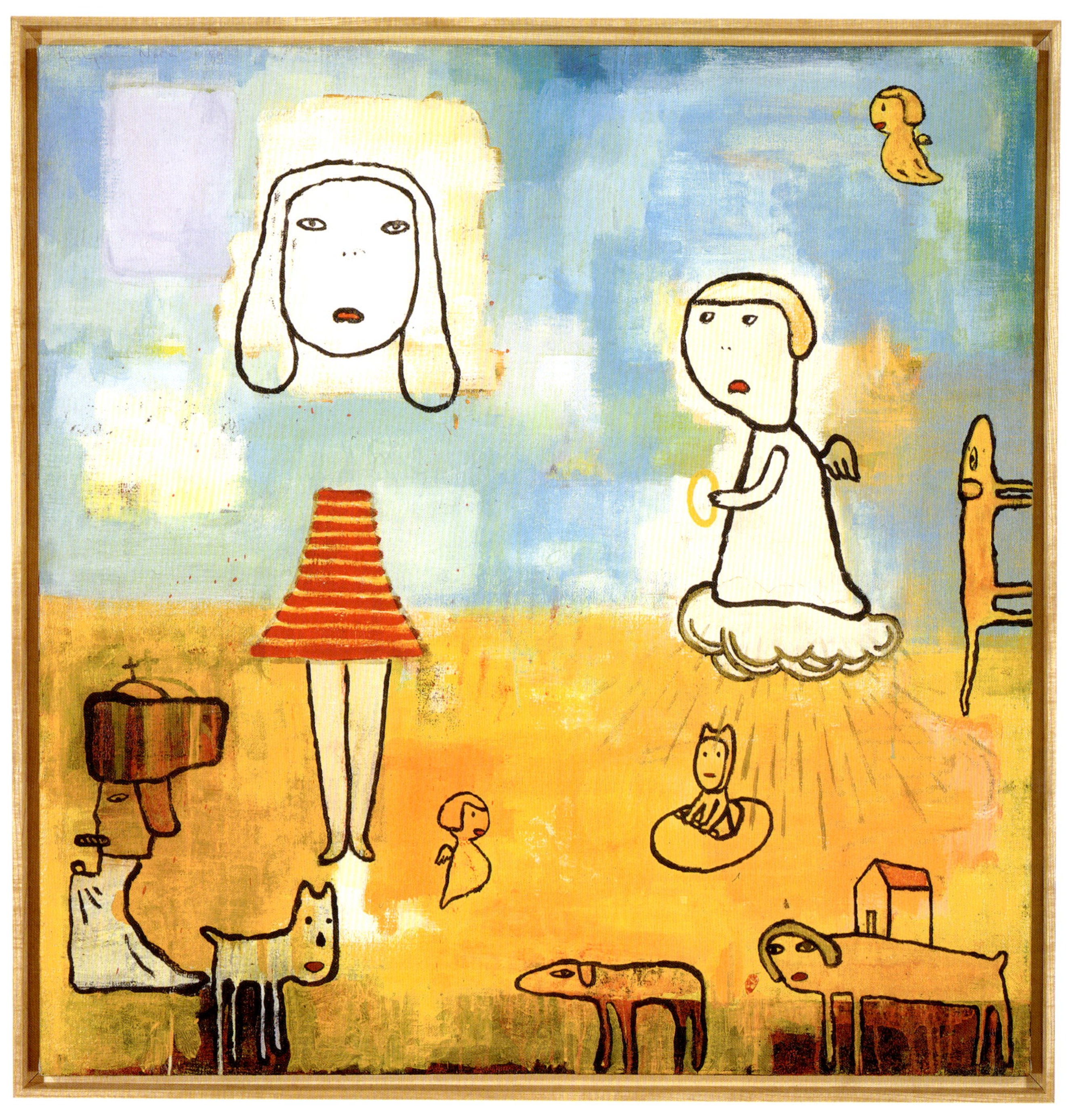

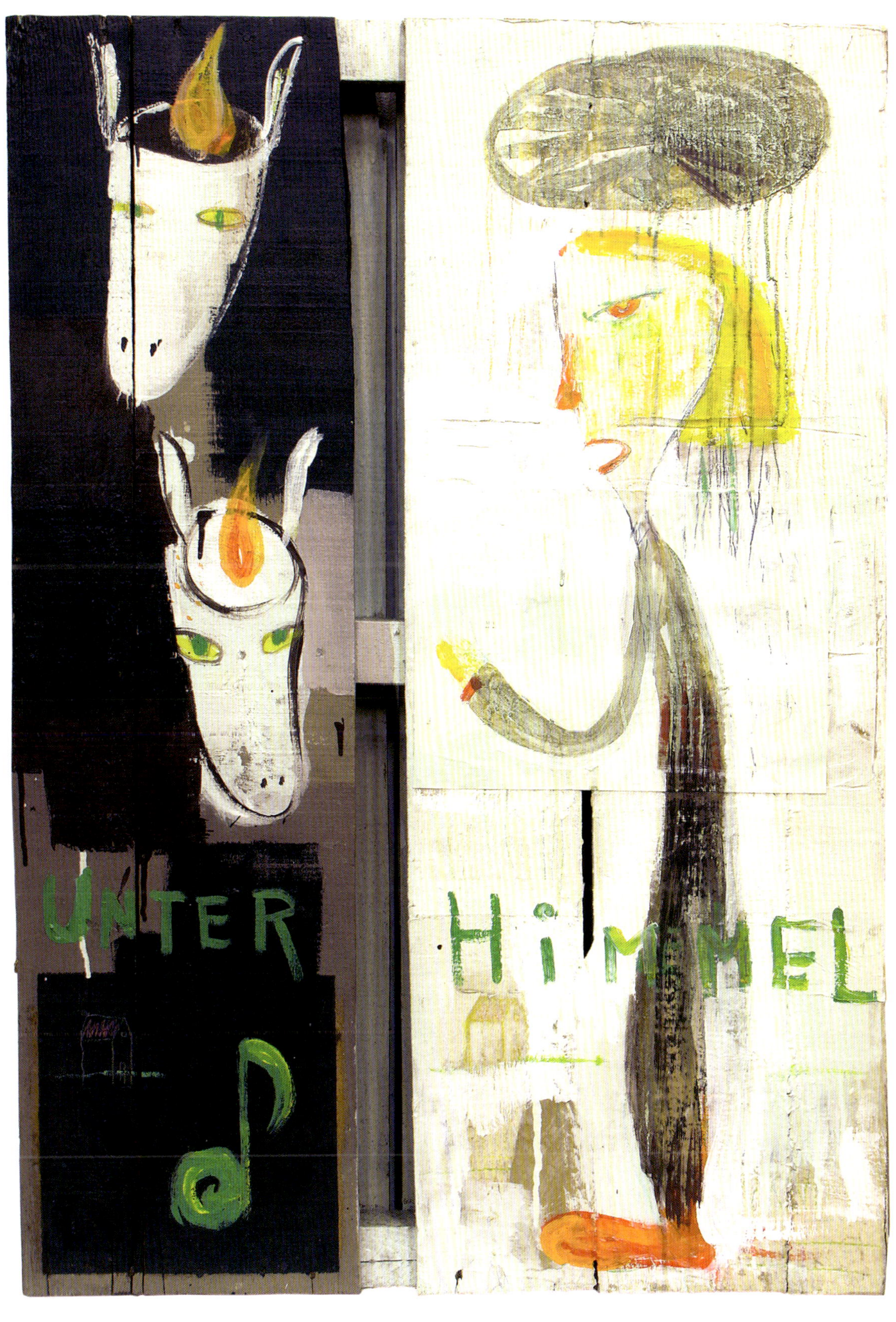
UNTER
HiMMEL

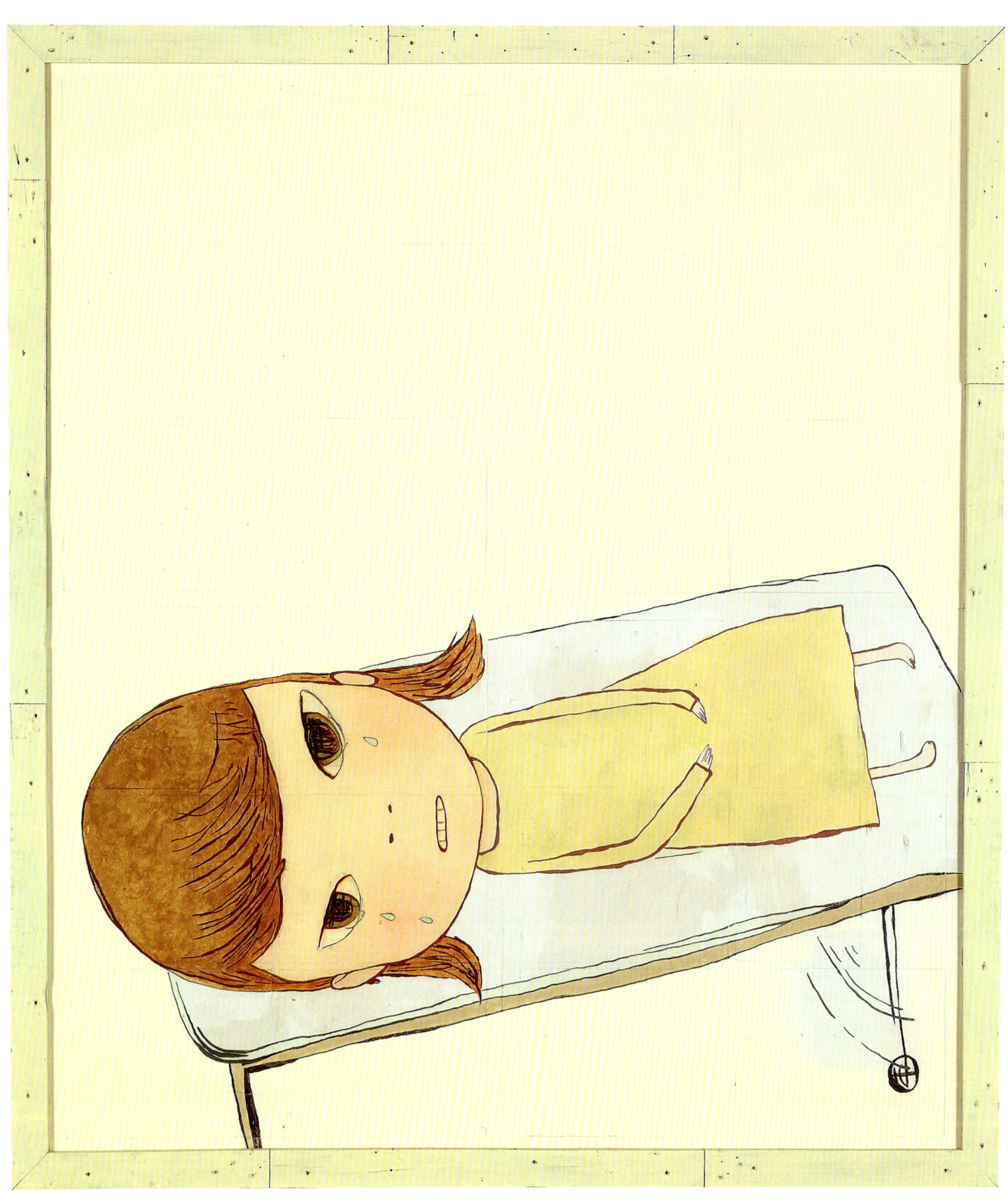

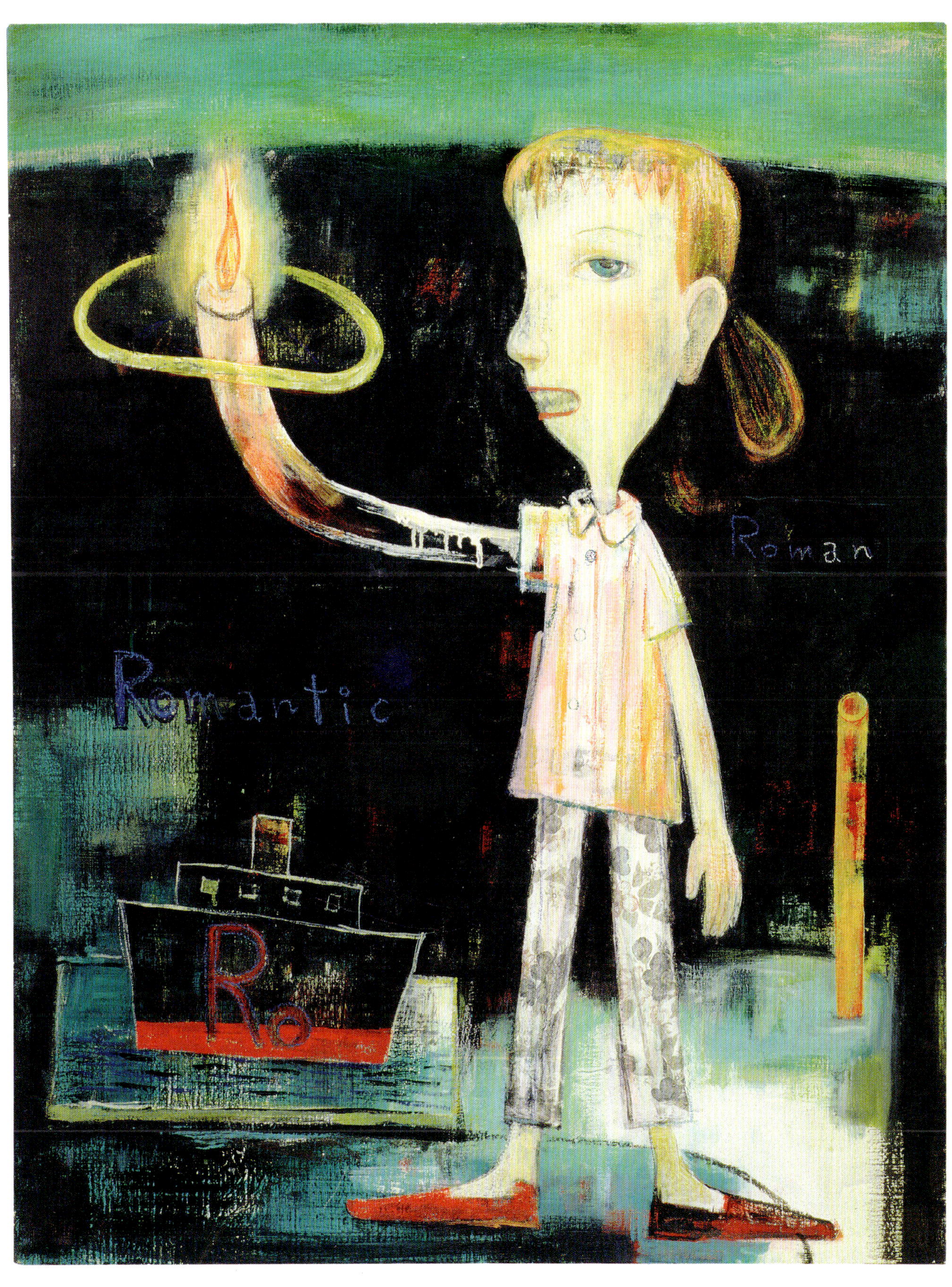
Roman
Romantic
Ro

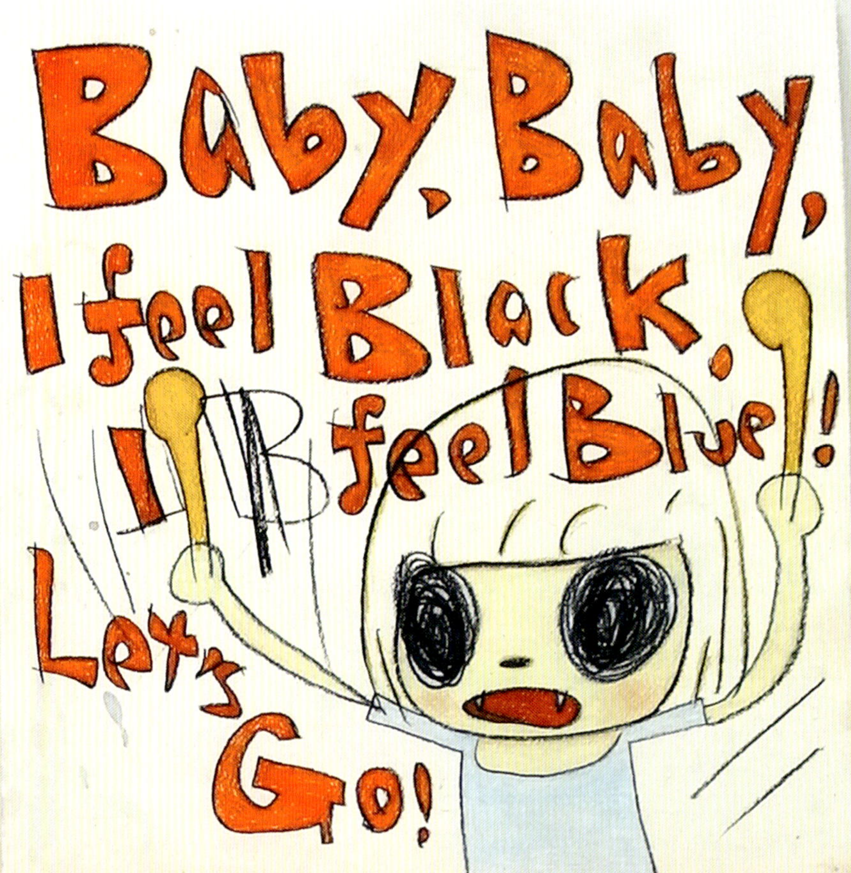
Baby, Baby,
I feel Black,
I feel Blue!
Let's
Go!

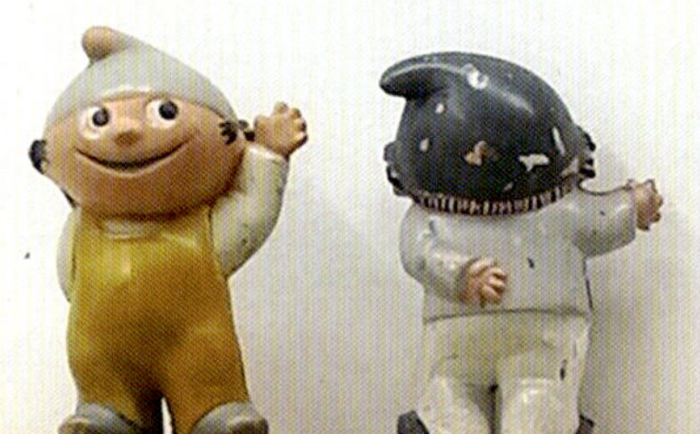

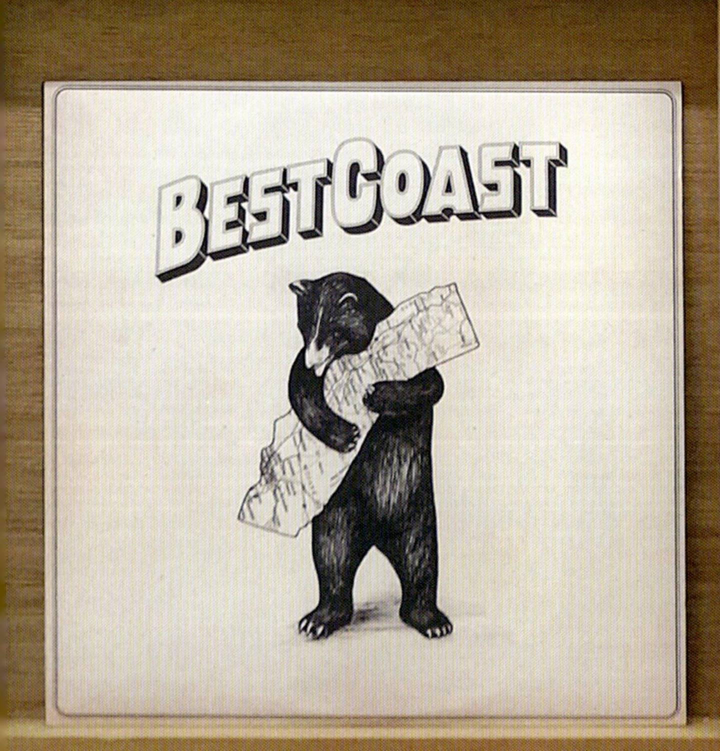
BEST COAST

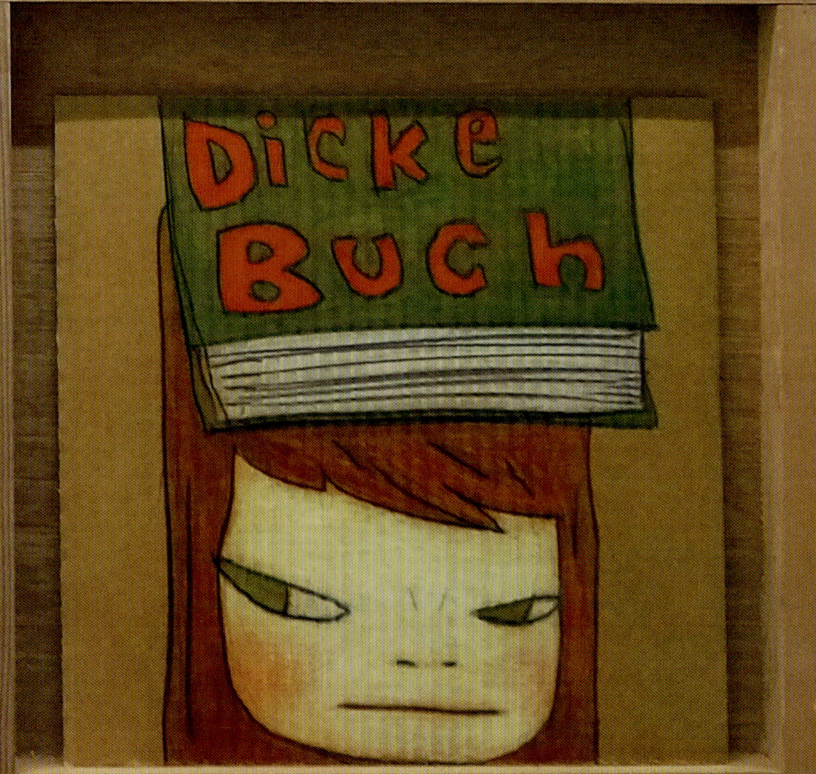
Dicke
Buch

III

I DON'T CARE A FUCK ABOUT EVERYTHING

Untitled, 1985–88
Untitled, 1985–88
Untitled, 1988
Ships in Girl, 1992
Untitled, 1988
Untitled, 1988
Schallplatten, 2012
Untitled, 2013
Fuckin' Street, 2013
Thinking about a Little Star, 2014
Untitled, 2012
Untitled, 2013
Untitled, 2013
Untitled, 2013
Untitled, 2013
Untitled, 2011
Rock You!, 2012
My Skull, 2013
Solid Fist, 2011
Untitled, 1989
Untitled, 2010
Untitled, 2010

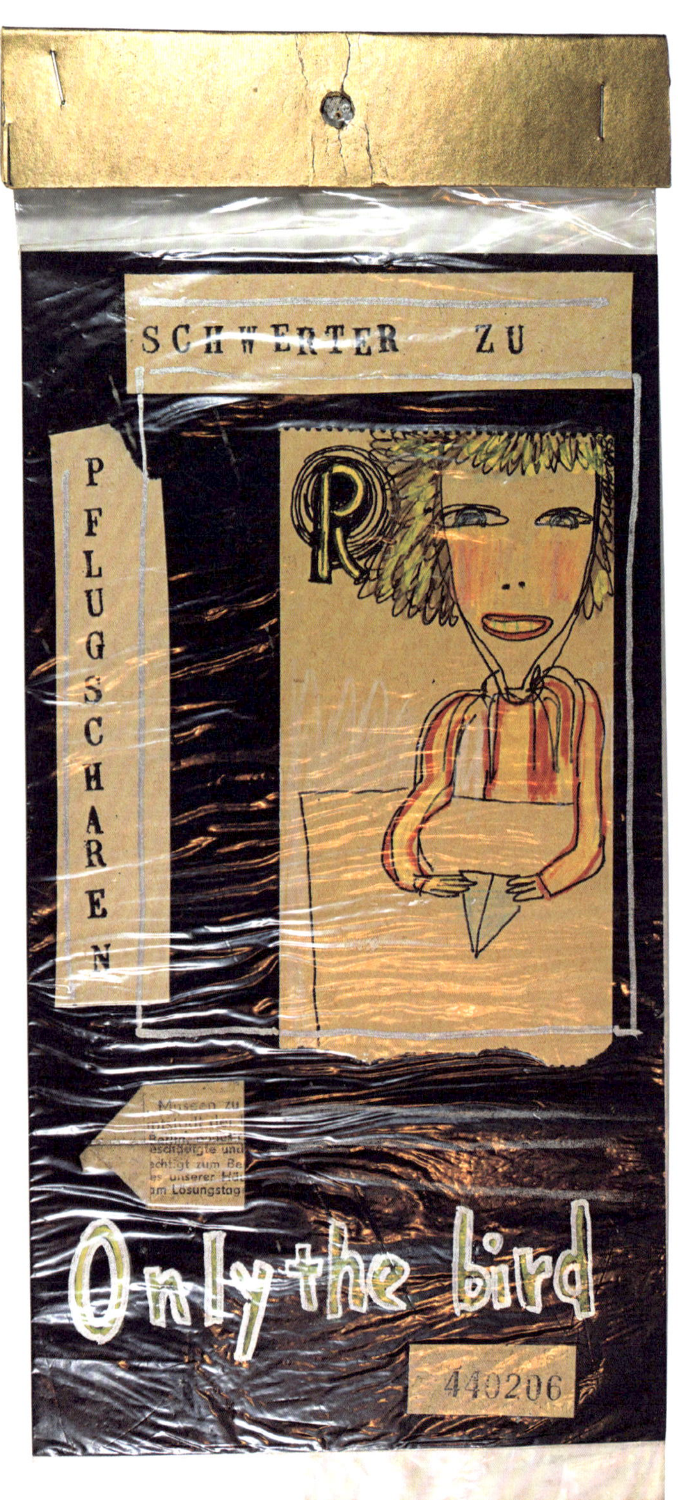
SCHWERTER ZU
PFLUGSCHAREN
Only the bird
440206

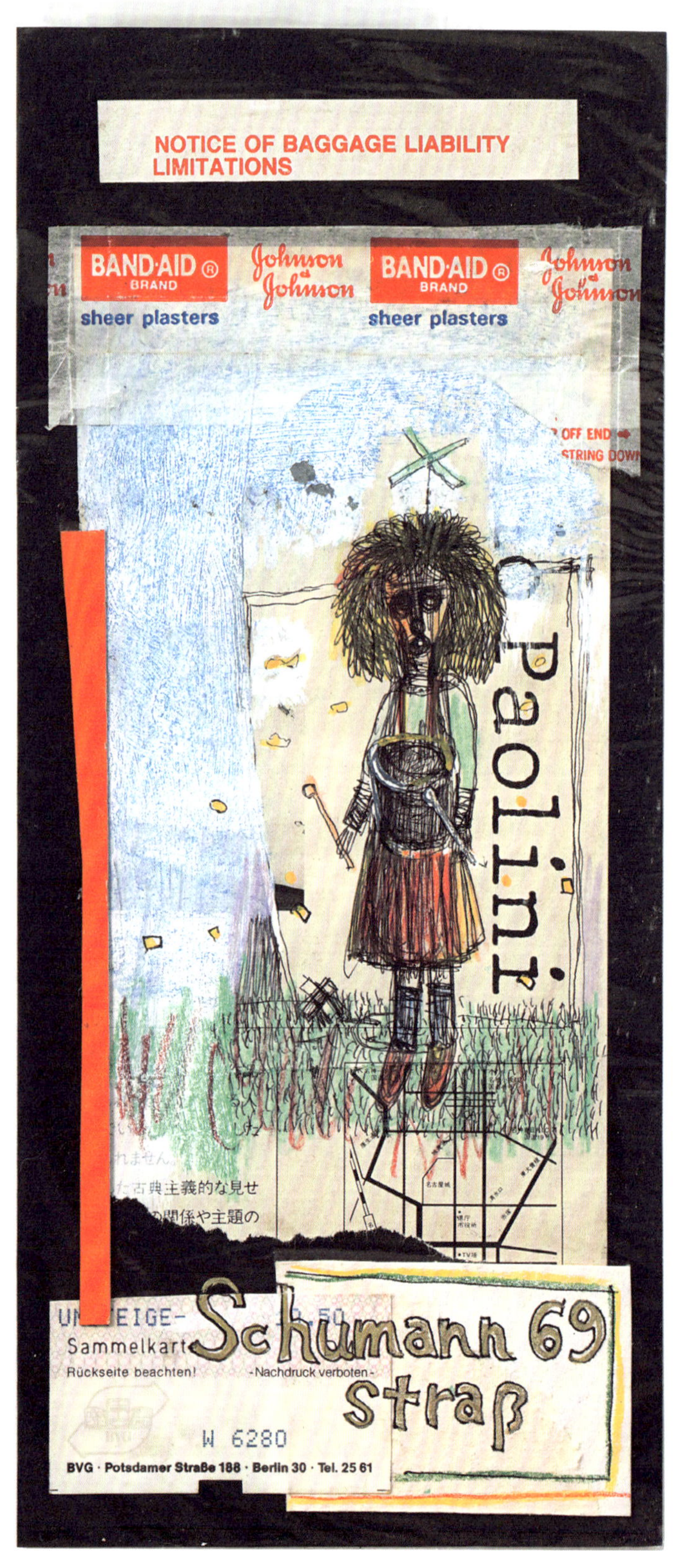
NOTICE OF BAGGAGE LIABILITY
LIMITATIONS
BAND-AID BRAND
Johnson & Johnson
sheer plasters
Paolini
Sammelkarte
Rückseite beachten!
-Nachdruck verboten-
W 6280
BVG · Potsdamer Straße 188 · Berlin 30 · Tel. 25 61
Schumann 69
strap

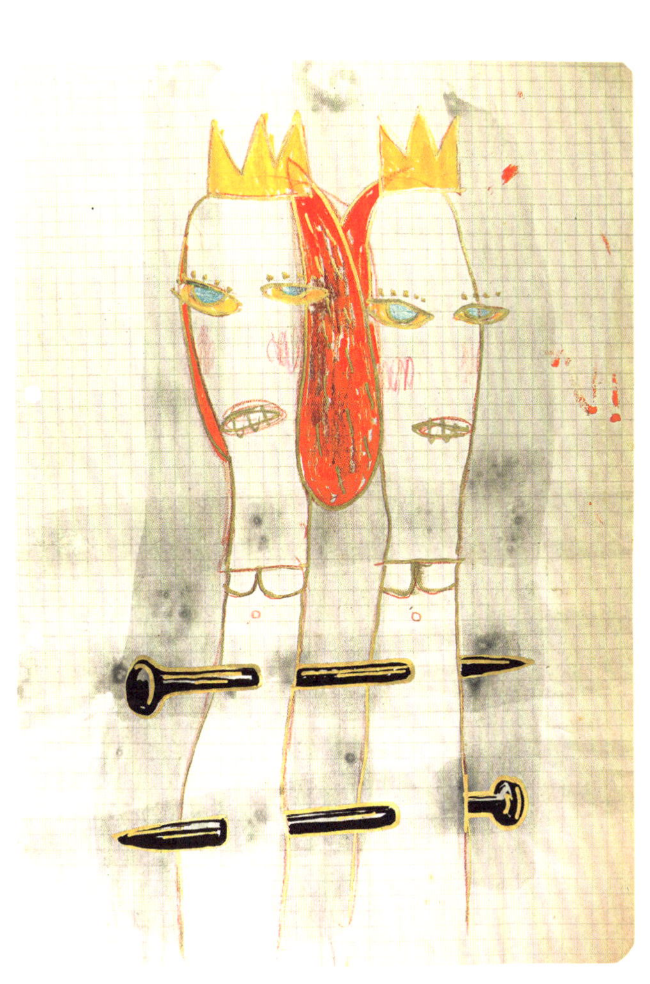

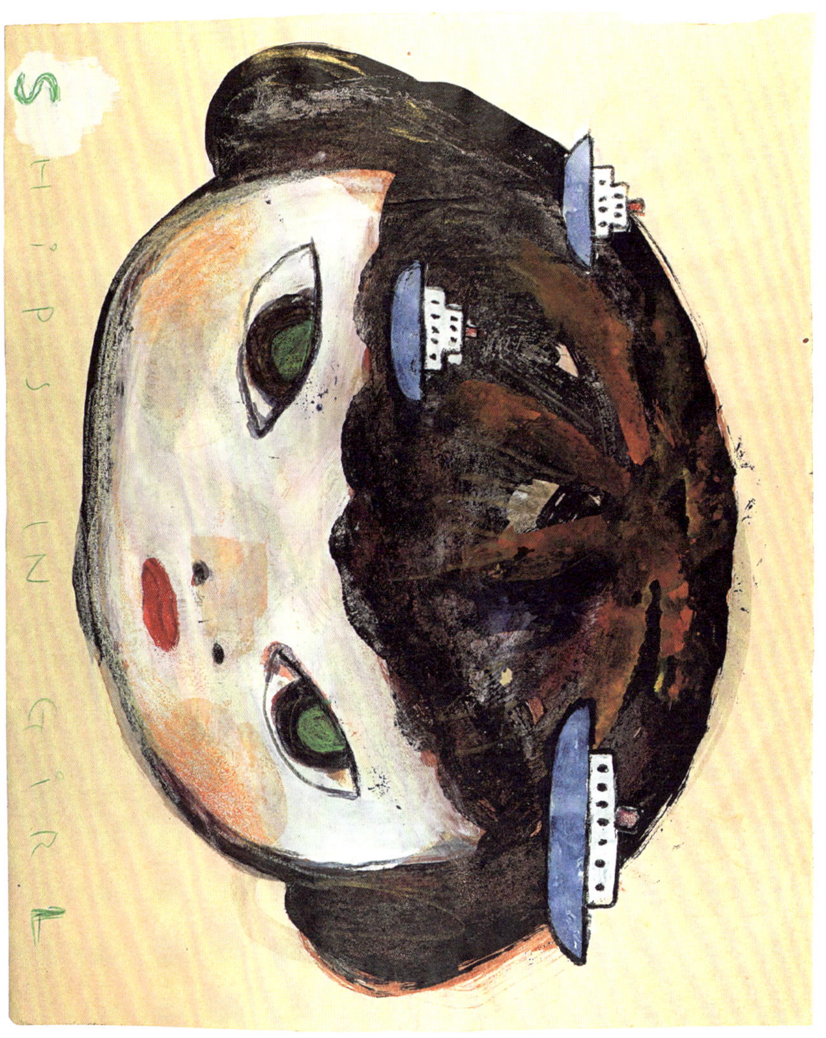
SHIPS IN GIRL

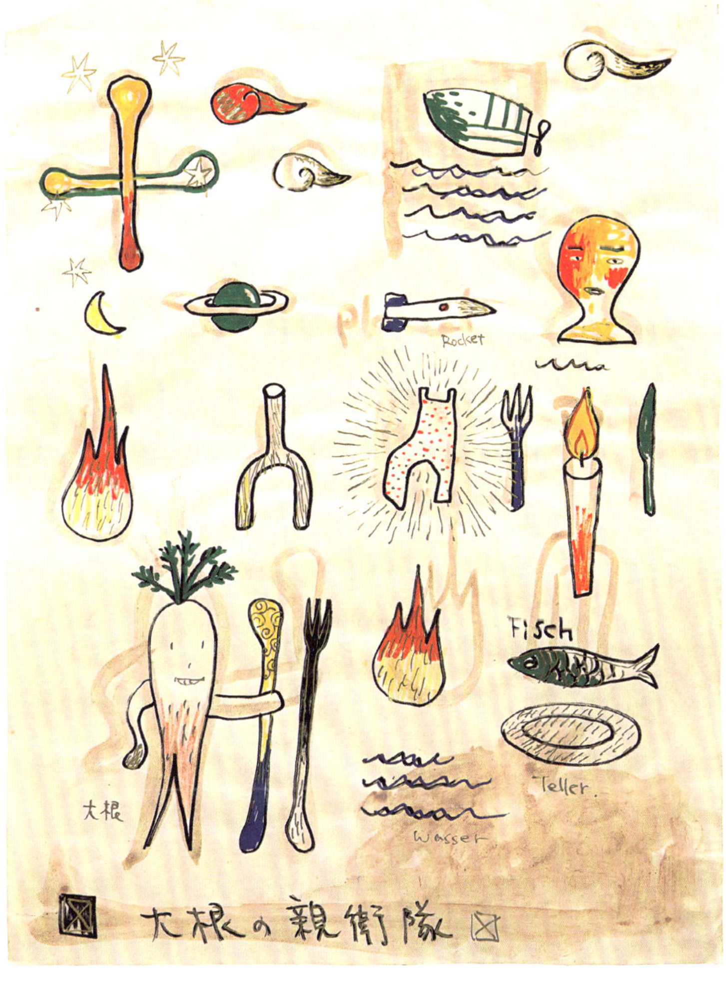
Rocket
Fisch
大根
Teller
Wasser
大根の親衛隊

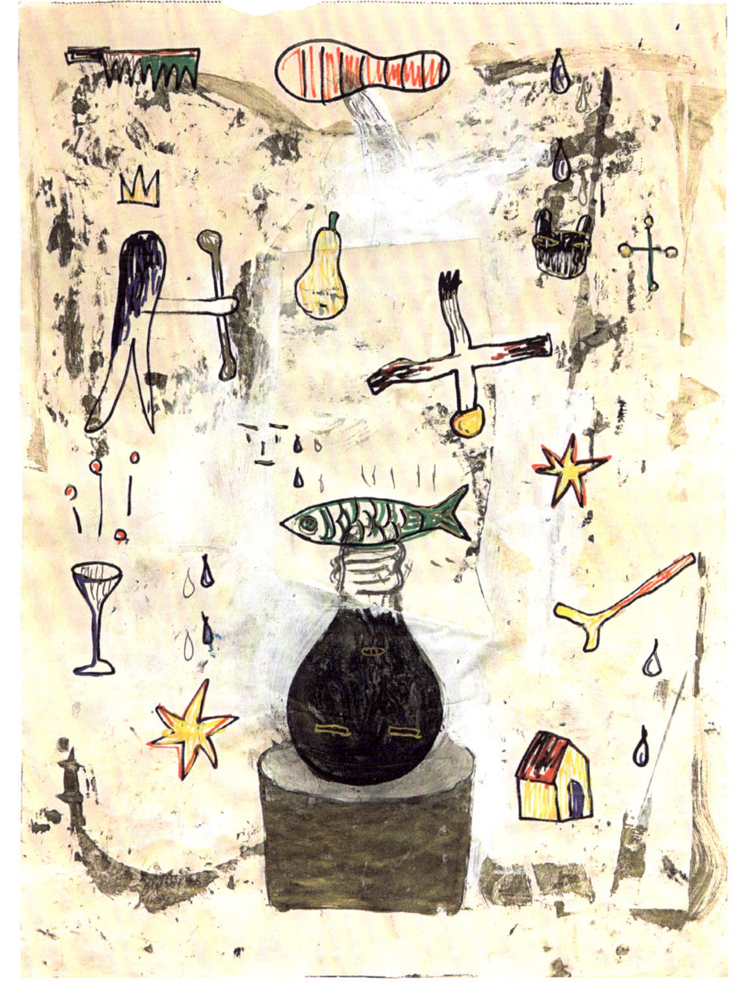

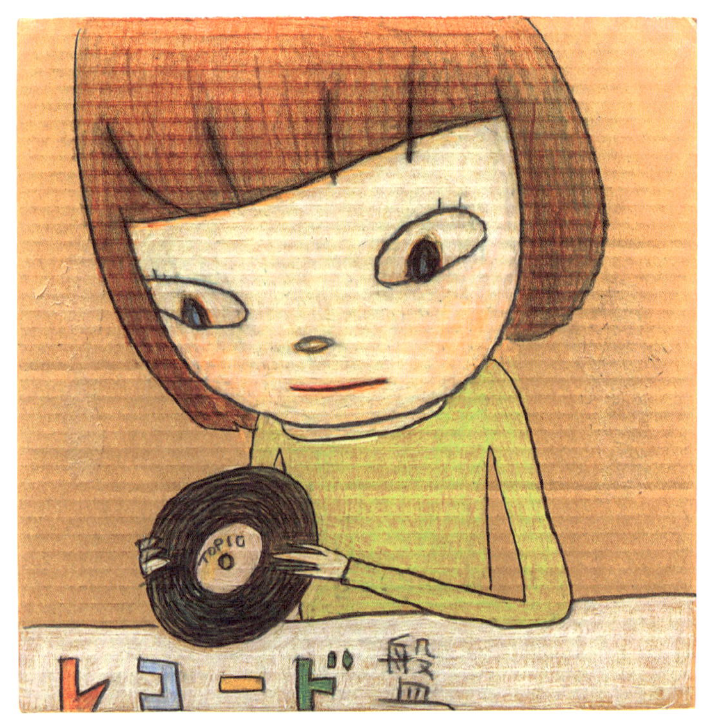
レコード盤

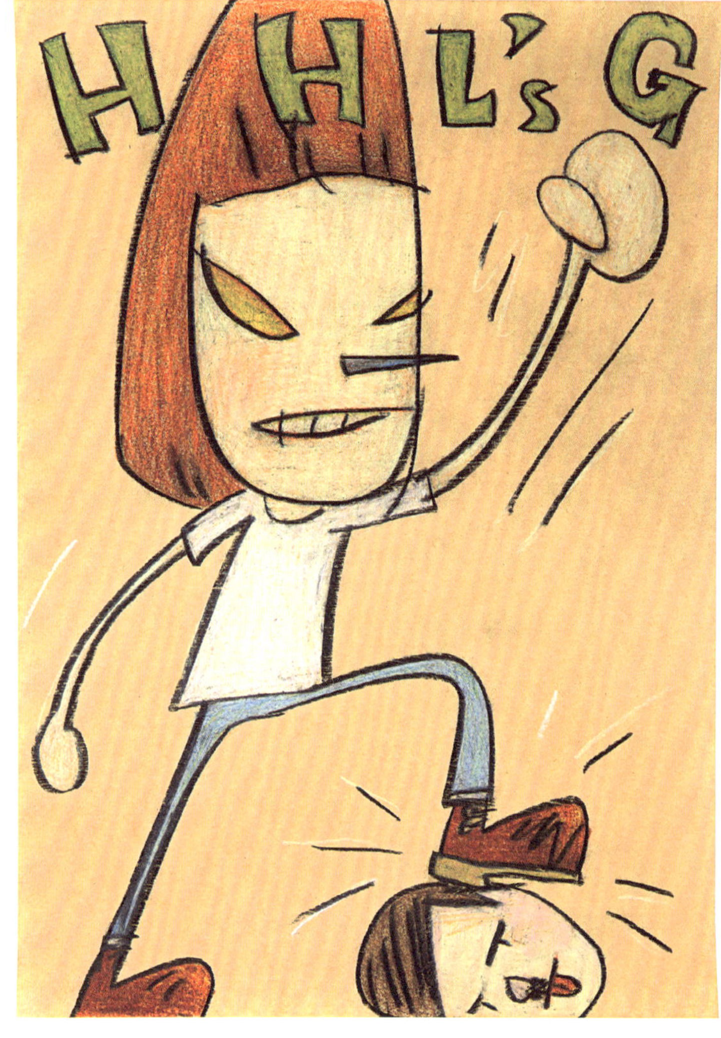
H H L's G

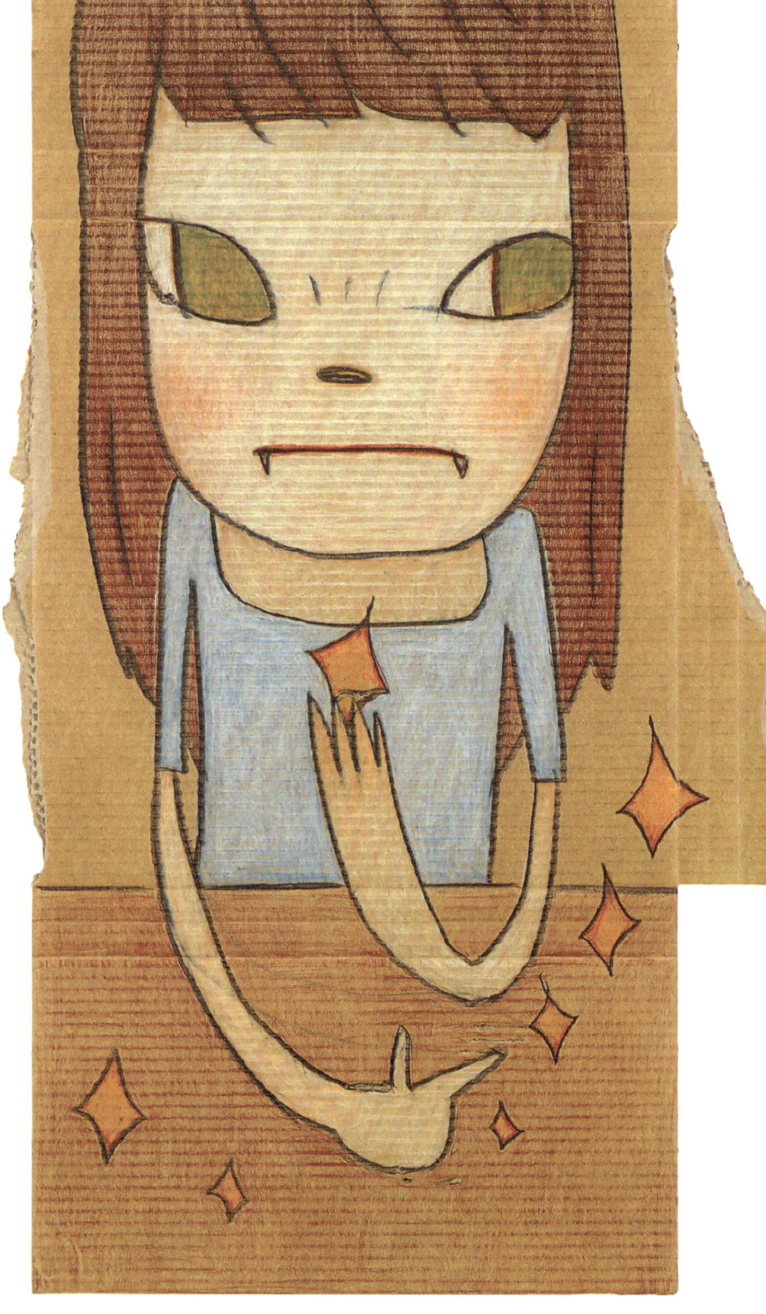

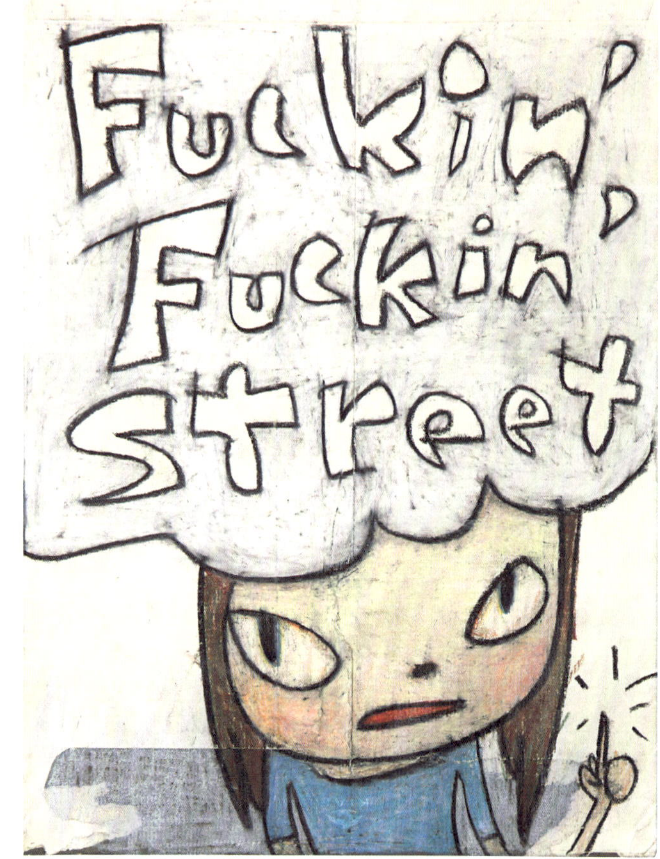
Fuckin'
Fuckin'
Street

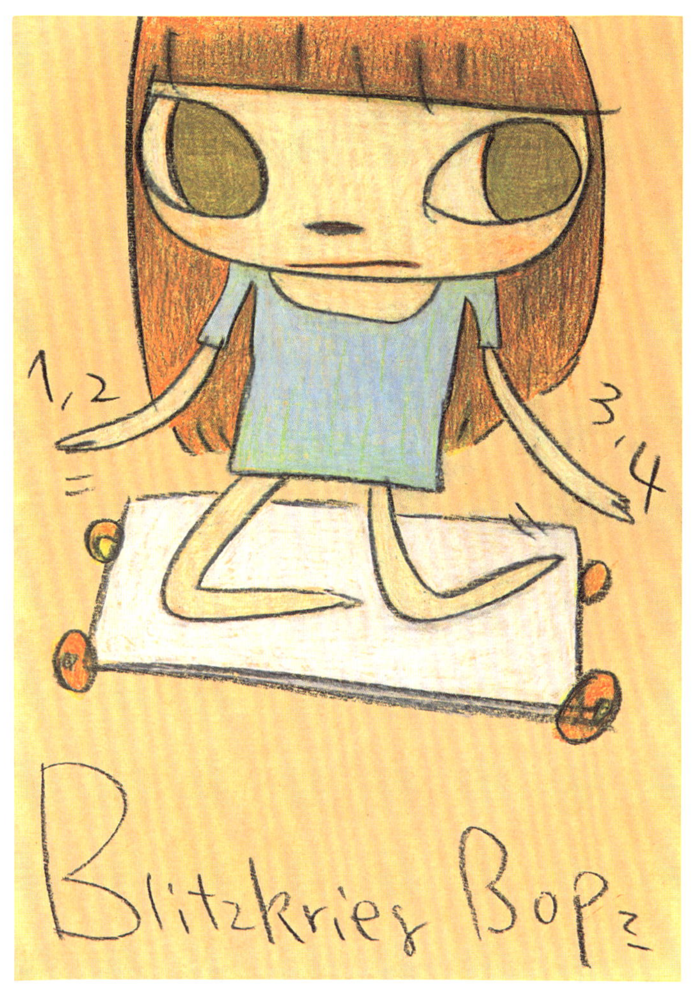
1,2
3,4
Blitzkrieg Bop

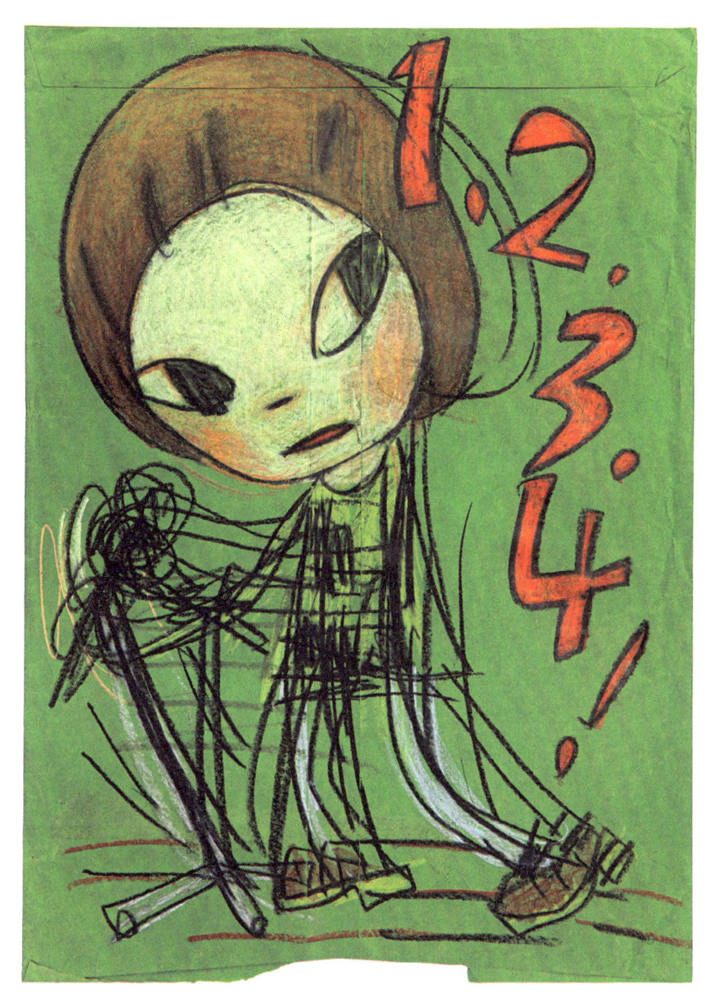
1.2.3.4!

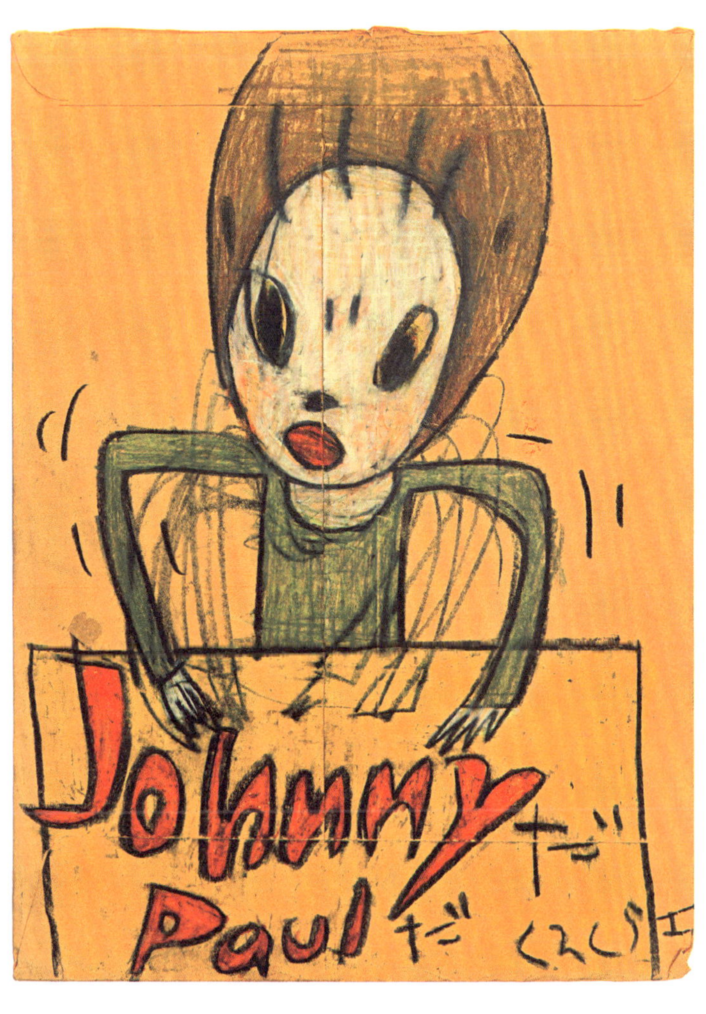
Johnny
Paul

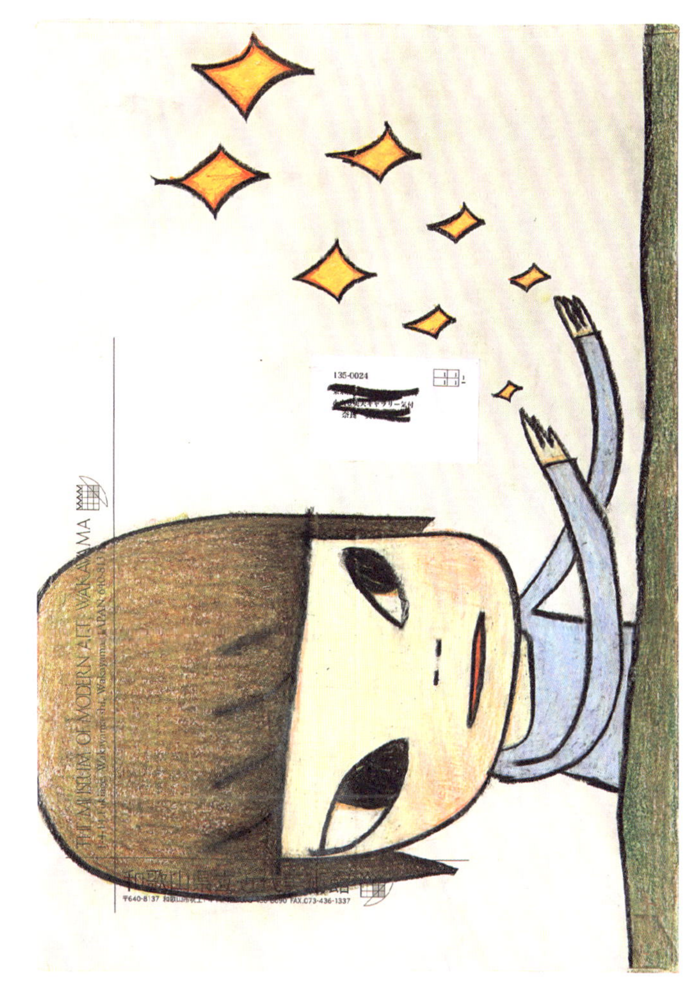

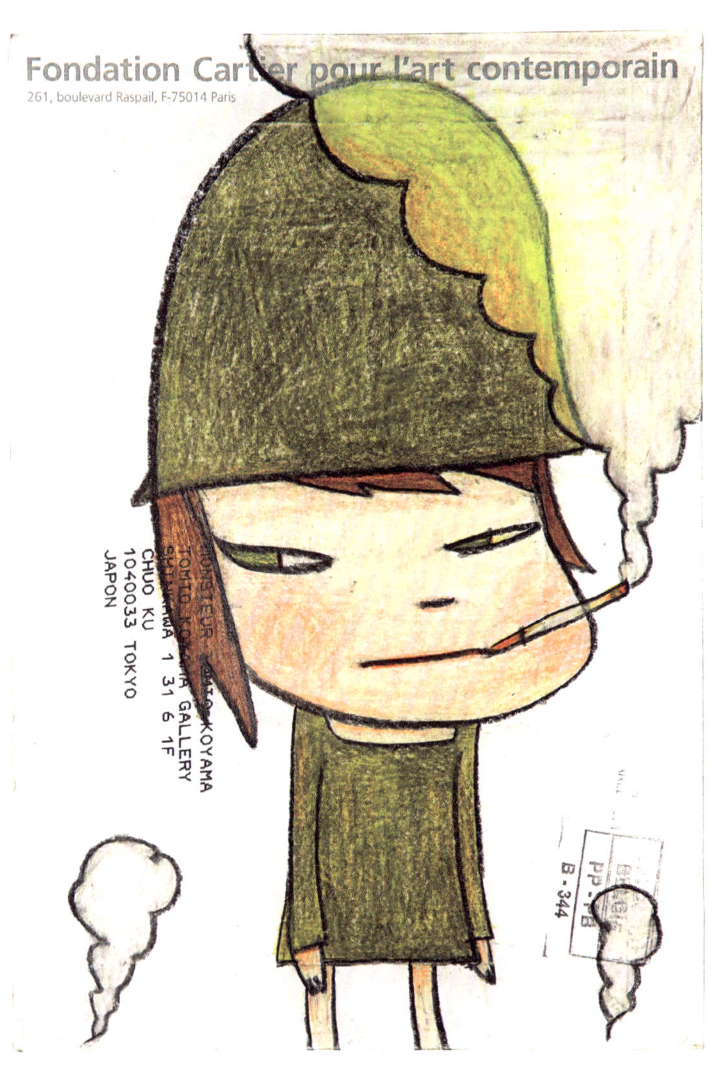
Fondation Cartier pour l'art contemporain
261, boulevard Raspail, F-75014 Paris
CHUO KU
1040033 TOKYO
JAPON

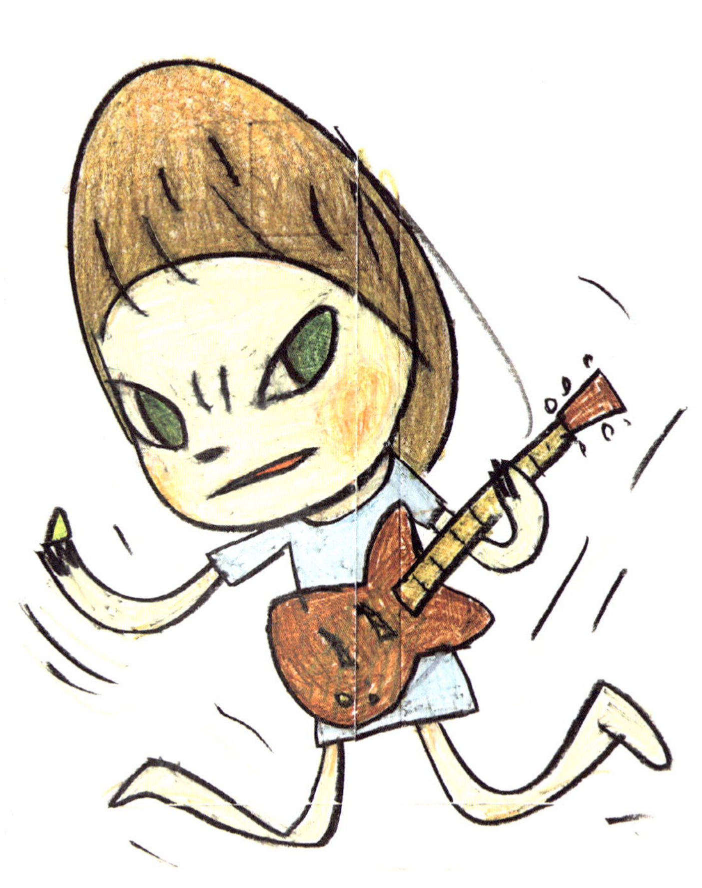

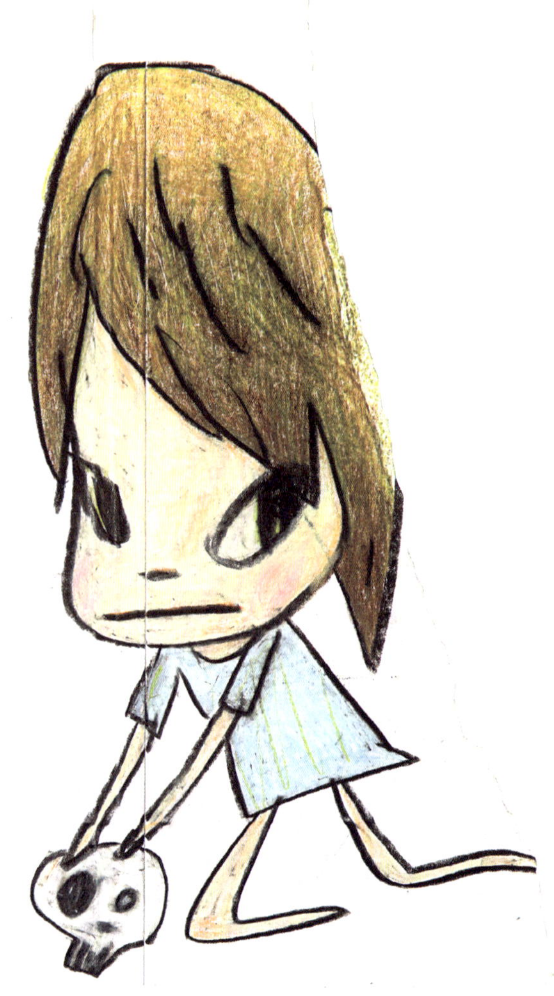

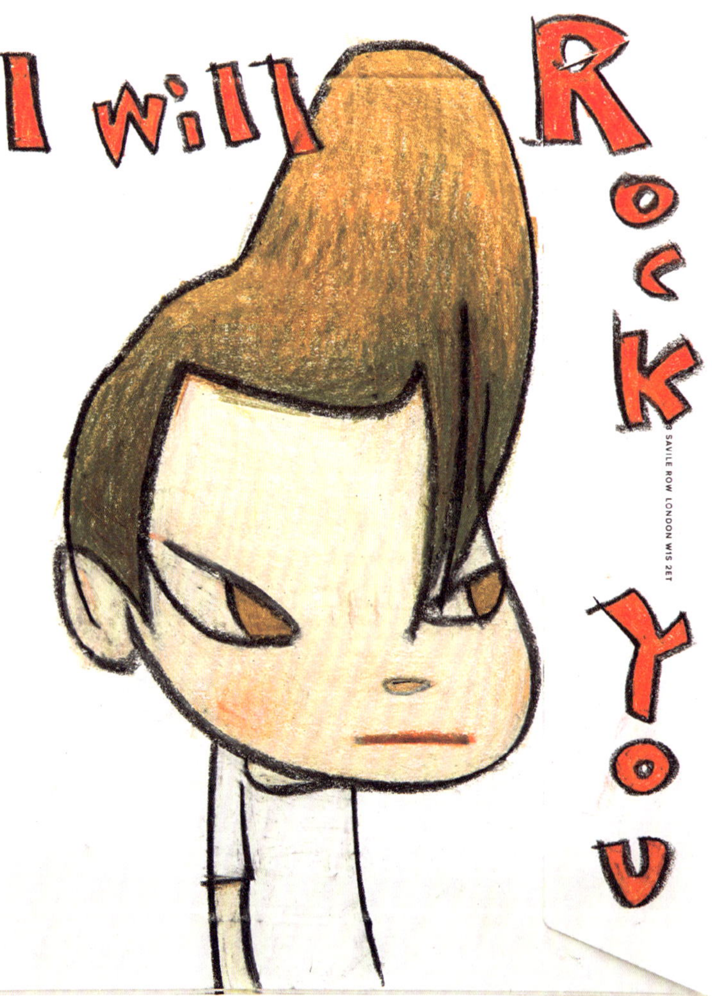
I will Rock You
SAVILE ROW LONDON W1S 2ET

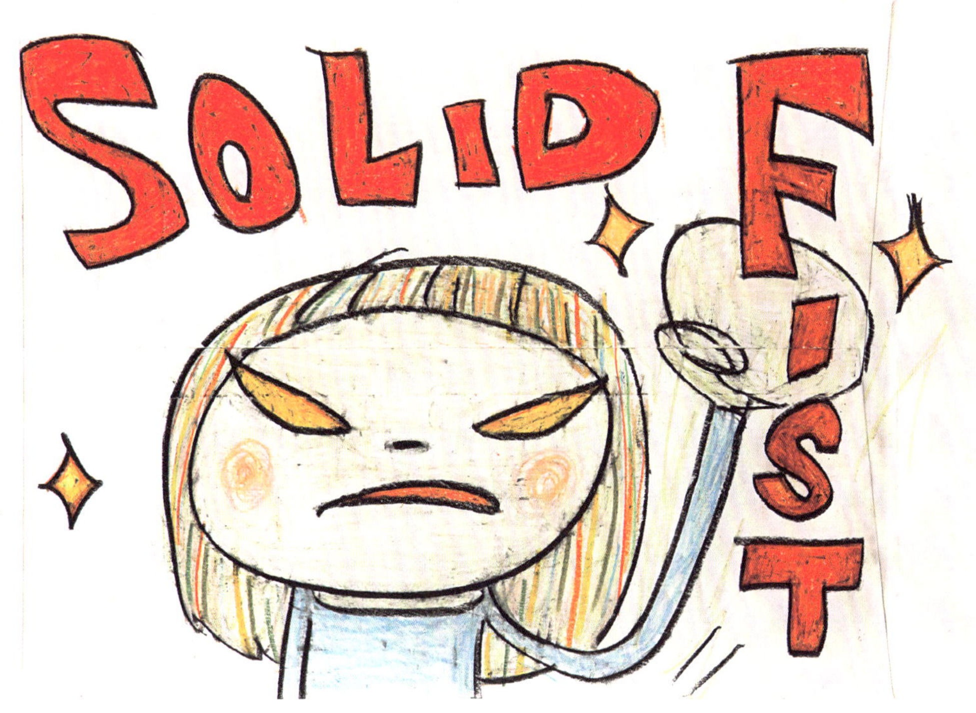
SOLID FIST

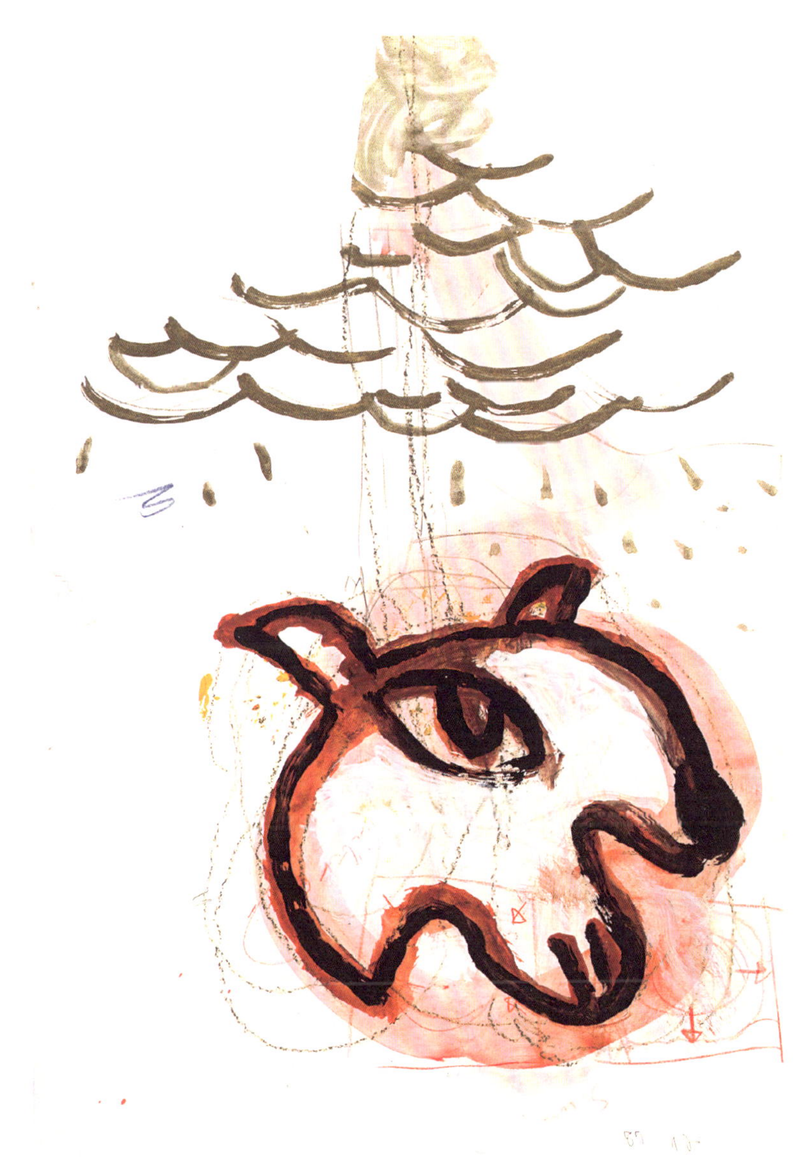

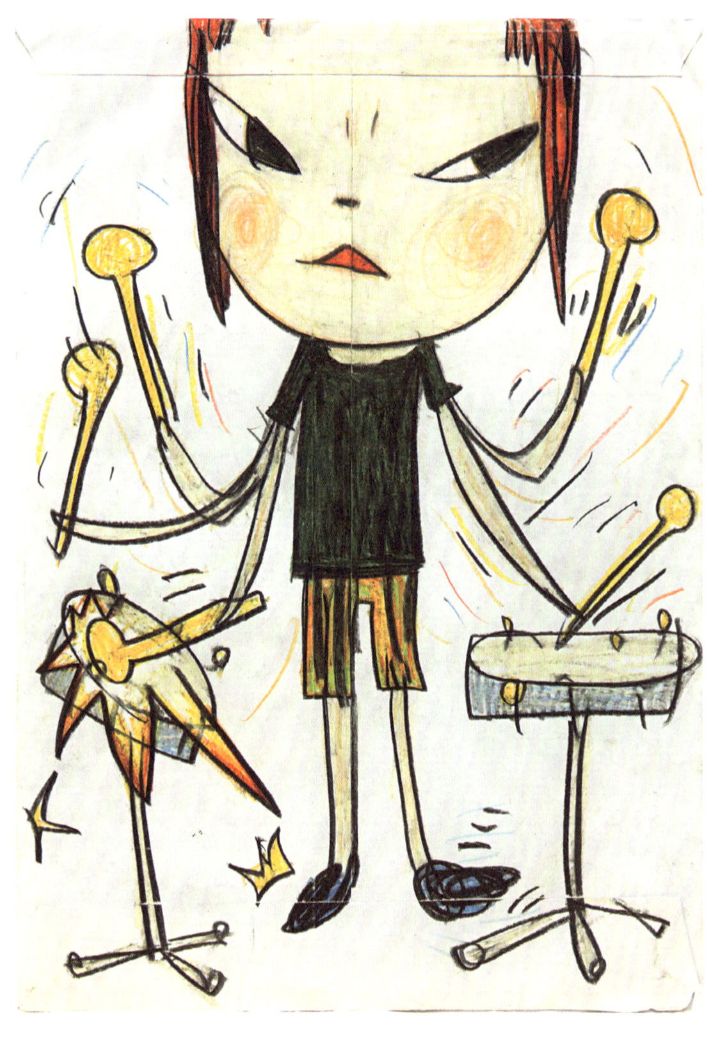

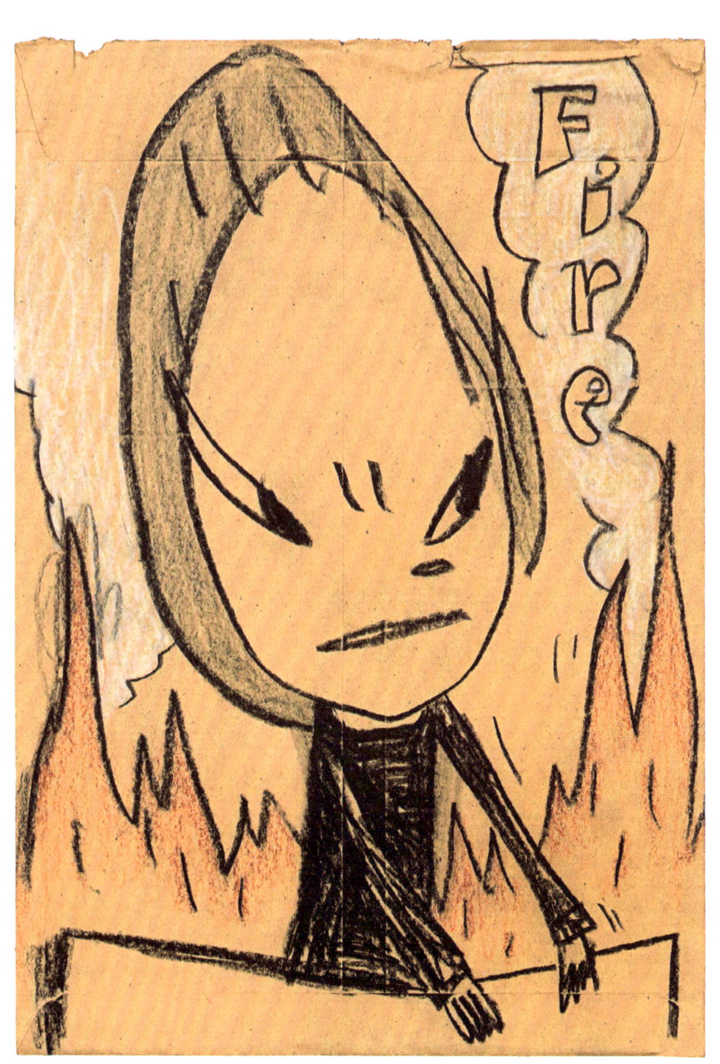
Fire

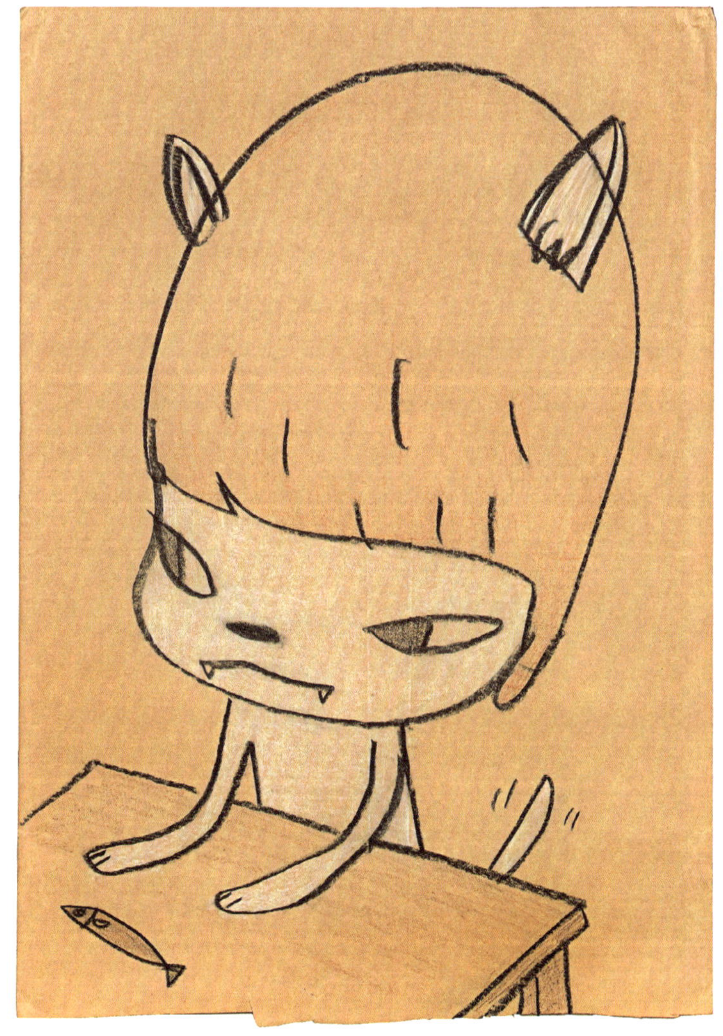

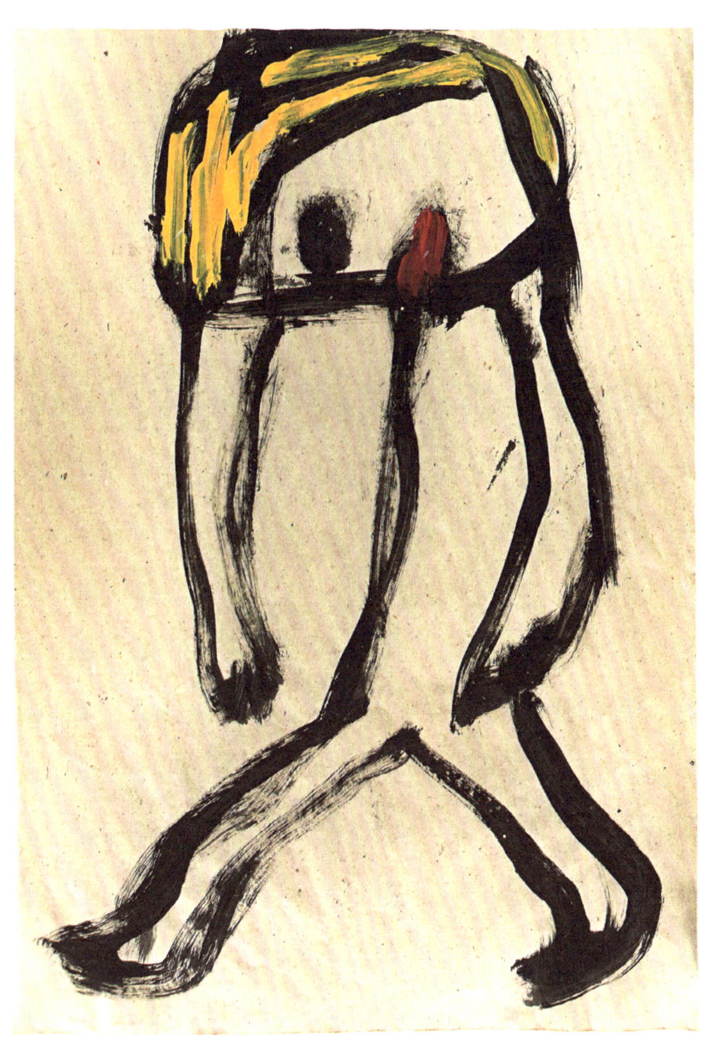

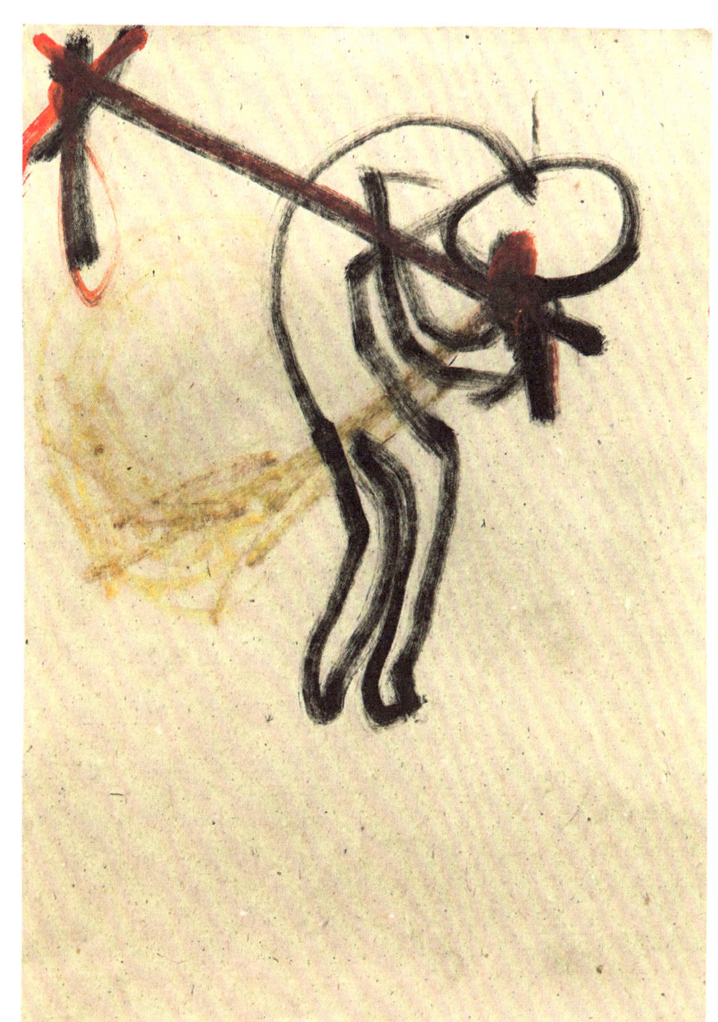

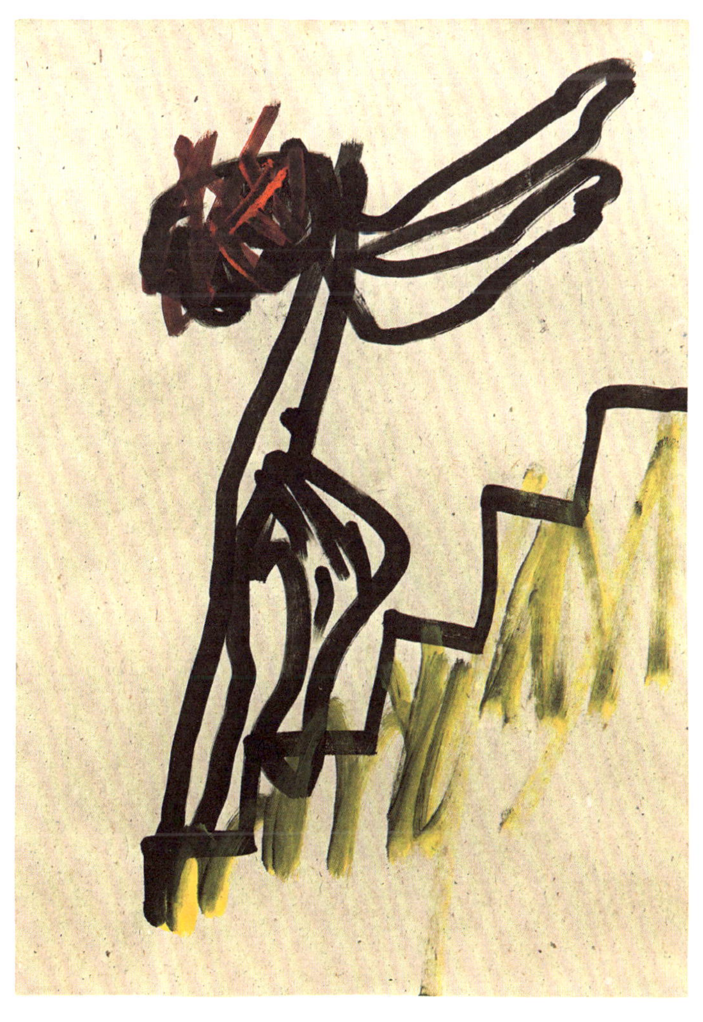

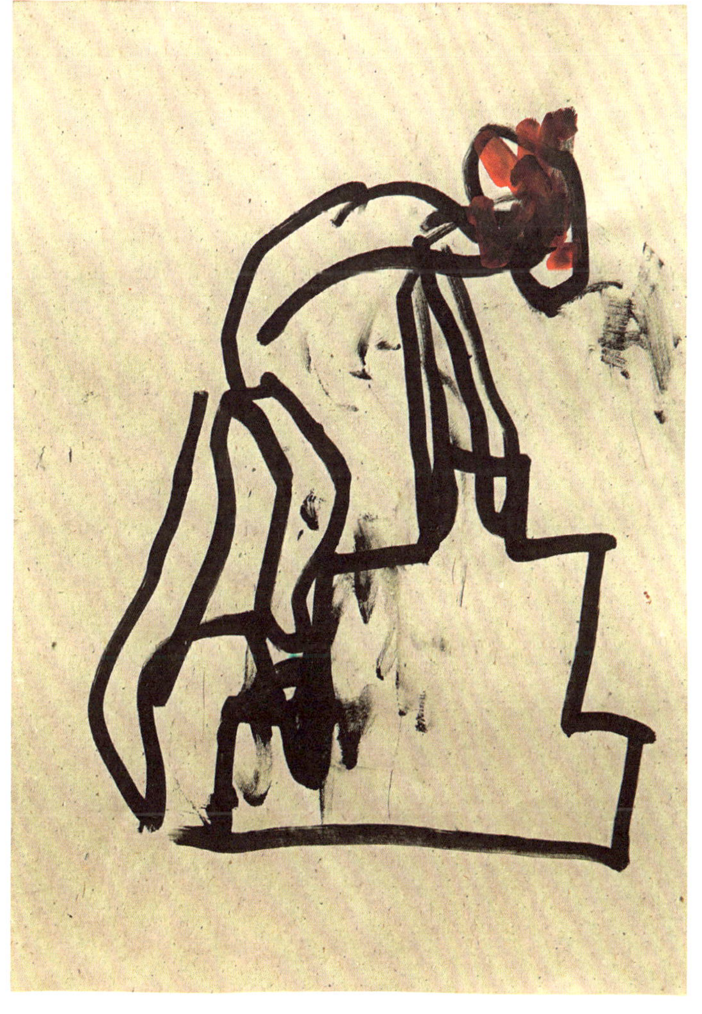

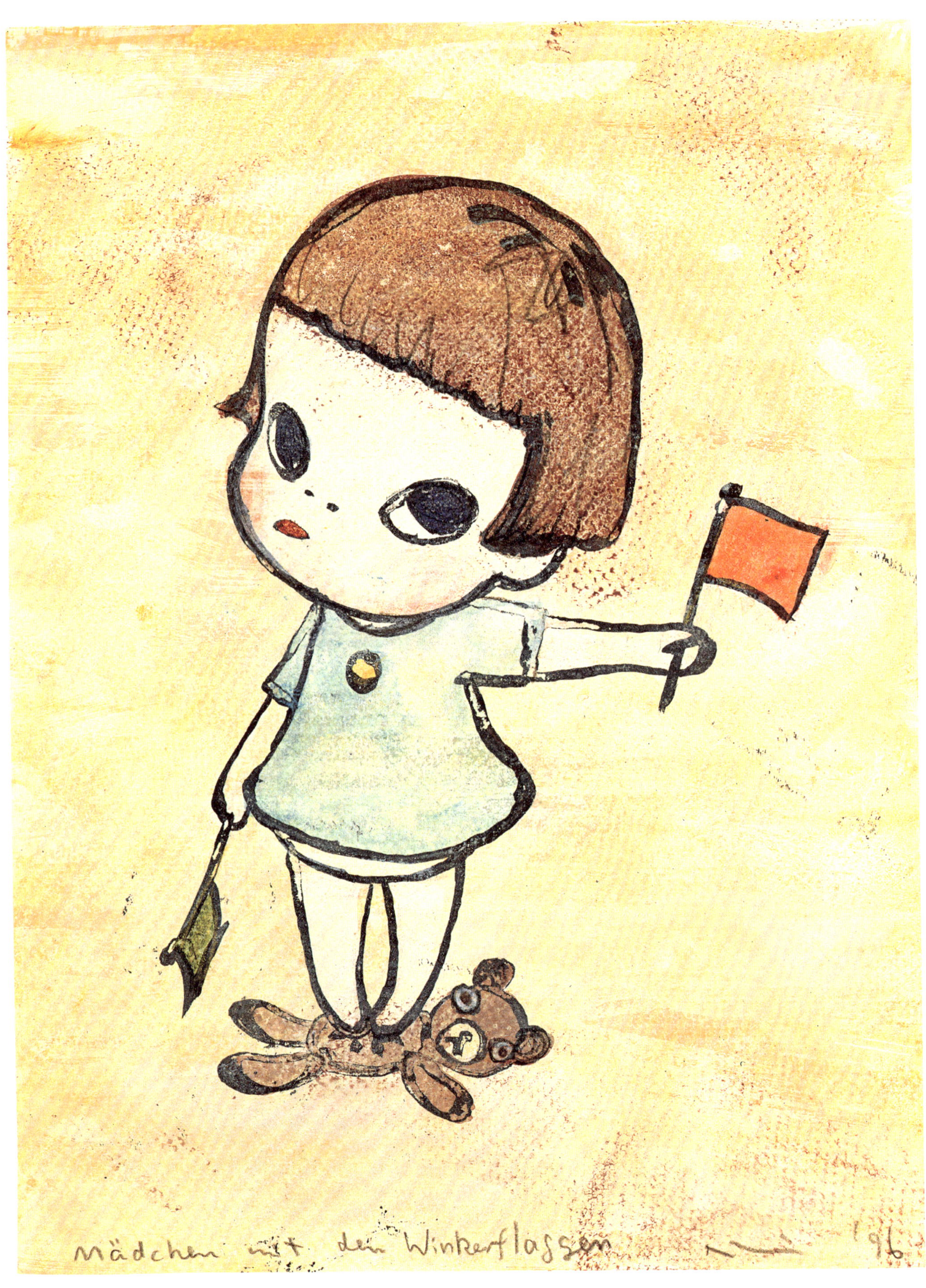
Mädchen mit den Winkerflaggen '96

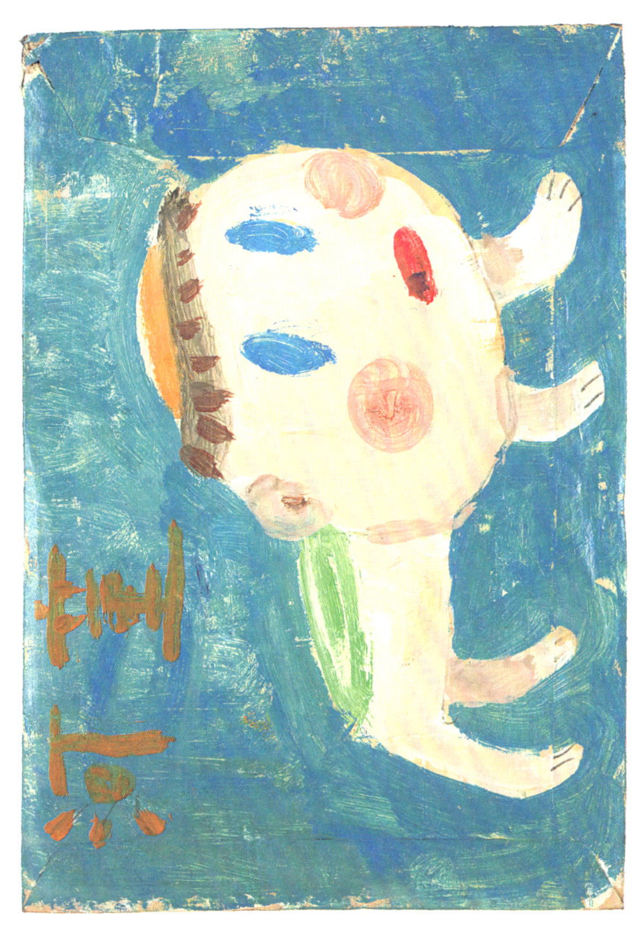

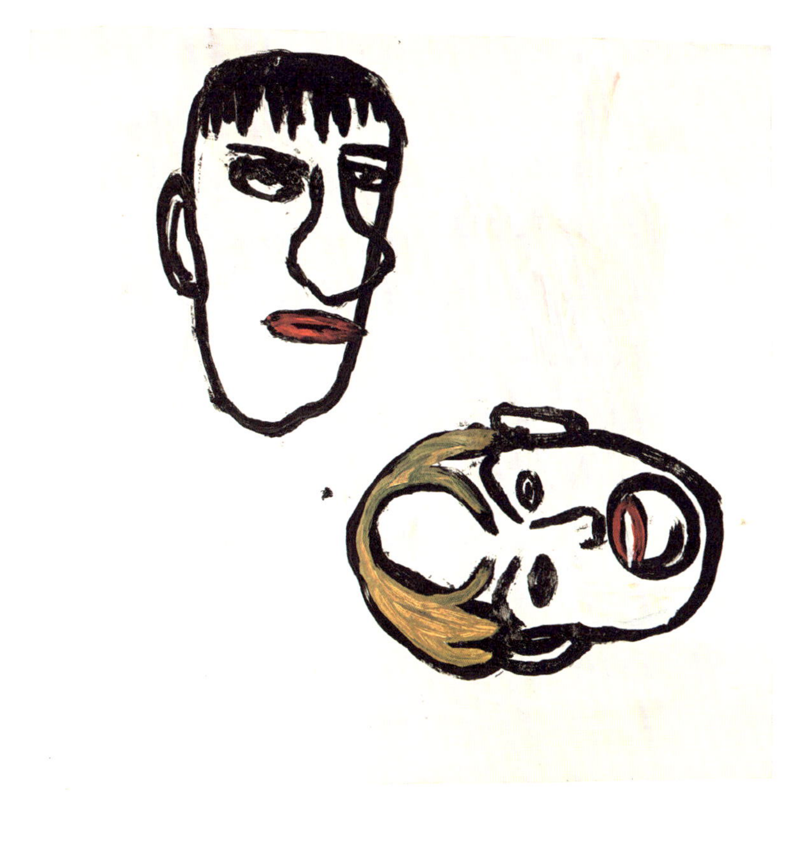

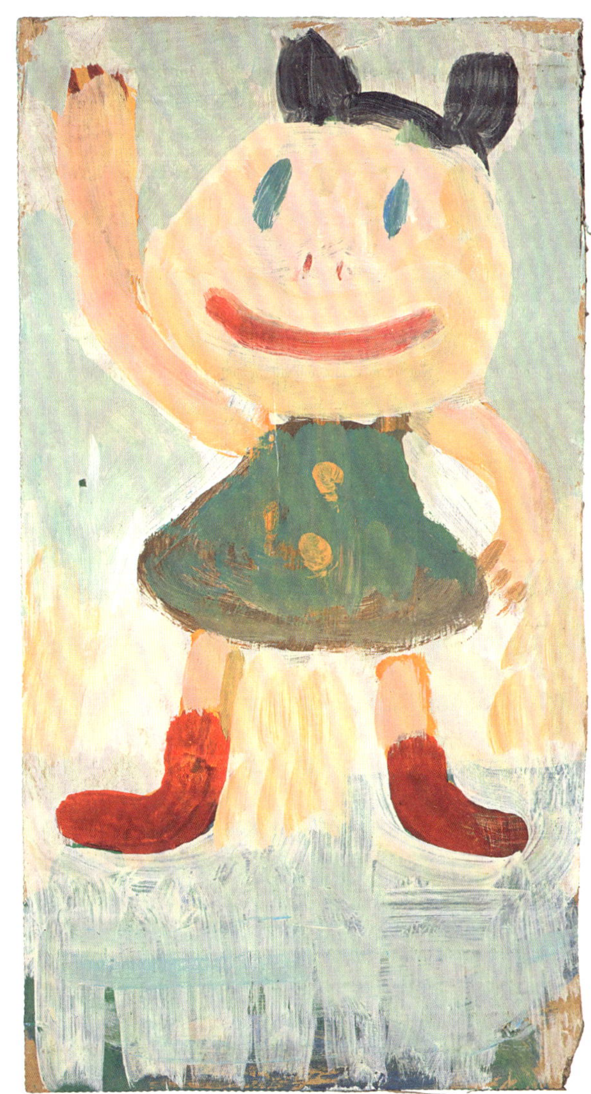

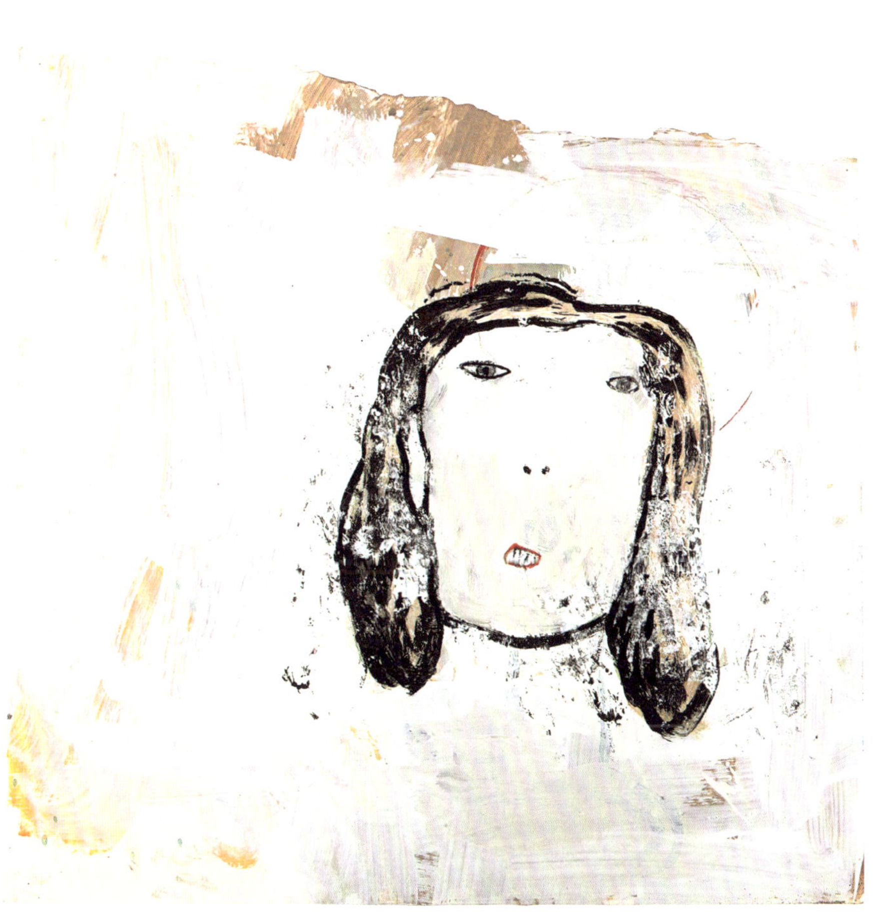

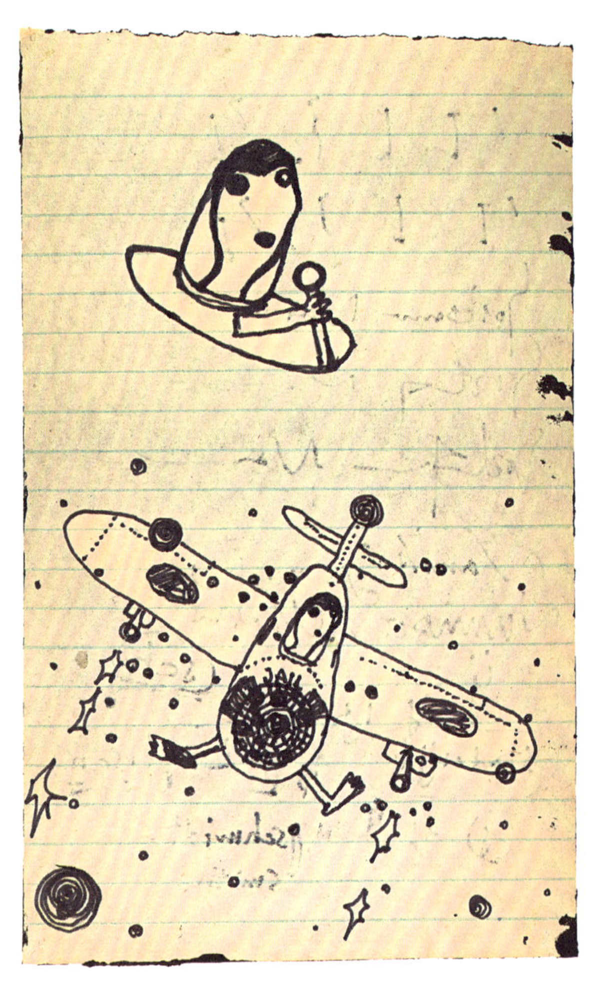

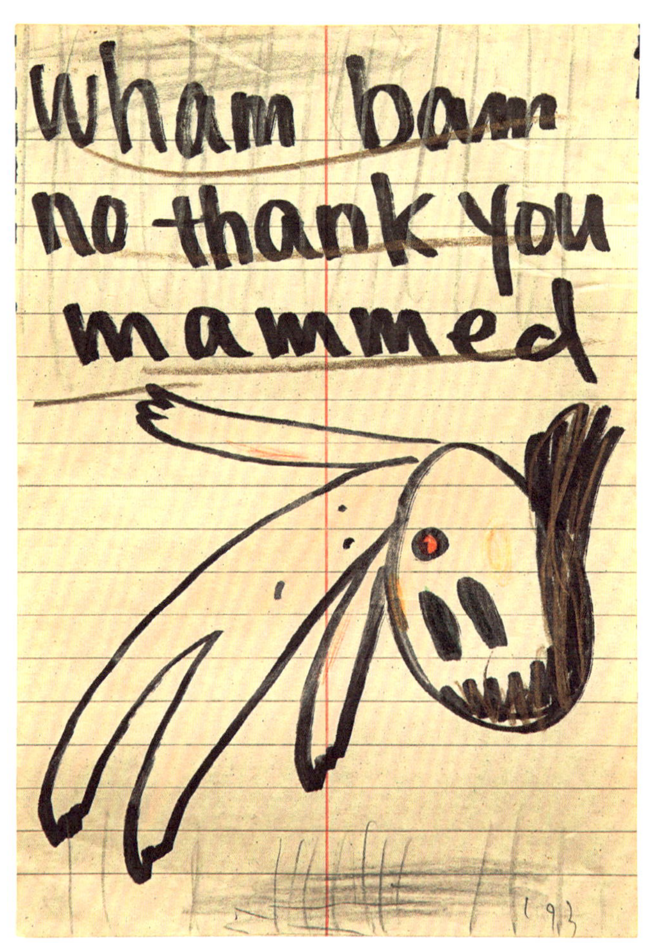

wham bam
no thank you
mammed

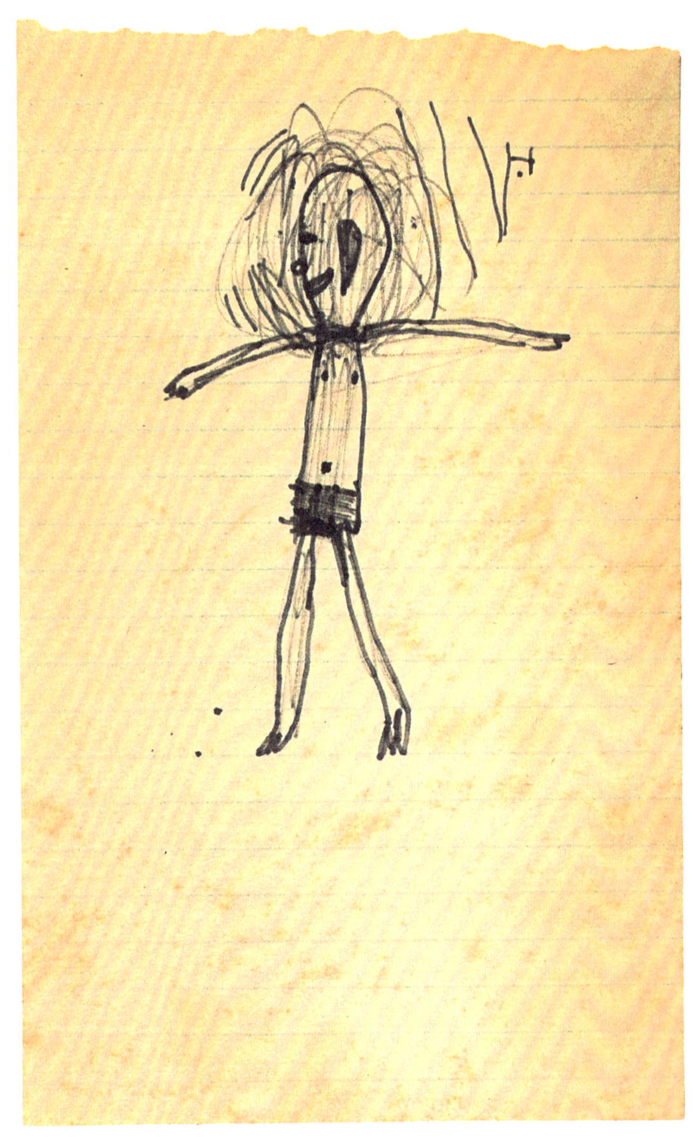

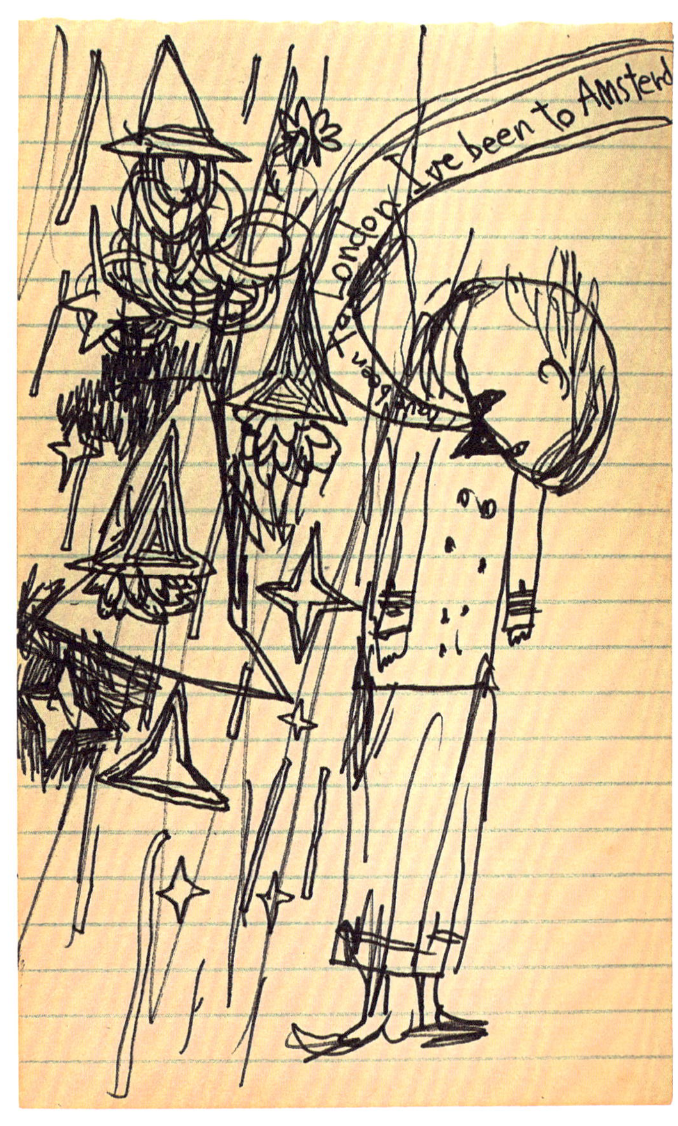

Ive been to Amsterd
London

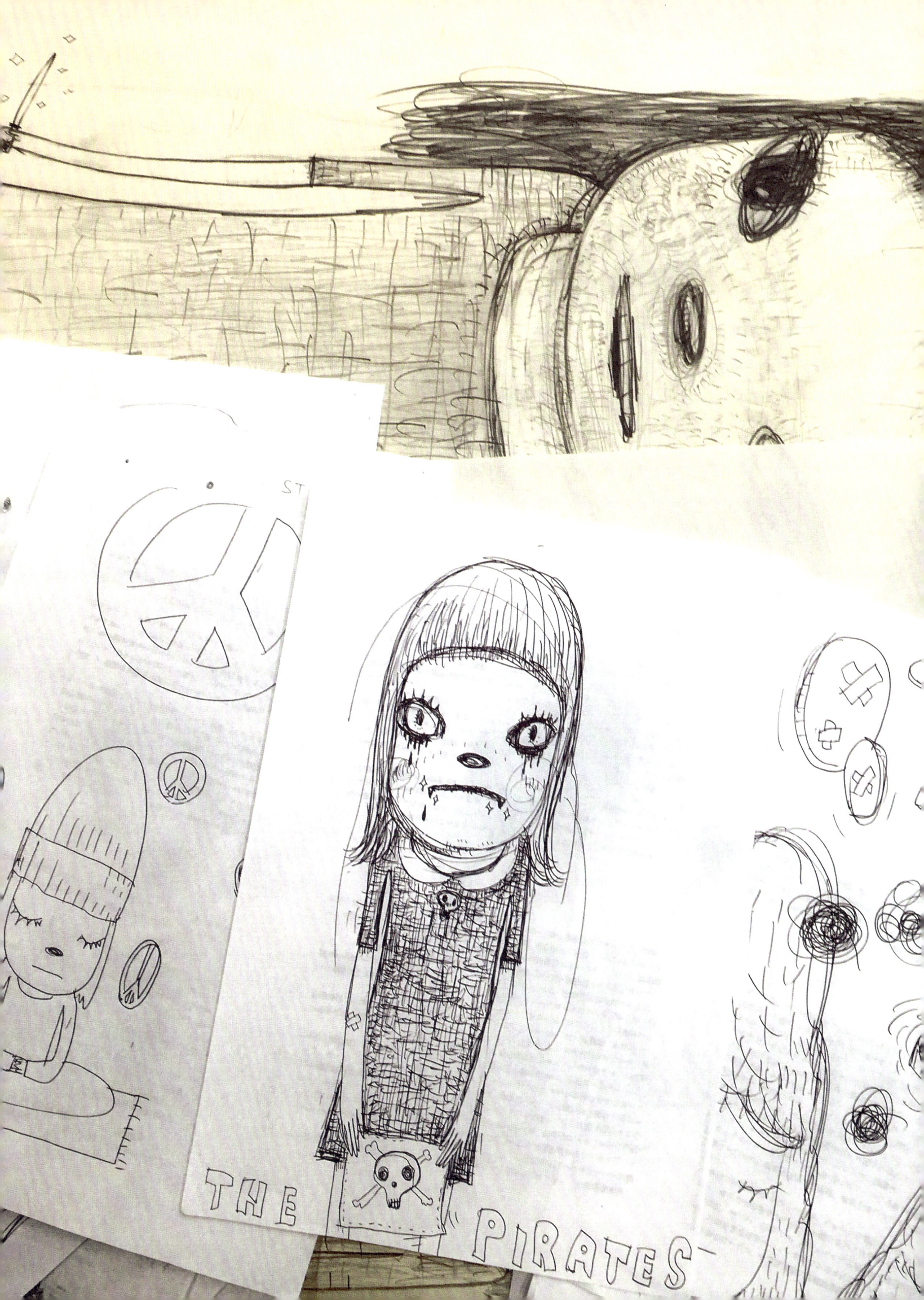
THE
PIRATES

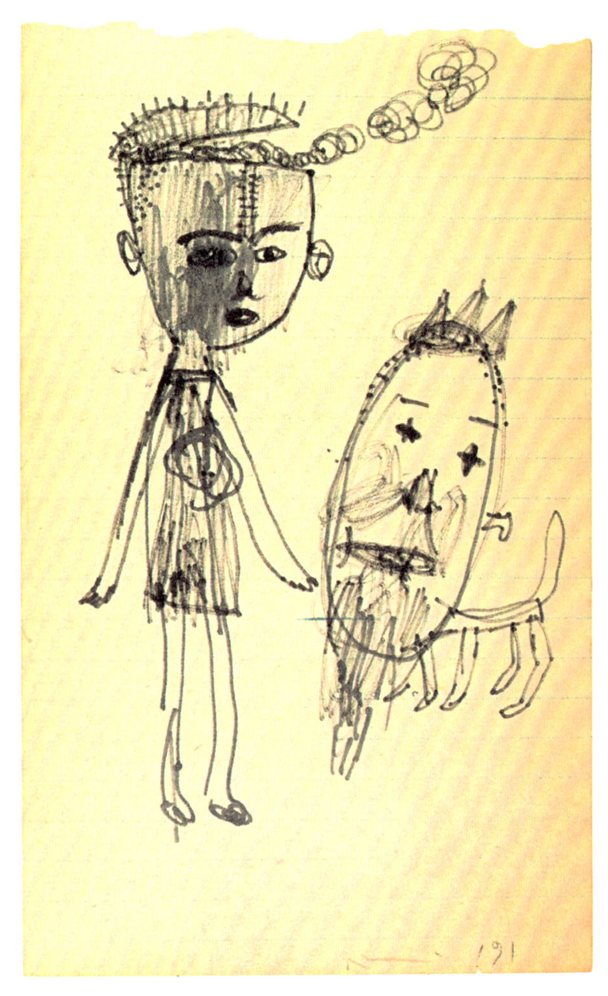

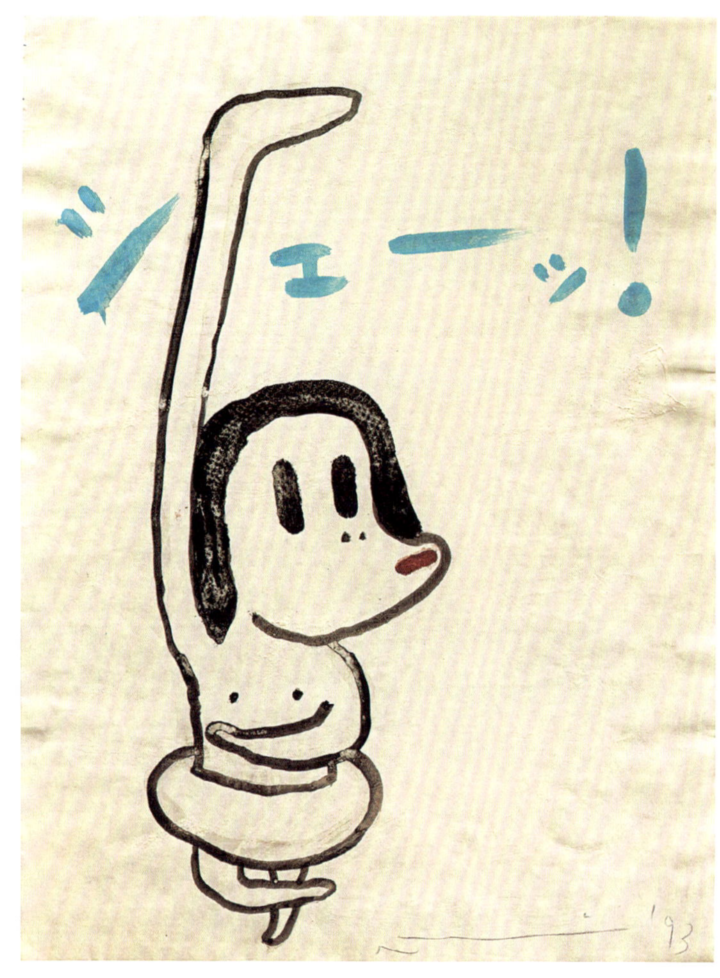
ジェーッ!

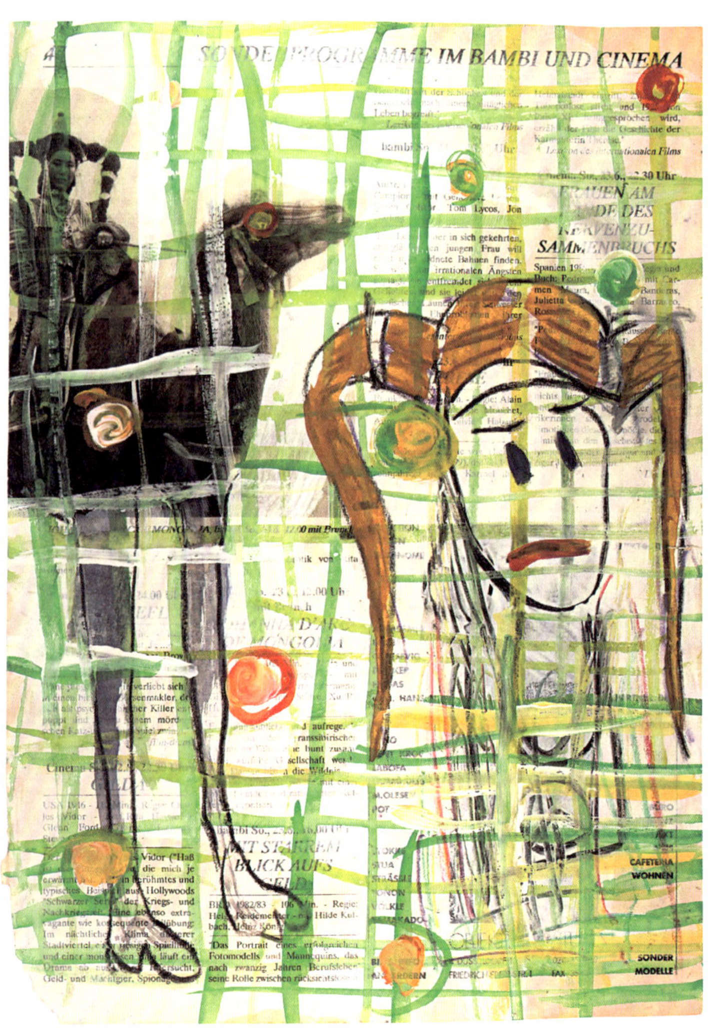
IM BAMBI UND CINEMA
CAFETERIA
WOHNEN
SONDER
MODELLE

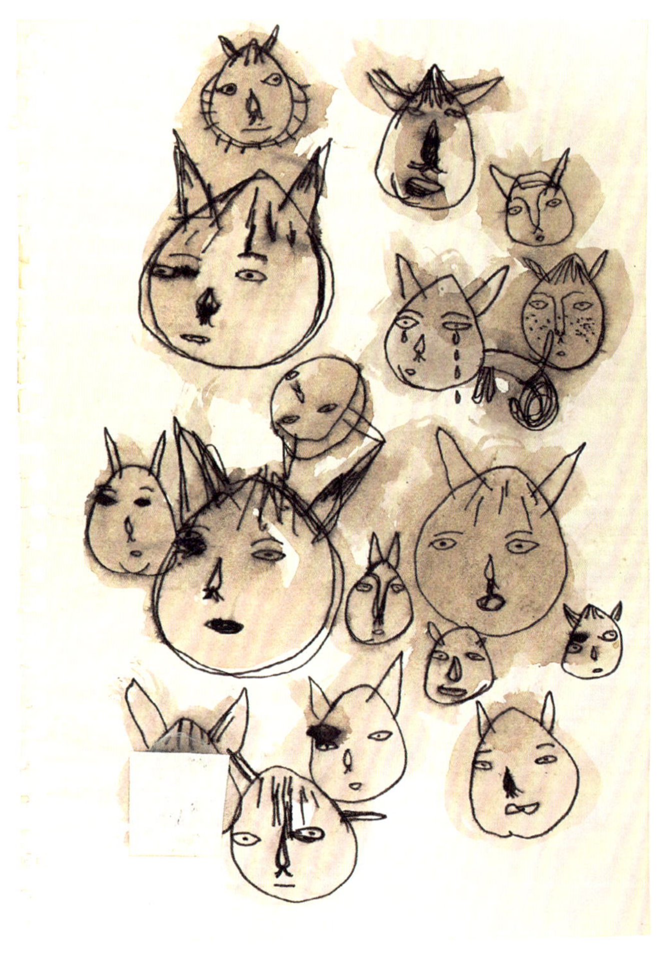

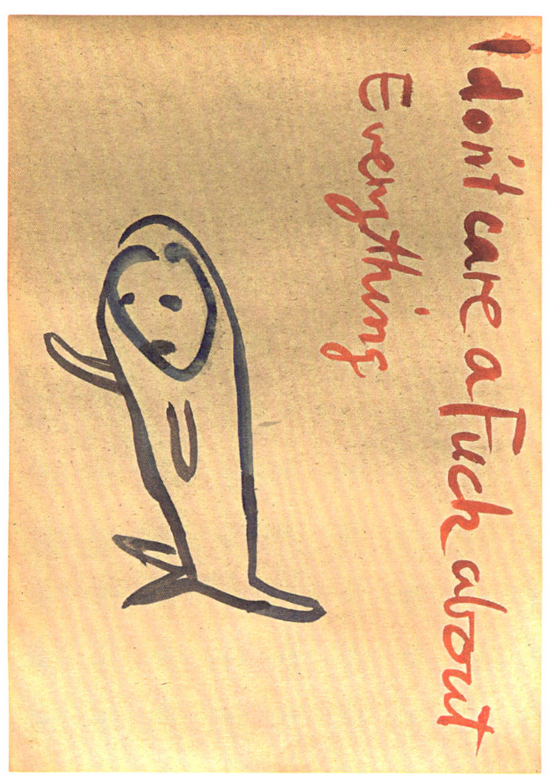
I don't care a Fuck about
Everything

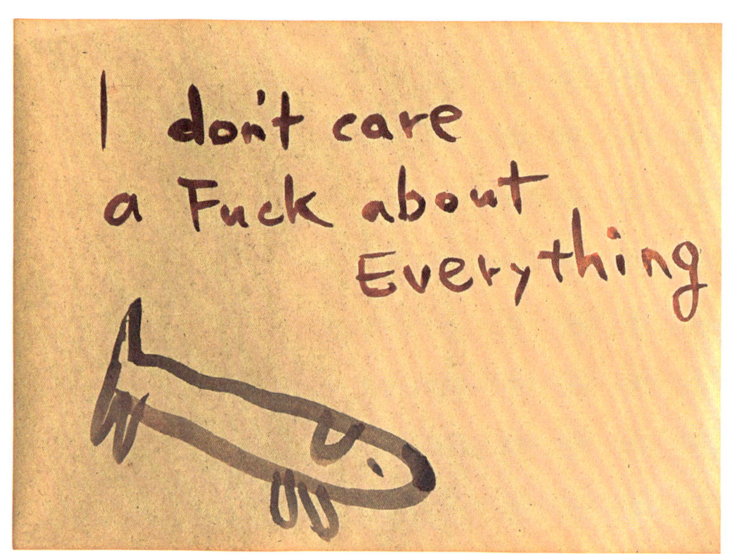
I don't care
a Fuck about
Everything

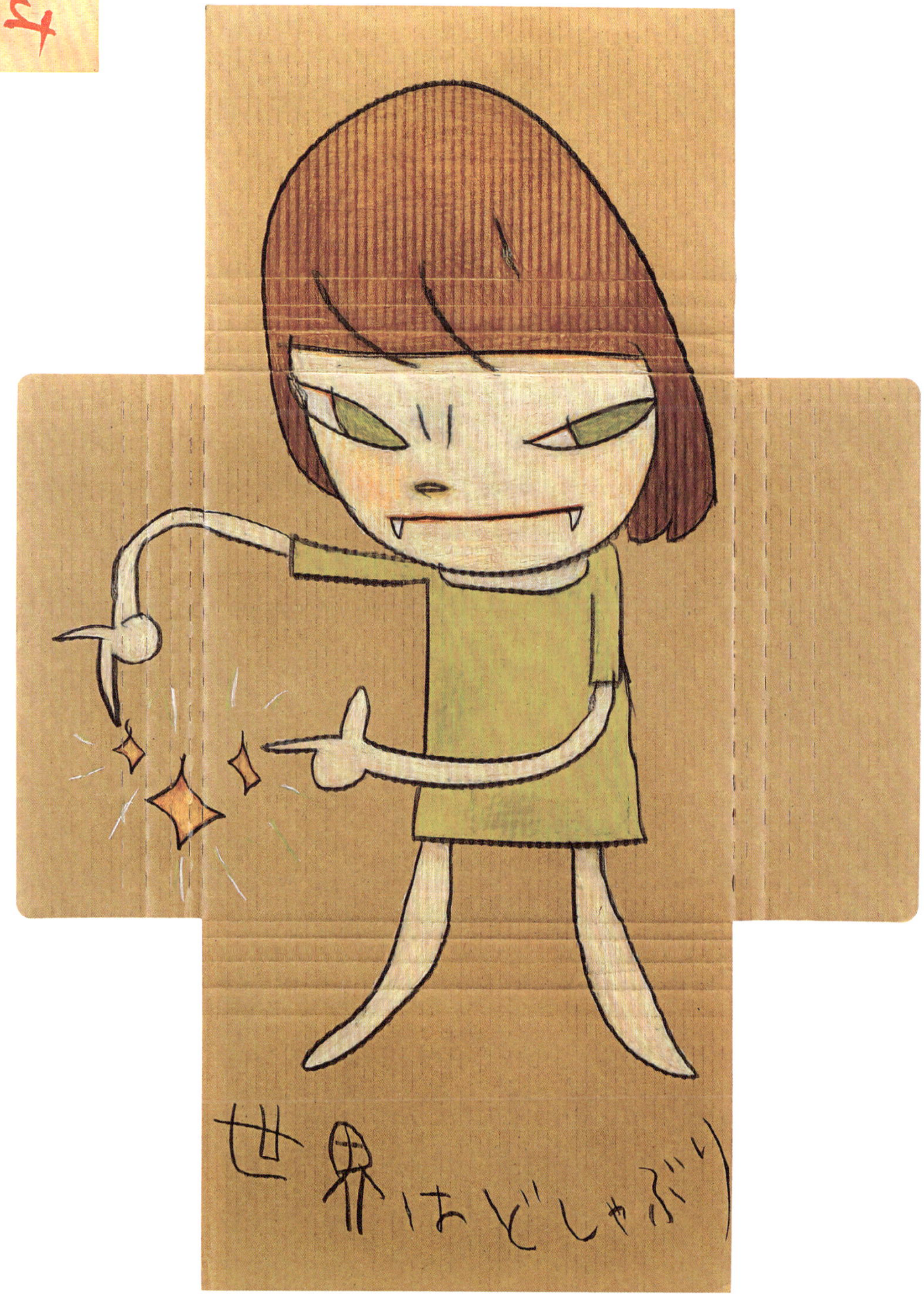

世界はどしゃぶり

Fire, 2010
Untitled, 1989
Untitled, 1989
Untitled, 1989
Untitled, 1989
Mädchen mit den Winkerflaggen, 1996
Untitled, 1990
Untitled, 1991
Untitled, 1991
Untitled, 1990
Untitled, 1991
Untitled, 1993
Untitled, 1991
Untitled, 1991
Untitled, 1991
Untitled, 1993
Untitled, 1991
Untitled, 1992
I Don't Care a Fuck about Everything, 1989
I Don't Care a Fuck about Everything, 1989
Hard Rain, 2014

IV

MY DRAWING ROOM

My Drawing Room, 2008

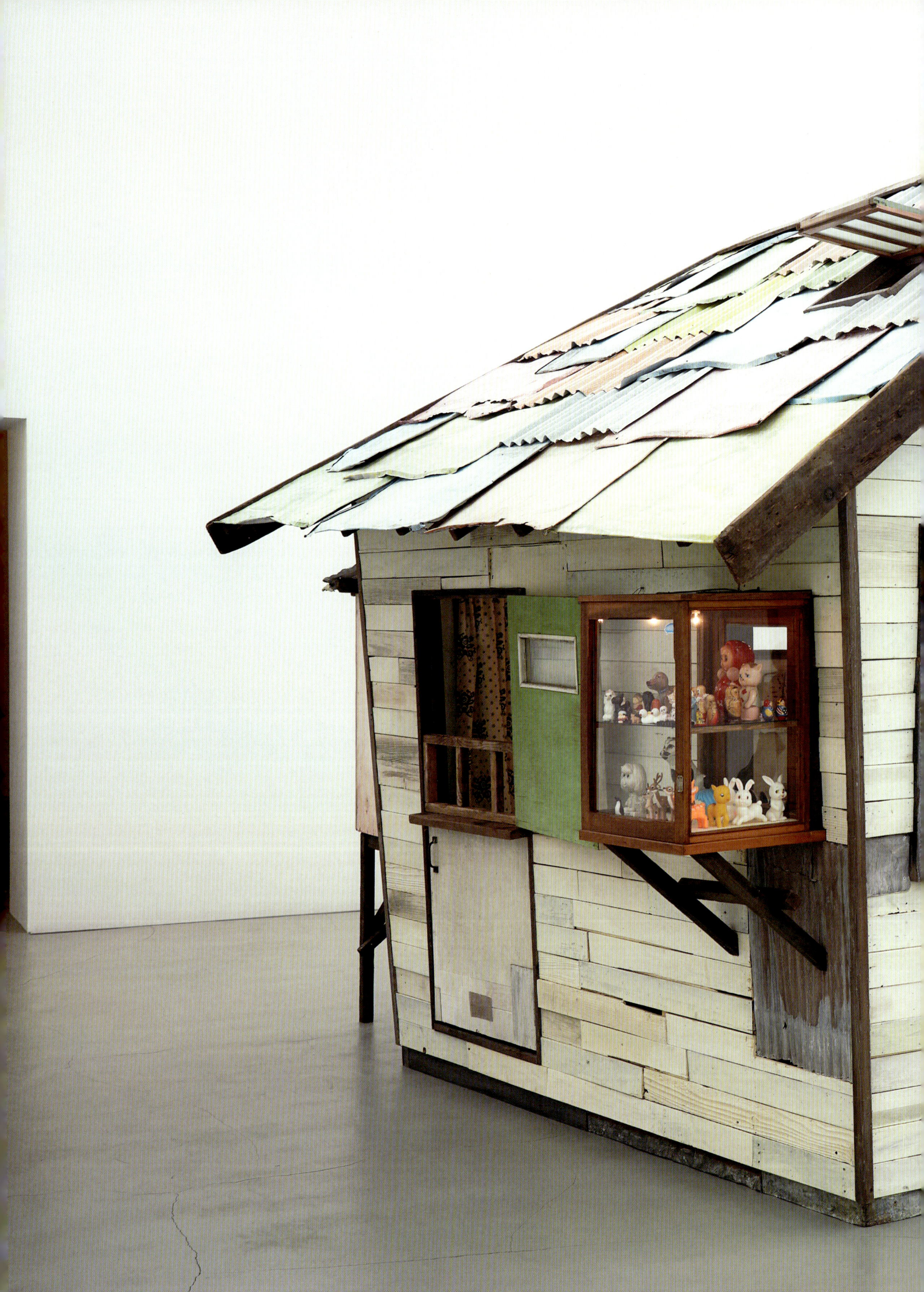

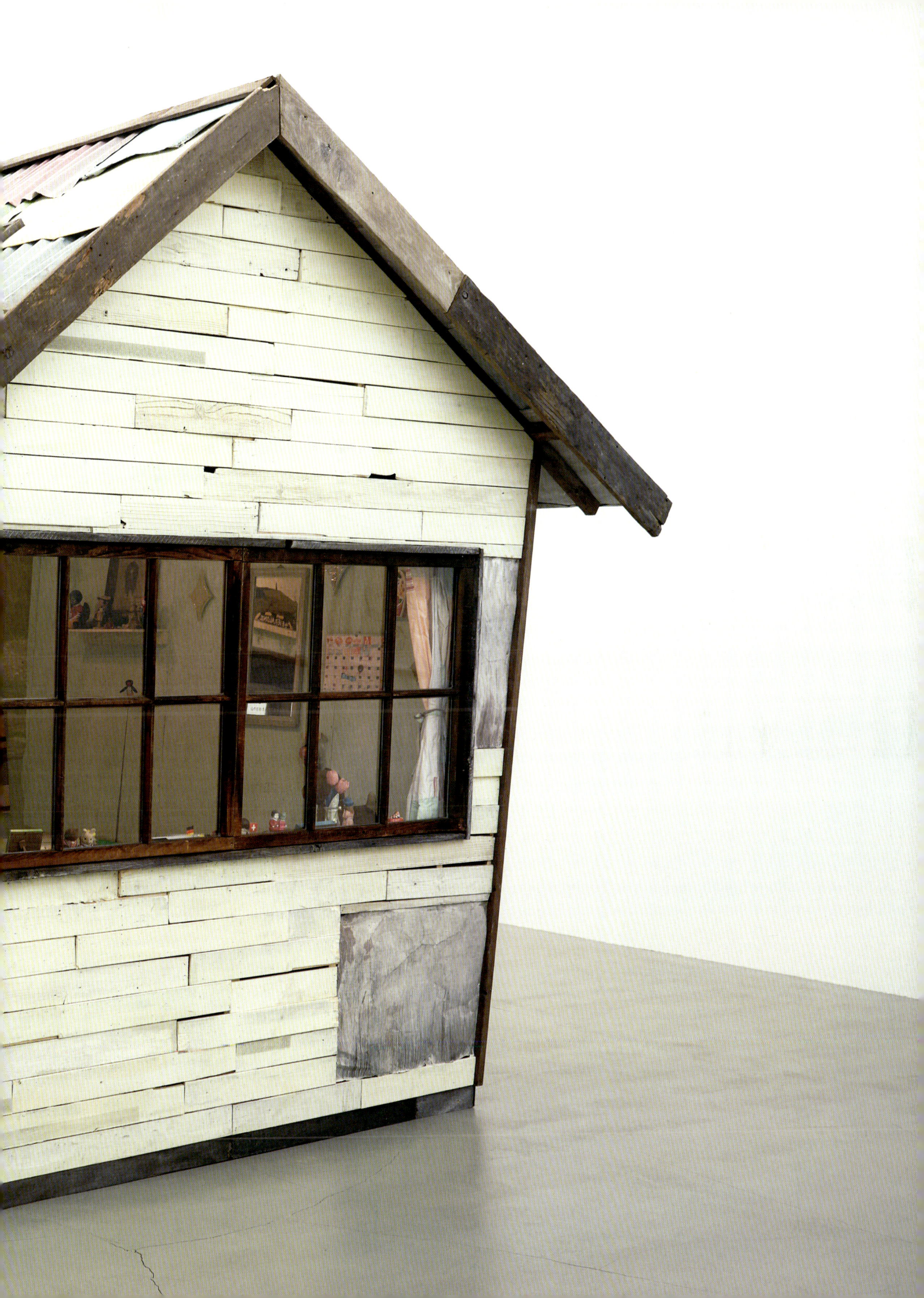

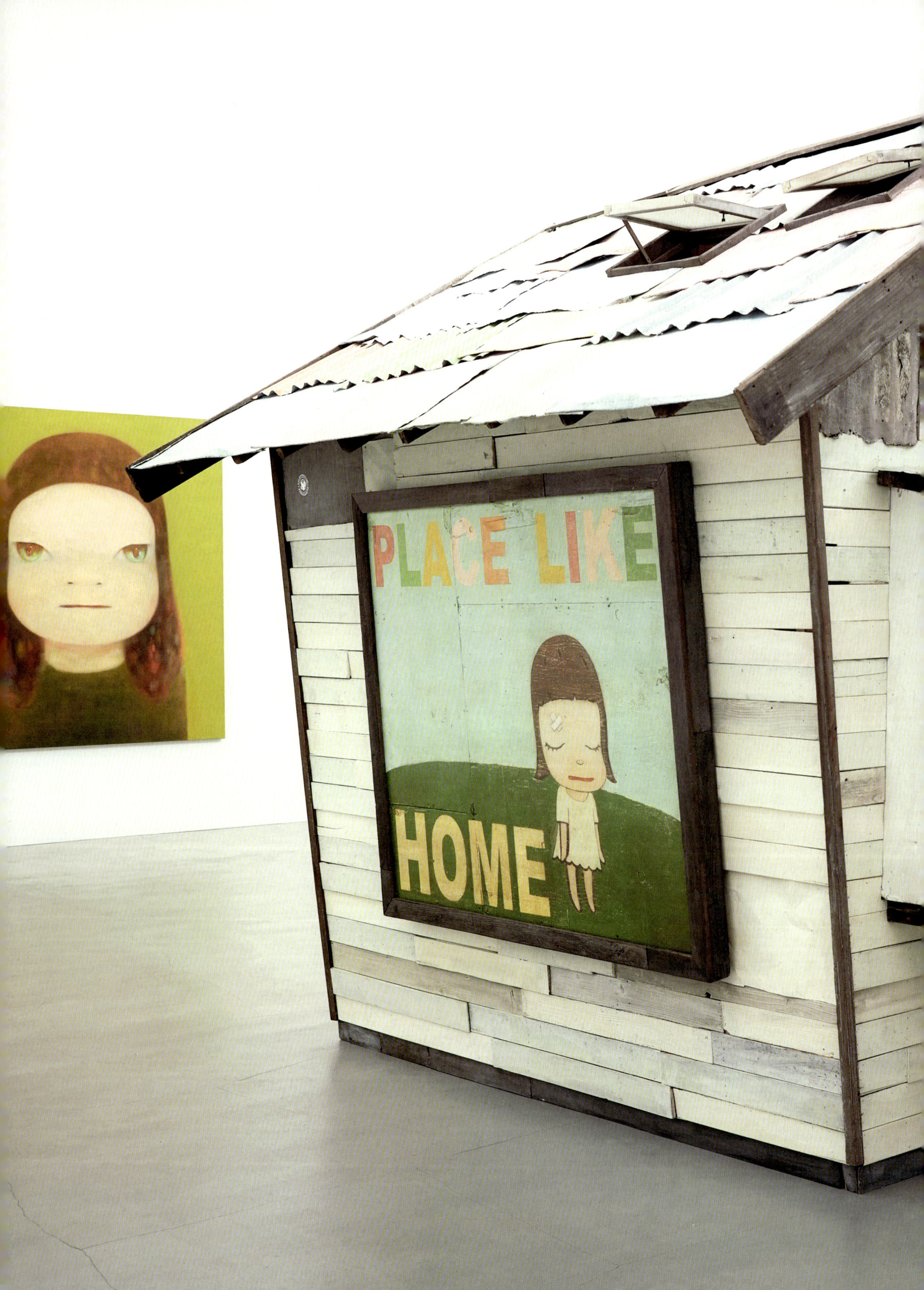
PLACE LIKE
HOME

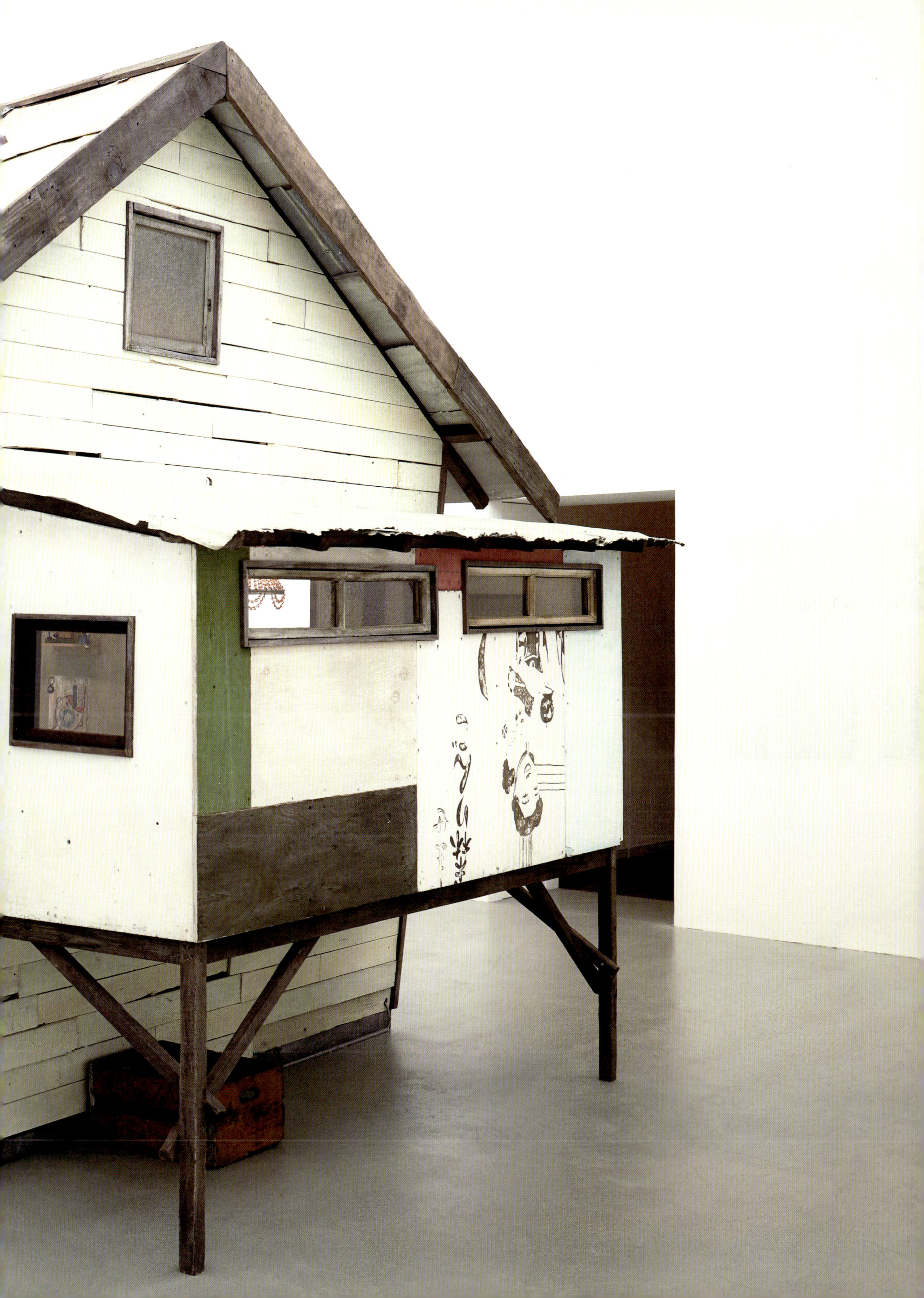

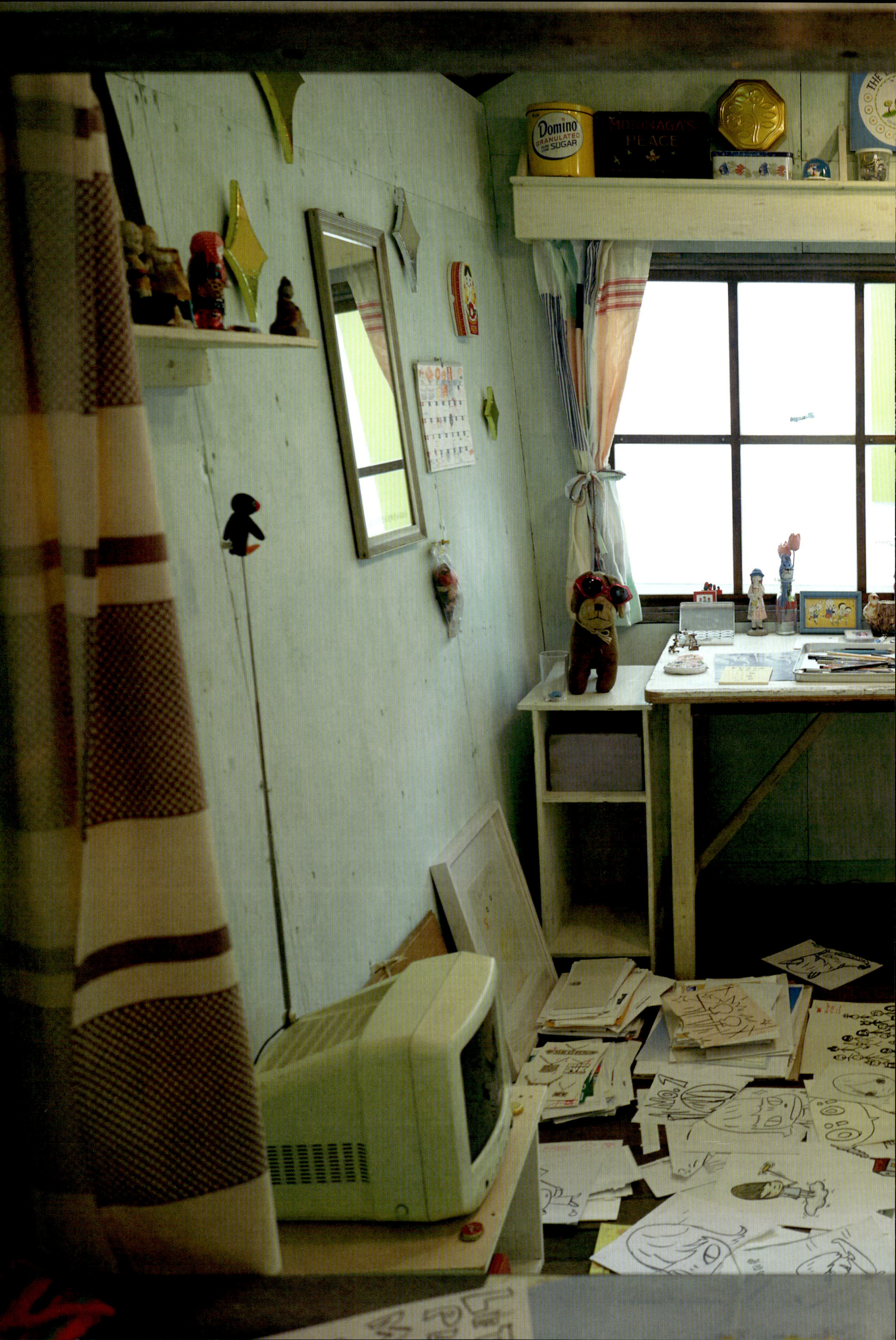
Domino
GRANULATED
SUGAR
MORINAGA'S
PEACE

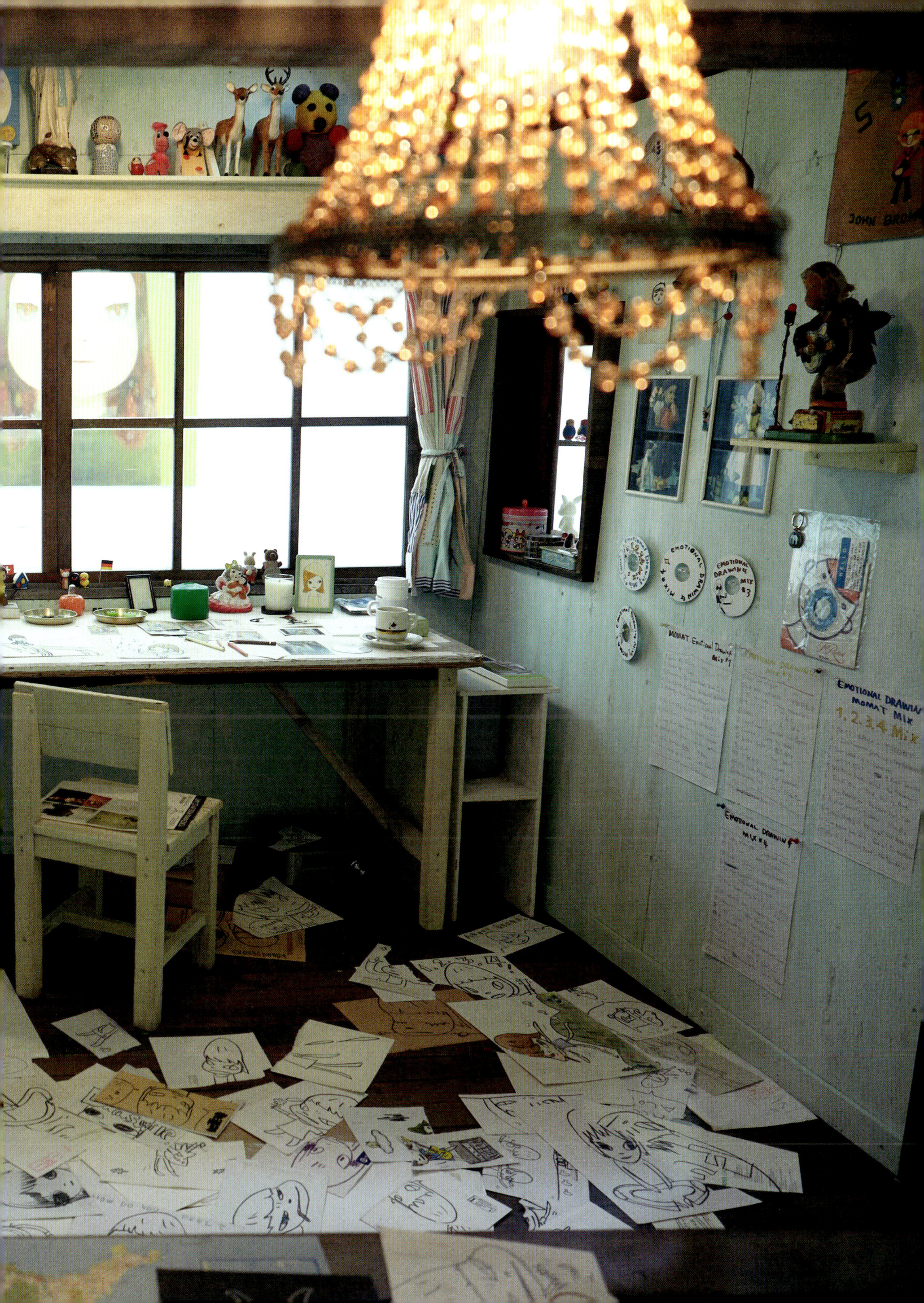

EMOTIONAL DRAWING MIX #3
MOMAT Emotional Drawing Mix #1
EMOTIONAL DRAWIN
MOMAT MIX
1.2.3.4 Mix
EMOTIONAL DRAWING
MIX #4

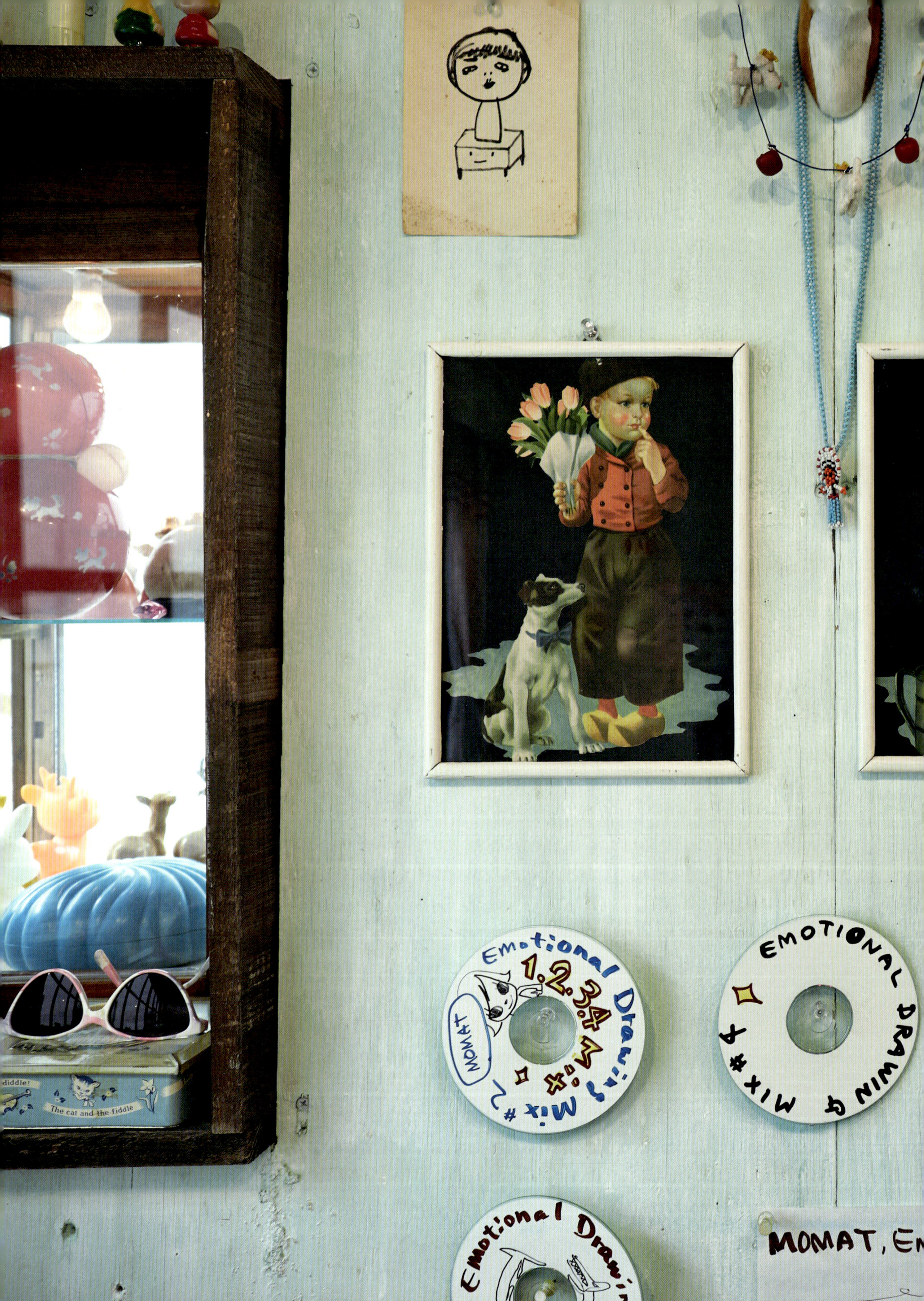
Emotional Drawing Mix #2
1.2.3.4
MOMAT
EMOTIONAL DRAWING MIX #4
The cat and the fiddle
MOMAT, E

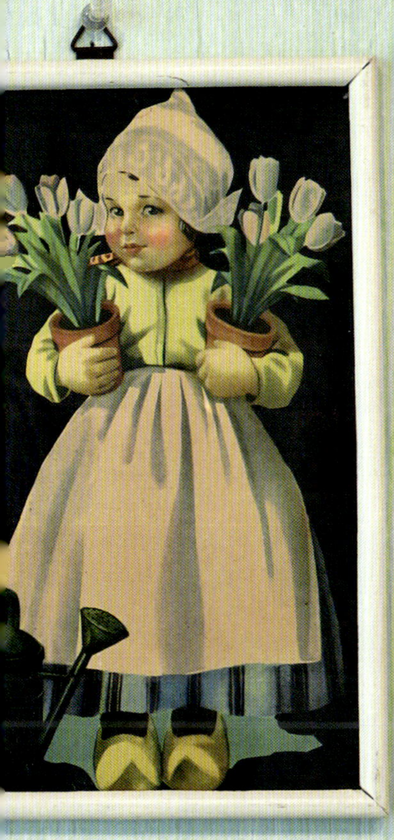

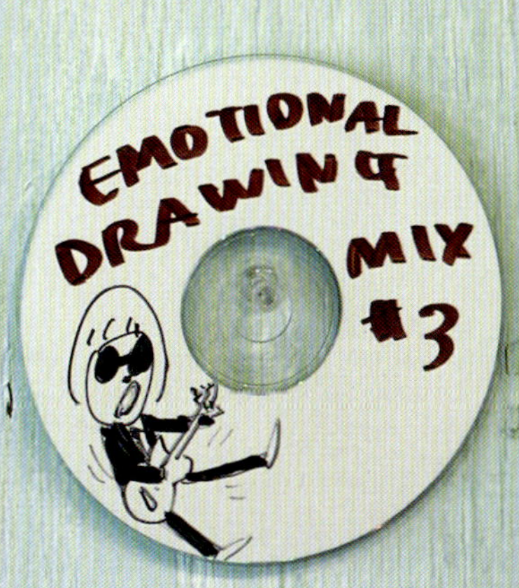
EMOTIONAL DRAWING MIX #3

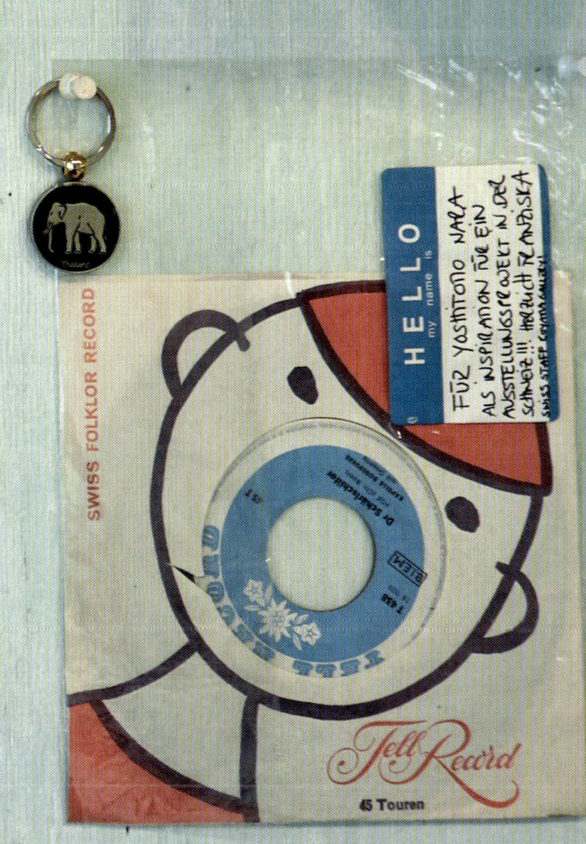
SWISS FOLKLOR RECORD
HELLO my name is
Tell Record
45 Touren

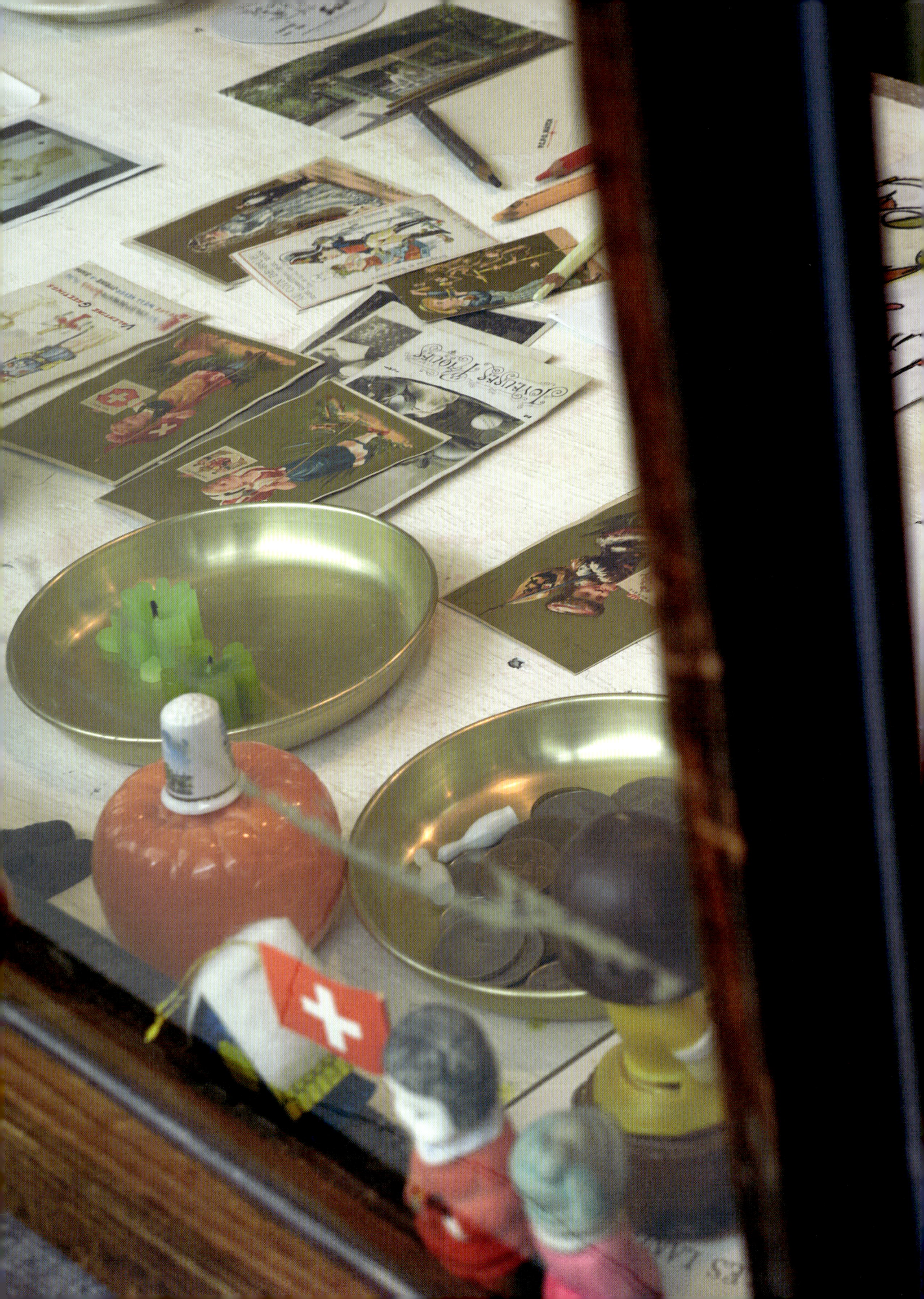

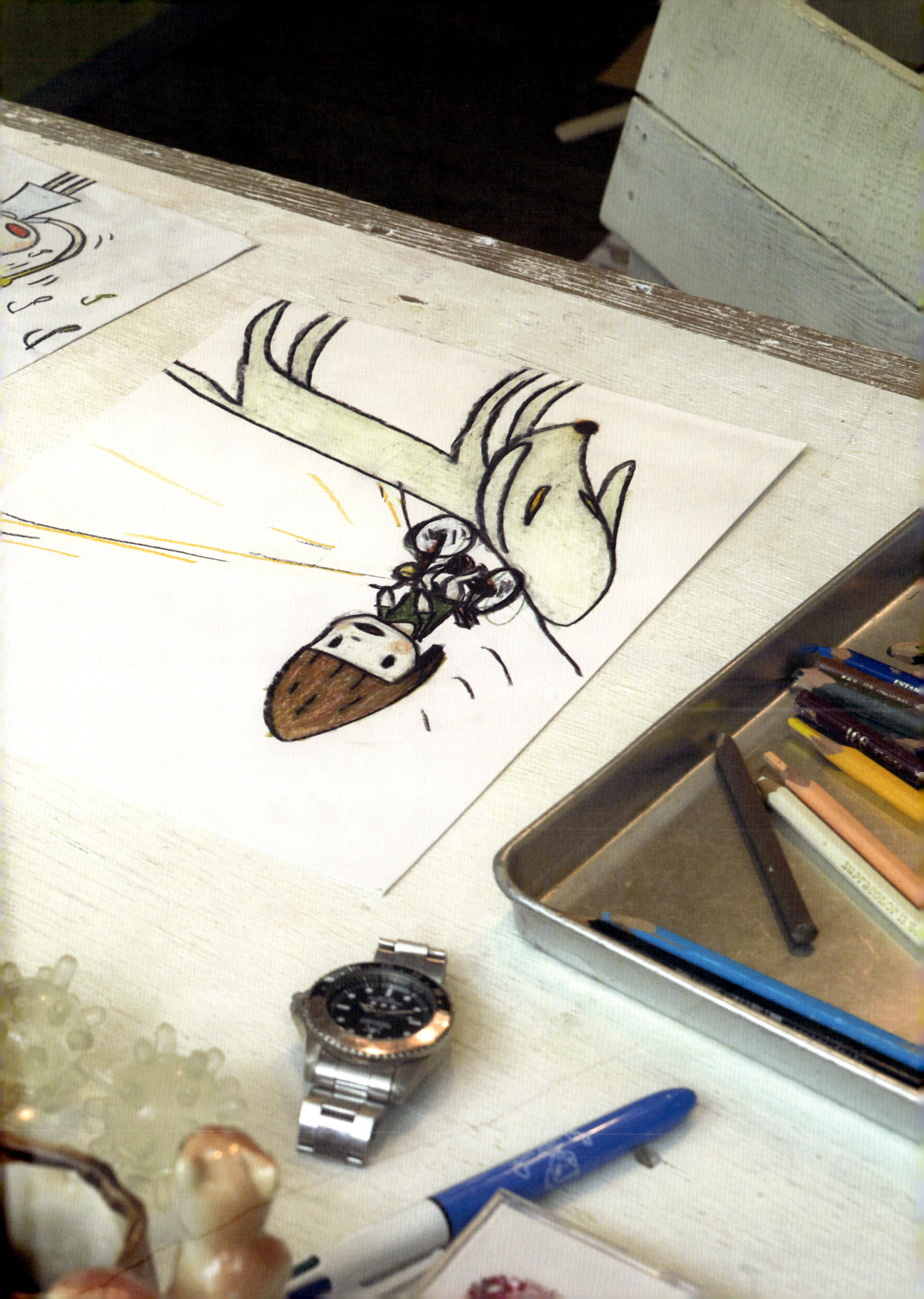

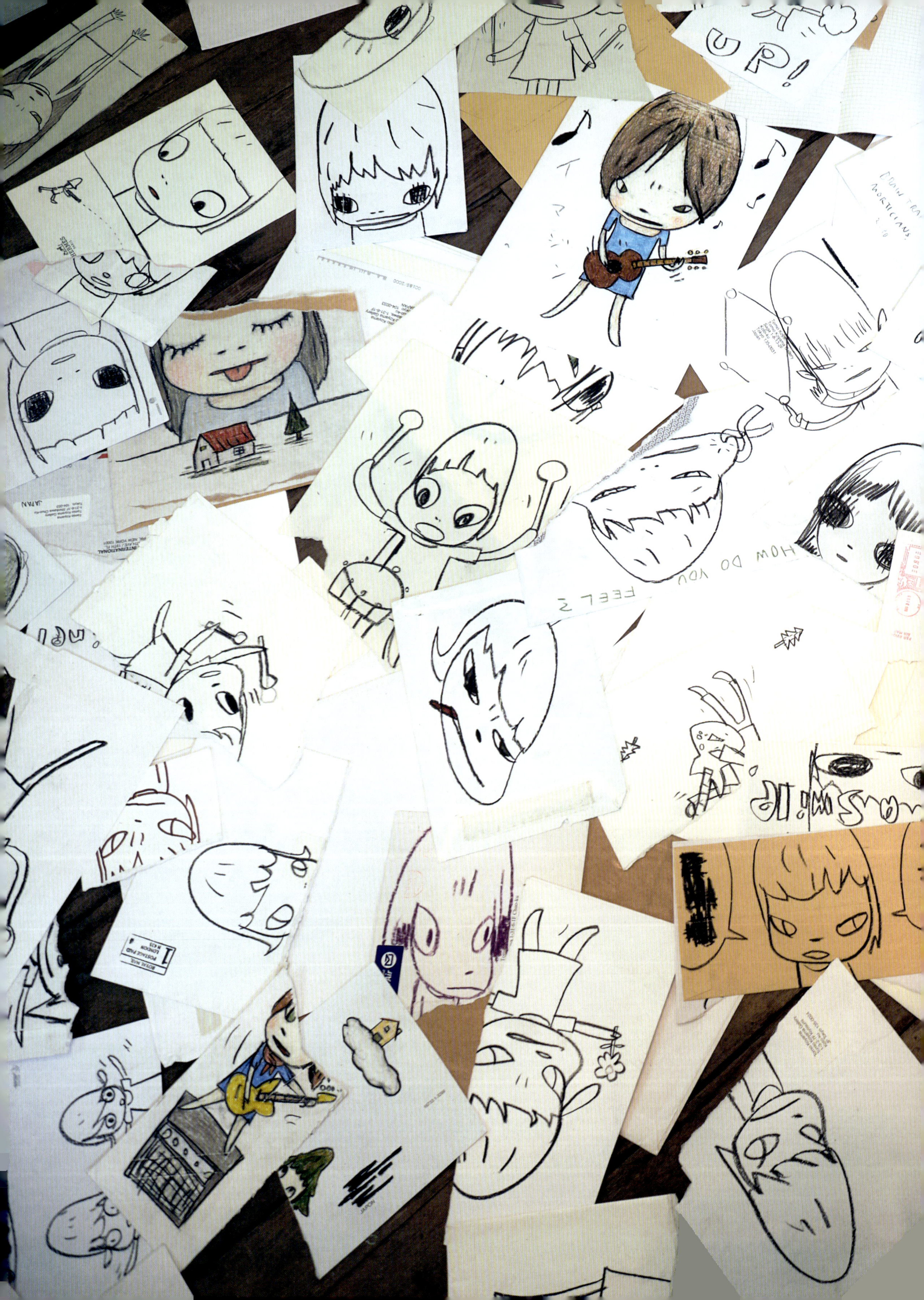
UP!
HOW DO YOU FEEL ?

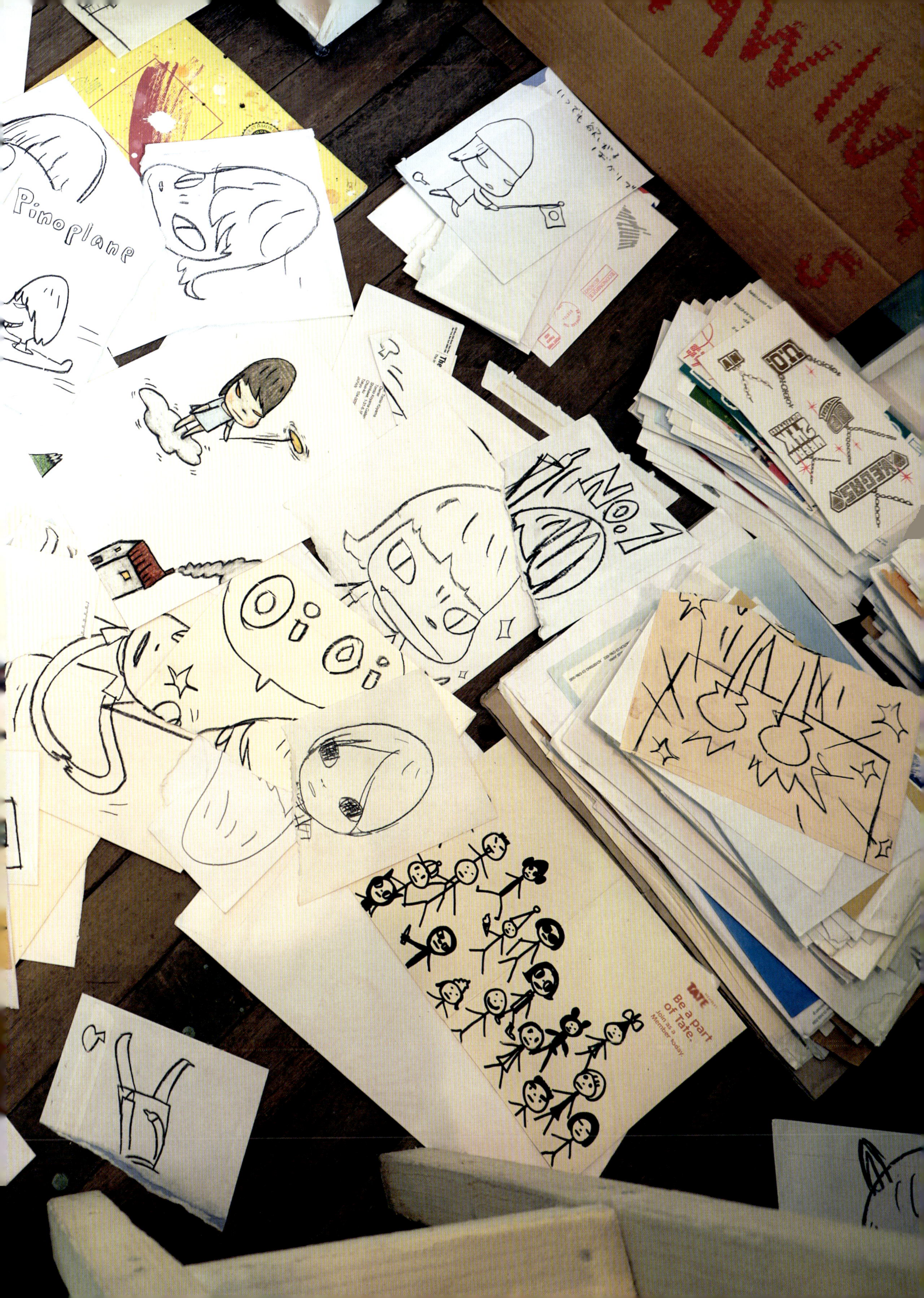
Pinoplane
No.1
TATE
Be a part of Tate.
Join as a Member today.

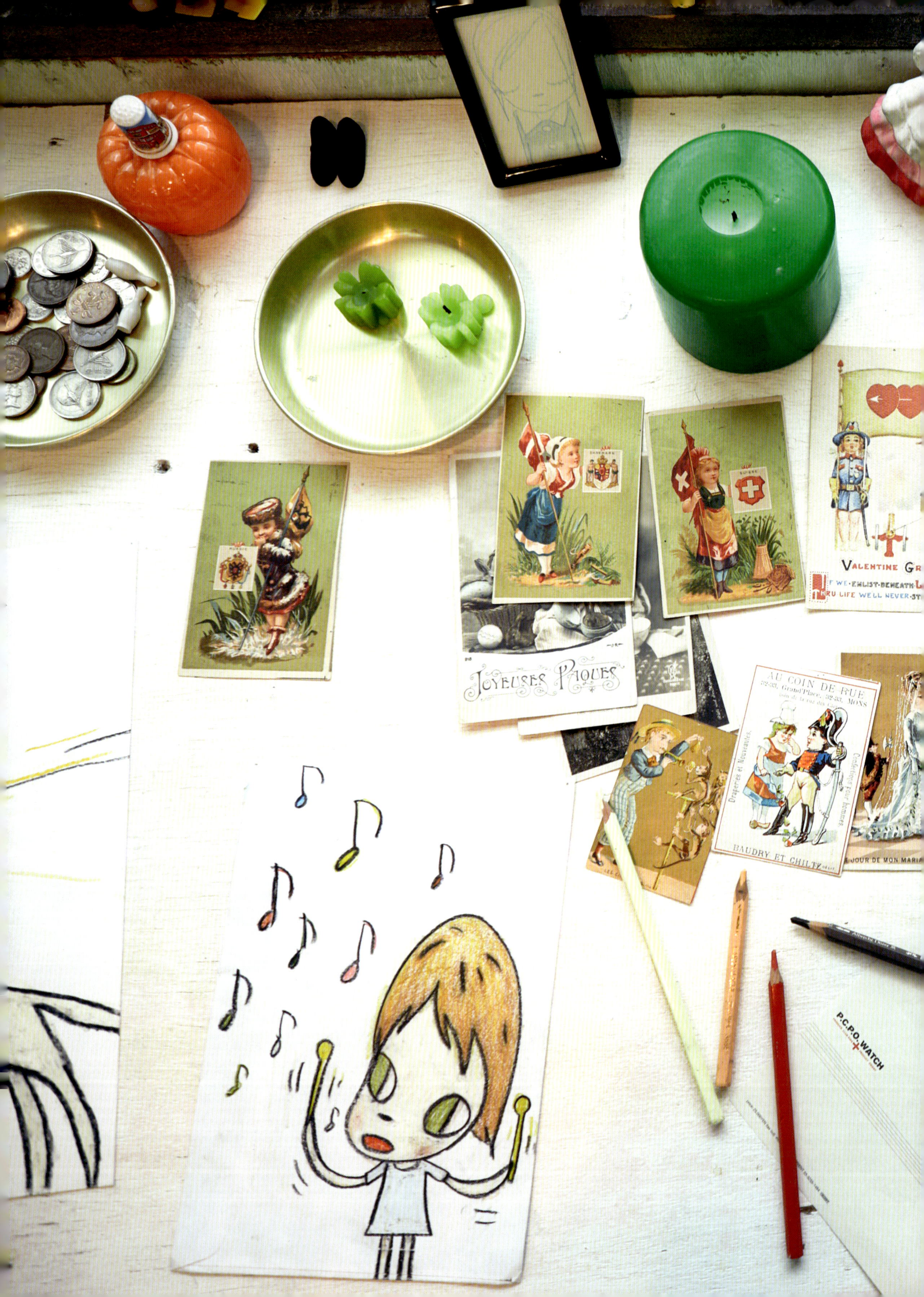

JOYEUSES PAQUES
AU COIN DE RUE
32-33, Grand'Place, 32-33, MONS
Draperies et Nouveautés
Confections pour hommes
BAUDRY ET CHILTZ
P.C.P.O. WATCH

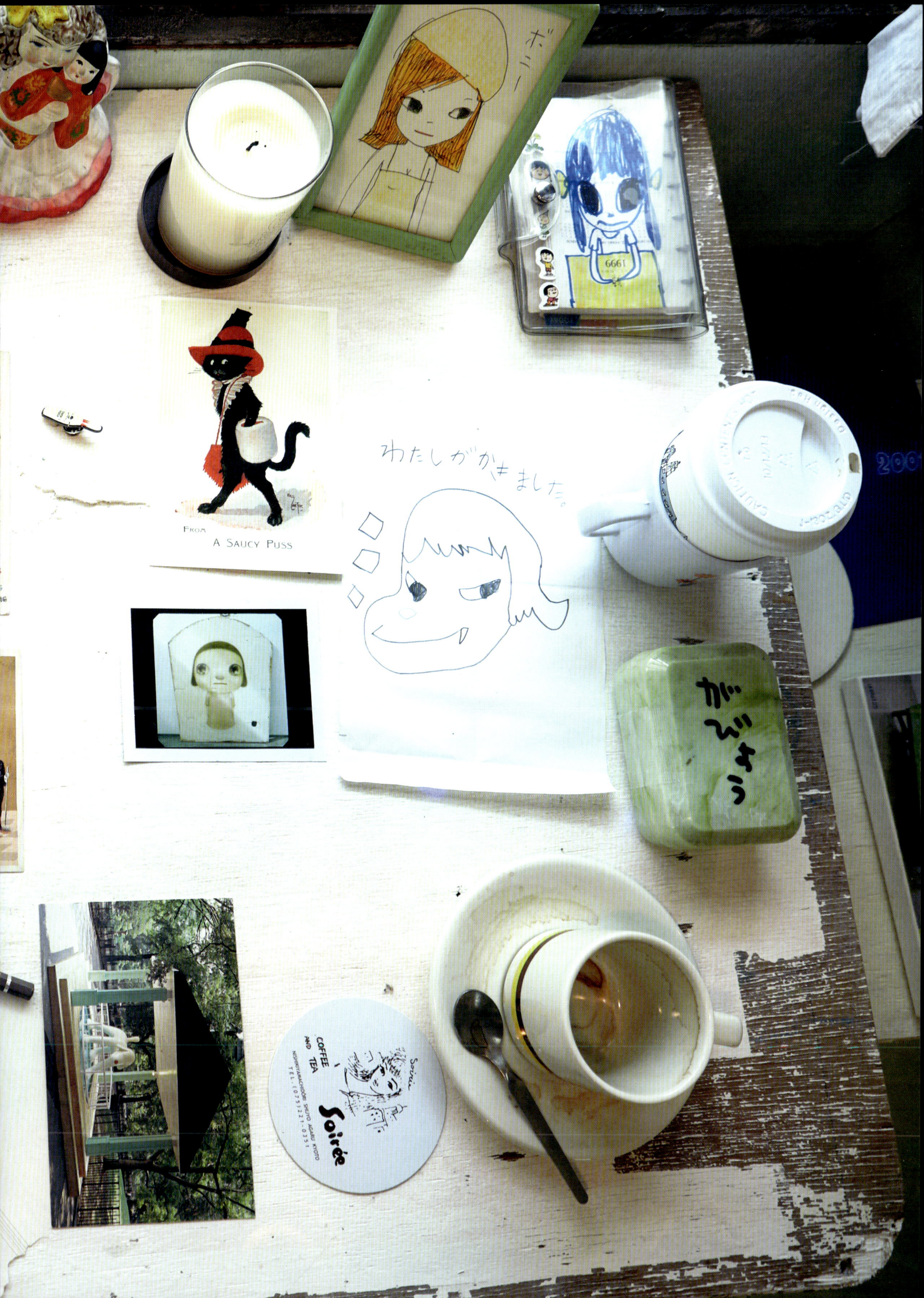
ボニー
FROM
A SAUCY PUSS
わたしがかきました。
がびょう
COFFEE
AND TEA
Soirée

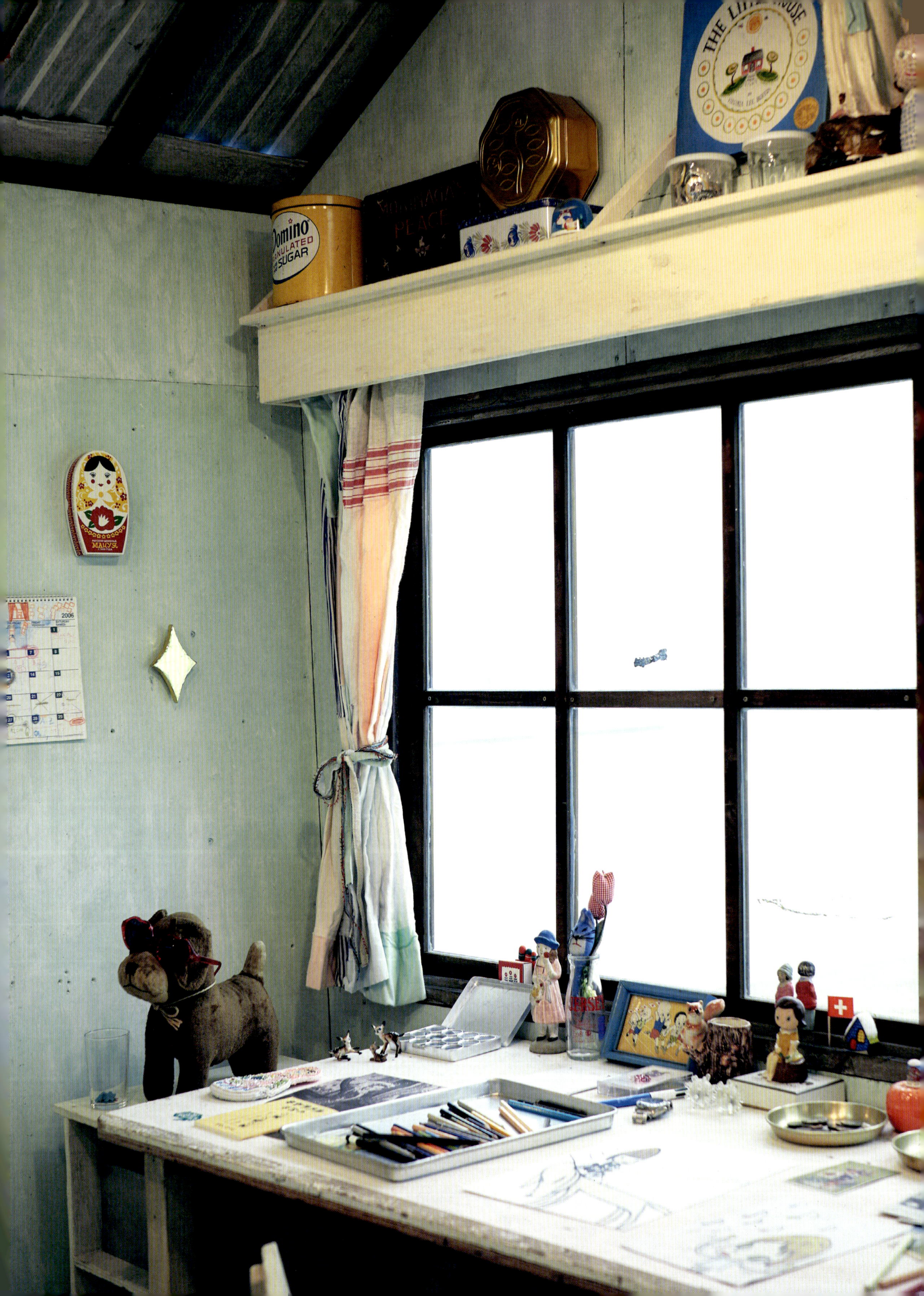
Domino
SUGAR

V

CAN'T WAIT 'TIL THE NIGHT COMES

In the White Room, 2003
Black Eyed Cat, 2003
Missing in Action—Girl Meets Boy—, 2005
Princess of Snooze, 2001
Sprout the Ambassador, 2001
White Night, 2006
After the Acid Rain, 2006
Shallow Puddles, 2006
Wounded, 2014
Miss Margaret, 2016
Dead of Night, 2016
No Means No, 2014
Blankey, 2012
Can't Wait 'til the Night Comes, 2012
In the Milky Lake/Thinking One, 2011

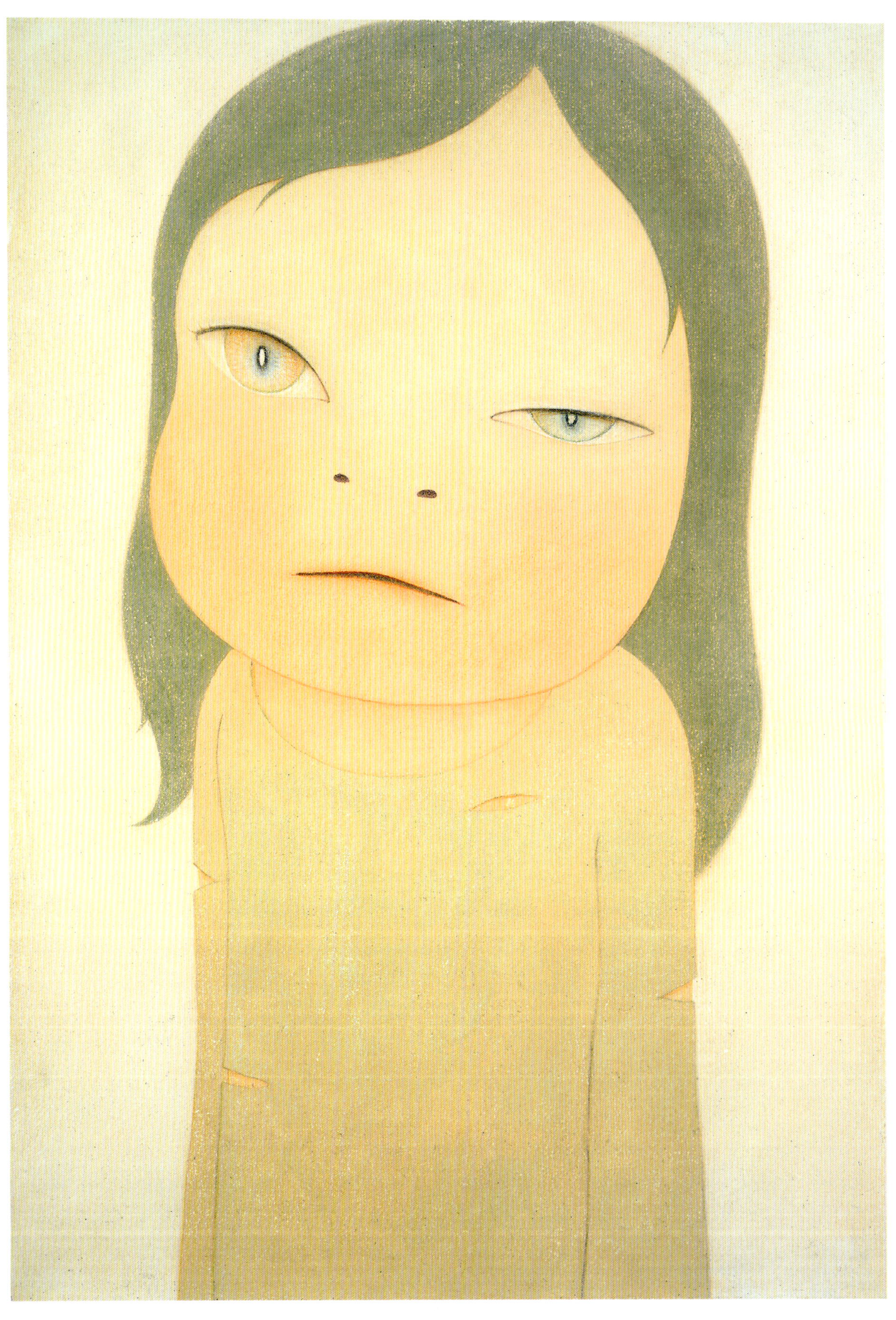

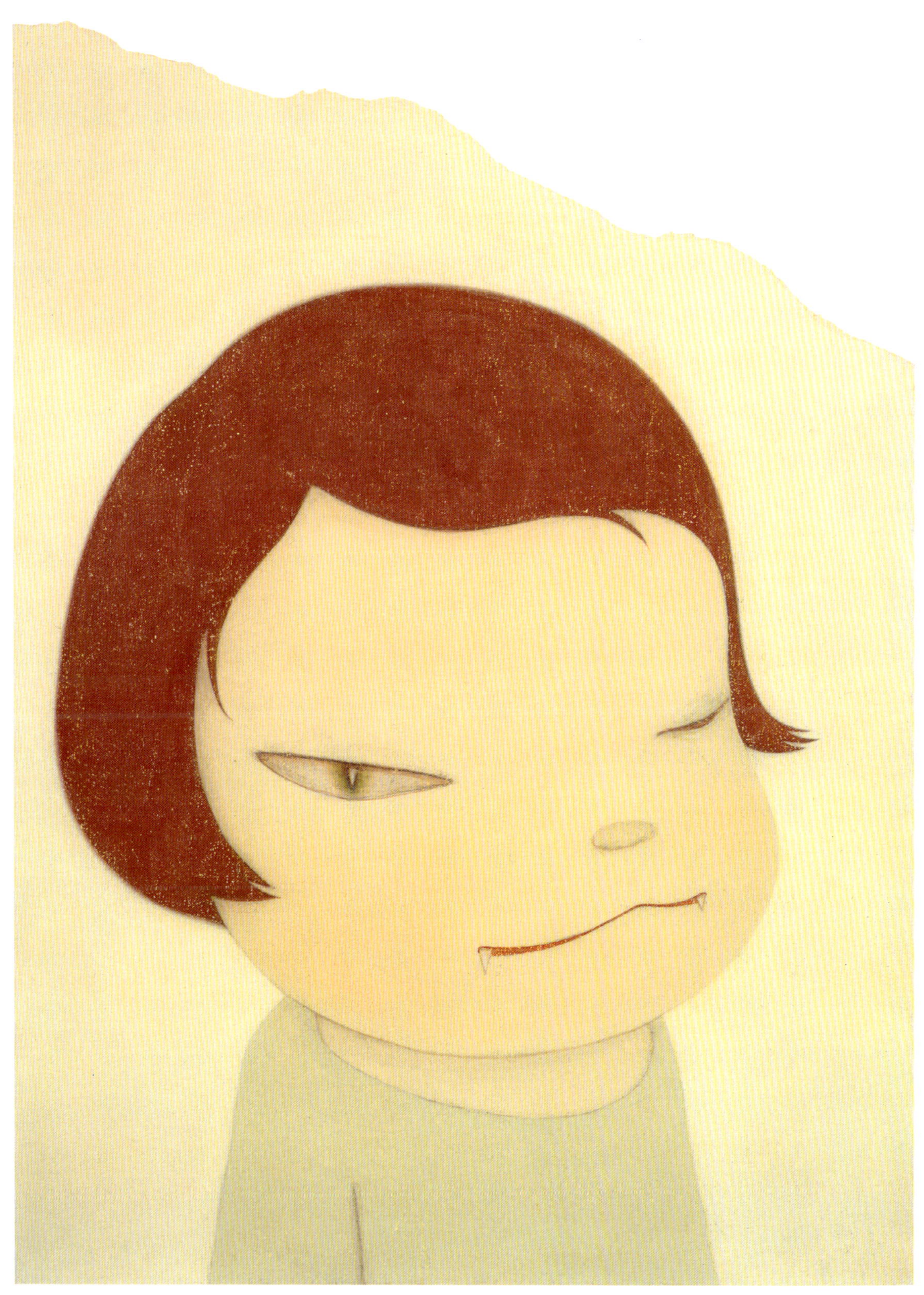

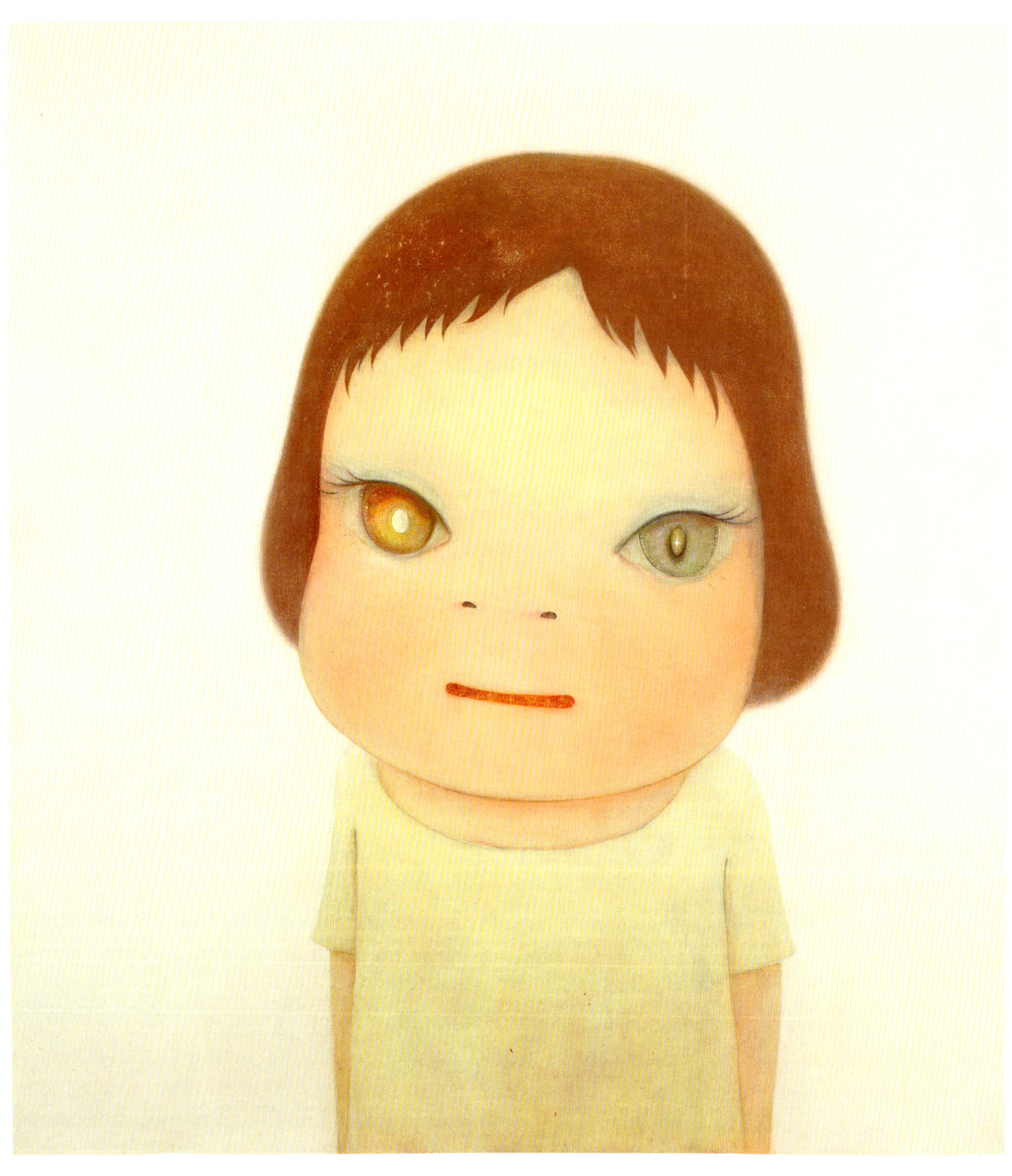

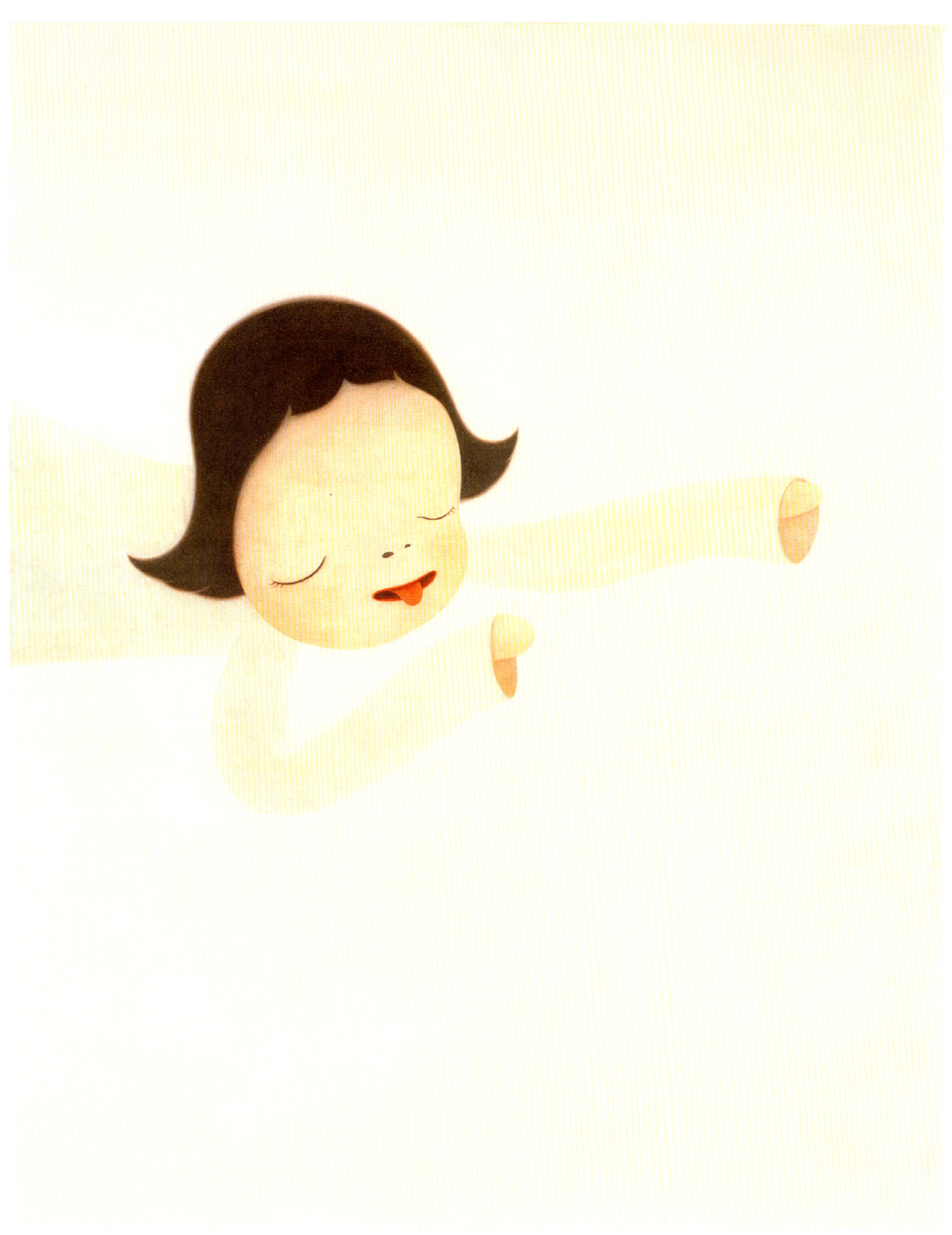

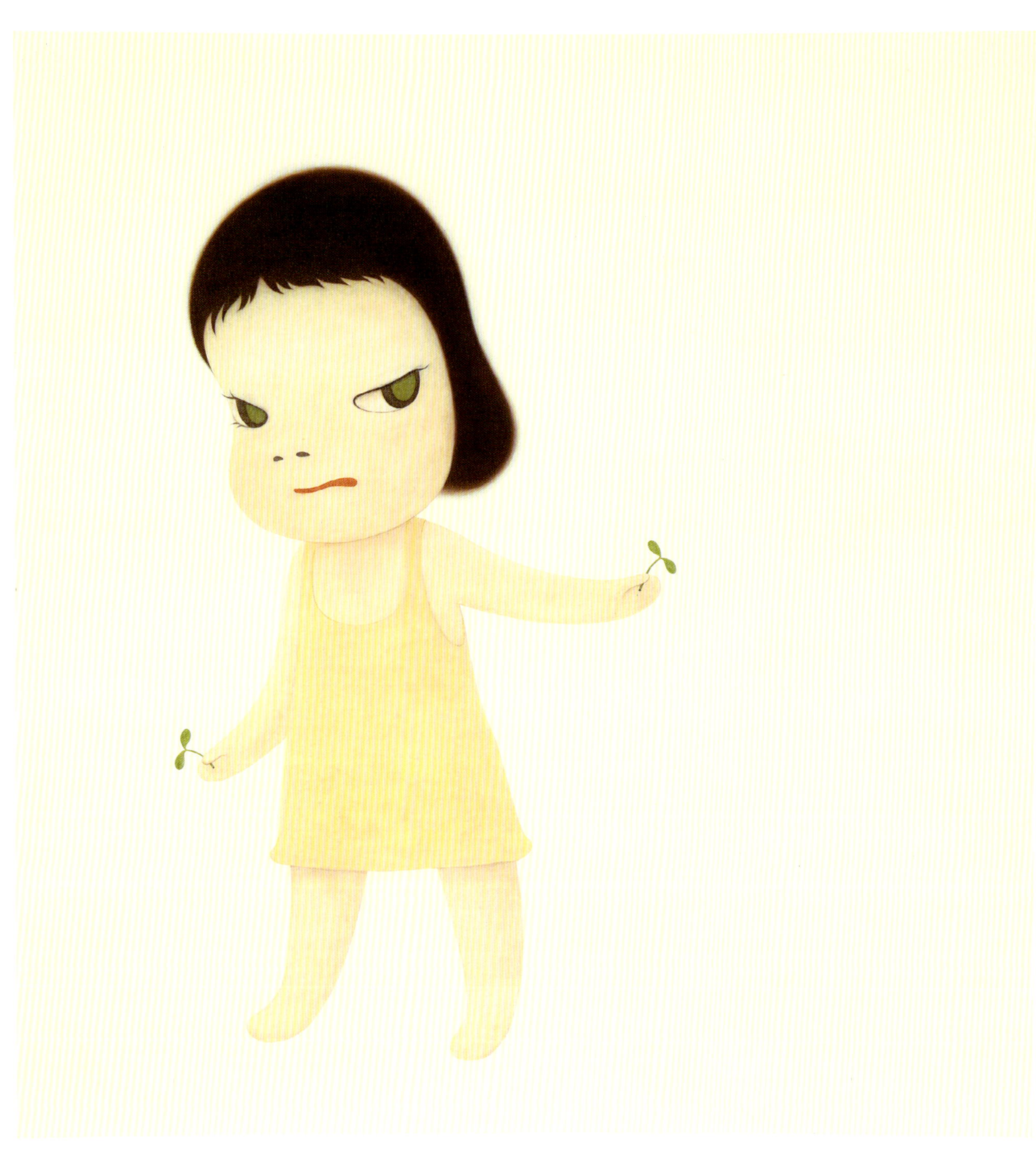

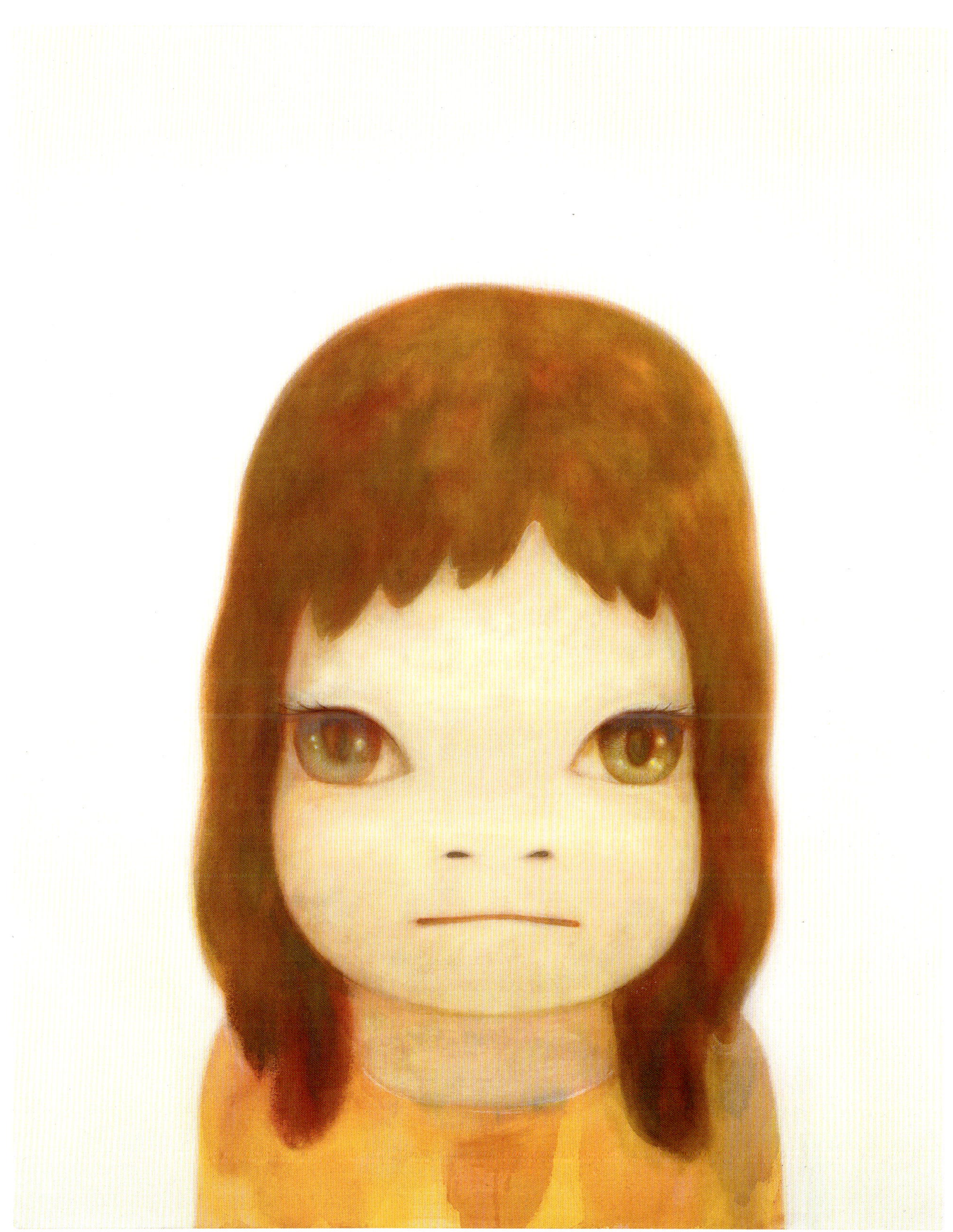

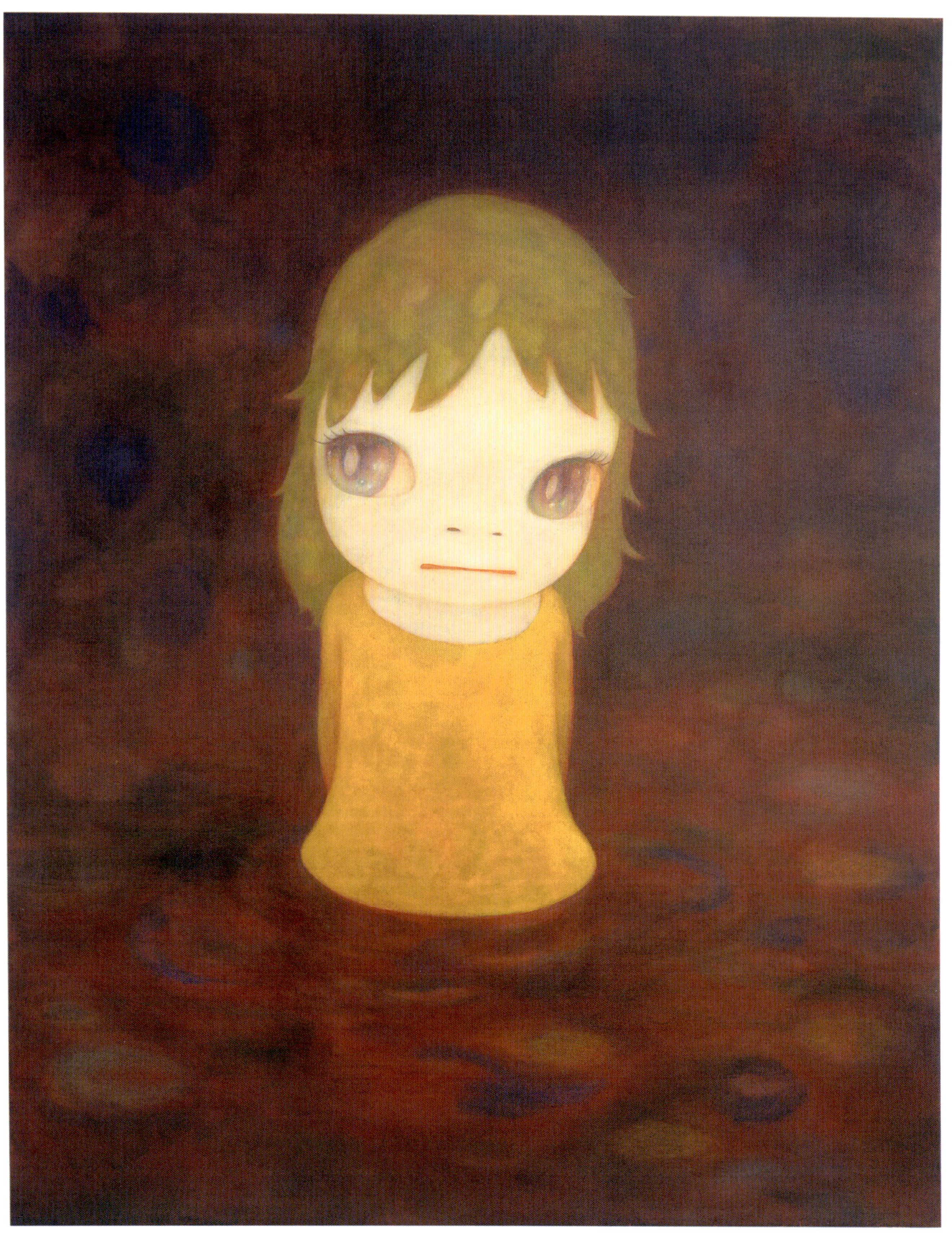

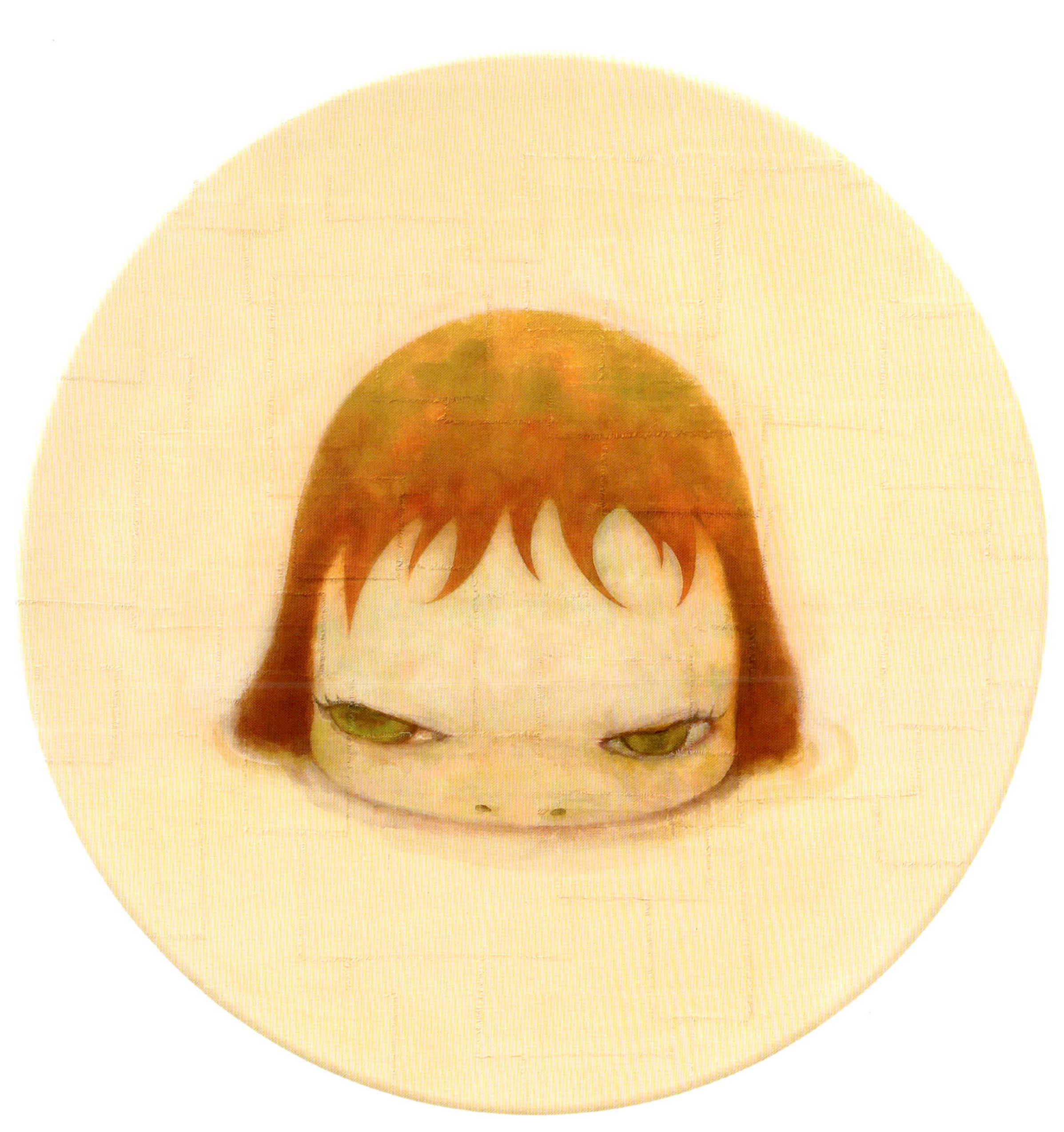

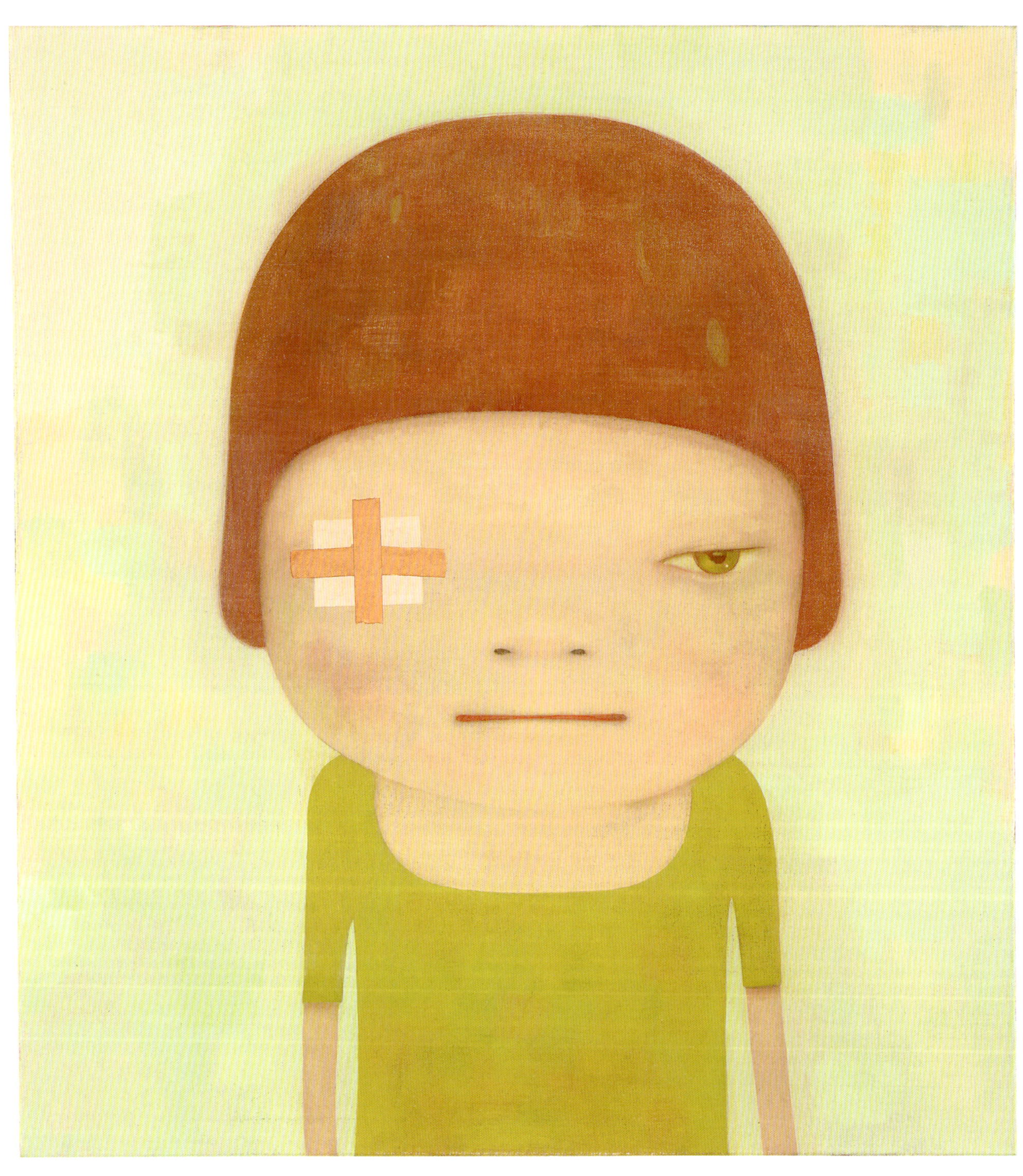

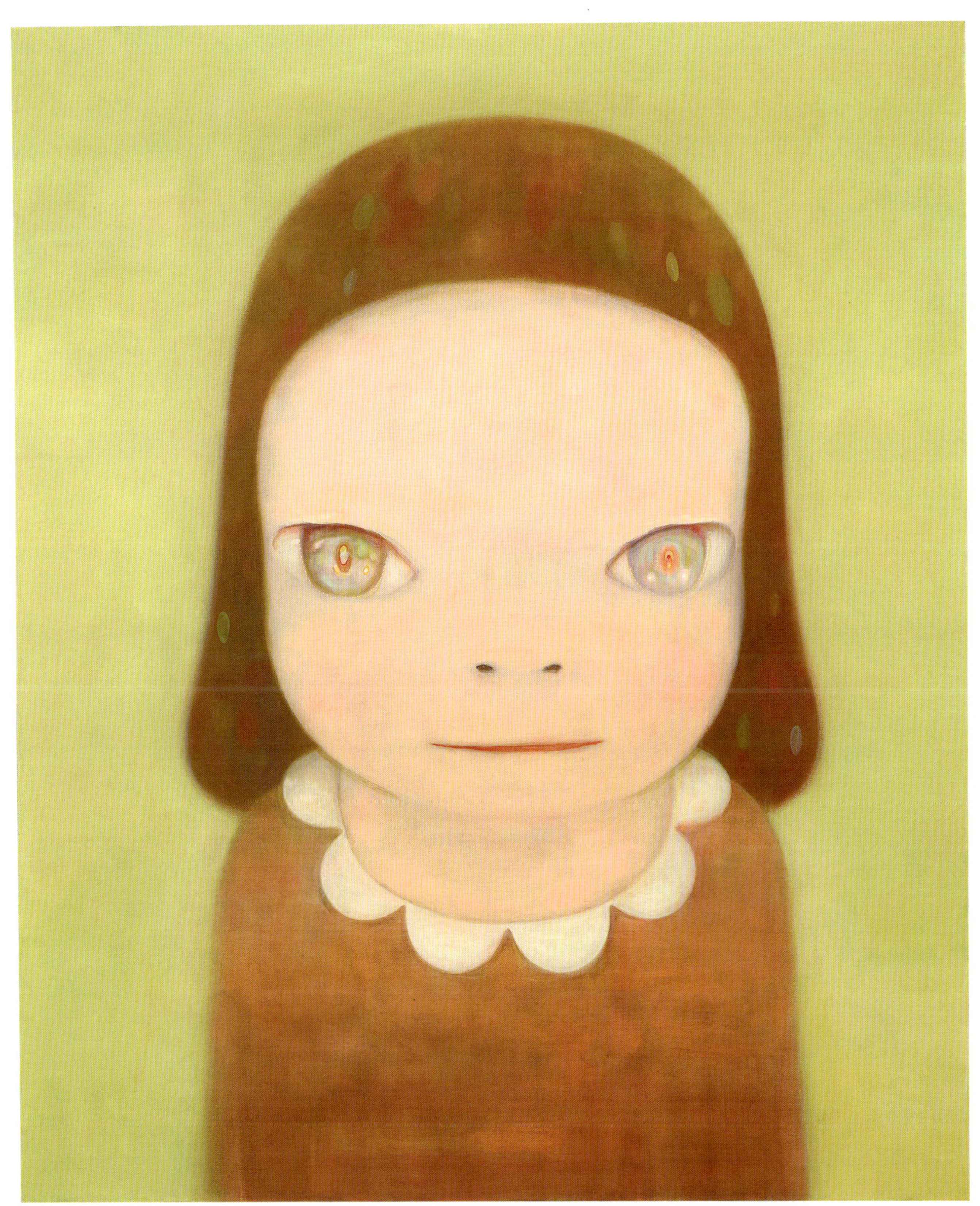

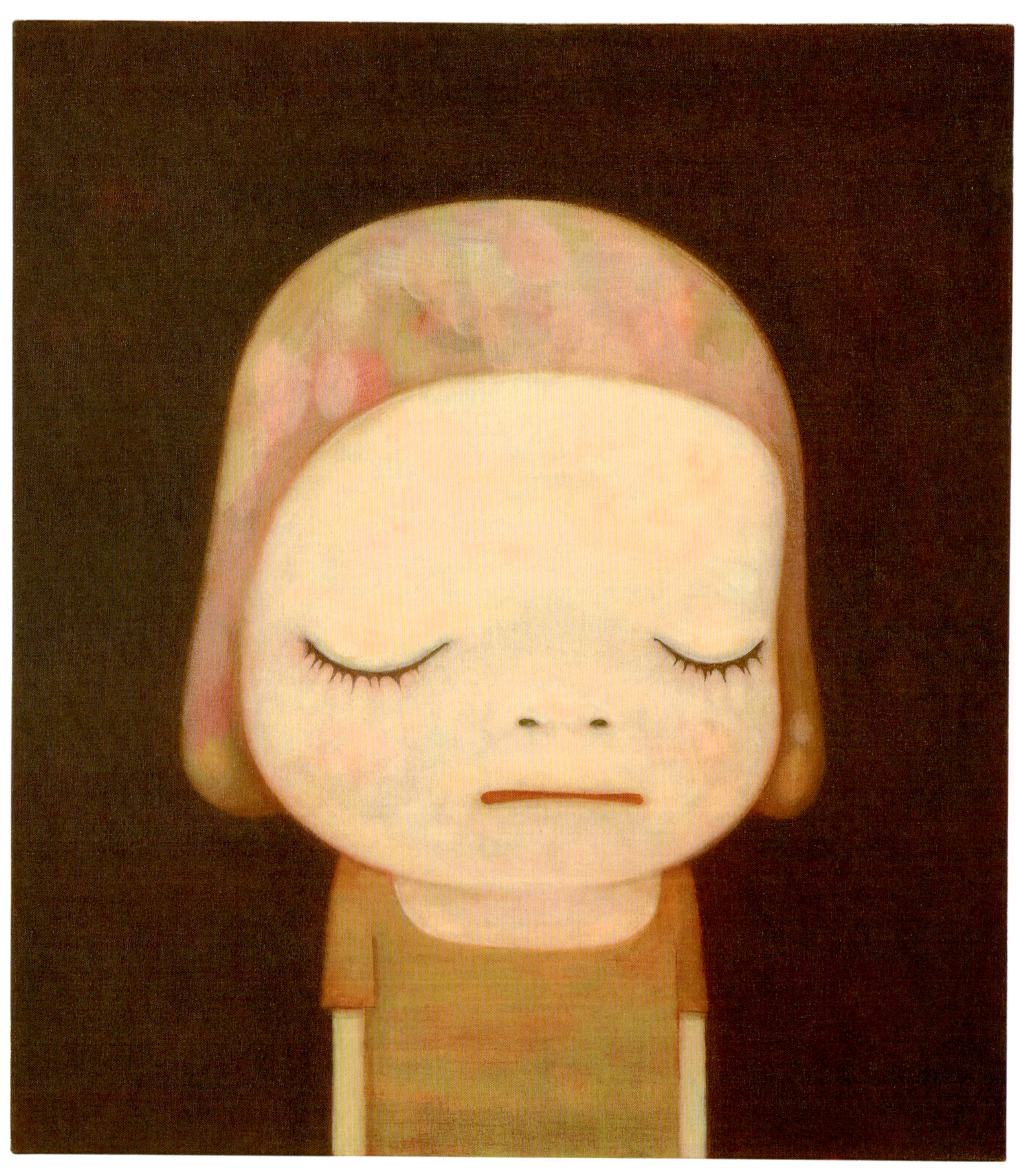

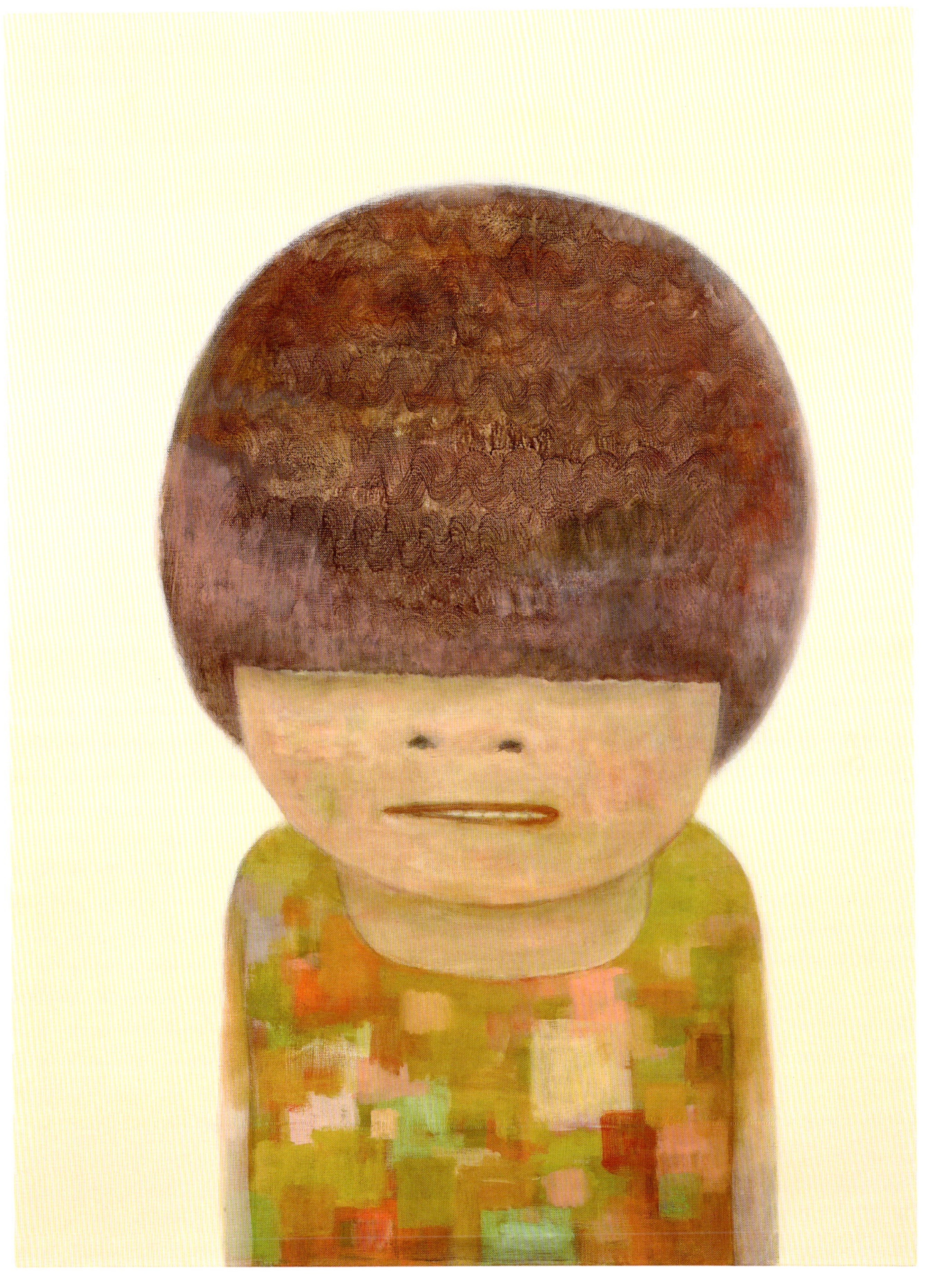

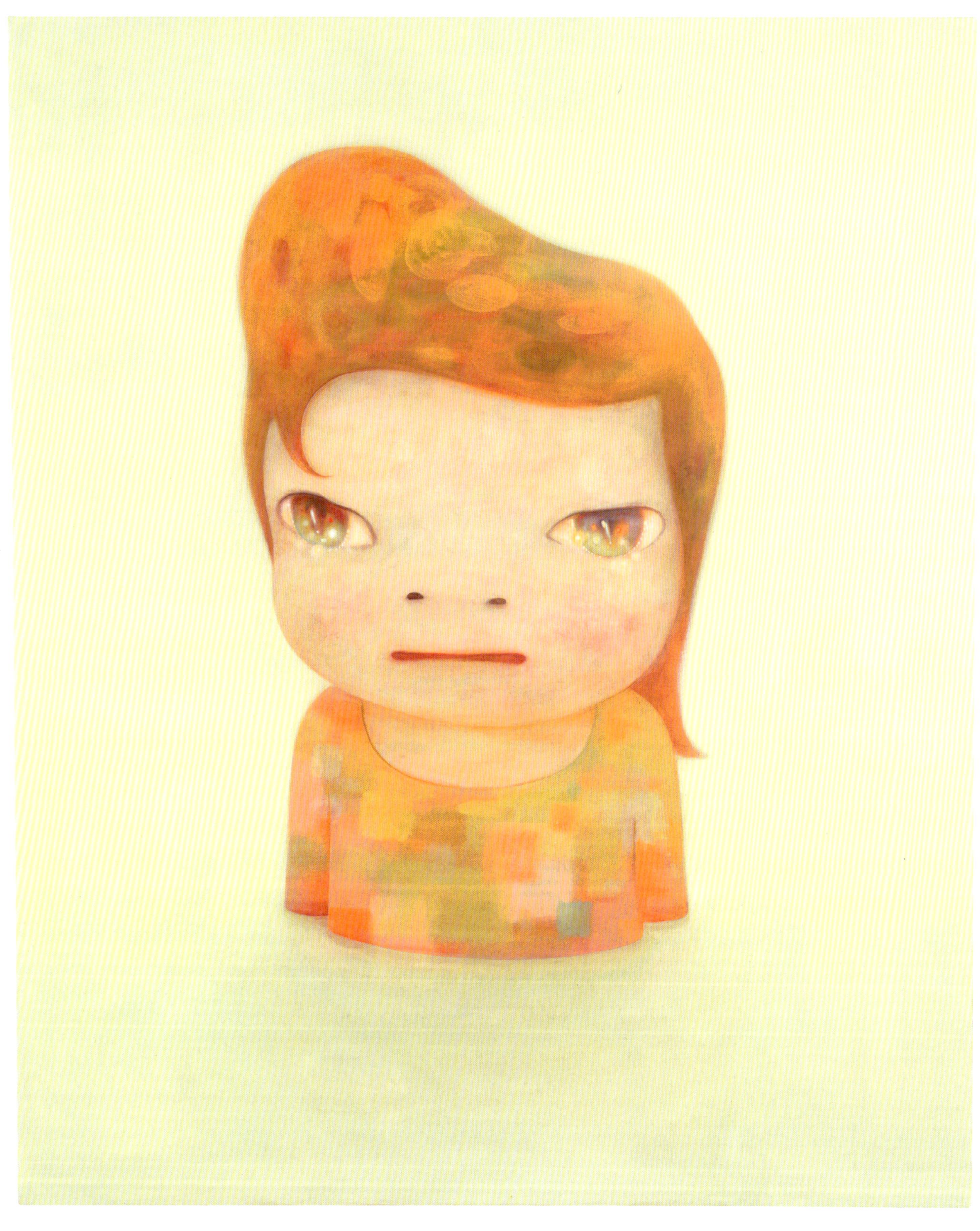

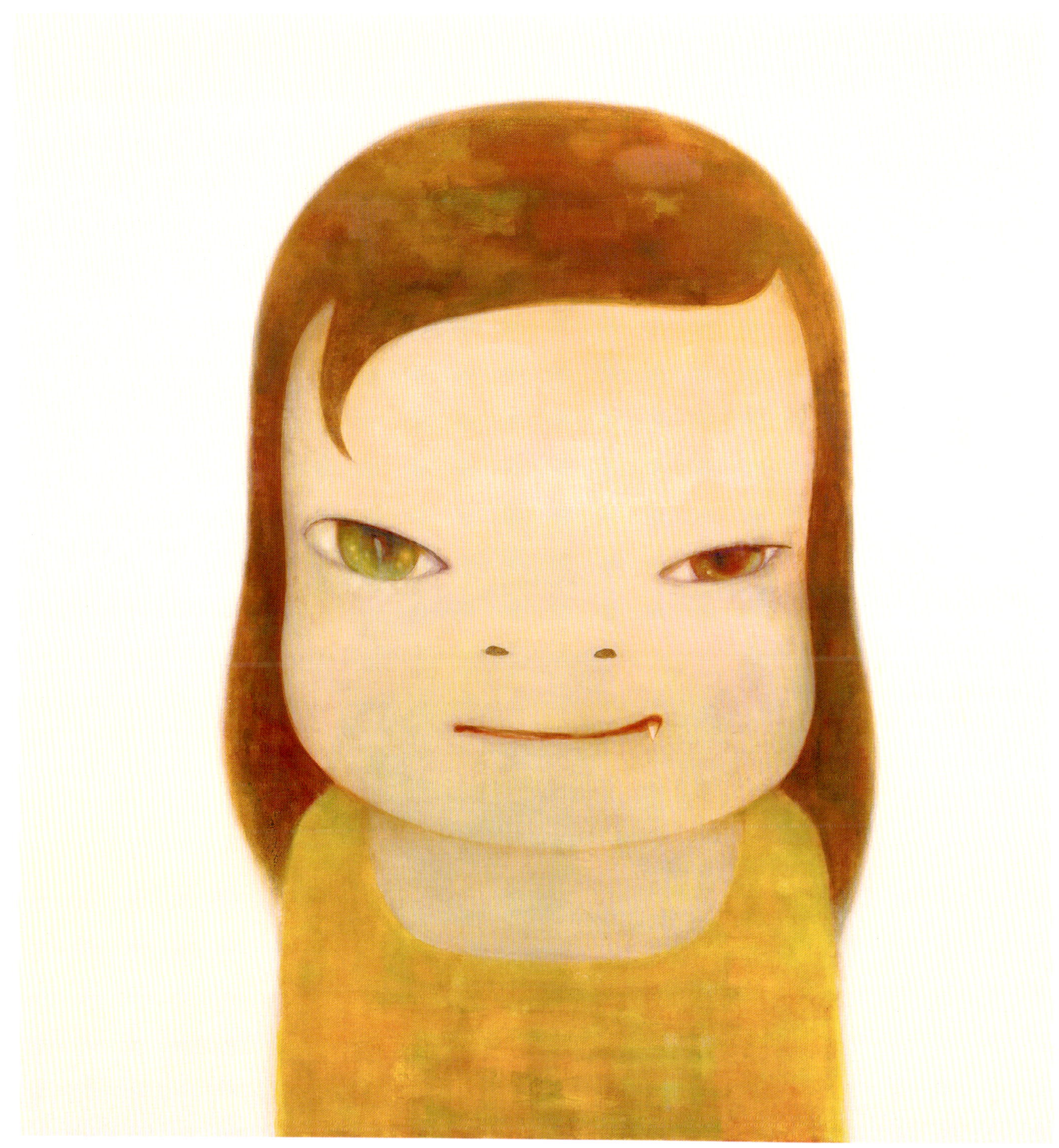

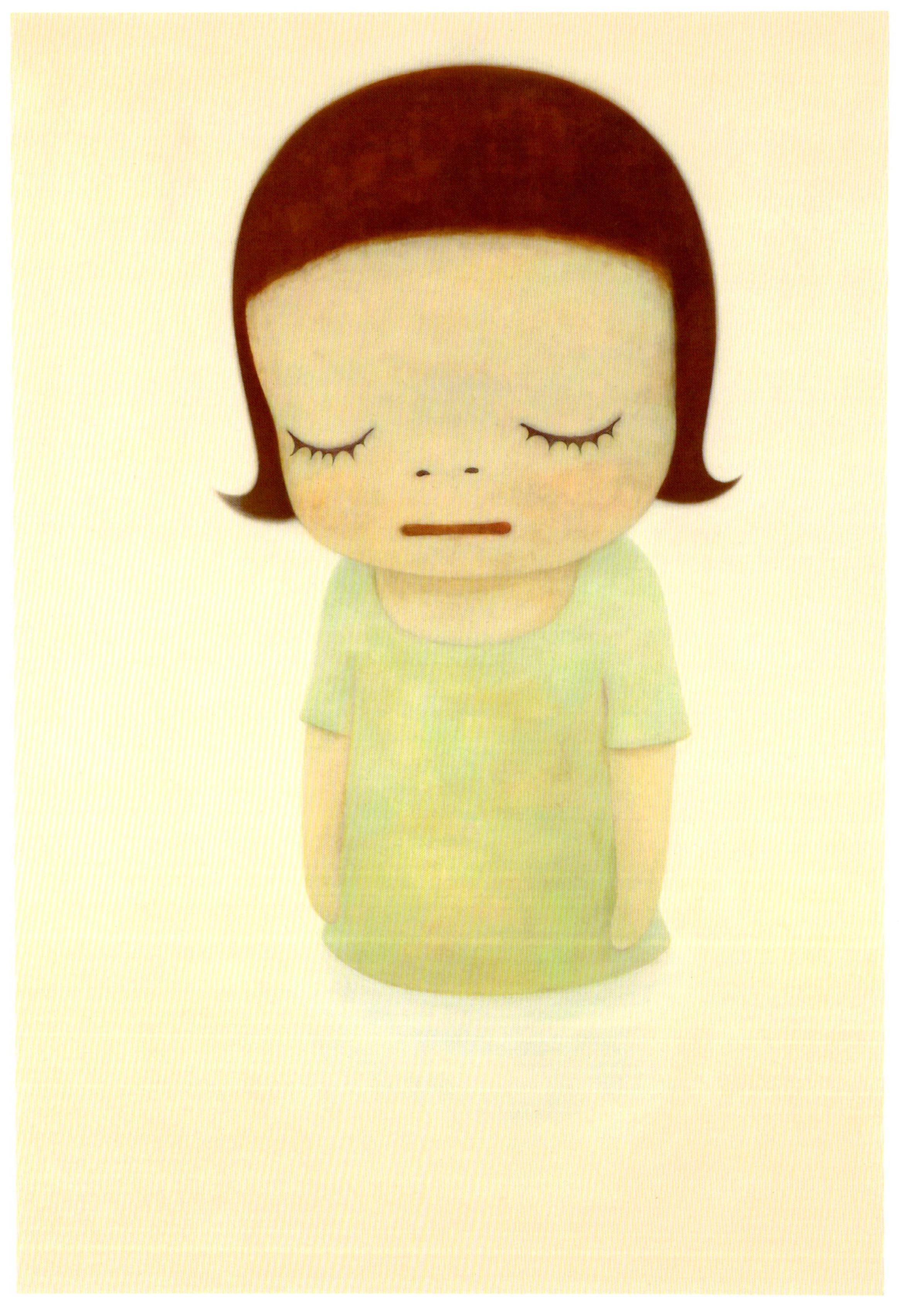

VI

SEARCHING

Untitled, 2010
Untitled, 2010
X Company, 2010
Untitled, 2010
Untitled, 2010
Untitled, 2010
Untitled, 2010
Untitled, 2010
Arabic Ship, 1989
Zero Fighter Plane, Dogfight, 1989
Girl at the Harbor, 1989
Searching, 2011
Untitled, 2011
Untitled, 2010
On the Building, 2015

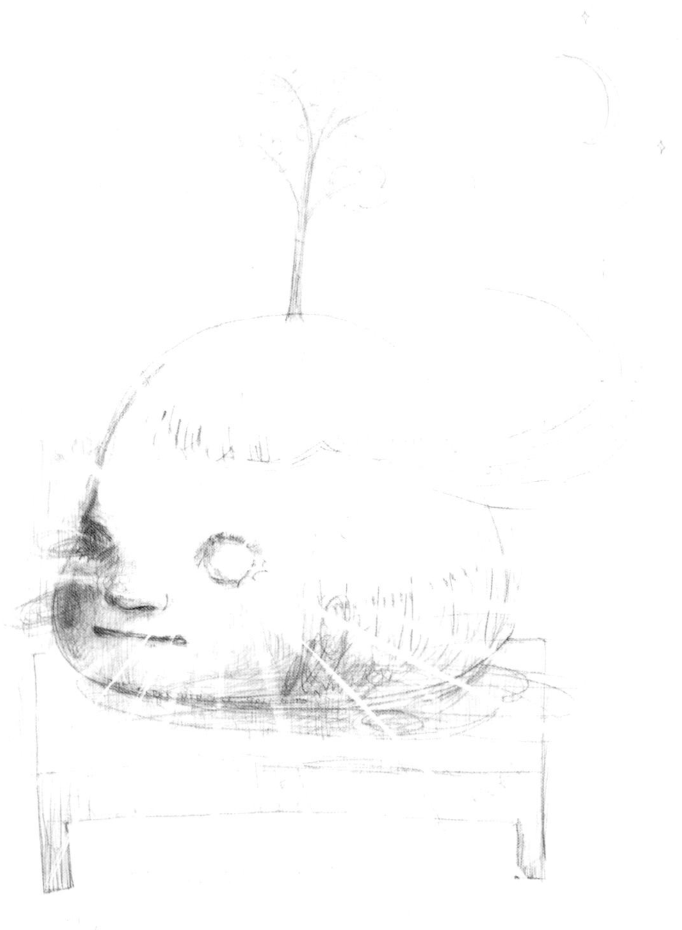

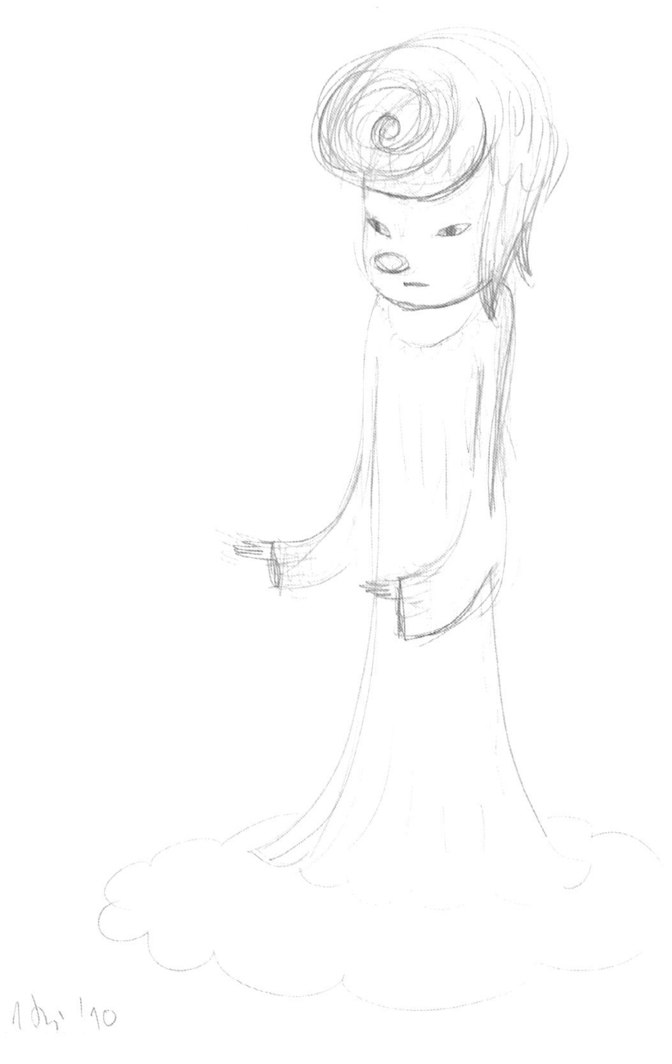

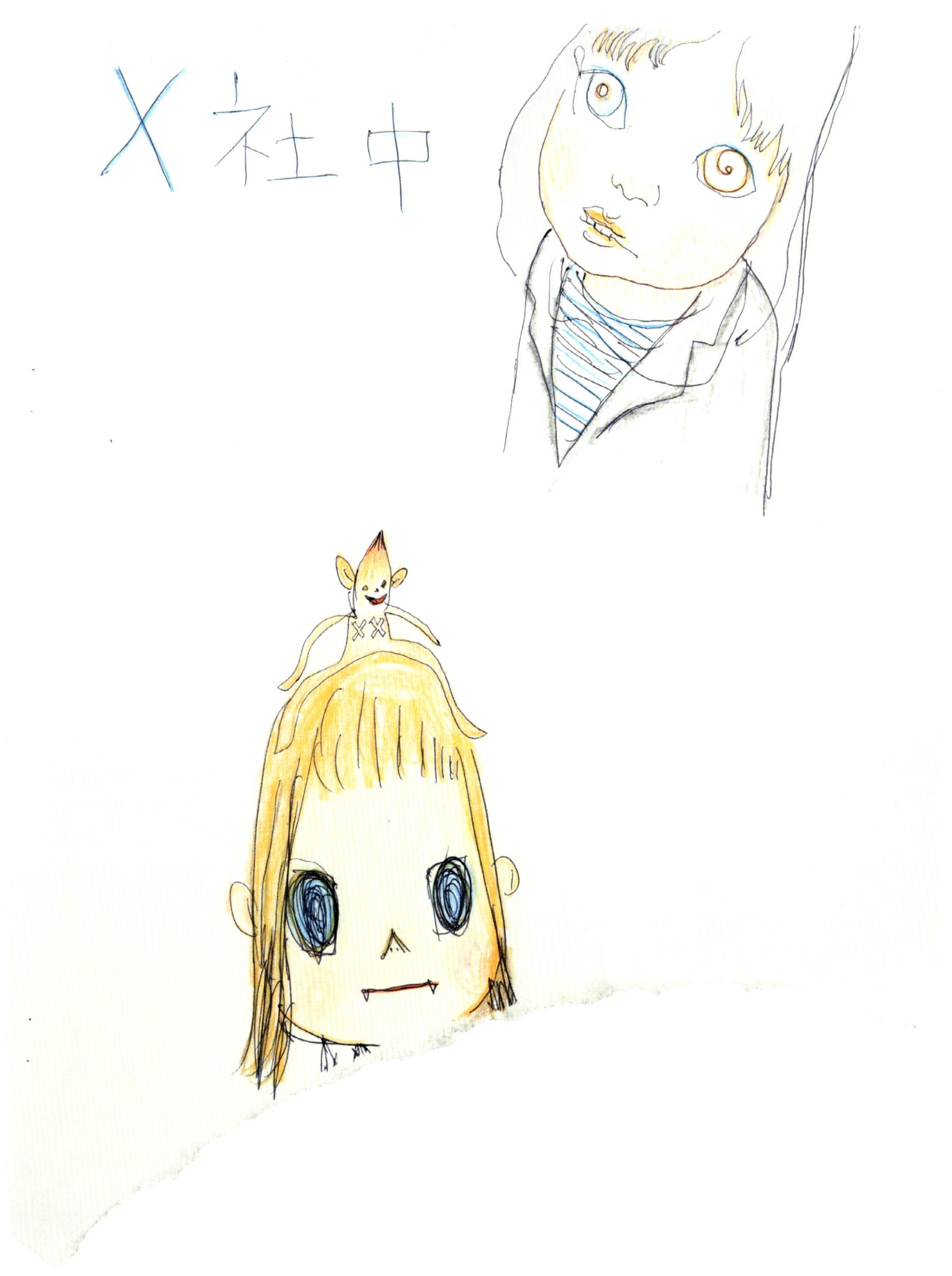
X社中

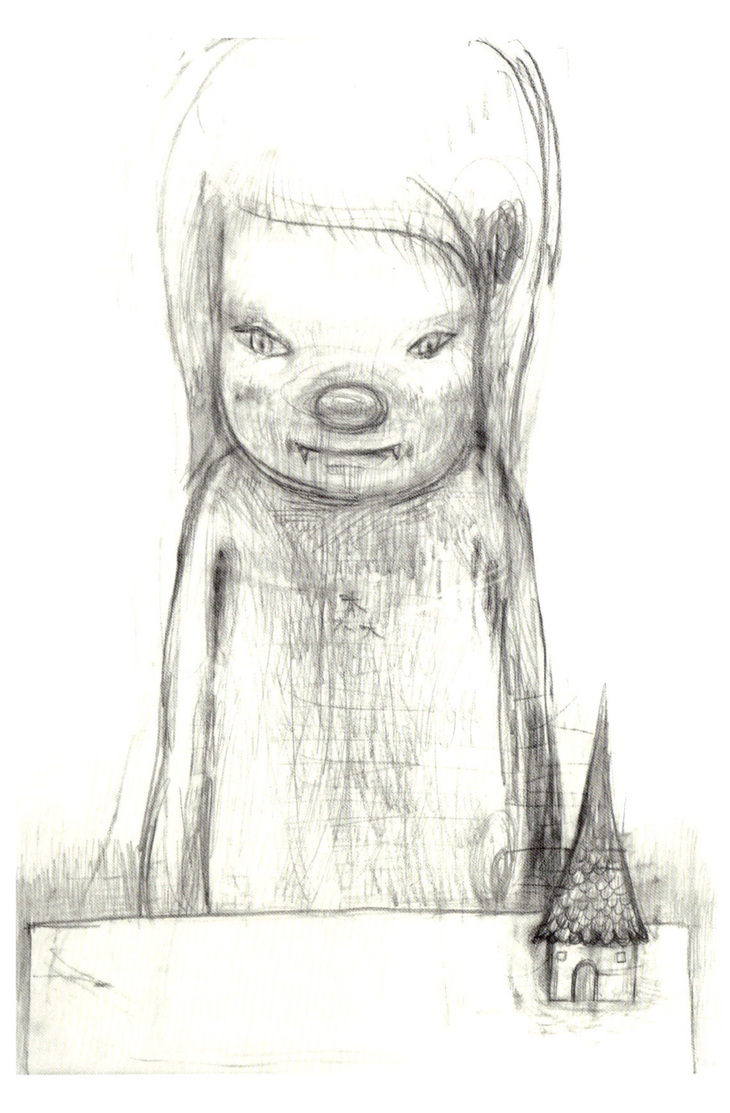

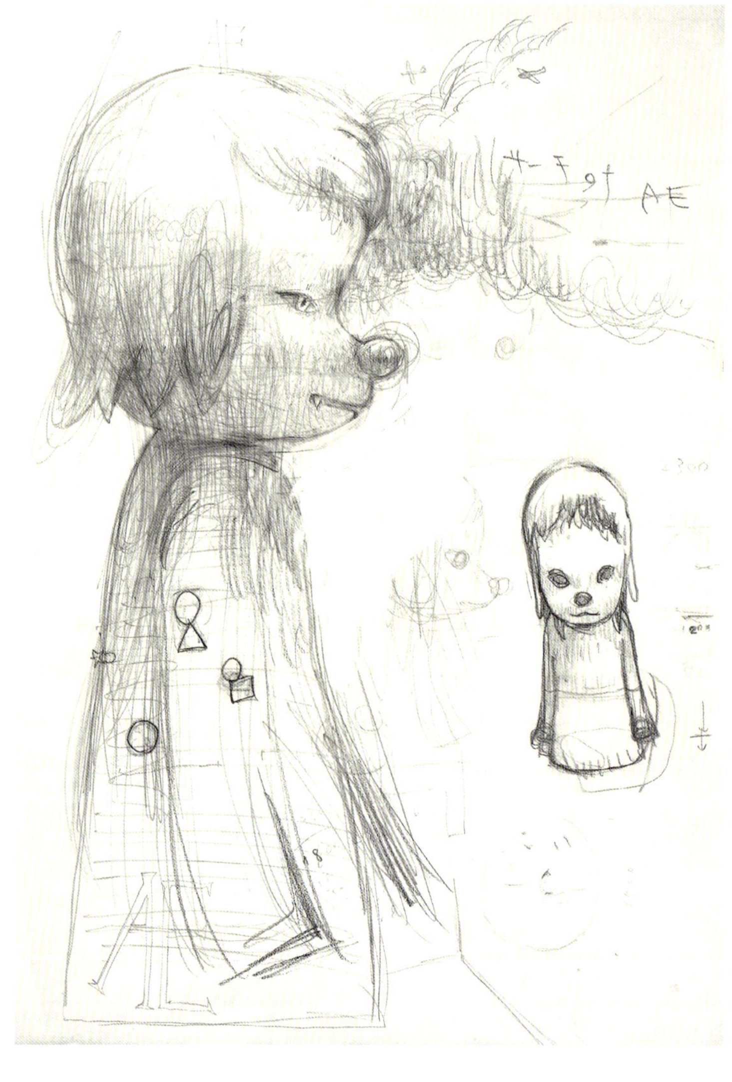

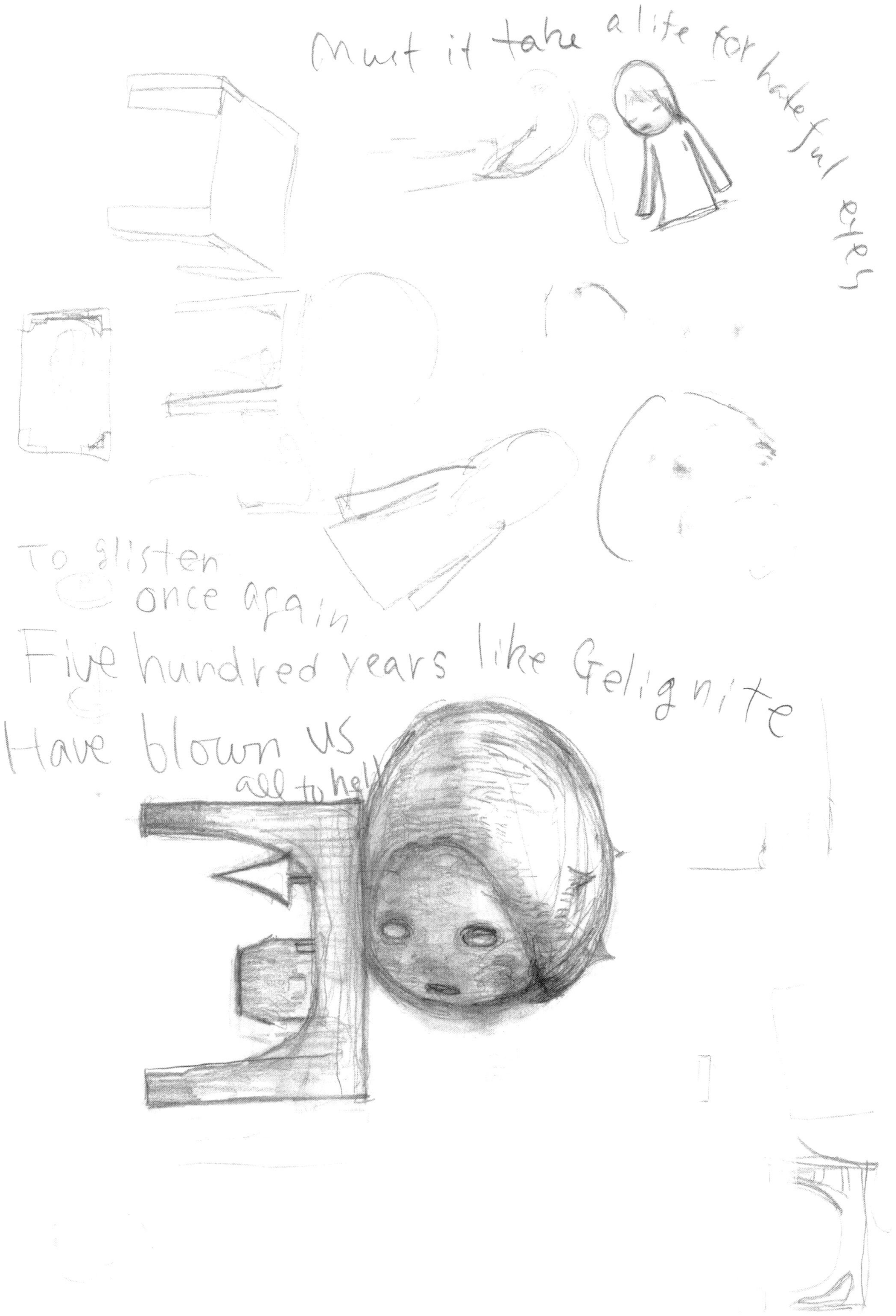
Must it take a life for hateful eyes
To glisten once again
Five hundred years like Gelignite
Have blown us all to hell

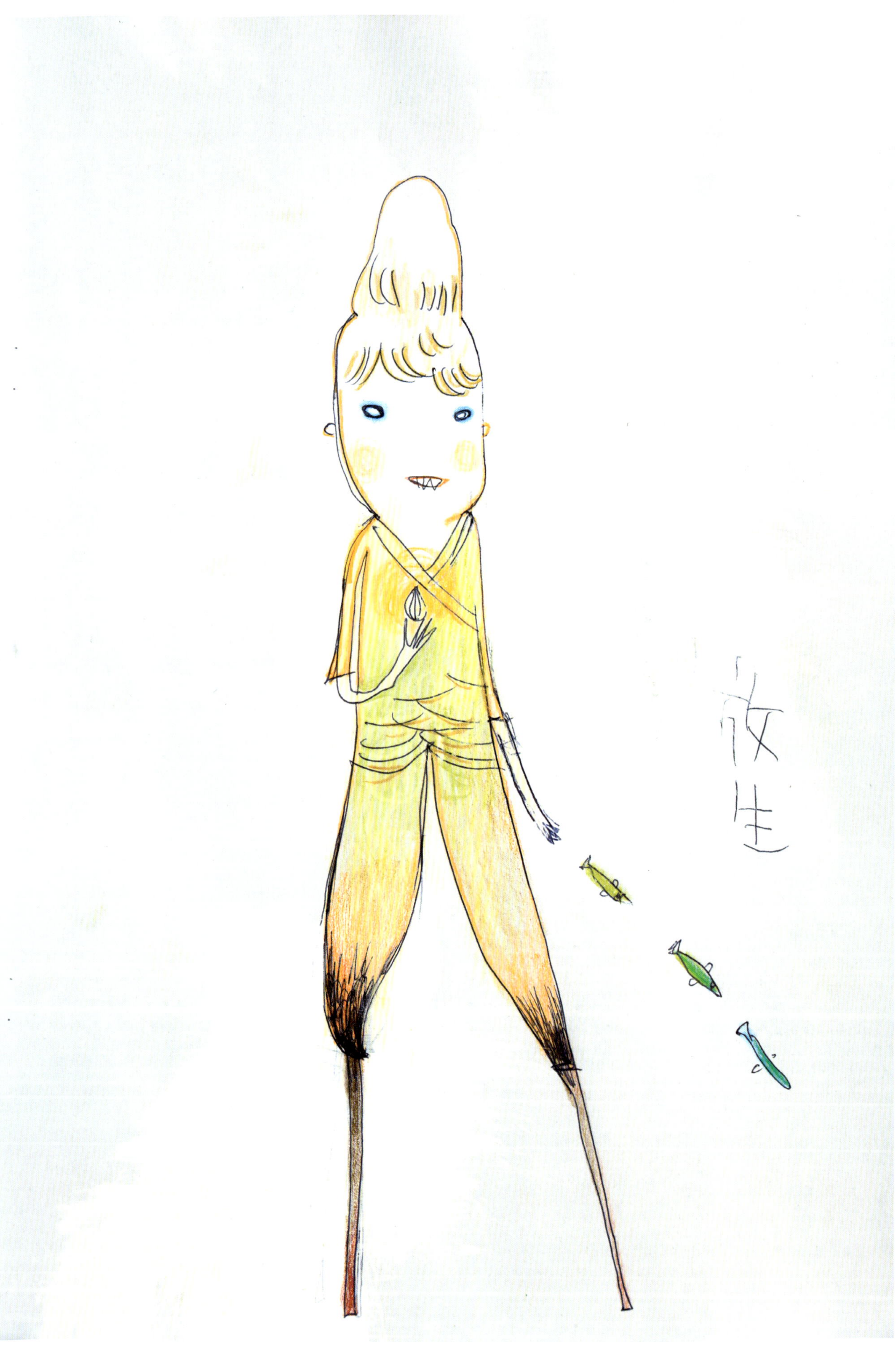
夜生

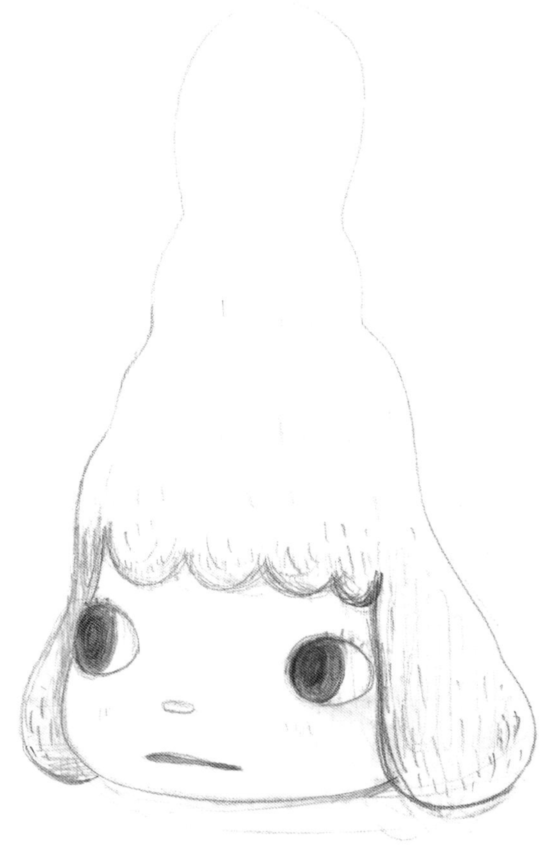

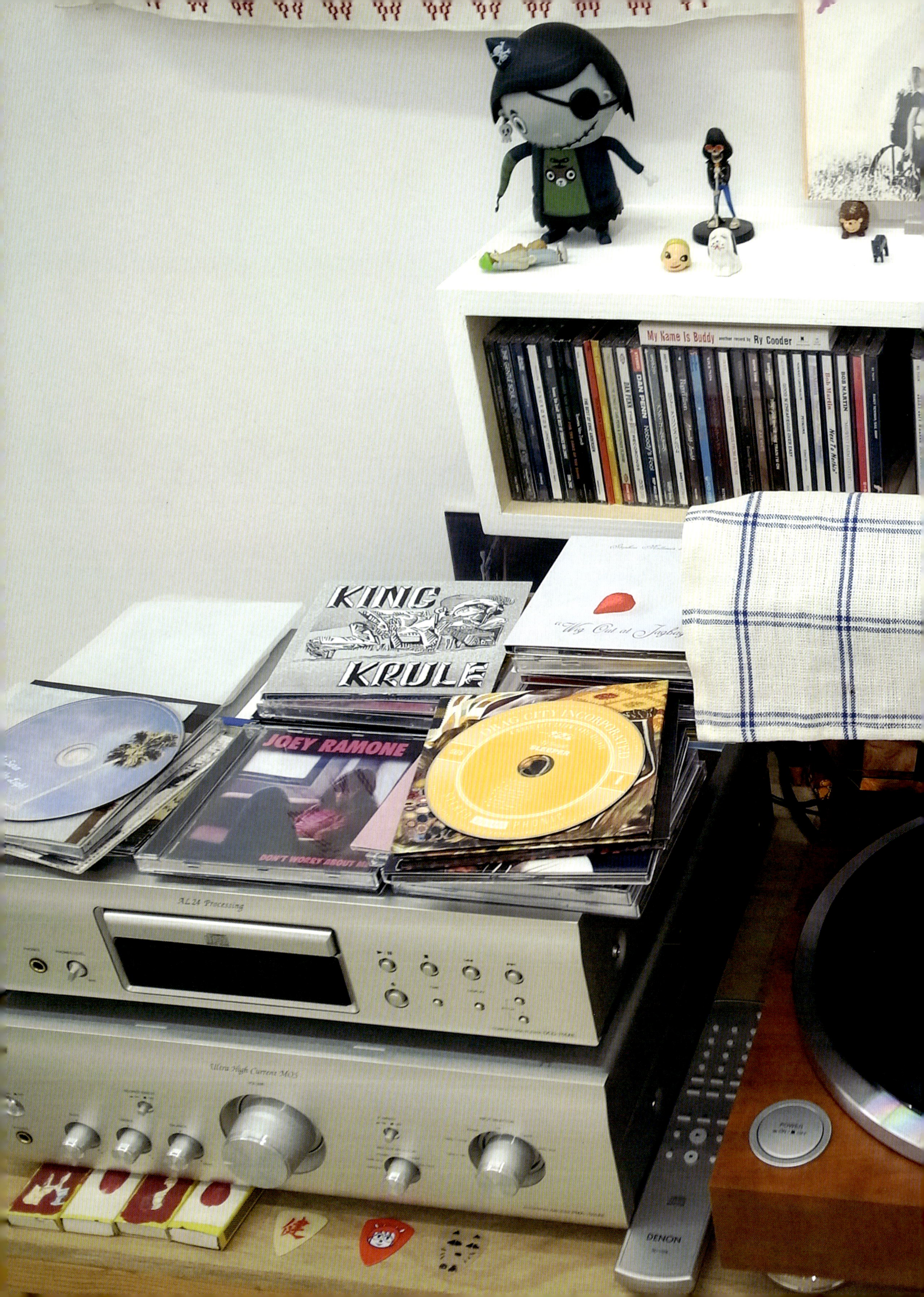

My Name Is Buddy
another record by Ry Cooder
KING
KRULE
JOEY RAMONE
DRAG CITY INCORPORATED
AL24 Processing
Ultra High Current MOS
DENON

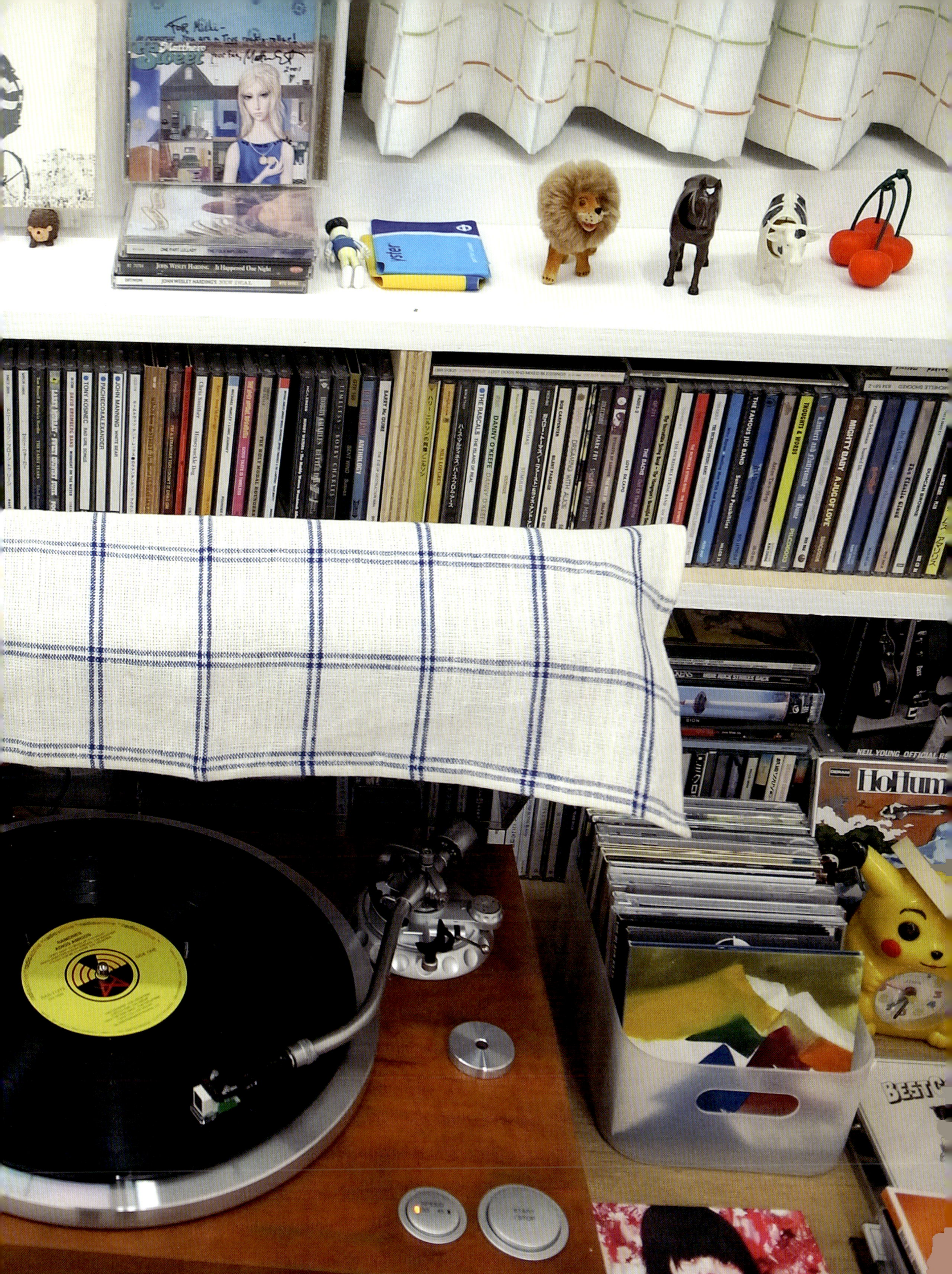

Matthew Sweet
JOHN WESLEY HARDING It Happened One Night
DANNY O'KEEFE
THE RASCALS
THE FAMOUS JUG BAND
MIGHTY BABY A JUG OF LOVE
NEIL YOUNG OFFICIAL
HoHum

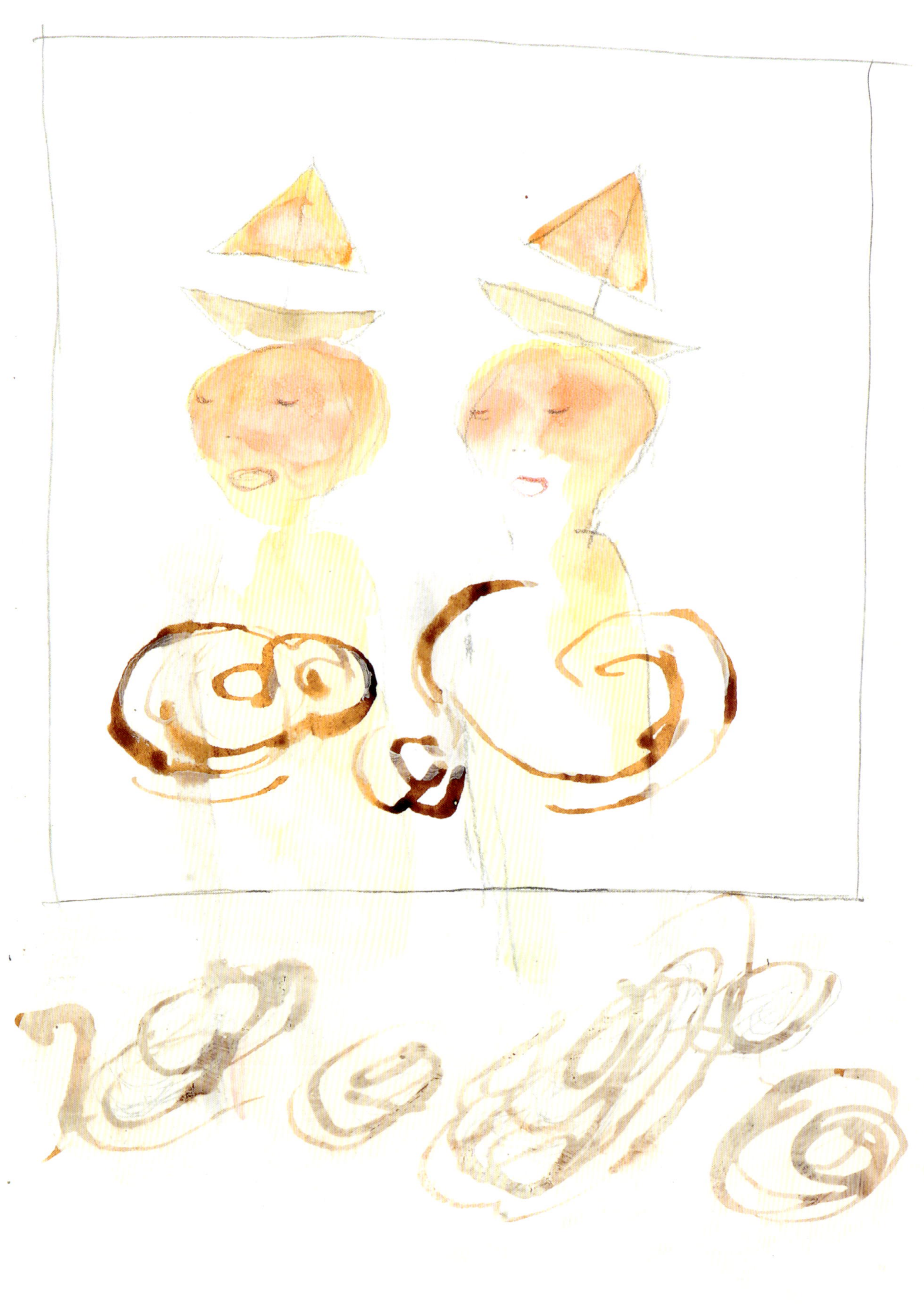
アラビアの船
NARA '89

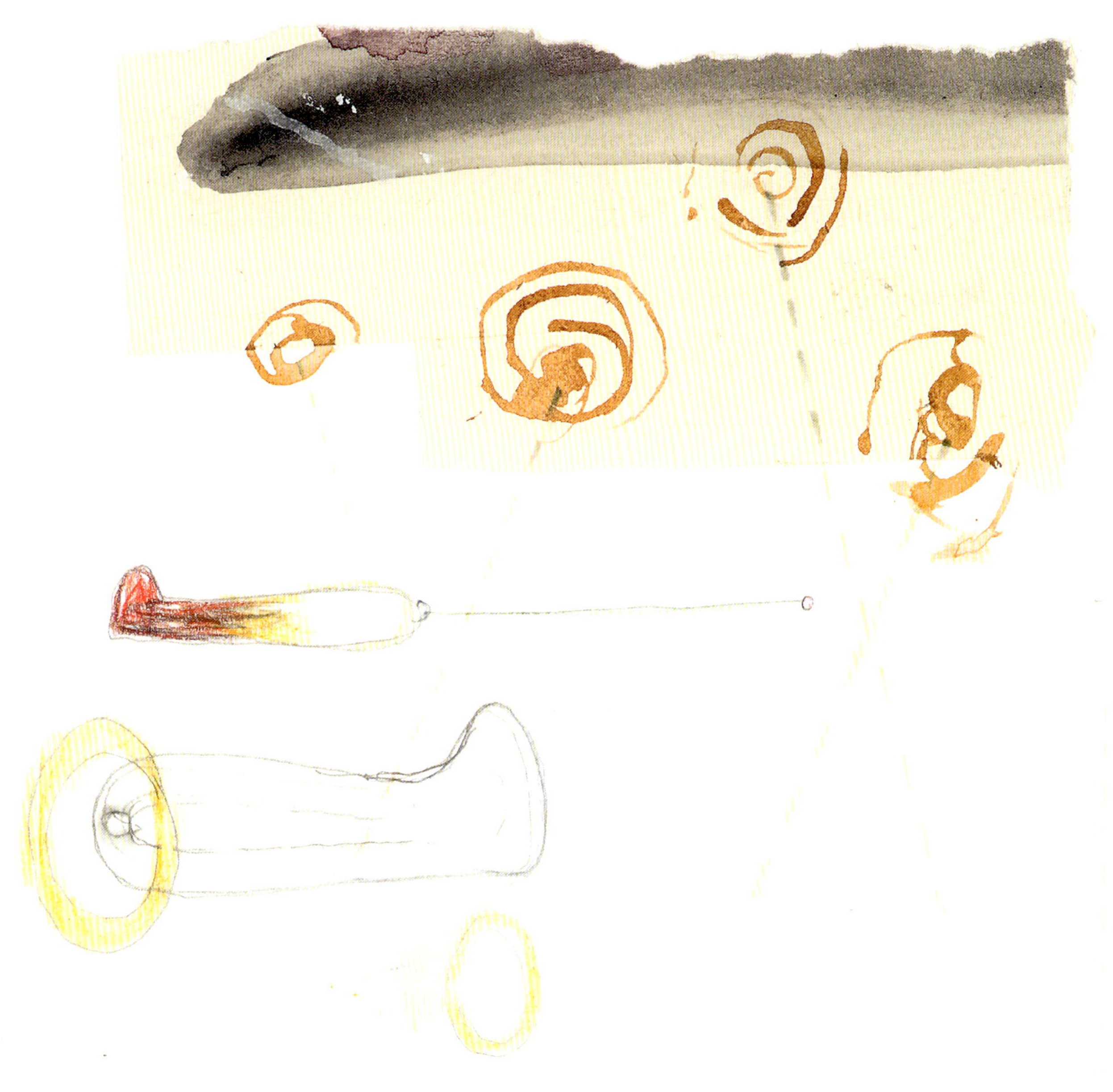
ゼロ戦 空中戦
NARA '80

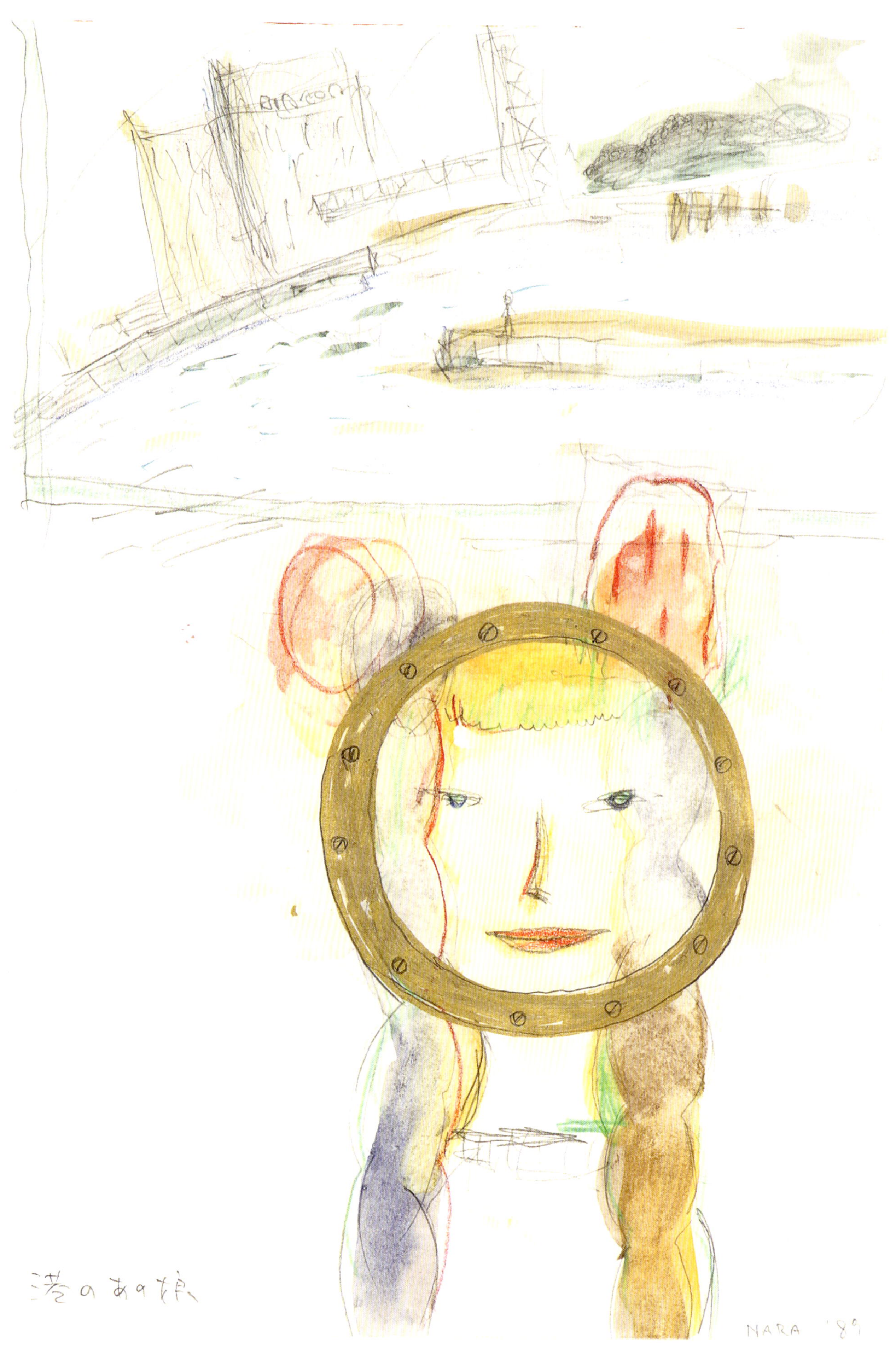
港のあの娘
NARA '89

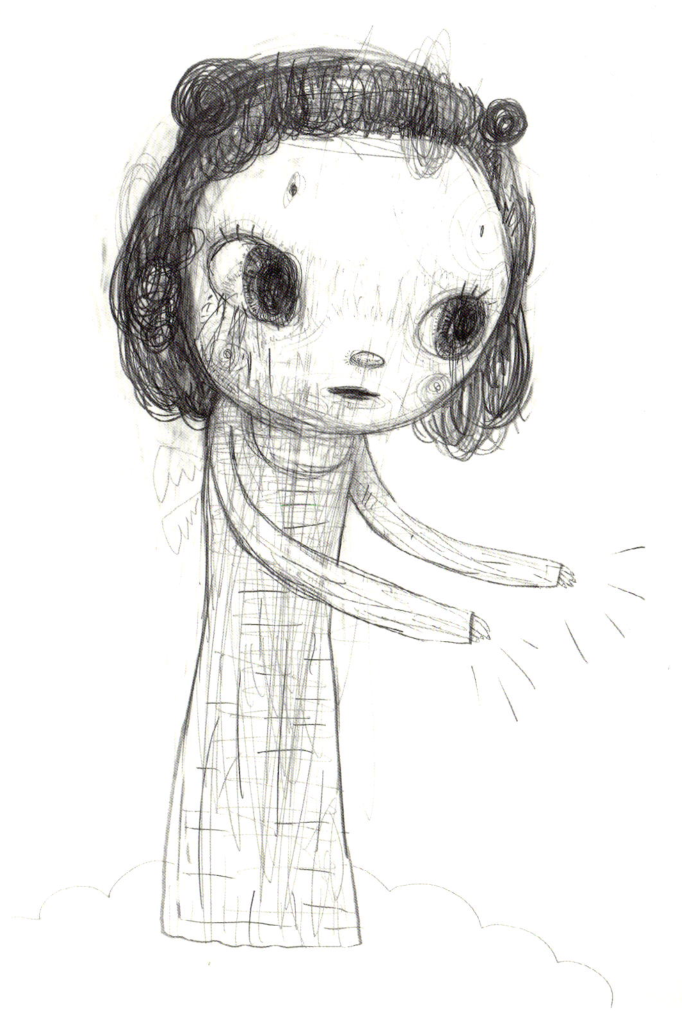

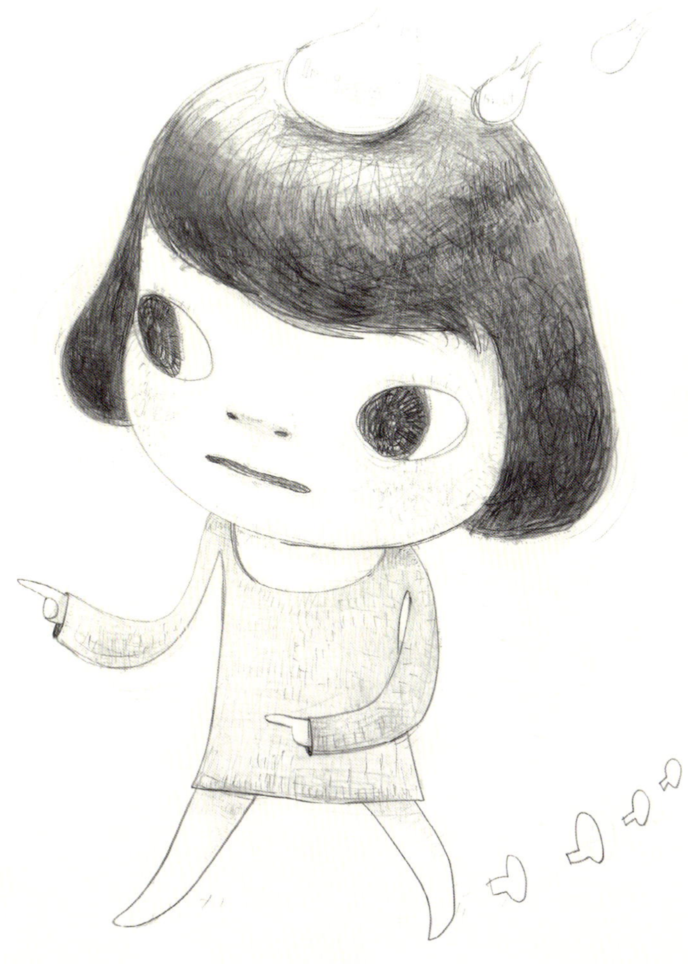

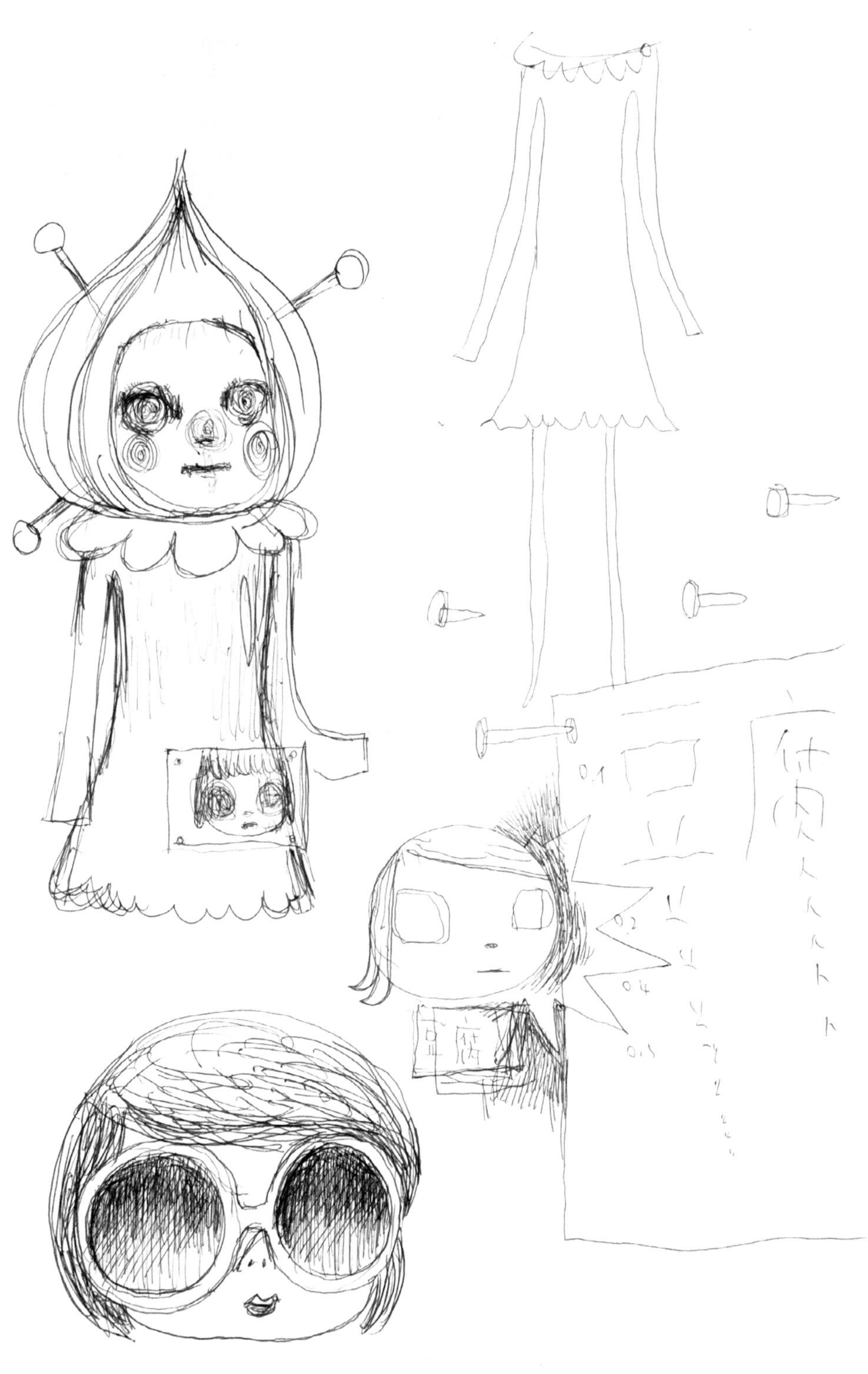

0.1
0.2
0.4
豆腐

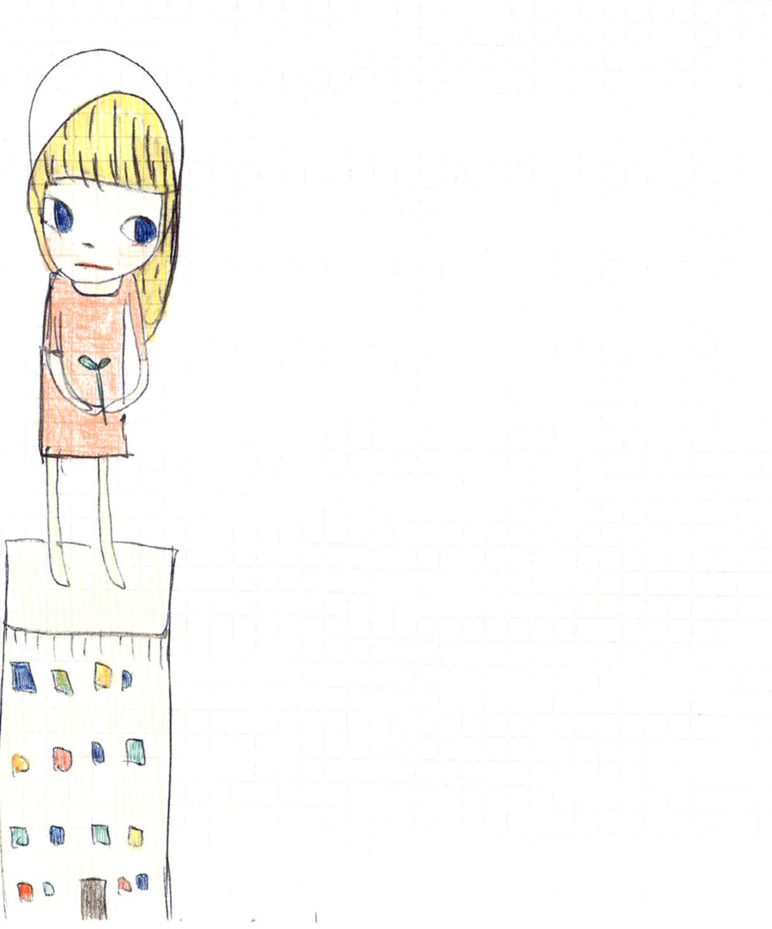

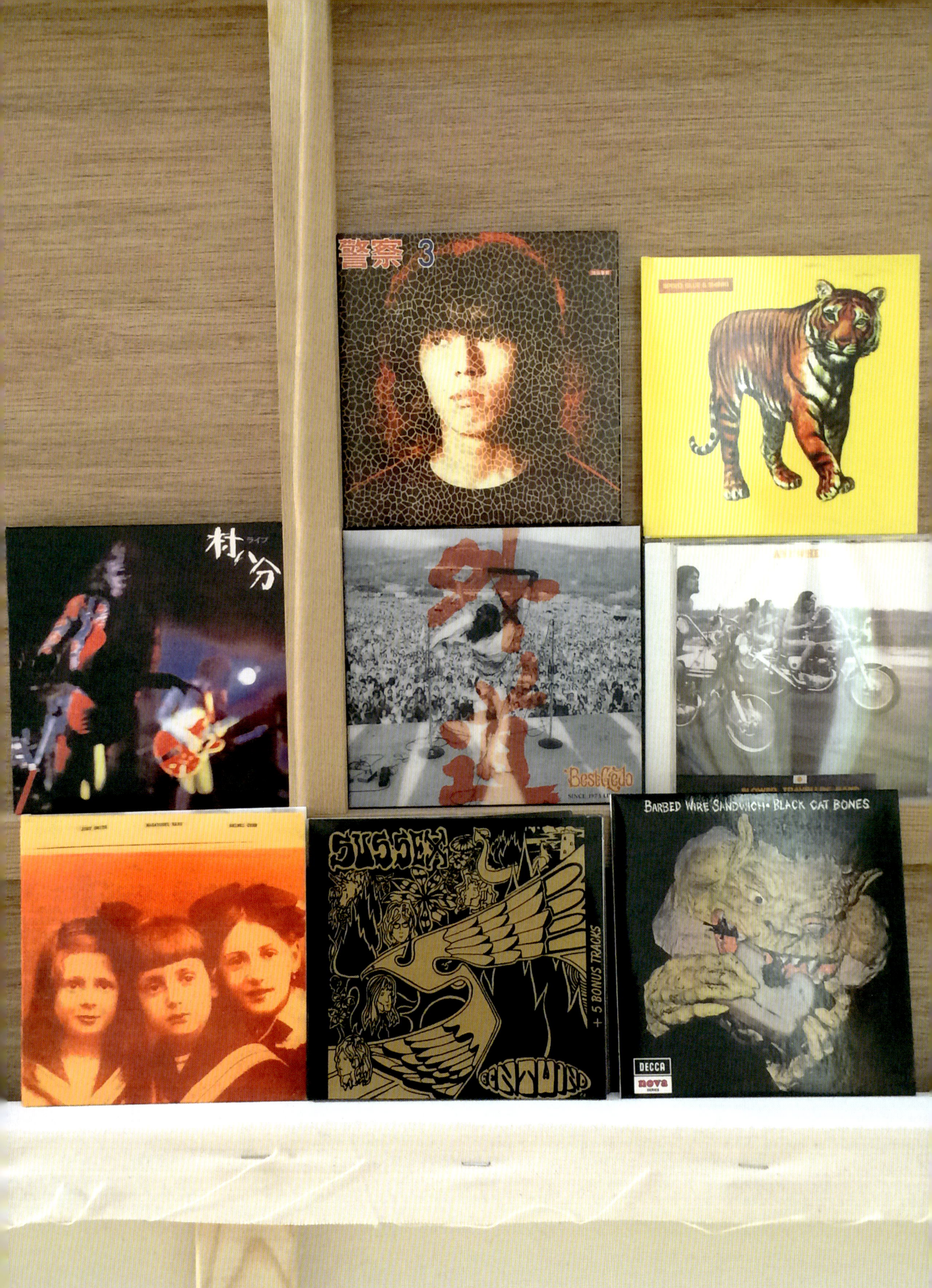

警察 3
村八分
ライブ
BestGedo
SUSSEX
+ 5 BONUS TRACKS
BARBED WIRE SANDWICH • BLACK CAT BONES
DECCA
nova

VII

LITTLE THINKER IN SILENCE

Headache, 2012
Miss Forest, 2010
Midnight Truth, 2017
Untitled, 2008
Untitled, 2008
Little Thinker in Silence, 2016
Peace of Mind, 2019
HOME, 2017
FROM THE BOMB SHELTER, 2017
SWEET HOME GATE, 2017
PEACE GIRL, 2017
Dream of Zero Fighter Plane, 1989
West and East, Two Rabbits, 1989
Girl Left Behind the Night, 2019
Little Thinker in Garden, 2016

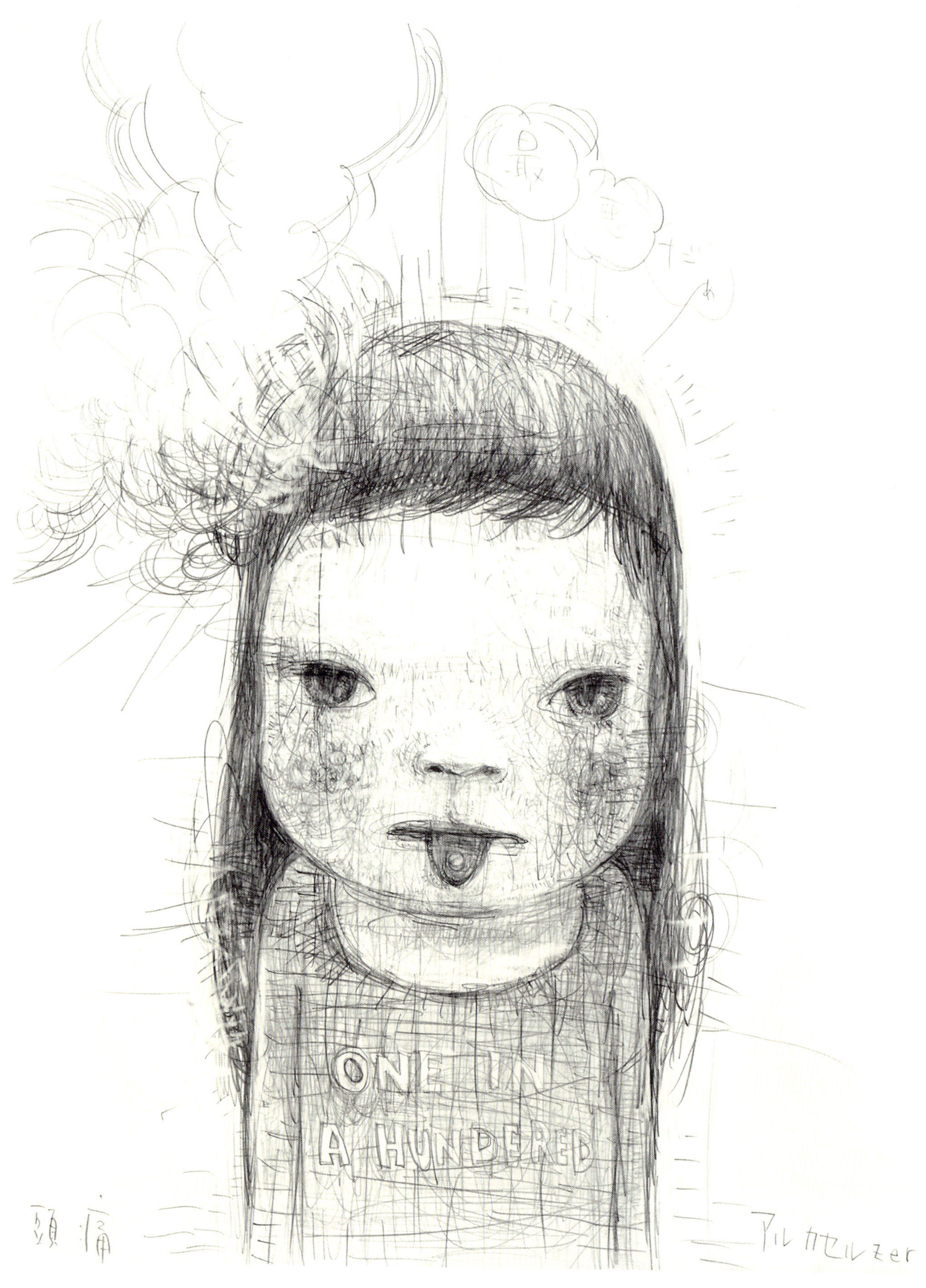
ONE IN
A HUNDRED
頭痛
アルカセルzer

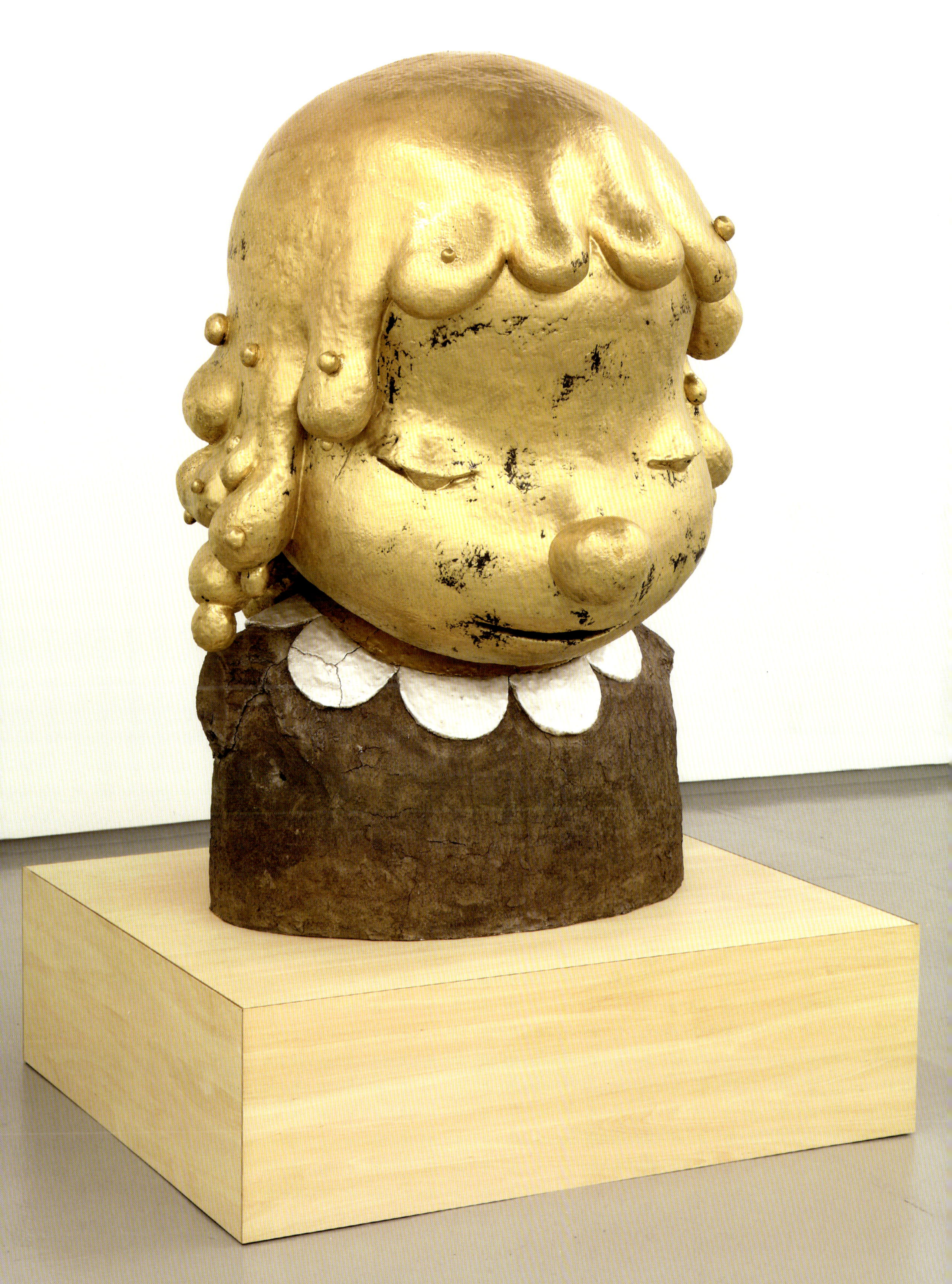

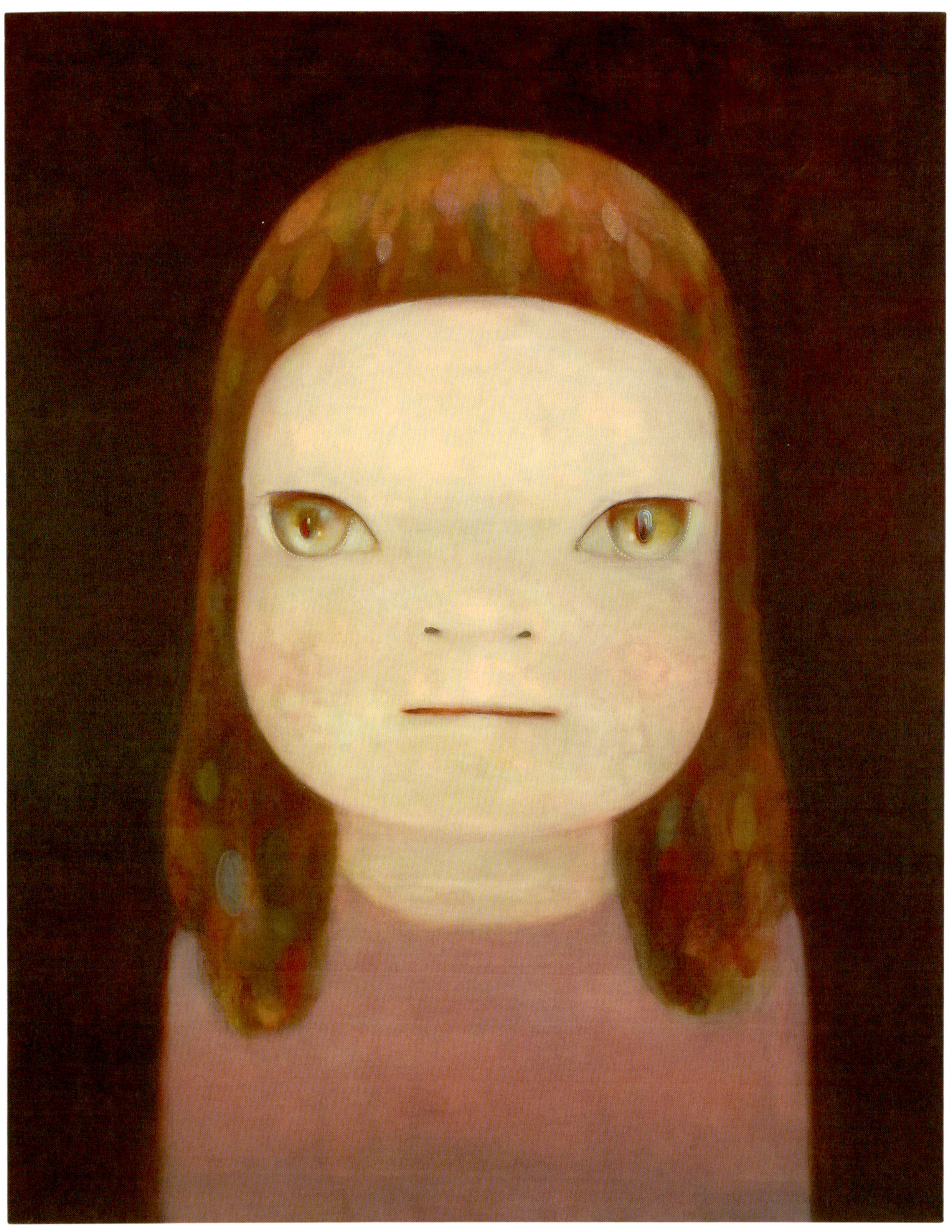

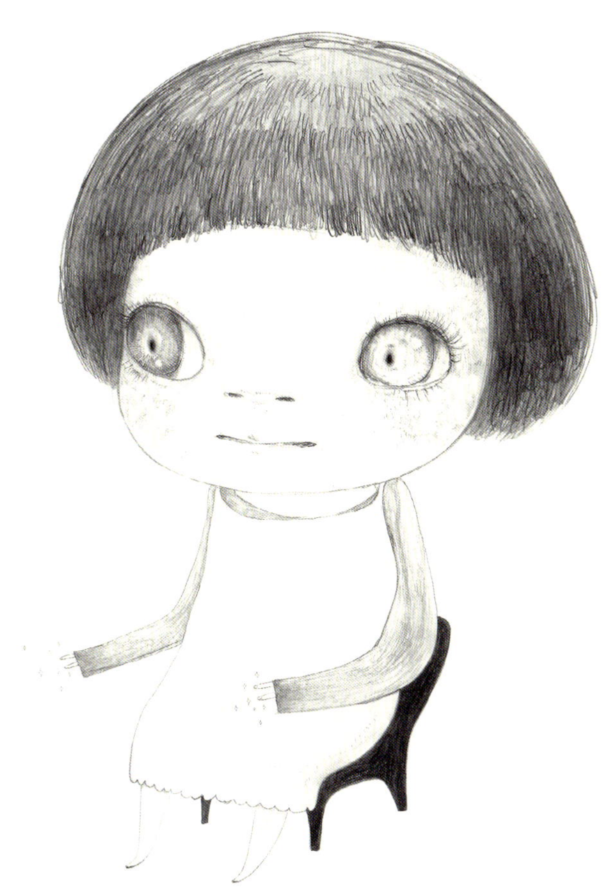

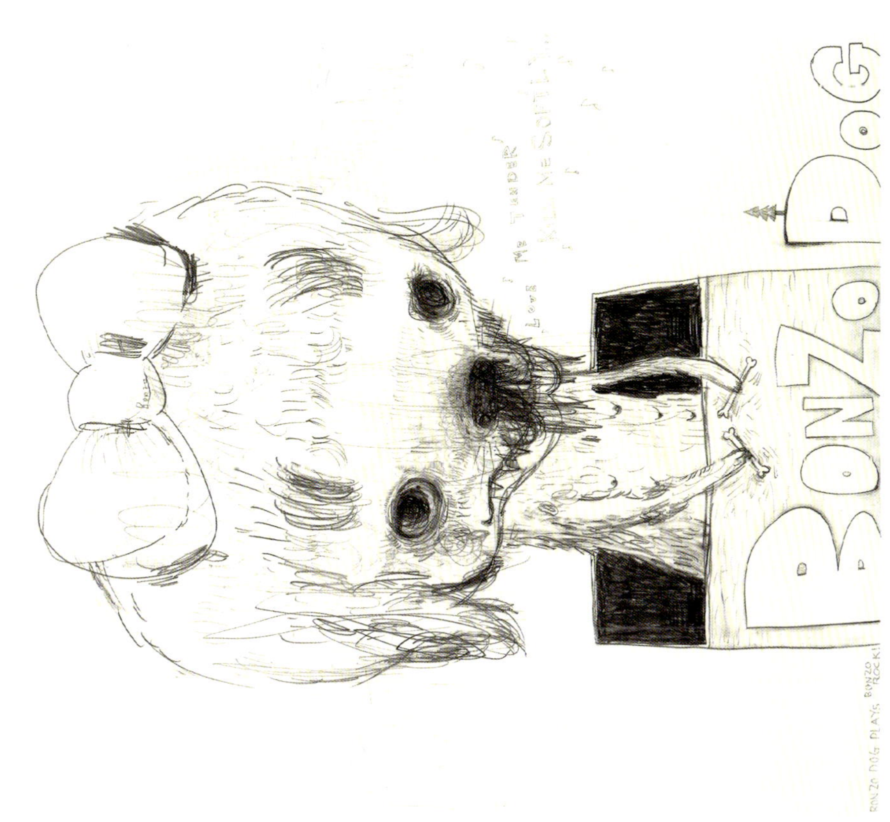
BONZO DOG

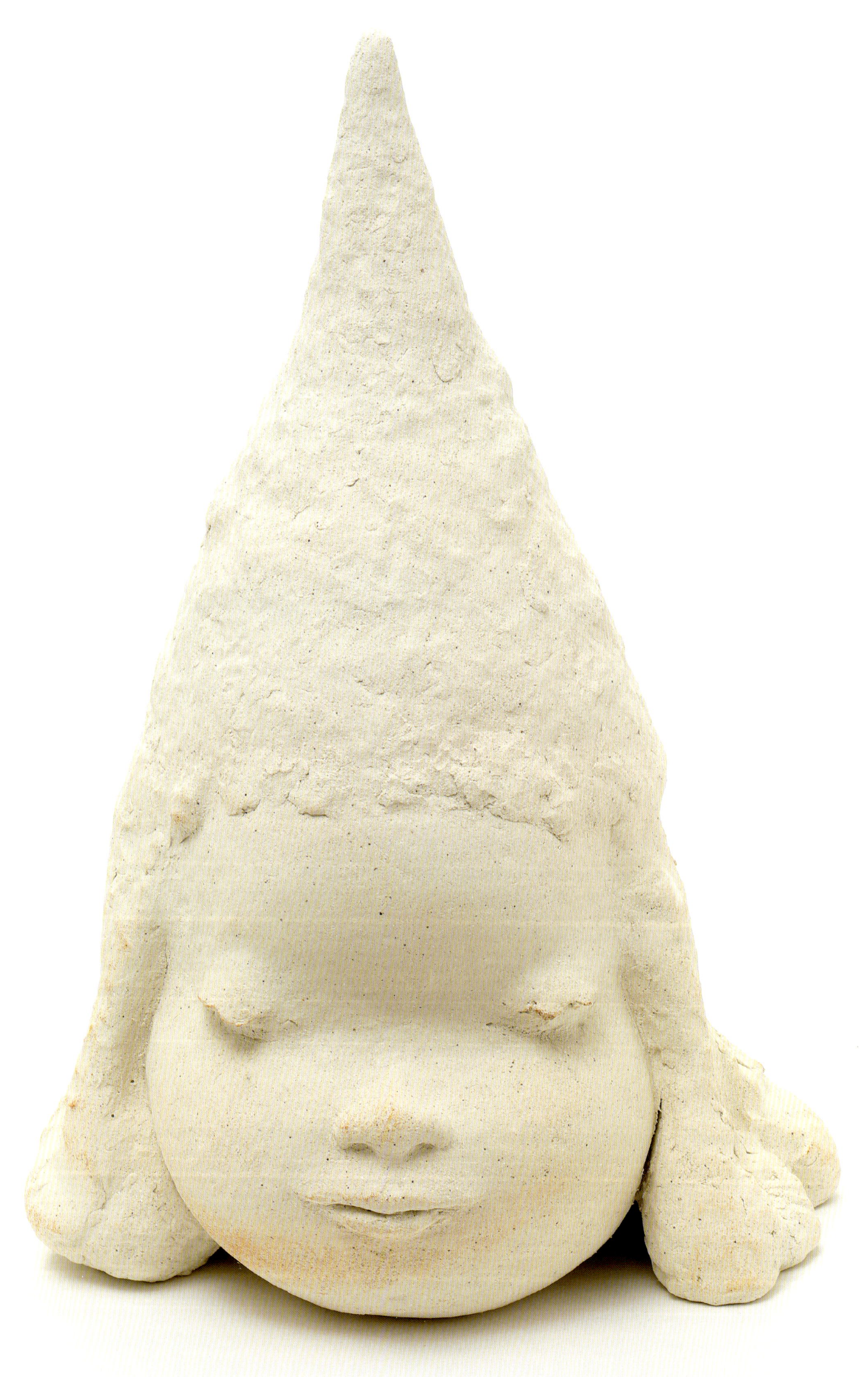

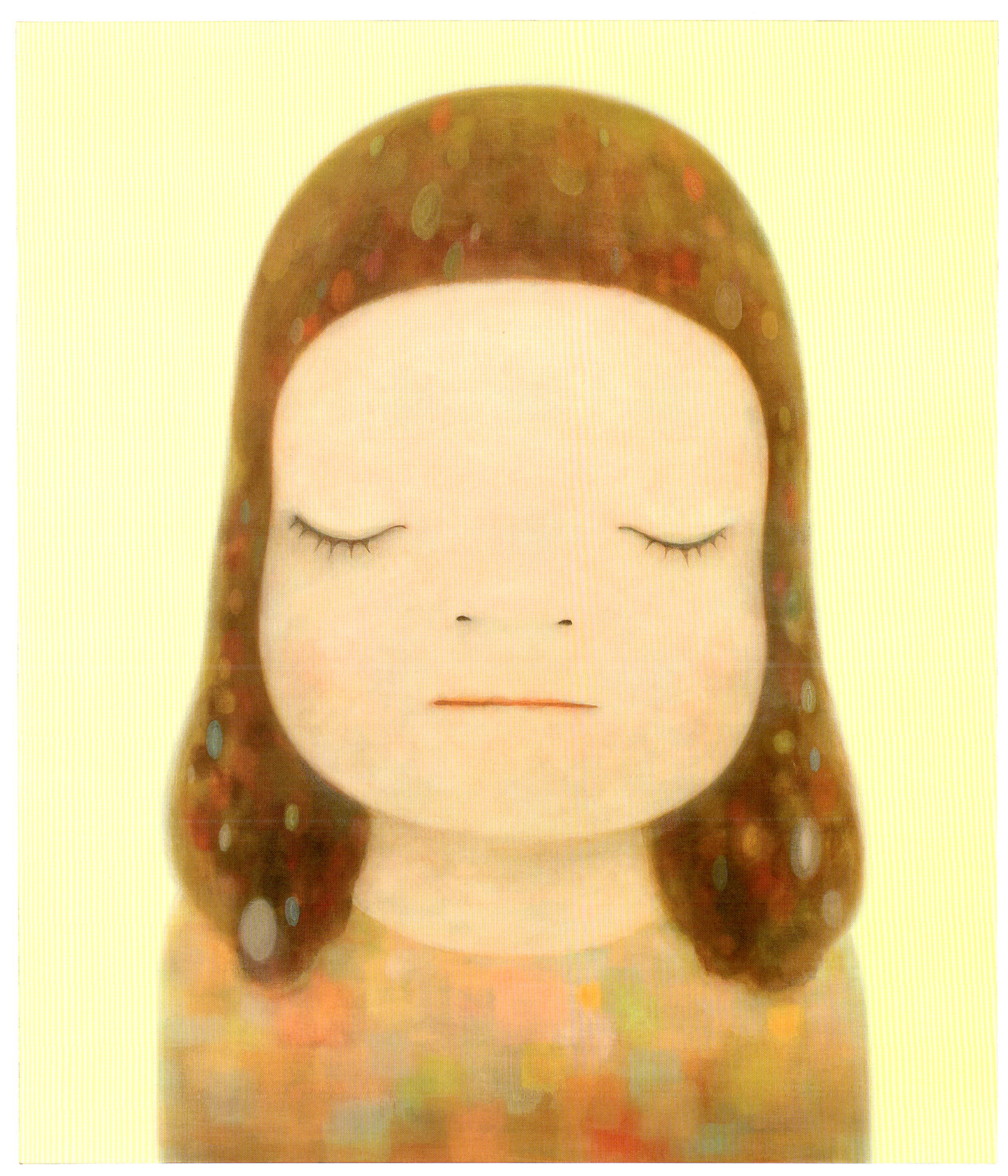

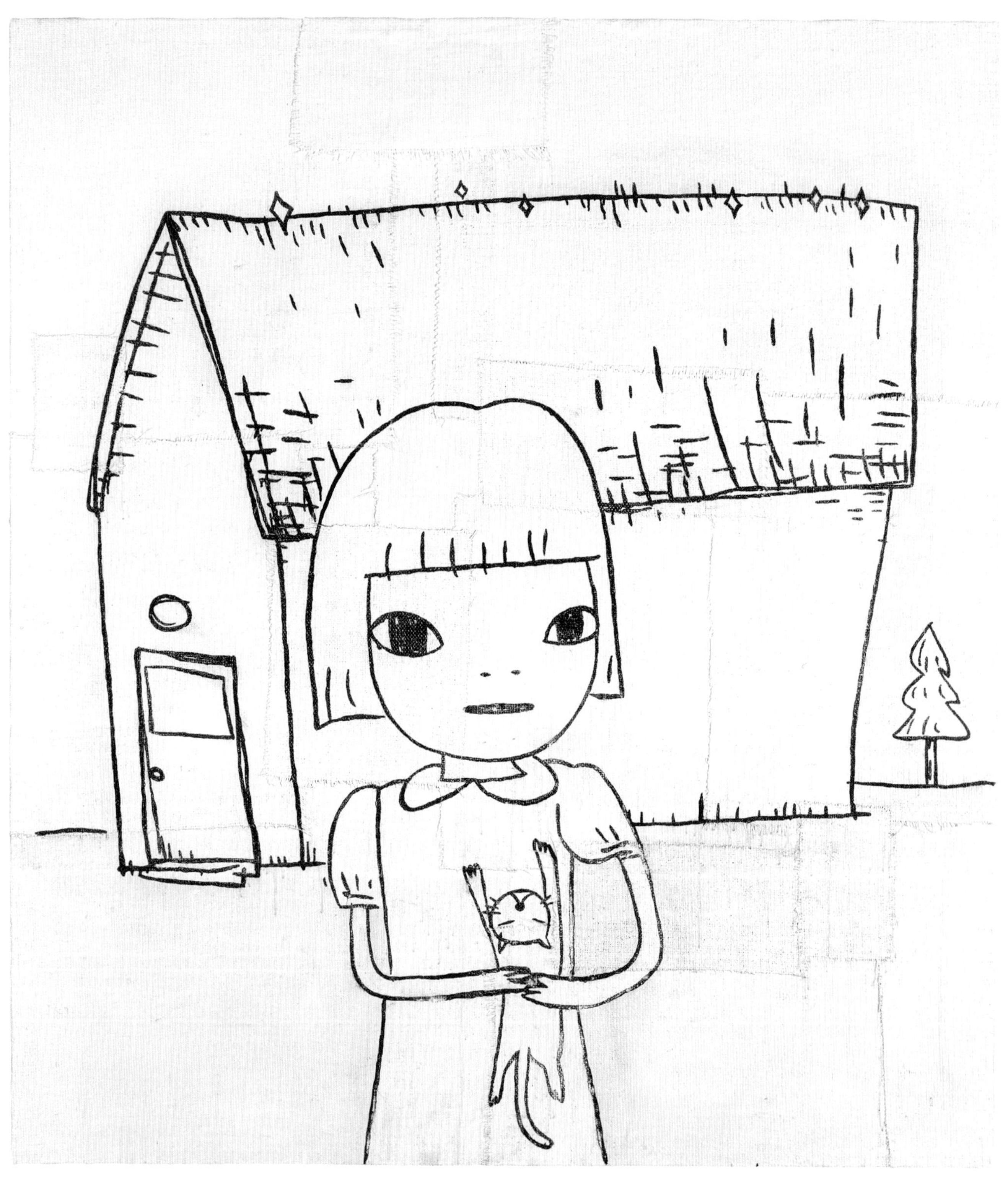

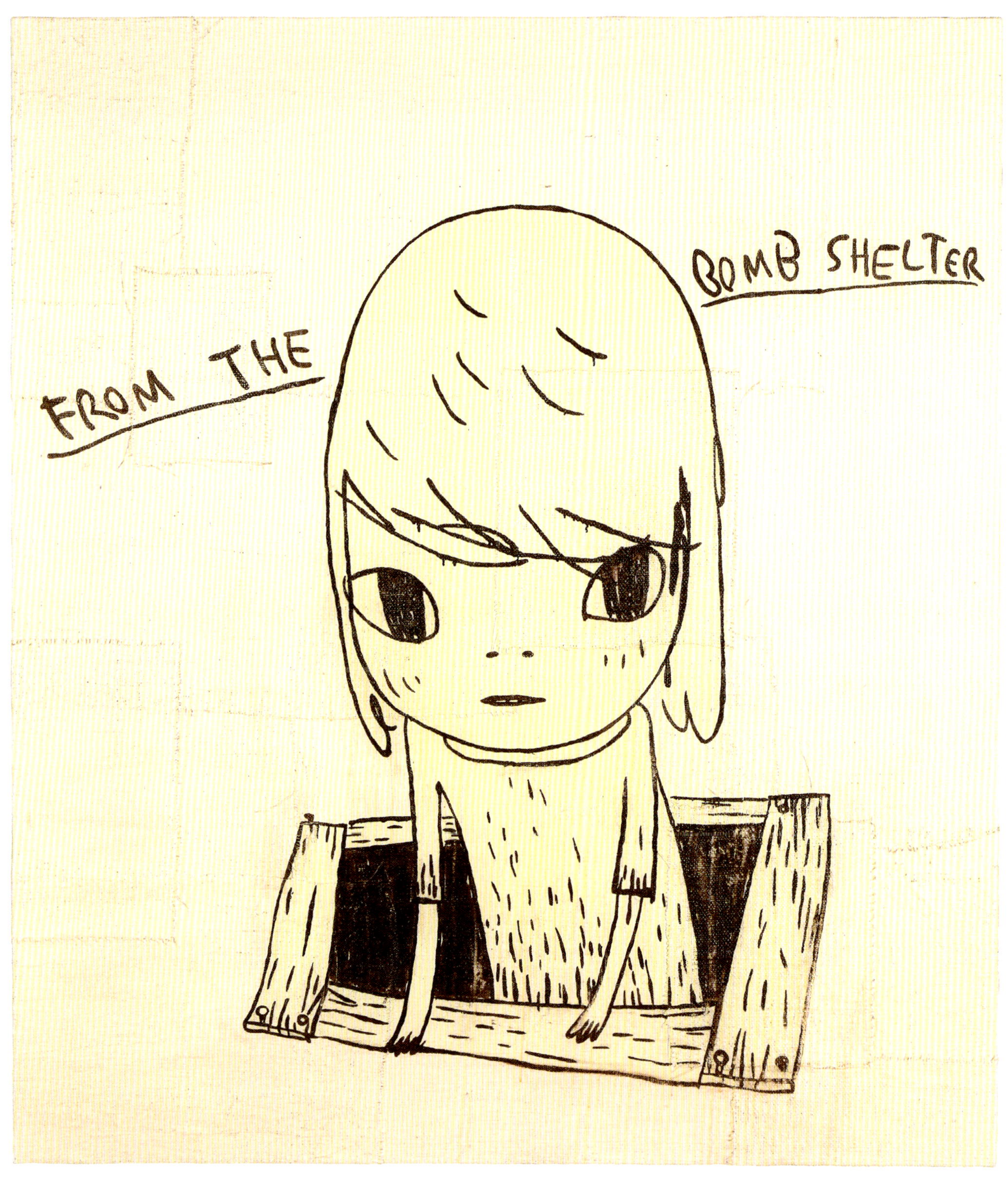
FROM THE
BOMB SHELTER

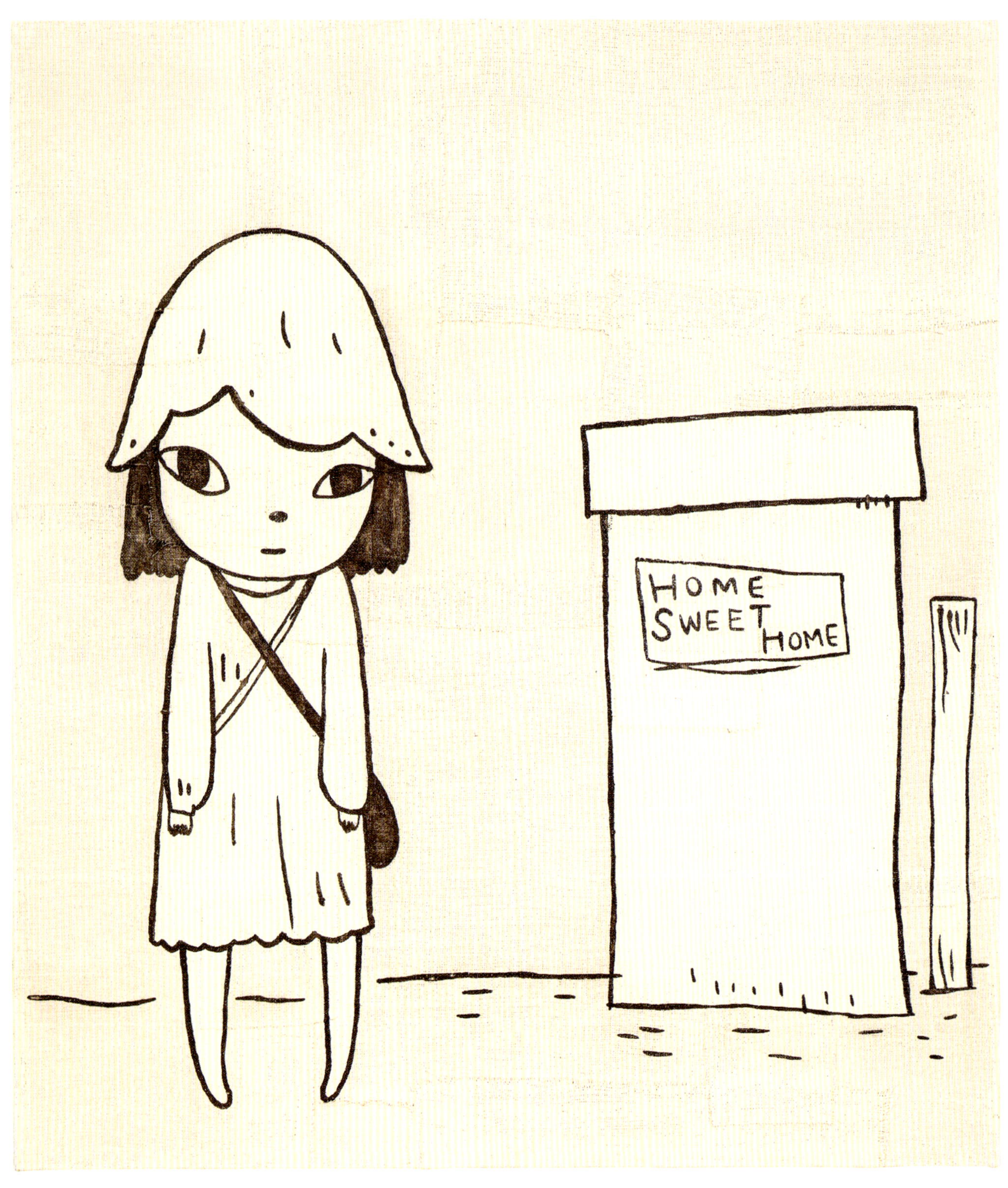
HOME
SWEET HOME

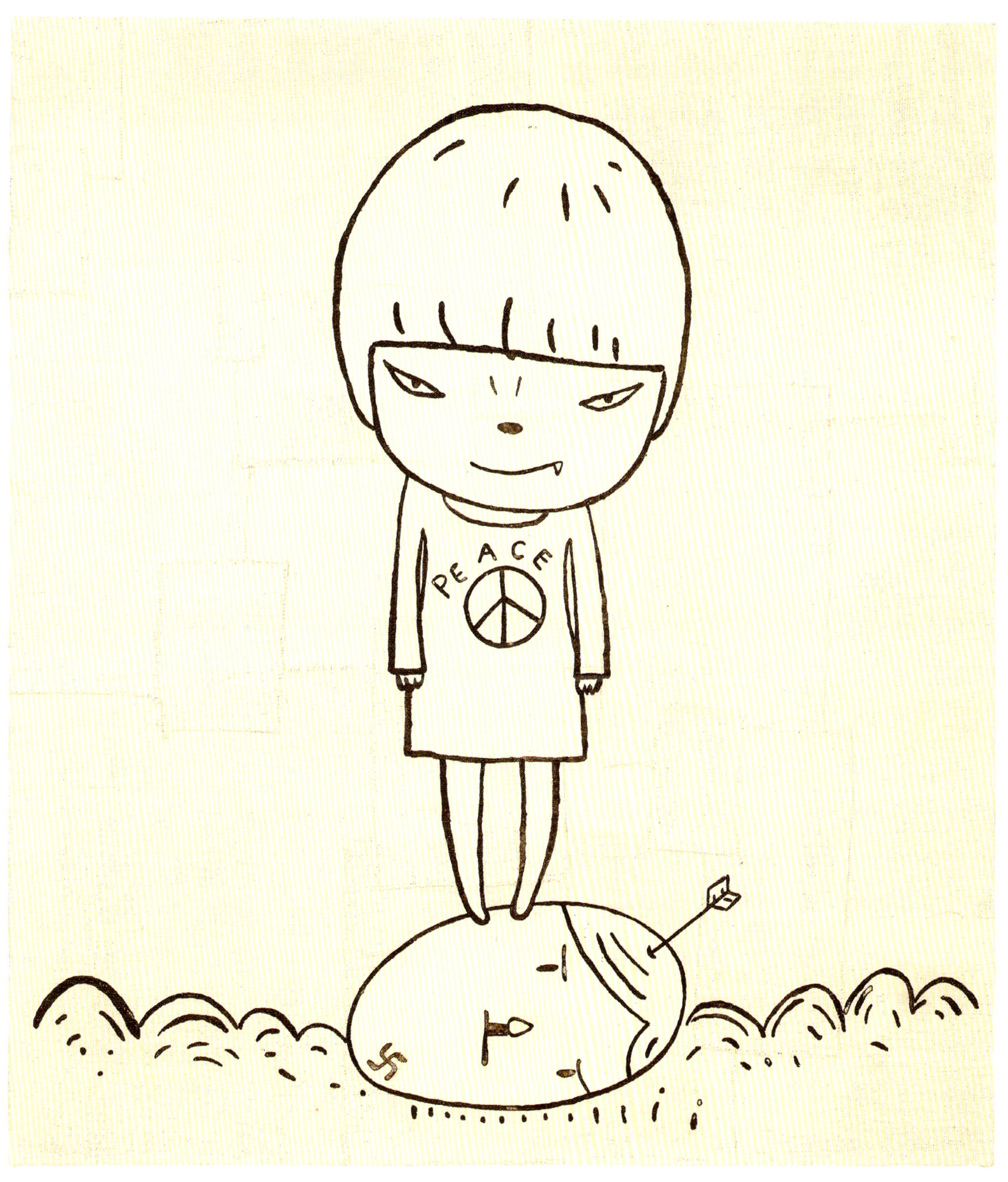
PEACE

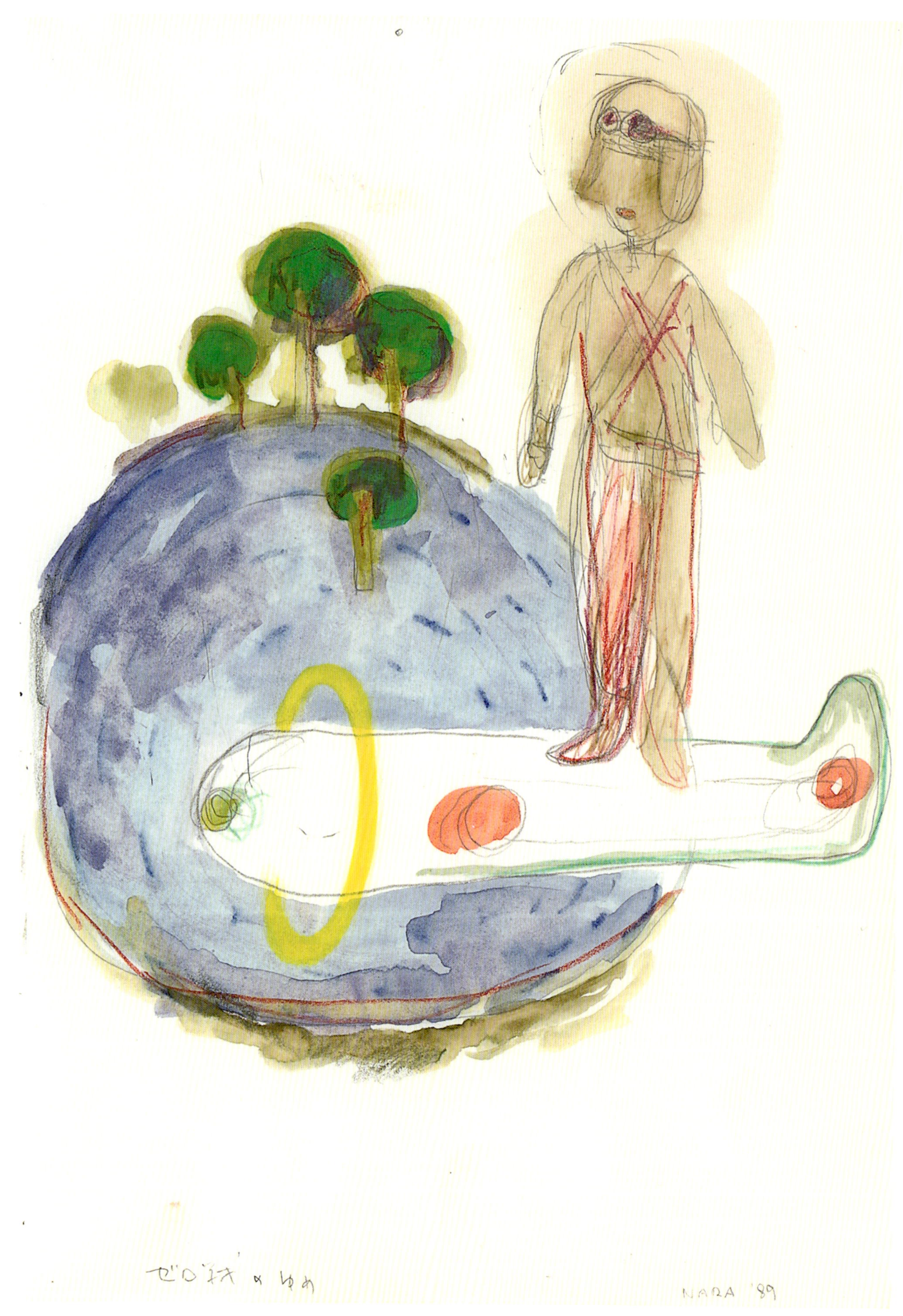
NARA '89

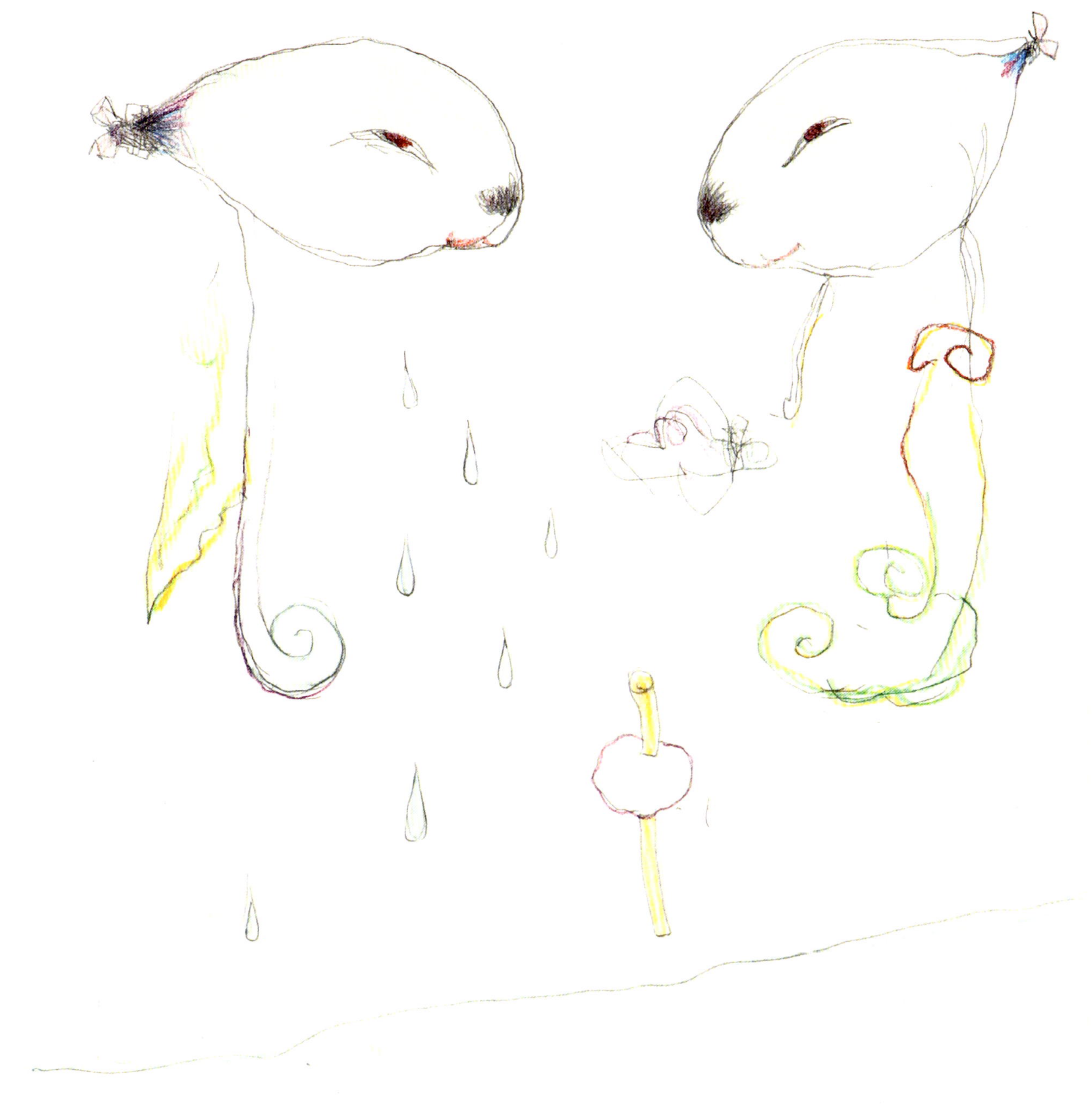
2匹の兎
西と東
NARA '89

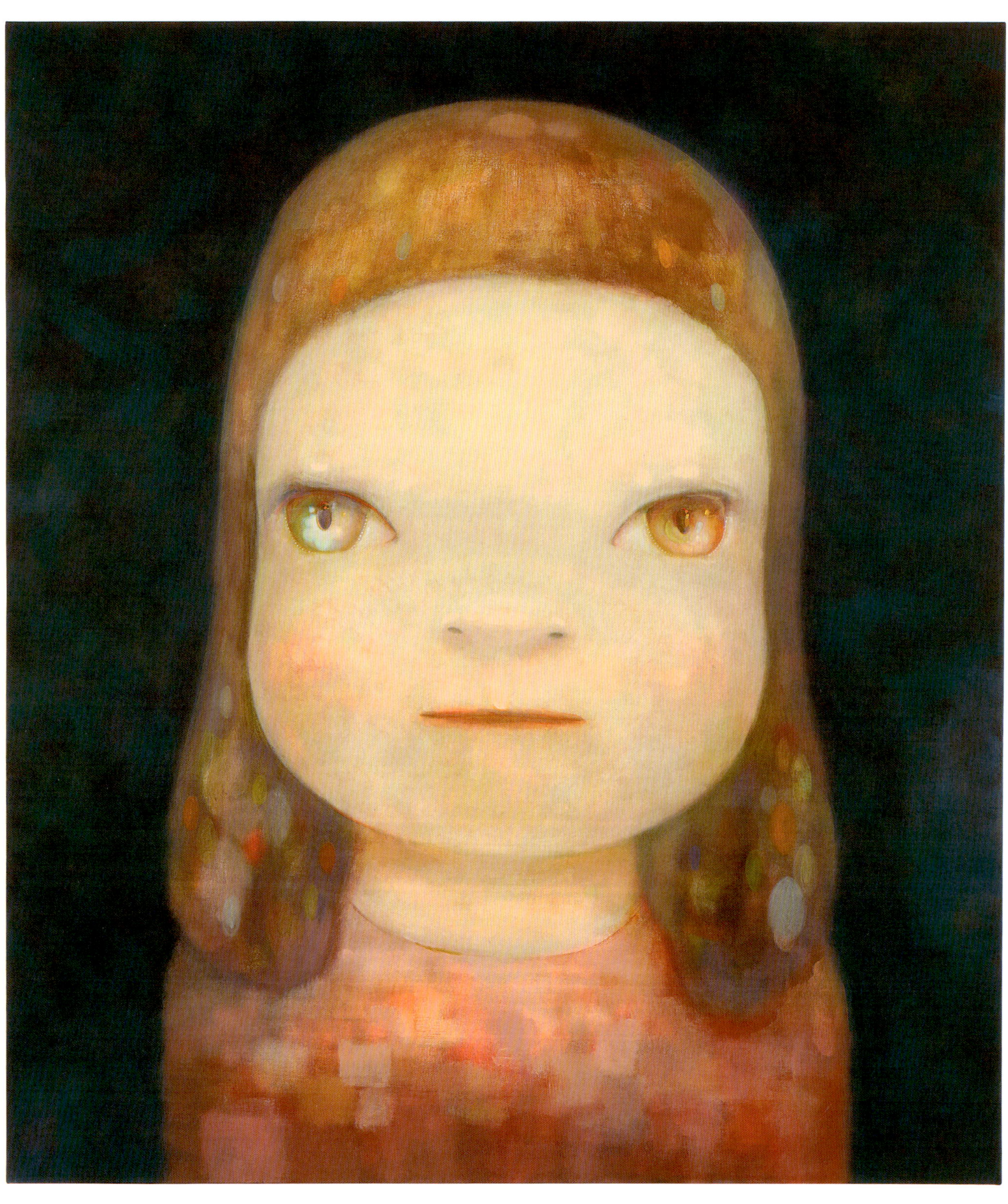

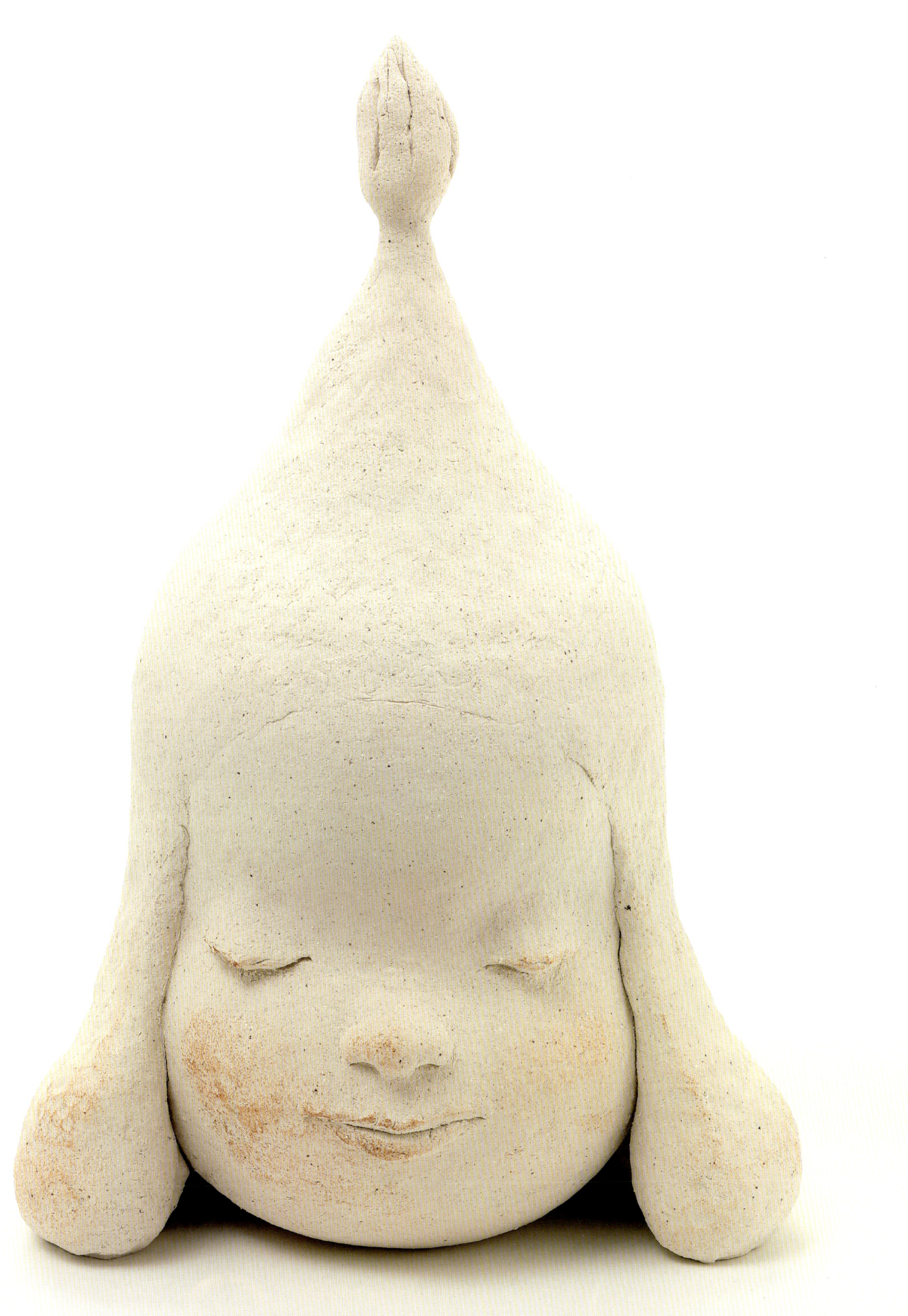

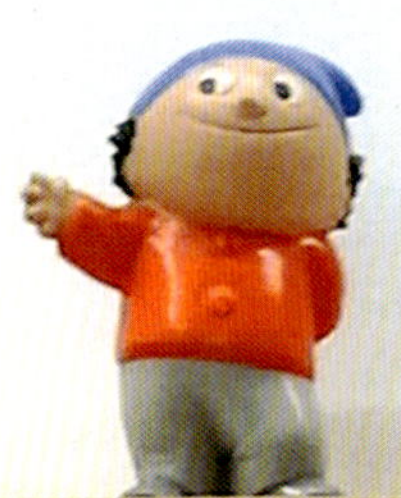

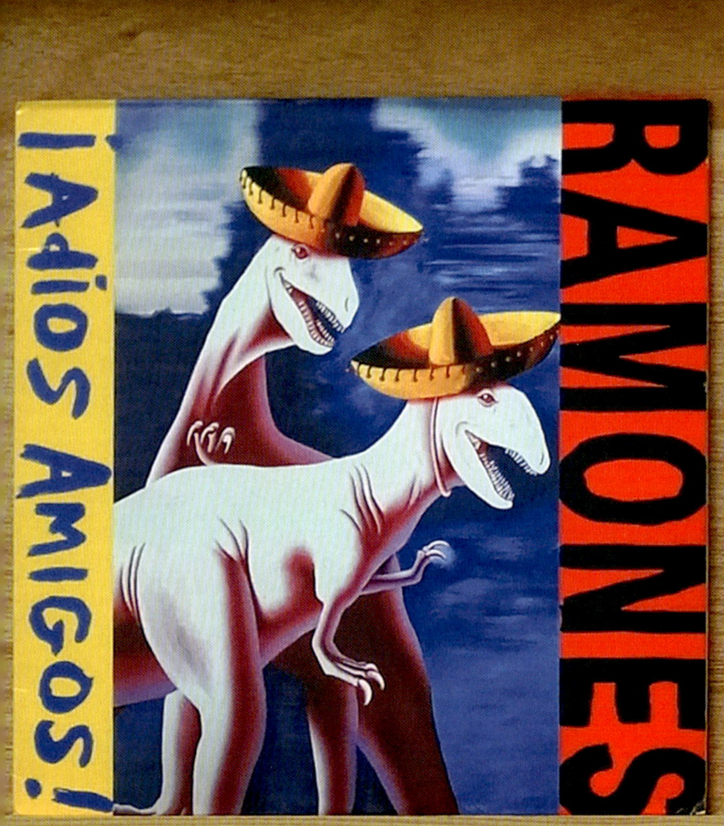

¡ADIOS AMIGOS!
RAMONES

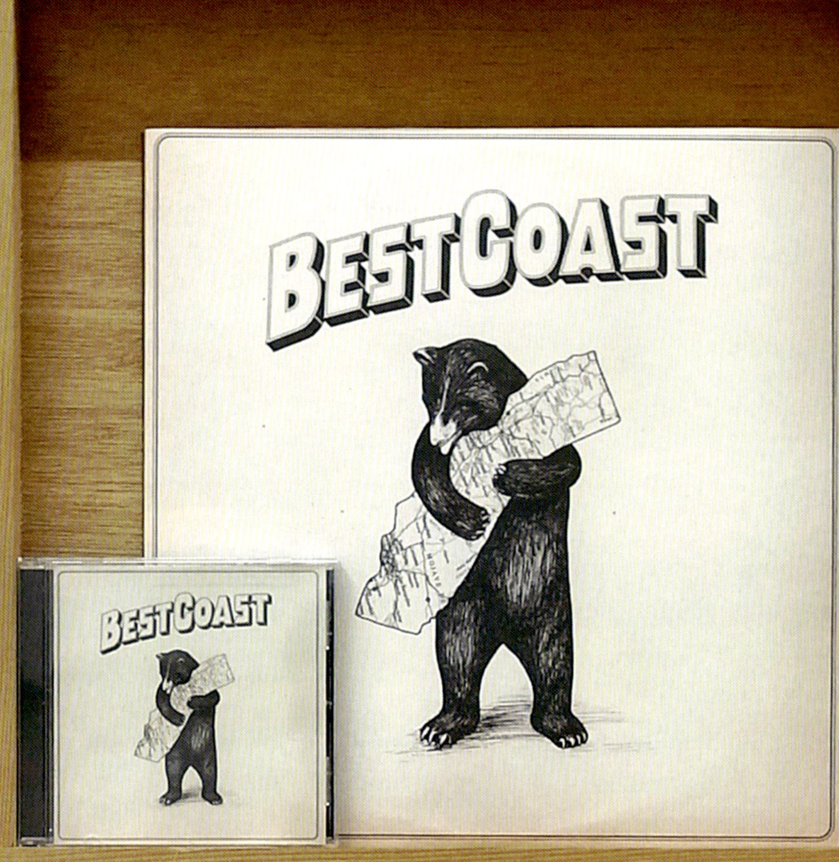

BEST COAST
BEST COAST

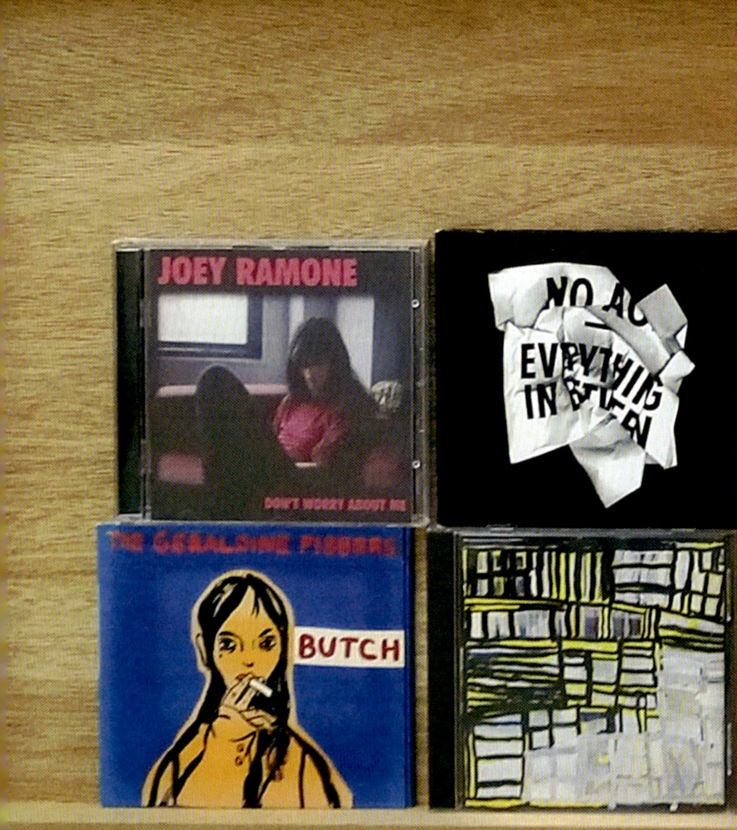

JOEY RAMONE
DON'T WORRY ABOUT ME
BUTCH

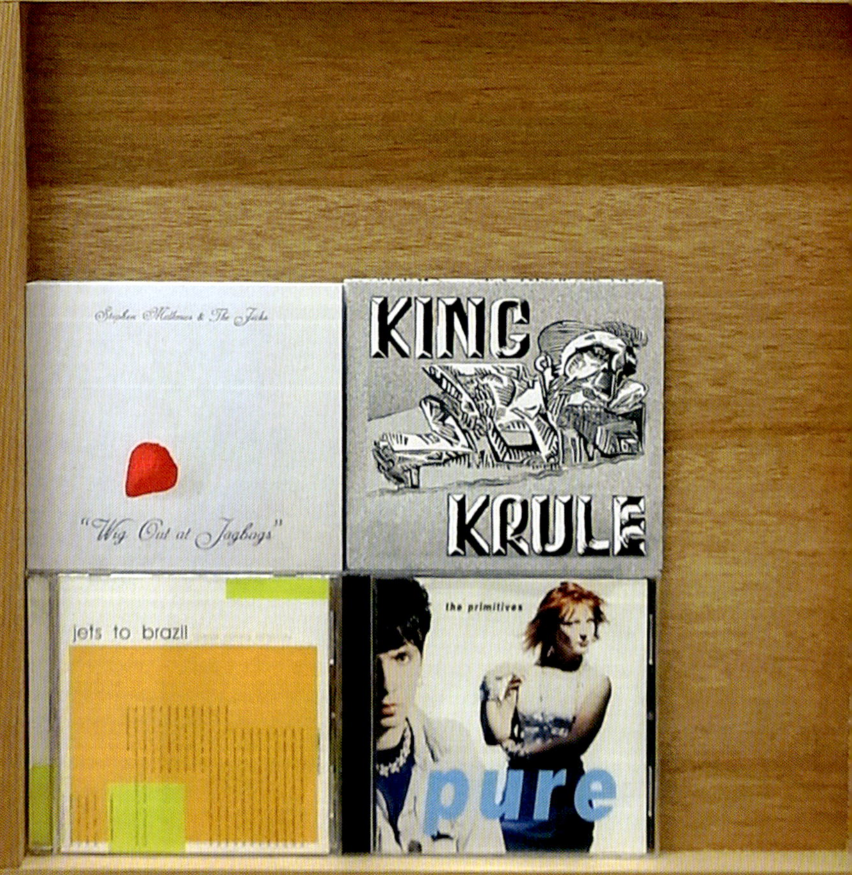

Stephen Malkmus & The Jicks
"Wig Out at Jagbags"
KING KRULE
jets to brazil
the primitives
pure

VIII

IN MY TEENS, I STUDIED ART THROUGH RECORD JACKETS

YOSHITOMO NARA

YOSHITOMO NARA wrote "In My Teens, I Studied Art through Record Jackets" as a monthly feature for the Japanese art magazine Bijutsu Techō *(*BT*) between 2013 and 2015. In each issue Nara discussed a different album from his record collection, thoughtfully considering the work of the artists, designers, illustrators, and photographers who created the jacket covers alongside personal anecdotes about the music. Of the thirty that were published, fifteen are reproduced in the following pages in English, with translations by Chisato Uno. The text below appeared as Nara's final column in the magazine.*

The albums I've talked about have almost all been Western. I was a huge Western music fan in my teens, but if you asked if I had properly understood the lyrics, the answer would have to be a definitive NO! Of course I would sometimes buy the Japanese versions that included translations, but more often I bought the cheaper import versions, and with minor-label releases that didn't even have Japanese versions, they didn't include any liner notes at all. So, how was it that this music reached the heart of a country boy who only understood Japanese? I want to think back to that time (oh, it really feels like the end of the series!).

I was born and raised at the very northern tip of Honshū, in Aomori Prefecture. There is an American air base there because of the proximity to the former Soviet Union (now Russia). U.S. bases in Japan had their own radio stations and would broadcast in their areas. I think they were primarily for emergency broadcasts, but most of the programs were ordinary, ranging from local information to Japanese lessons, and a lot of music by request. The music covered a wide range, from 1950s pop to country to the newest rock. A lot of the requests were for popular, catchy songs, and even though I didn't understand English at all, I found myself singing along to the choruses and dancing. I was kind of a precocious elementary school kid, but when I started studying English in middle school, I wanted to sing along properly to the words I had memorized as Japanese-ish sounds. For example, "do re mi daaa" became "don't let me down," and I was so excited because I felt like I got it, I could get it!

When I started middle school, I'd run to the record shop whenever I got my allowance. I'd sing the hooks to the songs that had stayed in my heart since elementary school, and have them help me find those records. This is how I began my collection. Since the import versions were cheaper, I mostly bought those even though they didn't come with any translations. Of course, not all of it was easily understood like "don't let me down" (crying), but even if I didn't understand it, the sounds vibrated into my body, and even acoustic folk songs were seared into this kid's heart.

At the time, I was determined to understand this music, if not with words then with my body and soul. I'd gaze endlessly at the record jacket as I listened to the music. I stared at every inch of the square jacket and tried to tie all that visual information to the songs. I was forging my own mental connections between the music and visual art. This is how, during the long performances, I would embark on a journey with the songs and the jacket to an imaginary world. I'd create my own translations of the lyrics in a way that had nothing to do with the English language, while I transformed the jacket image in my mind, kind of like imagining a music video.

All of the long hours spent doing this resulted in training my imagination and creativity. (That's what I wanted to say with this series!) This was not something you're taught, like technique or art history. Looking back now, I think that this had trained me subconsciously, bit by bit. Of course, this has been put to good use today in my creative work and thought processes, but even if I had not chosen the path of art, I am sure that this experience would have been invaluable to me as a member of the only species to possess creativity.

Even now, I listen to records and I'll line up the jackets while I work. But I no longer stare at the jacket while getting deep into the songs. The music gets sublimated into the paintings and drawings I'm thinking about. I used to be just on the receiving end of creations like these, but now I'm on equal footing with the people who produced the jackets, sending out my creations to an audience I've never met. Part of me wants to proudly stand shoulder to shoulder with these jackets and songs, but the records and CDs let me know, "Hey, not yet! You've still got a long way to go!"

Even when I'm gone from this world someday,
Not for the sake of anyone else
I want to record these days that I've lived with this air around me,
I want to leave it within the history of this world.
I feel this deeply.
(@michinara3, Twitter, April 6, 2015)

So with that, goodbye, readers!

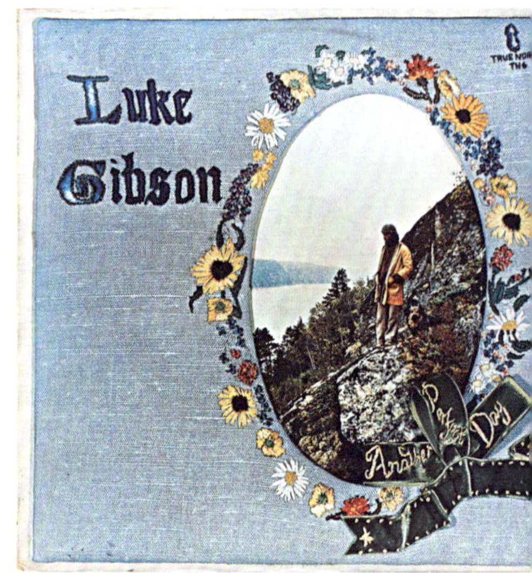

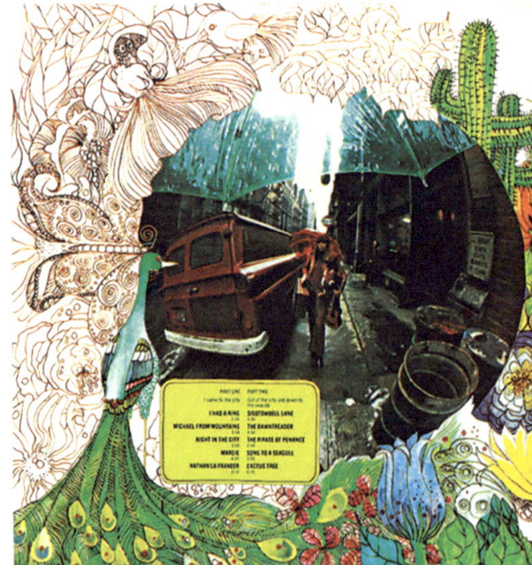

LUKE GIBSON
Another Perfect Day (1971)

Luke Gibson was born in Canada. This record was released in 1971 from True North Records, the same label as that of Canada's top singer-songwriter, Bruce Cockburn. This is the first solo album from Gibson, who was also in the bluesy rock band Luke & The Apostles, and the folk rock band Kensington Market. Full of Canadian folk music's honest kindness, the entire record has a simple, refreshing feel throughout.

Now, it's hand sewn. It's a record jacket with little wildflowers embroidered on it. Within an oval frame surrounded by sweet flower embroidery stands the singer in the midst of the great Canadian wilderness. It looks to be fall, based on the clothing. By his side is a dog that is camouflaged into the landscape. The jacket is square to begin with, and there sits an oval to the right of center. Within that oval, we see the diagonal of the mountain ridge, and a person standing vertical against gravity. In the background we see the horizon line, perhaps a lake. The green ribbon with the album title is also positioned just right. The square, round, diagonal, horizontal, and vertical are all composed in subtle perfection...and yet, the analog feel of the fabric and embroidery makes this very structured composition down to earth, and makes it look natural.

Whenever I come across modern artworks with embroidery or the act of sewing incorporated as a vital element, I'm reminded of the jacket of this album, *Another Perfect Day*.

Looking at the back cover, a painting of a well-worn country road with what looks like the entrance to a farm is contained within a window-like square frame. The credits say a woman named Sarah Burnett did the painting and embroidery, but I couldn't find anything about an artist by that name in my internet searches. But this doesn't change the fact that this painting and embroidery, done by an unknown artist (or maybe not), remains in my heart.

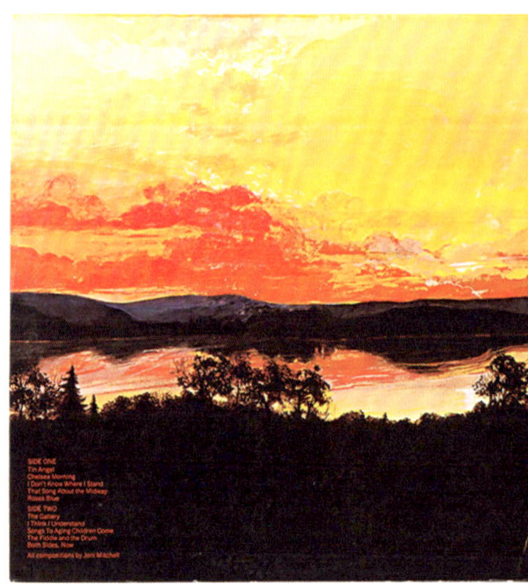

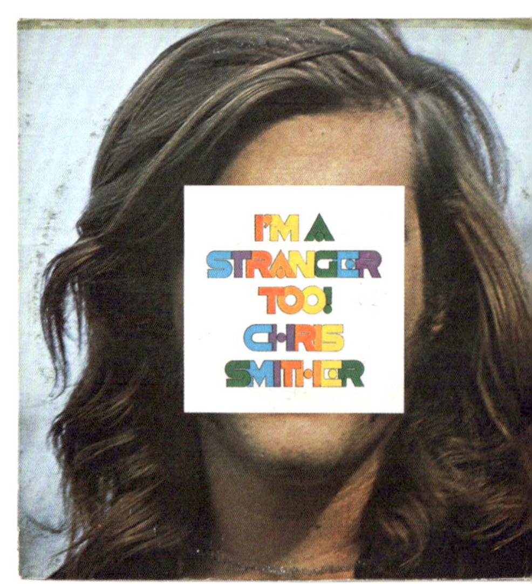

JONI MITCHELL
Song to a Seagull (1968)
Clouds (1969)

Joni Mitchell's* debut album (*Song to a Seagull*) and sophomore album (*Clouds*). Hailing from Canada, she is not only a trailblazer as a singer, but also a remarkable songwriter. She wrote "The Circle Game" from the film *The Strawberry Statement*, sung by Buffy Sainte-Marie, as well as "Woodstock" by Crosby, Stills, Nash & Young, and "Both Sides Now" by Judy Collins. She won her first Grammy with her second album, and has gone on to win several more times.

I think there are a lot of musicians who have studied art, but

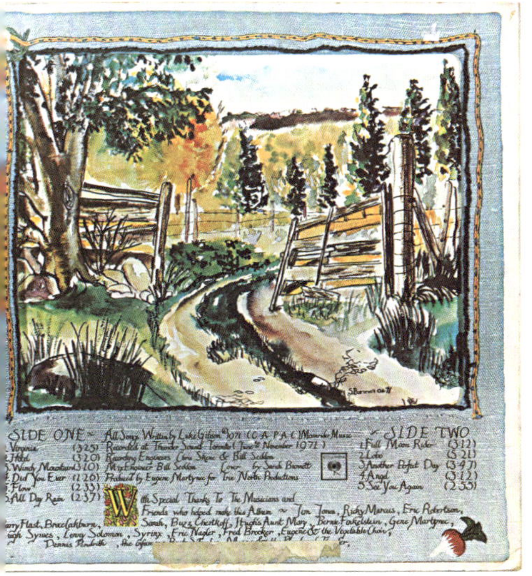

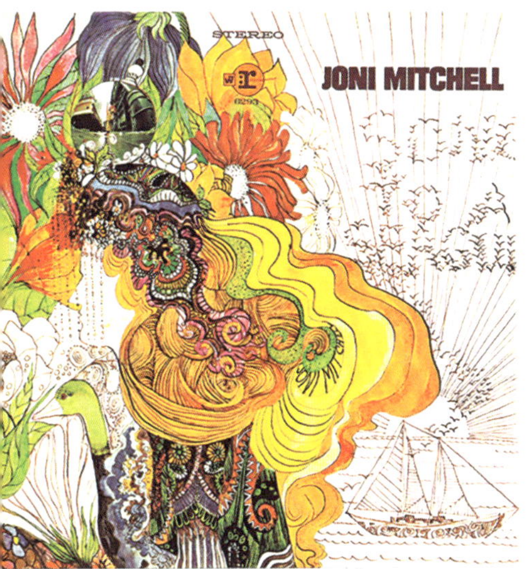

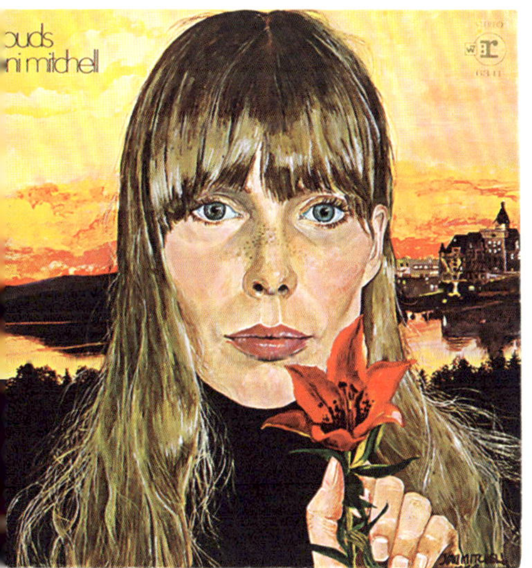

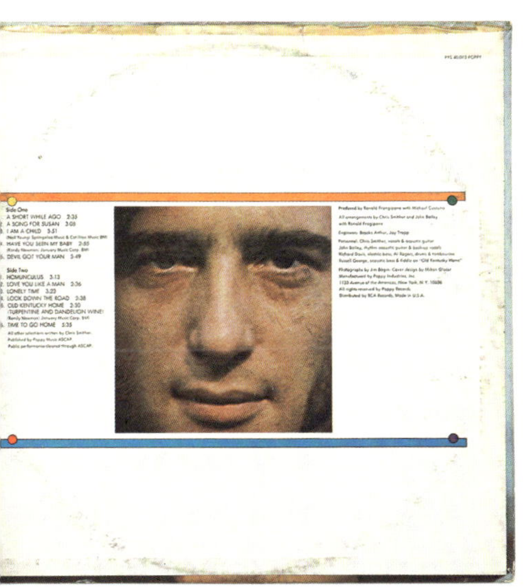

Joni Mitchell is someone who is the epitome of "a person who chose expression." The jacket of her second album *Clouds* gives a bold impression due to its composition, but if you look closely at details like the hair, you can clearly see a confident attention to detail. Listening to the record and looking through the credits, I was stunned to learn that Joni Mitchell herself painted this image. So I checked and discovered that she also painted the image for her debut album. I remember being utterly astonished by this revelation.

The fact is that she is not just a musician, but also truly an artist. Not only is she widely respected by countless musicians across generations and genres, but she has also shown in many exhibitions as an artist. What surprised me back then was how good she was at painting even though she was a singer. But her painting skills effectively make use of her sensibilities just as her music does, and after understanding this, her songs sounded even more amazing to me.

P.S. Her 1994 album, *Turbulent Indigo*, has her face inserted into a Vincent van Gogh self-portrait, and won Best Album Package at the 1995 Grammys.

* Singer, songwriter, painter. Born in 1943 in Alberta, Canada. Discovered folk music while studying at the Alberta College of Art and Design and became a musician. Debuted in 1968. Inducted into the Rock & Roll Hall of Fame in 1997. Won nine Grammys between 1969 and 2015.

CHRIS SMITHER
I'm A Stranger Too! (1970)

Debut album of Chris Smither, born in 1944 and raised in New Orleans. He became obsessed with Mississippi John Hurt and Lightnin' Hopkins in his late teens, and decided to become a musician after meeting the white blues legend Eric Von Schmidt. This first album—which includes covers of Neil Young's "I Am a Child" and Randy Newman's "Have You Seen My Baby?," as well as "Old Kentucky Home"—along with his second album, *Don't It Drag On*, released the following year—which is recognized as a masterpiece of acid folk—cement his place in music.

The entirety of the album jacket is filled with our protagonist's face, yet the most vital part in the center is cut out, and in that square sits the title in a colorful hippie font. So where is the center of his face? Turn over the jacket and there he is, the musician looking out at us. It's a small thing, but has great impact.

This was a "you got me!" kind of jacket. I recalled this album later, when I encountered the work of John Baldessari* and thought, "That jacket design might have come from a place like this."

I remember most albums being sold in Japan at that time did not have a trace of this kind of art. How do I say this? It's like a commercial design that uses conceptual art as a foundation, almost like an intellectual game.

In America and Europe in the 1960s and 70s, rock was at the forefront of avant-garde expression, even more so than fashion. They still maintained some distance from commercialism that would use expensive advertising to sell things. I think the designers were genuinely inspired by art, rather than using it as "gimmicks," and were paying homage by borrowing. In contrast, I feel like nowadays everything all over the world is built on a foundation of commercialism and has nothing to do with art or design.

I feel there's an earnest design spirit in this first album jacket, but also in his second album, *Don't It Drag On*, with his portrait shot by Duane Michals.** Of course, it was much later that I learned that the name of the photographer was Duane Michals...

* Modern artist. Born in 1931. Since the mid-1970s, known for his prints that obscure people's faces with colorful dots in graphic representation. Based in L.A.

** Photographer. Born in 1932. Known for photograph sequences (a series of photographs that create a story) and other works combining photography and text. Worked on many album jackets, photographing for *Synchronicity* (1983, The Police) and *Clouds Over Eden* (1993, Richard Barone), among others.

"When you open it up, you see the stumps of all the trees.... That violent image is in ironic juxtaposition with the outer image."

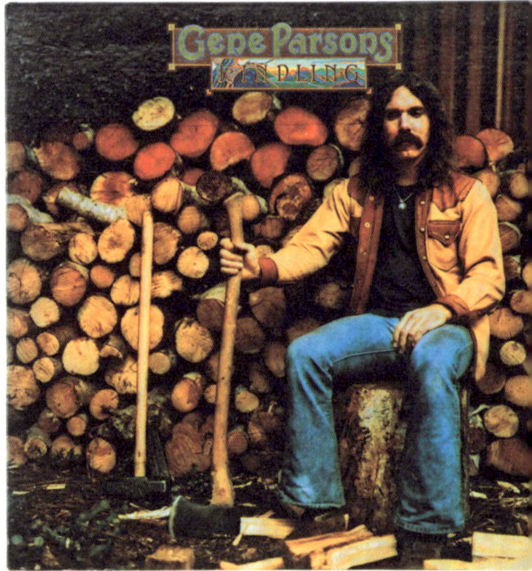

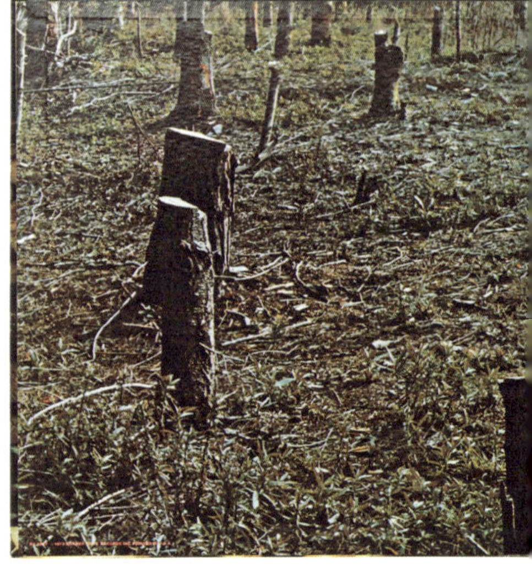

GENE PARSONS
Kindling (1973)

The first solo album by Gene Parsons, who joined the Byrds after being invited by the guitarist, Clarence White, for *Dr. Byrds & Mr. Hyde* (1969). Parsons remained the drummer for the Byrds until they dissolved in 1973. He supported the latter half of the band's career with his unique drumming style. Parsons used to work in a music store and was originally a banjo player but was skilled at all instruments, and this album showcases his multi-instrumental talents. This album's masterpiece is probably the cover of Little Feat's "Willin.'" The gentle vocals and soft instrumentals are joined by Nick DeCaro's accordion. Full of earthy sounds with country flavor, an enjoyable album you can relax to.

If you, the reader, are a guitar nerd, you may know the name "Parsons/White StringBender." It's a normal electric guitar that's been developed to sound like a pedal steel guitar. As the name suggests, it was invented by Gene Parsons and Clarence White, who were in the Byrds together. The two of them play together nicely on this solo album by Gene Parsons, which came out after the Byrds broke up. The sound is relaxed, comfortable country rock. However, it appears the creator was not as carefree as I may have thought.

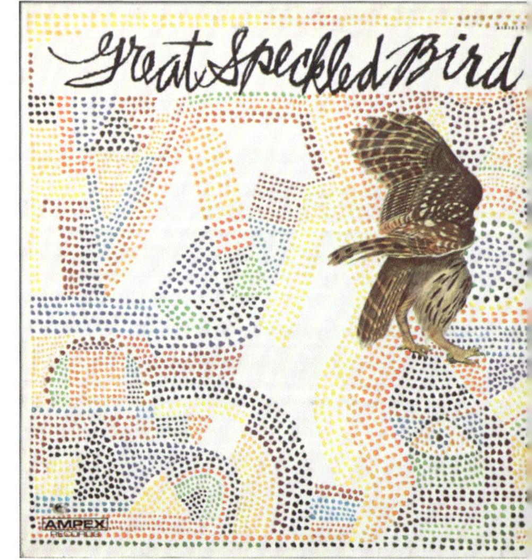

"'Great Speckled Bird' is a code name for amphetamines in America, and if you think about this fact, the oddly drawn bird and the colorful dots seem to have deeper meaning."

The jacket shows a kind-smiling man with an axe (Gene Parsons himself) in front of a pile of firewood, but when you open it up, you see the stumps of all of the trees that were cut down. That violent image is in ironic juxtaposition with the outer image. And on one of those stumps is a small TV, its screen showing the formerly green, lush forest...

What seeing this made me think at the time as a middle school student is important, but there's no point in discussing it here. I digested all of it naturally and without words, without pushing it into the category of art, but still most definitely appreciated it.

GREAT SPECKLED BIRD
Great Speckled Bird (1970)

After gaining popularity in the 1960s with hits like "Four Strong Winds," the Canadian folk duo Ian & Sylvia formed a band and debuted with this album in 1970. During their folk duo days, they were scouted by Albert Grossman, who managed Bob Dylan. After relocating to New York, their sound became more rock and they formed a band. Other members like Amos Garrett from Hungry Chuck and N. D. Smart joined them two years later. This album was recorded in Nashville, and produced by Todd Rundgren at Bearsville Records in Woodstock. Bearsville was a label founded by Albert Grossman, but the album was sold by Ampex. The relationship between Bearsville and Ampex didn't last long, so despite the wonderful music and performances, this album disappeared from the market after only a short while. By the way, the band name, Great Speckled Bird, comes from old country gospel song performed by Roy Acuff.

The colorful dot work is reminiscent of Native American patterns, and creates a natural feel. Laid on top of this is an oddly angled bird, perhaps a bird of prey. Both the drawing and design were done by Bob Cato,* a designer well versed in modern art of that time.

The more you look at it, the weirder the bird looks. "Great Speckled Bird" is a code name for amphetamines in America, and if you think about this fact, the oddly drawn bird and the colorful dots seem to have deeper meaning.

P.S. Unrelated, but I love how cute the Bearsville logo is!

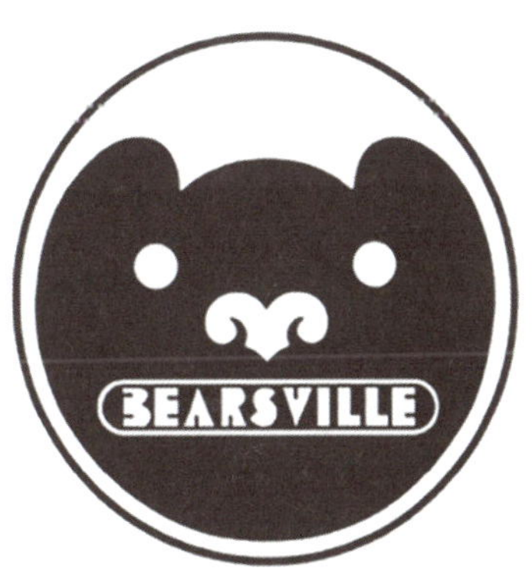

* Art director, photographer, illustrator, sculptor. Born in 1923 in New Orleans. Died in 1999. Apprenticed with Mexican painter José Clemente Orozco during his teens. After World War II, apprenticed with László Moholy-Nagy, then assisted Alexey Brodovitch. Started designing covers for Columbia Records in the 1960s. Promoted the work of Andy Warhol and Robert Rauschenberg, among others. Won the Best Album Cover Grammy for Barbra Streisand's *People* (1964) and Bob Dylan's *Bob Dylan's Greatest Hits* (1967).

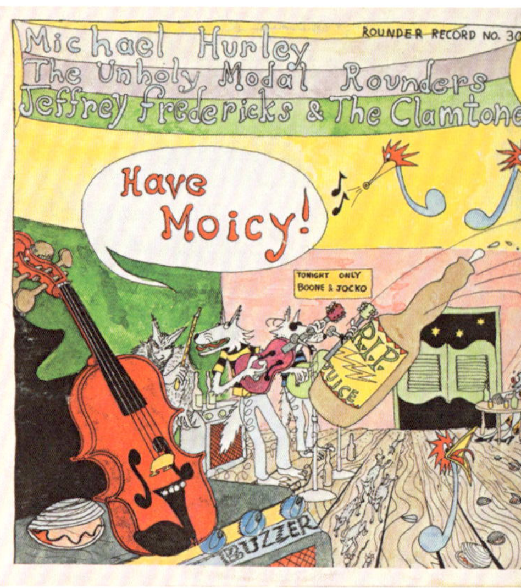

MICHAEL HURLEY
Have Moicy! (1976)

THE HOLY MODAL ROUNDERS
Good Taste Is Timeless (1971)

Michael Hurley's* drawings have long been respected by music lovers and all of his jackets feature great images. His fourth album, *Have Moicy!*, is a collaboration with Peter Stampfel of the Holy Modal Rounders and Jeffrey Frederick, and is also a musical masterpiece.

It's impossible to discuss acid folk without mentioning the Holy Modal Rounders, a band created by Peter Stampfel and Steve Weber from New York's underground scene. *Good Taste Is Timeless* is their fifth album, and with its increasing acid-ness it's considered to be one of the finest exemplars of their style.

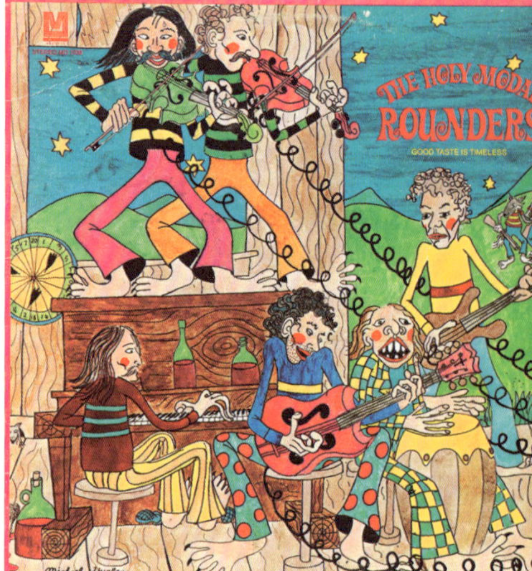

In 1980s Japan when I was in my twenties, there was a trend in illustration called *heta-uma*. It was people who are actually skilled purposefully drawing poorly, and I remember quite a few illustrators using this technique. I was a student at the time (I started university [at Aichi Prefectural University of the Arts] in 1981) and it was right in the middle of the *heta-uma* trend, but I remember having no interest in it. The reason for this is because I had already seen a lot of *heta-uma*-style record jackets back in high school, and it was basically just déjà vu for me.

There were a lot of very DIY-looking jackets that made you want to ask, "Are you sure you're okay with this?," especially among minor-label releases, and they were fun for what they were. Within these, Michael Hurley's jackets from Rounder Records were the extreme of this *heta-uma*. They possessed a quality of freedom that his music shared, and were head and shoulders above all the others.

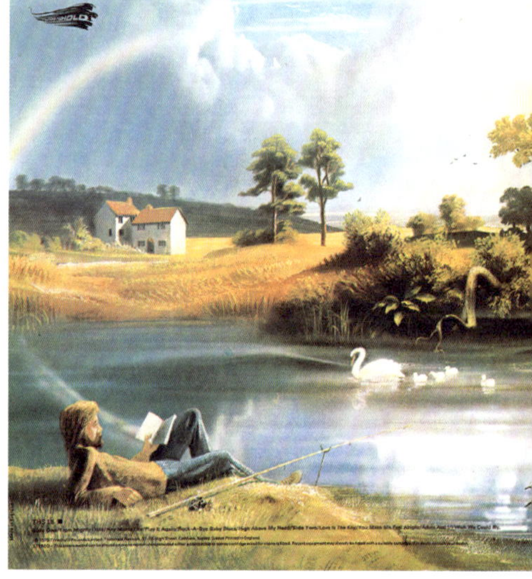

When *heta-uma* became popular in Japan, I immediately recalled the record jackets that Hurley had drawn—for example, his jacket for *Have Moicy!*, which some call a masterpiece, and the design for the Holy Modal Rounders' *Good Taste Is Timeless*, which he also did. I felt that these were illustrations not done cunningly with *heta-uma* as a gimmick (at least to me), but with a love for music above all else, a feeling of "I'm a musician!"

That said, it turns out that *heta-uma* style was a global trend. Tom Tom Club, founded by members of the post-punk band Talking Heads, had James Rizzi** create a New York version of *heta-uma* for their 1981 debut album...but to me, it seemed transparent, and looked like just a trendy band.

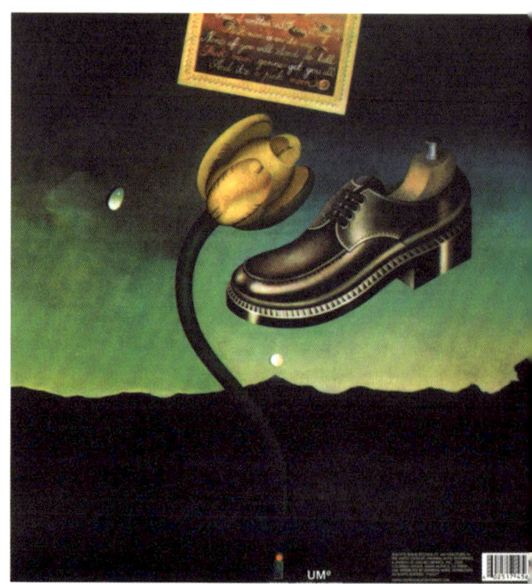

* Singer-songwriter. Born in 1941 in Pennsylvania. Has released over twenty albums so far. Often creates his own album artwork.

** Artist. Born in 1950 in New York. Died in 2011. Produced official artwork for the 1996 Olympics in Atlanta and the 1998 Olympics in Nagano.

"Michael Hurley's jackets. . .were the extreme of this *heta-uma*. They possessed a quality of freedom that his music shared, and were head and shoulders above all the others."

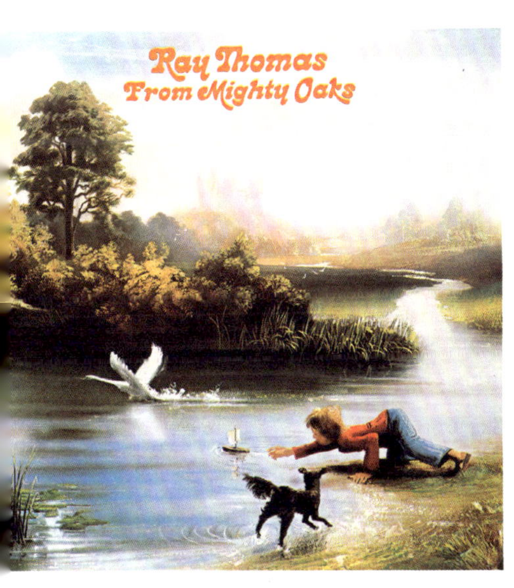

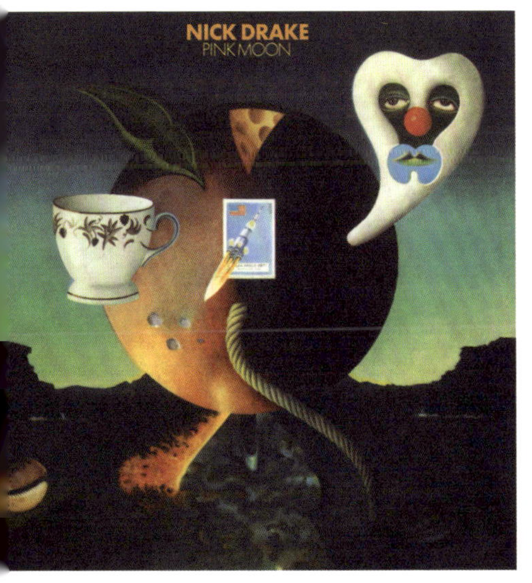

RAY THOMAS
From Mighty Oaks (1975)

The first solo album from Ray Thomas, the vocalist and flautist of the Moody Blues. Along with Pink Floyd, the Moody Blues were the leading pioneers of progressive rock. (Jimmy Page has said that the only true prog bands are Pink Floyd and the Moody Blues.) At the time this solo album was released, the band was on hiatus, so fans starved for their sound were overjoyed.

It looks like a classical landscape painting (or maybe a souvenir shop oil painting?), perhaps because of the way the trees are rendered or the aerial perspective, but the worldview depicted here is really appealing. A child and his dog play at the water's edge with a toy boat, and a hippie-looking father reads a book while fishing. In the distinctively British mist, we see a castle faintly in the distance. The inside of the jacket is a photo of the real Thomas family relaxing by the water, so no doubt this painting is depicting them, or they set up the photo to look like the painting. As the title of the album is *From Mighty Oaks*, the trees in the painting are likely oak trees.

At the time, I had a kind of Pop impression of this image. It was refreshing to see people in modern dress inside of this old-looking (yet very happy) painting. The coloration of the child's red clothing and the father's dusk-colored outfit gave me a sense of familiarity. This painting was done by Phil Travers, who previously created album artwork for the Moody Blues. But unlike the other art he created for progressive rock, this painting is full of a comforting sense of security. Travers continues working to this day, and apparently he is still painting English countryside landscapes like this one.

P.S. After I started to study art, I understood that Travers employs references to a wide range of artists, but this is a story for another time...

NICK DRAKE
Pink Moon (1972)

British singer-songwriter Nick Drake passed away at the young age of twenty-six on November 25, 1974, from an overdose of antidepressants. Ironically, his work became acclaimed after his death. *Pink Moon* was the third and final album released during his lifetime. His introspective vocals and simple instrumentals reach deep into your heart.

A voice seems to slide through the gaps in an endlessly gray, cloudy sky. This was perfect listening for a boy holed up in his room alone, lying on his back and staring at the cracks in the ceiling. Listening to this album on repeat, I'd imagine that if this room were the universe, I could throw away this whole world into the trash can in the corner of the room.... This album's surreal painting helped to endlessly stoke my imagination. Even for an optimist like me, there were also some depressive boyhood days.

This mysterious painting, which invites you into the depths of your soul, was done by Michael Trevithick, a friend of Nick Drake's sister, Gabrielle. Trevithick also did the jacket for Spooky Tooth's *Tobacco Road* (1968). This jacket had an image of a pipe with leaves growing out of it, and when you flipped it over, it was all ash.... Trevithick may be more accurately described as an illustrator, rather than a painter. He's illustrated a number of covers for Penguin Books, a famous British publishing house known for its penguin logo.

P.S. In 1970–71, before this album was released, Nick's sister, Gabrielle, appeared as an actress on the TV show *UFO* (as Lieutenant Gay Ellis).

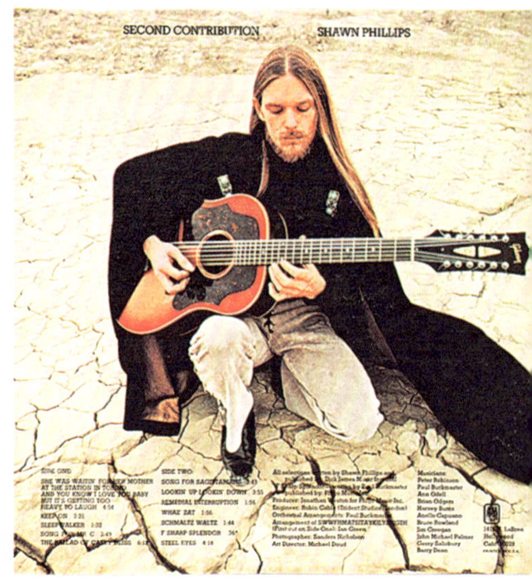

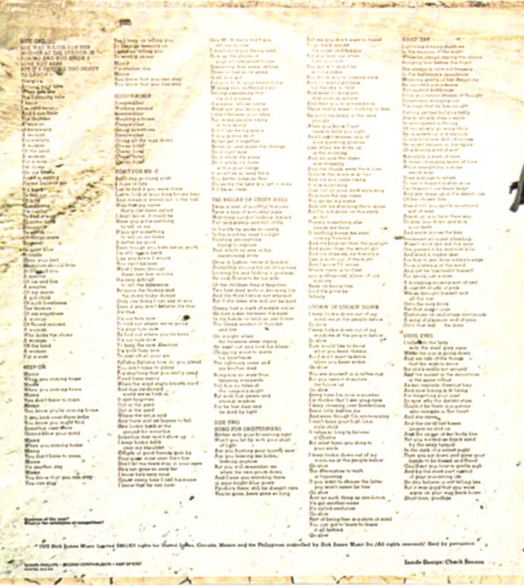

SHAWN PHILLIPS
Second Contribution (1970)

The fourth album from Shawn Phillips, who, despite being American, was a nomad in England. A follow up to 1970's *Contribution*, this album eventually became the second in a trilogy. The third part was released in 1971 and is titled *Collaboration*.

We see the back of a figure in a black cloak, squatting on dried-up earth and holding a guitar.... The black of the cape is not in gradation but a flat, dark field, and brings out the cracked details on the earth in the background. It's a powerful image that sears into your brain at first glance, but if you turn this jacket over, you'll see a hippie-looking singer. But that back view is mysterious and full of wonder. In fact, his music is full of a progressive feel, and can't be pigeonholed into the category of folk. On this acid-feeling album, one can also sense a sensitive British dampness, which may be because he's backed by British musicians. But it may be Phillips's true sensibility expressing itself; though he is American, he had chosen England as the land he wanted to wander as a nomad.

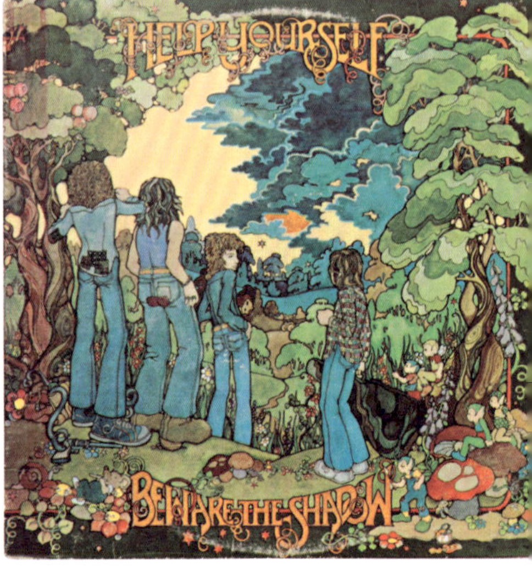

If we were to think about this jacket photo like a painting, the black cape is a flat painted field of solid color, the dried-up earth in the background is detailing, and the hair is a gradation.... It was much, much later that I realized this had such a classical painting composition, but it may be that everything that looks good always has this kind of underlying structure.

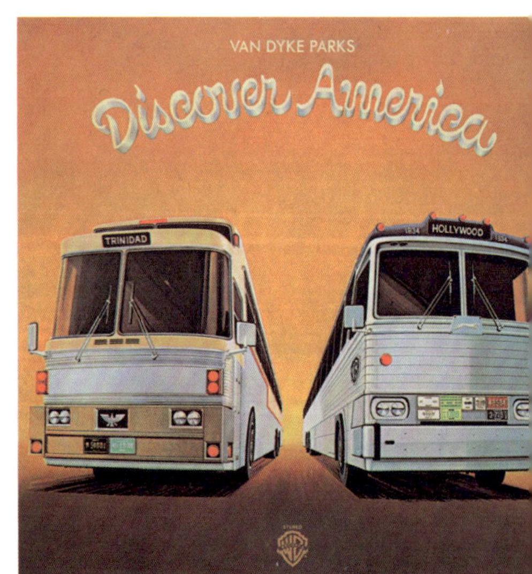

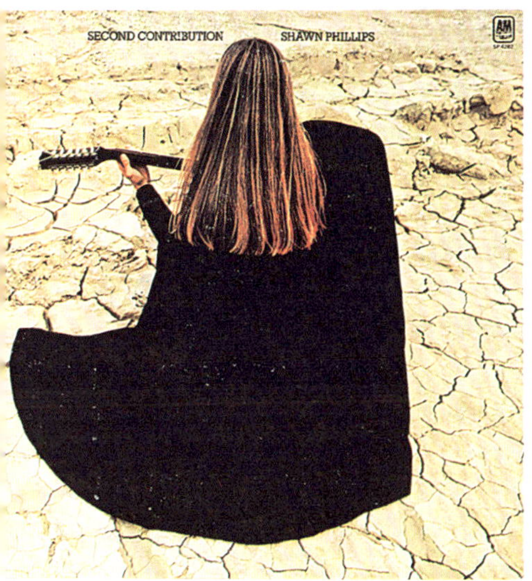

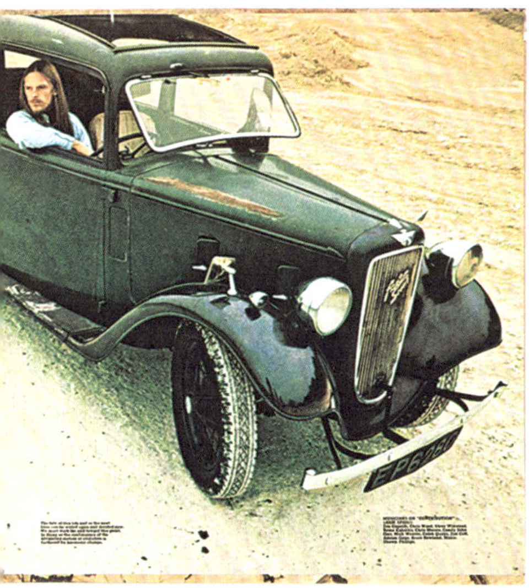

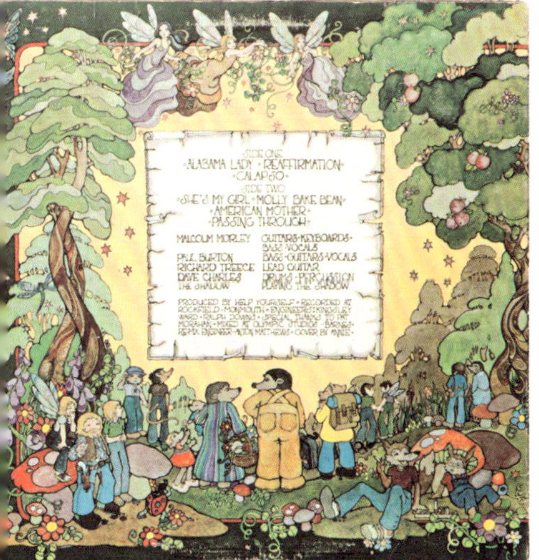

HELP YOURSELF
Beware the Shadow (1972)

The third album from British pub-rock pioneers Help Yourself. At the time in the UK there were quite a few musicians who looked up to American rock. By American rock, I don't mean rock and roll that people dance to, but music that is more folk-flavored, earthy, and distanced from mainstream hit charts.

This band was known for having that kind of American flavor without it being overly assertive, while also having some British progressive-y long songs. Pub rock refers to music that was played in pubs and small venues in the 1970s, away from the commercialized music scene. One could call it rock for the working class. There are a lot of punk musicians who came out of this scene, like Joe Strummer, the drummer for the Clash.

The moon is rising or the sun is setting, and there are stars twinkling in the sky. It's probably a bright starry night. The image is reminiscent of an old picture book. Four long-haired youngsters in bell-bottoms, who may be the band members, are gazing at the view through the clearing in the forest. And around them are little antennaed fairies that they probably can't see. Flipping over the jacket, there are Tinkerbell-like fairies with wings, and anthropomorphized badgers and wolves in clothing hanging out.

I loved these images, which reminded me of early Osamu Tezuka. Listening to the music, I'd imagine endless stories from them. The credits list the artist as just Annie. These images were nostalgic but also had a touch of hippie culture. No dark shadows, just colors composed together, and the mushrooms and flowers add a kind of psychedelic feeling.

Later, when I discovered *Little Nemo in Slumberland*,* the early twentieth-century comic by Winsor McCay, I immediately remembered this album. Nemo's journey through the world in dreams, the colors, and the fantastical stories share something in common with hippie culture. I really love this band's debut album jacket, but unfortunately I don't have that one...

* American comic by Winsor McCay (1869–1934). Ran in color in the Sunday edition of the *New York Herald*, and then *New York American*, from 1905 to 1914. Known as an early comic book masterpiece.

VAN DYKE PARKS
Discover America (1972)

The sophomore album from Van Dyke Parks, who debuted in 1967 with *Song Cycle*. The calypso music featuring the steel drum, which he encountered in his travels to Trinidad and Tobago, must have been a bit of a culture shock to the rock scene of the time. I'm not going to go into depth about this, but there are many underdeveloped countries like Trinidad and Tobago near the U.S., and the U.S. prospers in part because of this. This album is Parks's cheer song rooting for those countries while also being an irony-filled strike directed at his home country of America.

The phrase "Discover America" comes from the United States Travel Service, from a campaign to promote domestic travel. Of course, my generation will be reminded of the Japan National Railways' (present day JR) slogan "Discover Japan," but of course Japan was the copycat...sad...

Putting that aside, with a title like *Discover America*, you might expect this album to have Native American music or old folk songs, but that's not the case at all. What leaps out of the speakers is calypso music with the light sounds of steel drums. Looking at the jacket, there are two Greyhound buses, American long-distance buses that are a staple of cross-country travel. The bus on the right is bound for "Hollywood," in California, the land of dreams, and the other one...if you look carefully, you can make out "Trinidad." That's right—this image is actually quite sardonic. And the calypso music is also all satirical and ironic.

This image, with its excellent symmetrical perspective, is credited only as Design Maru, but this was the design agency founded by Shusei Nagaoka,* who had gone to America in 1970. This is thought to be the first record design by Nagaoka, who is now known as a master of jacket art. He went on to do the Carpenters' *Now & Then* (1973), as well as albums by Earth, Wind & Fire and Deep Purple.

His jacket for Jefferson Starship's *Spitfire* (1976) won *Rolling Stone* magazine's Best Album Cover for 1976. This painting shows female vocalist Grace Slick riding astride a dragon. Earth, Wind & Fire's 1977 album *All 'n All* has a Nile temple theme; Ramses' pedestal has *fūrinkazan* letters mixed in with hieroglyphics, and is extremely interesting. But *Discover America* gives the impression of a high-quality American Pop art piece.... Well, I can say this now, but at the time, I just thought the buses in perspective with the sunset or sunrise behind them was so cool!

* Illustrator, painter. Born in 1936 in Nagasaki. Moved to America in 1970 and created a studio. Has worked on countless record jackets, movie promotions, and posters for corporations and municipal governments, continuing to the present day.

FAIRFIELD PARLOUR
From Home to Home (1970)

Originally debuting as Kaleidoscope in Britain in 1967, this psychedelic folk band's sound evolved away from the experimental. With stronger emphasis on British refinement and traditions, they renamed themselves Fairfield Parlour and released this album.

"An old woman reads a newspaper in an attic filled with an aura of history.... By the well-worn floor, we can tell it's not a luxurious life by any means. But still, the sunlight pouring in from the window gives us a sense of her simple happiness."

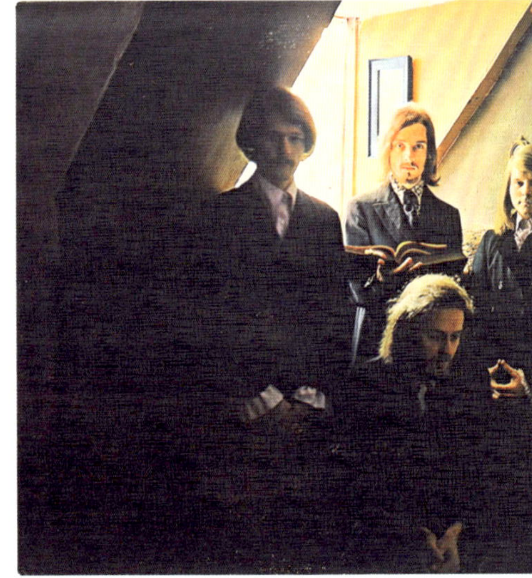

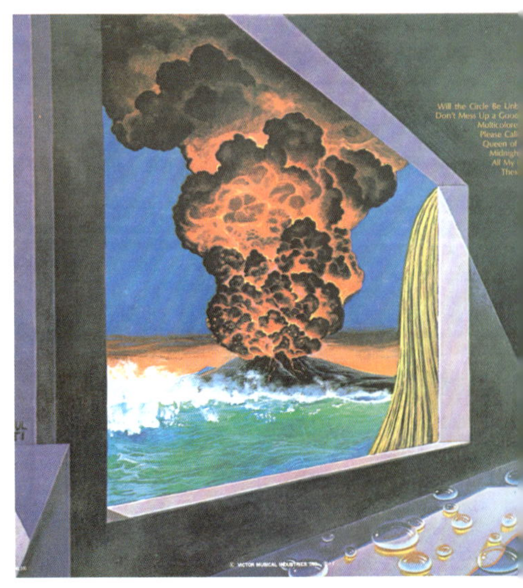

I think a film like *Melody* (1971) could have only come from England. If it had been American, it would have ended up with more pop action. And, above all, British traditions and history that are so strongly rooted within each citizen are what make this film landscape possible. That said, this movie didn't do well in the UK or in the U.S., and it was just in Japan that is was a huge hit, but it is the first film written by Alan Parker, who later went on to great success in Hollywood.

I know I just started off talking about a film from the time, but the point is that this album's contents and jacket are both also very British. The lyrical Mellotron, flute, cembalo, carillon, and other classical instruments go well with the gentle chorus.

The jacket is a photograph by Keef,* and unlike his usual direct and odd style, this jacket has a classical and relaxed atmosphere, like the band's sound. An old woman reads a newspaper in an attic filled with an aura of history. Instead of shooting from within the room, he takes the photo from outside the open door, giving us a peek into her little world. By the well-worn floor, we can tell it's not a luxurious life by any means. But still, the sunlight pouring in from the window gives us a sense of her simple happiness.

* Marcus Keef. Photographer, video director. From the late 1960s to early 1970s, produced popular jacket photography for albums such as Affinity's *Affinity* (1970) and Black Sabbath's *Black Sabbath* (1970). His style was often nostalgic and surreal. In 1978, Kate Bush hired him for the video for "Wuthering Heights," and he transitioned to directing.

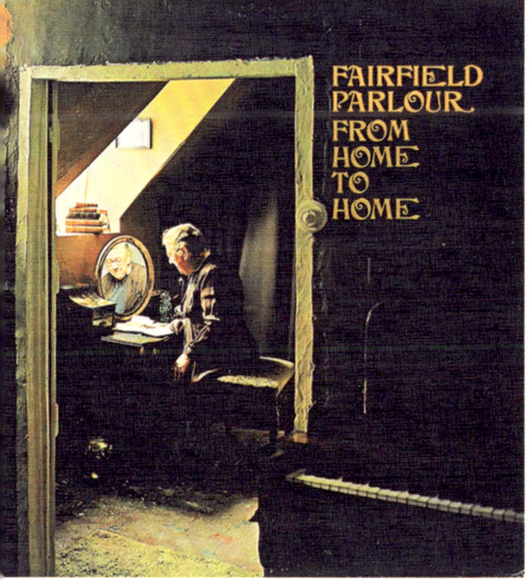

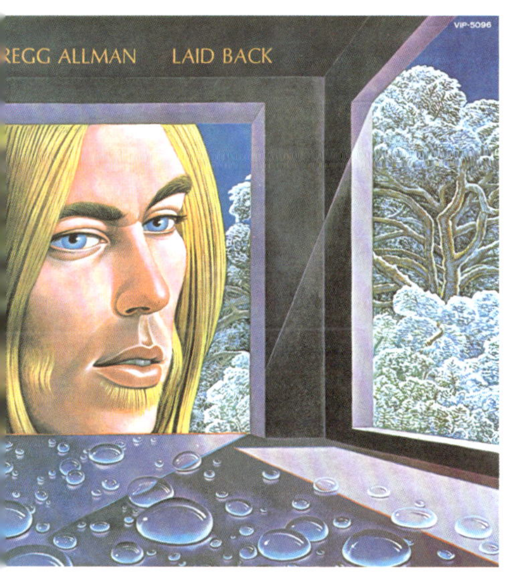

GREGG ALLMAN
Laid Back (1973)

The first solo album from Gregg Allman, the vocalist for the Allman Brothers Band, who established America's southern rock. The title phrase "laid back" became a popular saying in the music industry at the time. With subtle differences from the band sound, we can sense the depth of Gregg Allman's talent as a singer-songwriter.

In 1973 when this album came out, the Allman Brothers Band also released their fifth album, *Brothers and Sisters*, which hit number one on the Billboard charts. Of course, it was also a huge hit in Japan. But Gregg must have had issues with how Dickey Betts was pushing them away from blues and more toward country. Gregg's older brother and bandleader, Duane Allman, had died in 1971 in a motorcycle accident, after which the other guitarist, Betts, had become de facto leader. I wonder if that is why this solo album came to be.

As if to express those feelings, the jacket painting shows a world that is the opposite of the title *Laid Back*. The geometrically square room's floor is covered in large drops of water, and through the windows, open on all three sides, we see Gregg's large face. To the right of his face are trees covered in snow or frost, and on the left is a red, erupting volcano emerging from the ocean.

These contrasts between stillness and movement, cold and heat, may seem simple, but the inscrutable expression on Gregg's face, with his lips slightly parted, tells us that the answer may not be so straightforward. If I had to say, I would guess that it's not that he's between the contrasting extremes, but that he's disinterested in both, and in a disconnected place. And that's why it's "laid back"...

However, at the time, I wasn't living in such an intellectual world that I tried to understand this complexity. I couldn't quite get into the grown-up, weary sound, and to be honest, I didn't listen to the album that much. But I never regretted buying this album. That's because this unforgettable jacket continued to be displayed on my shelf, as something completely independent from the sound.

This painting with its mysterious power was the work of Abdul Mati Klarwein.* Abdul had previously done cover art for the second album from the pioneering Latin rock band Santana, *Abraxas*, and for jazz great Miles Davis's *Bitches Brew* (both 1970). It may be just me, but I felt there was something different in this painting for *Laid Back* from those others...

* Artist. Born in 1932 in Hamburg, Germany. Died in 2002. Known for his jacket art for Santana's *Abraxas* (1970), Miles Davis's *Bitches Brew* (1970), Miles Davis's *Live-Evil* (1971), and Joe Beck's *Beck* (1975). Was friends with Salvador Dali.

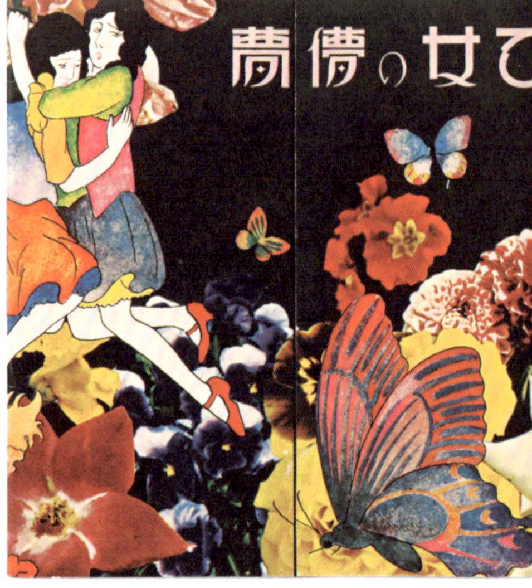

MORIO AGATA
Otome no Roman (1972)

The Japanese rock world of this time was heavily influenced by Europe and America, but this highly original concept album was created upon a unique foundation of *Taishō Roman* aesthetics. Backed by the band Hachimitsupai, led by Keiichi Suzuki, the album also has Shigeru Suzuki, Kenji Endo, and Masato Tomobe. Like Fairport Convention being influenced by the Band and seeking out British roots music, I think that Morio Agata, influenced by Fairport Convention, sought out his own roots through *Taishō Roman*.

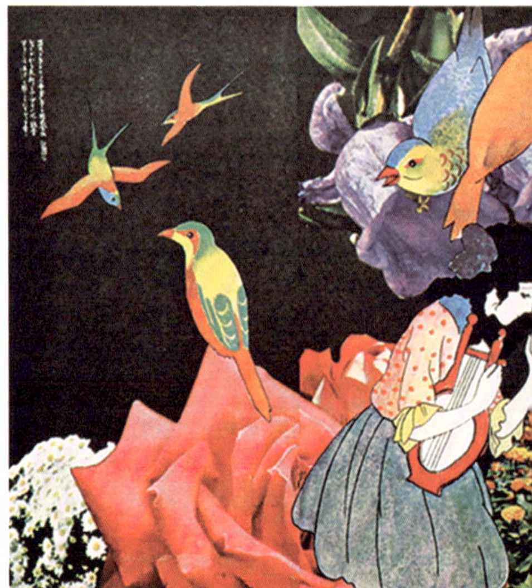

The first time I bought something that can be called an artwork was when I was nineteen. It was a woodblock print of girl in a kimono holding a paper balloon. The lines connecting her long neck to her profile and the expressiveness of the hands were graceful and beautiful. Even so, it was less about wanting a piece of art, and more like lusting after a poster of my favorite musician. The piece was by Seiichi Hayashi,* whose work I knew from the manga magazine *Garo* and the album jacket of Morio Agata's *Otome no Roman*.

“Flowers and girls, butterflies and beetles and birds, all collaged together against a jet-black background. It was beyond glorious for me as a middle school student.”

The first time I encountered Seiichi Hayashi’s work was before middle school, with the jacket of Agata’s debut single, *Red Colored Elegy*. That jacket was also so beautiful that you’d want to hang it up. And the following album, *Otome no Roman*, was like a bolt out of the blue for me, who had only known *Red Colored Elegy*. The distinctive title lettering design was by Genpei Akasegawa, whose work I encountered in high school reading *Garo*. I felt strongly that this album, including the jacket, was really a comprehensive piece of work. At the time, I’d skip school to hang out at a jazz cafe, and this place had all of the issues of *Garo*, starting with the first one. That’s where I learned about the works of Genpei Akasegawa, as well as Shinichi Abe, Ōji Suzuki, Masuzō Furukawa, Osamu Kanno, Mizumaru Anzai, and others.

Otome no Roman had a gatefold jacket, and both sides had Seiichi Hayashi’s flowers and girls, butterflies and beetles and birds, all collaged together against a jet-black background. It was beyond glorious for me as a middle school student. It was like the world of Henry Darger, though I didn’t know about his work at the time. I think I just fell in love with Hayashi’s paintings. And in the winter when I was nineteen, I saw a woodblock print of his in a gallery that I just happened to wander into, and couldn’t help but buy it. It cost almost as much as a whole month’s pay for me, but I felt like I had obtained something even more precious than a piece of art: for example, a really rare record or a giant, not-for-sale promotional poster of Neil Young.

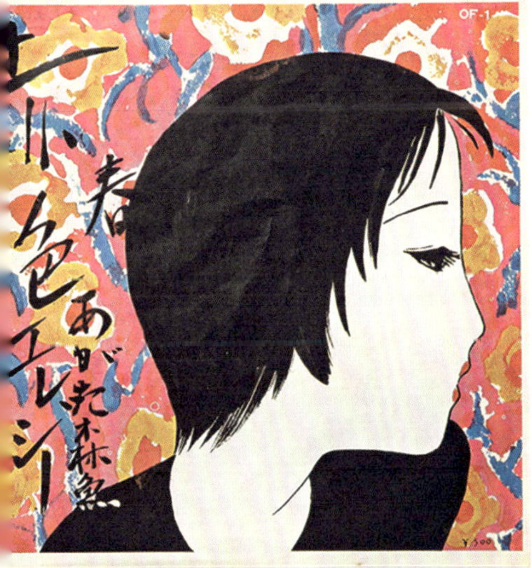

P.S. Since then, Morio Agata has always been one of my favorite musicians. Agata-san himself (!) reached out to me, saying, “I want to use your art for my next album,” so his album *Gusuperi Yōnenki* has my painting on the jacket! Yeah!

* Illustrator, painter. Born in 1945. Known for delicate *bijinga* (portraits of beautiful women) with a lyrical touch.

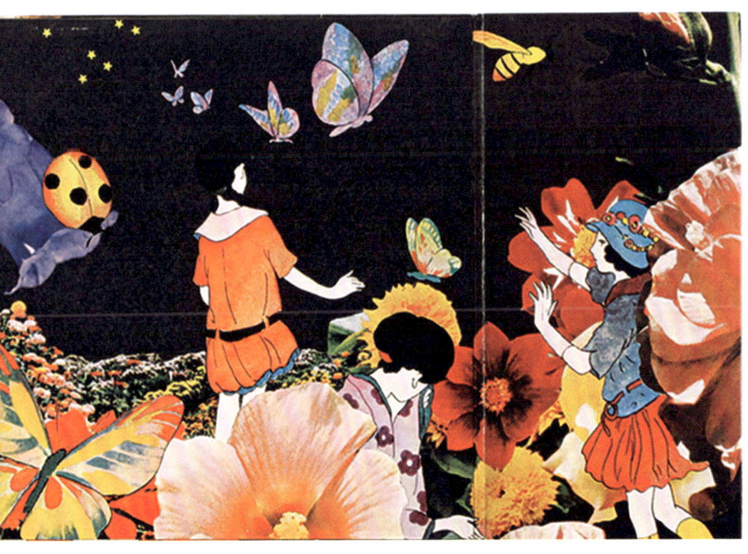

LUKE GIBSON
Another Perfect Day (1971)

JONI MITCHELL
Song to a Seagull (1968)
Clouds (1969)

CHRIS SMITHER
I'm A Stranger Too! (1970)

GENE PARSONS
Kindling (1973)

GREAT SPECKLED BIRD
Great Speckled Bird (1970)

MICHAEL HURLEY
Have Moicy! (1976)

THE HOLY MODAL ROUNDERS
Good Taste Is Timeless (1971)

RAY THOMAS
From Mighty Oaks (1975)

NICK DRAKE
Pink Moon (1972)

SHAWN PHILLIPS
Second Contribution (1970)

HELP YOURSELF
Beware the Shadow (1972)

VAN DYKE PARKS
Discover America (1972)

FAIRFIELD PARLOUR
From Home to Home (1970)

GREGG ALLMAN
Laid Back (1973)

MORIO AGATA
Otome no Roman (1972)

IX

LOVE IS THE POWER

No Fun!, 1999
Punk Ebizo, 1999
Slash with a Knife, 1999
To Hell and Back, 2008
Untitled, 2008
I'm Sorry, 2007
The Fool Dressed in Pink, 2006
Heads, 1998
No Nukes, 1998
Miss Spring, 2012
No Nukes!, 1999
Full Moon Night, 1999
Love Is the Power, 1999
UKIYO, 1999

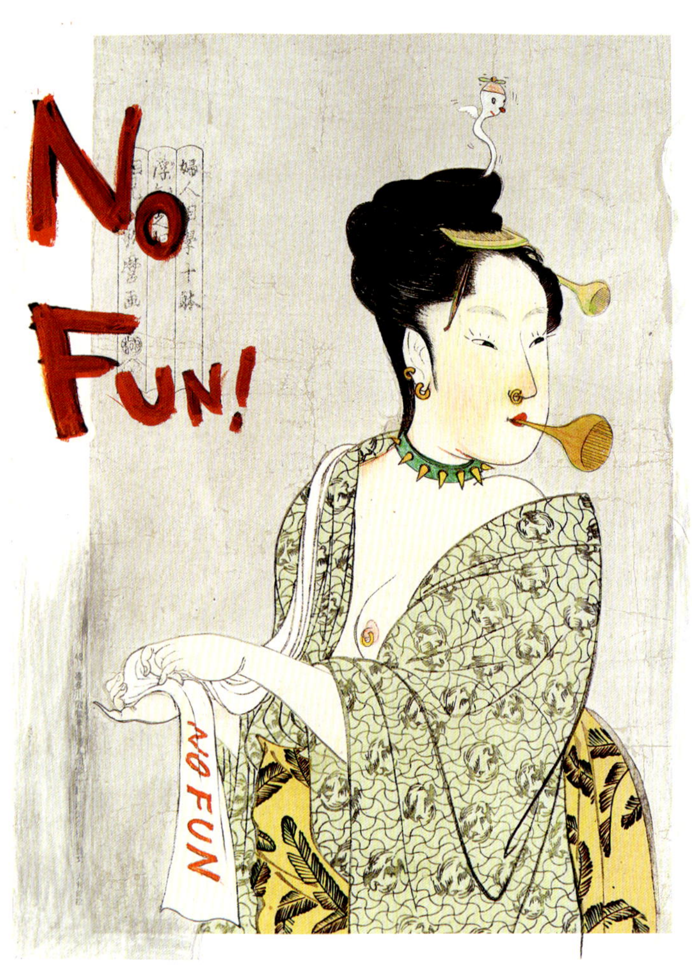
NO FUN!
NO FUN

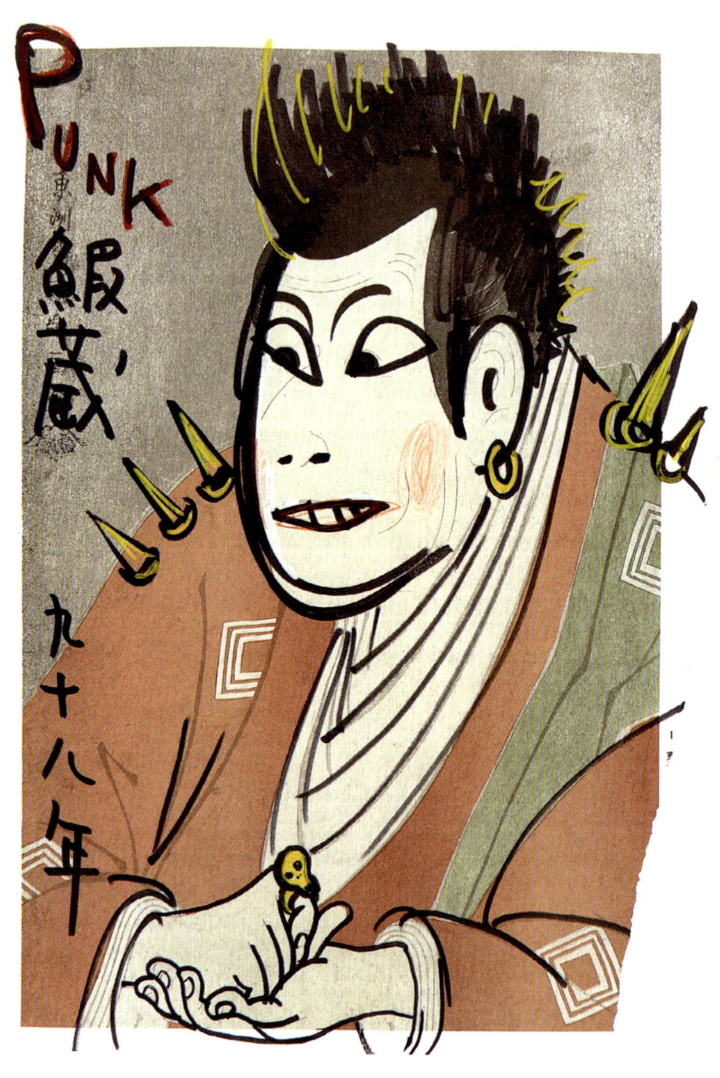
PUNK
鰕蔵、
九十八年

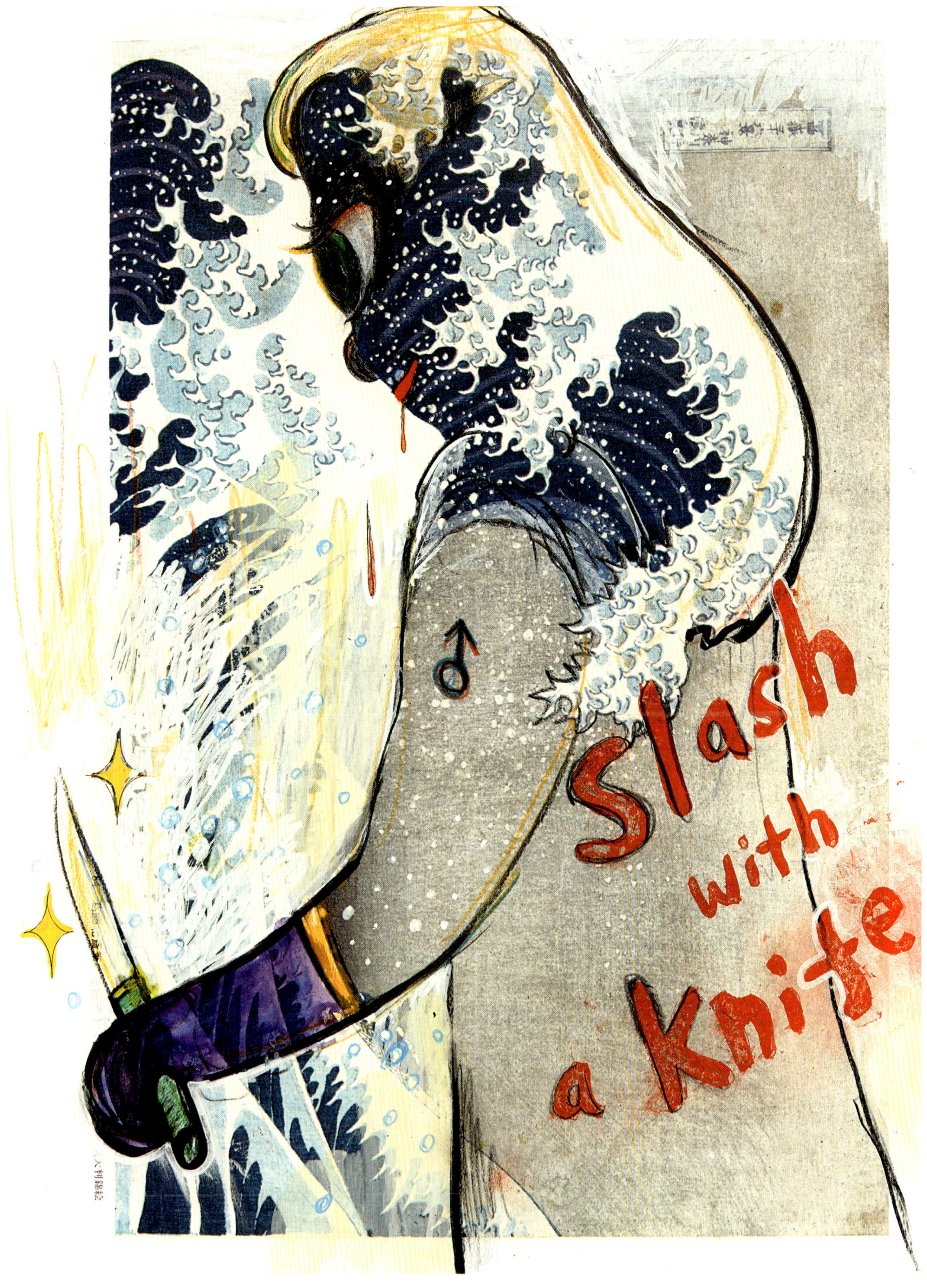
Slash
with
a Knife

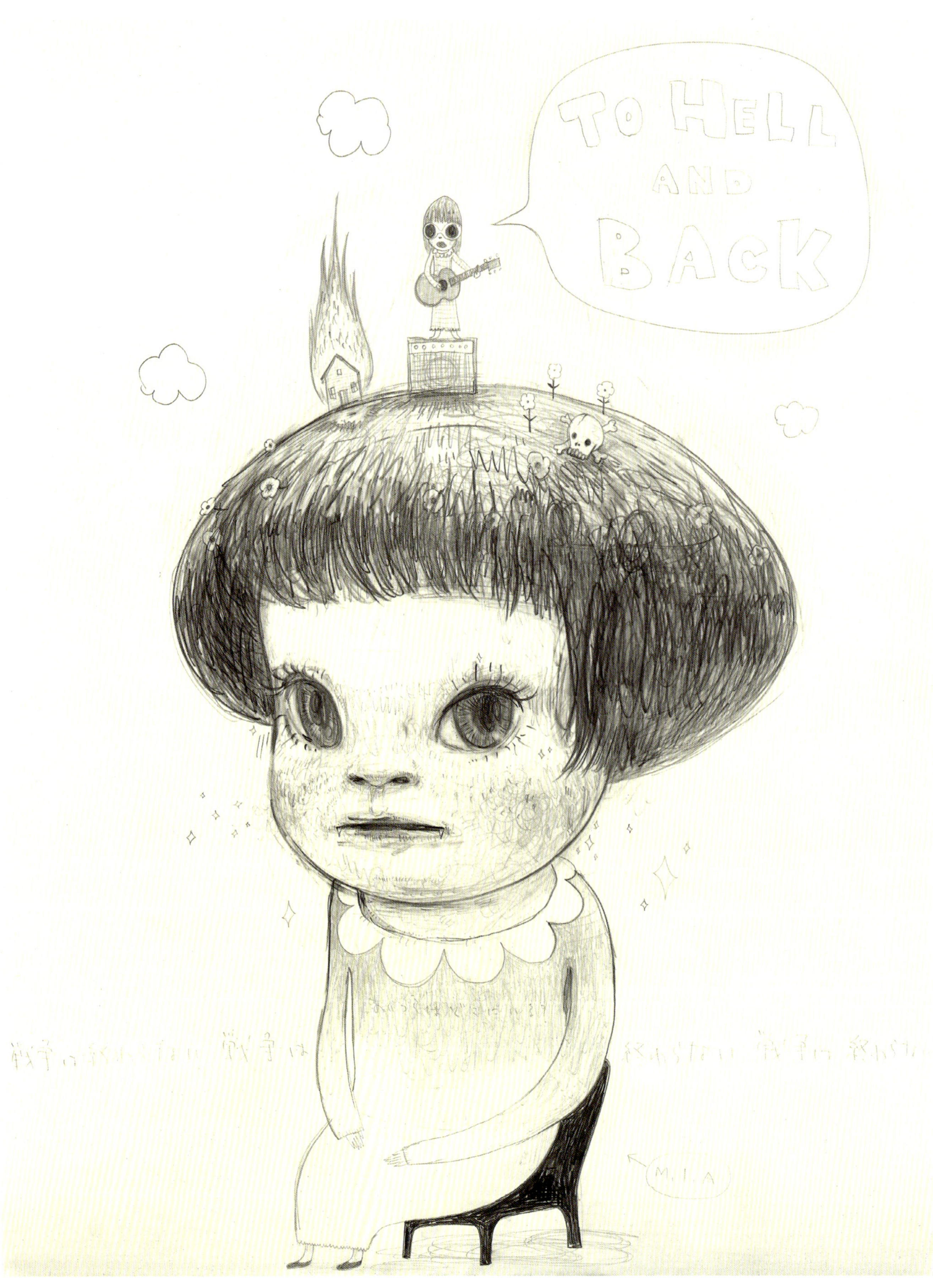
TO HELL AND BACK
M.I.A

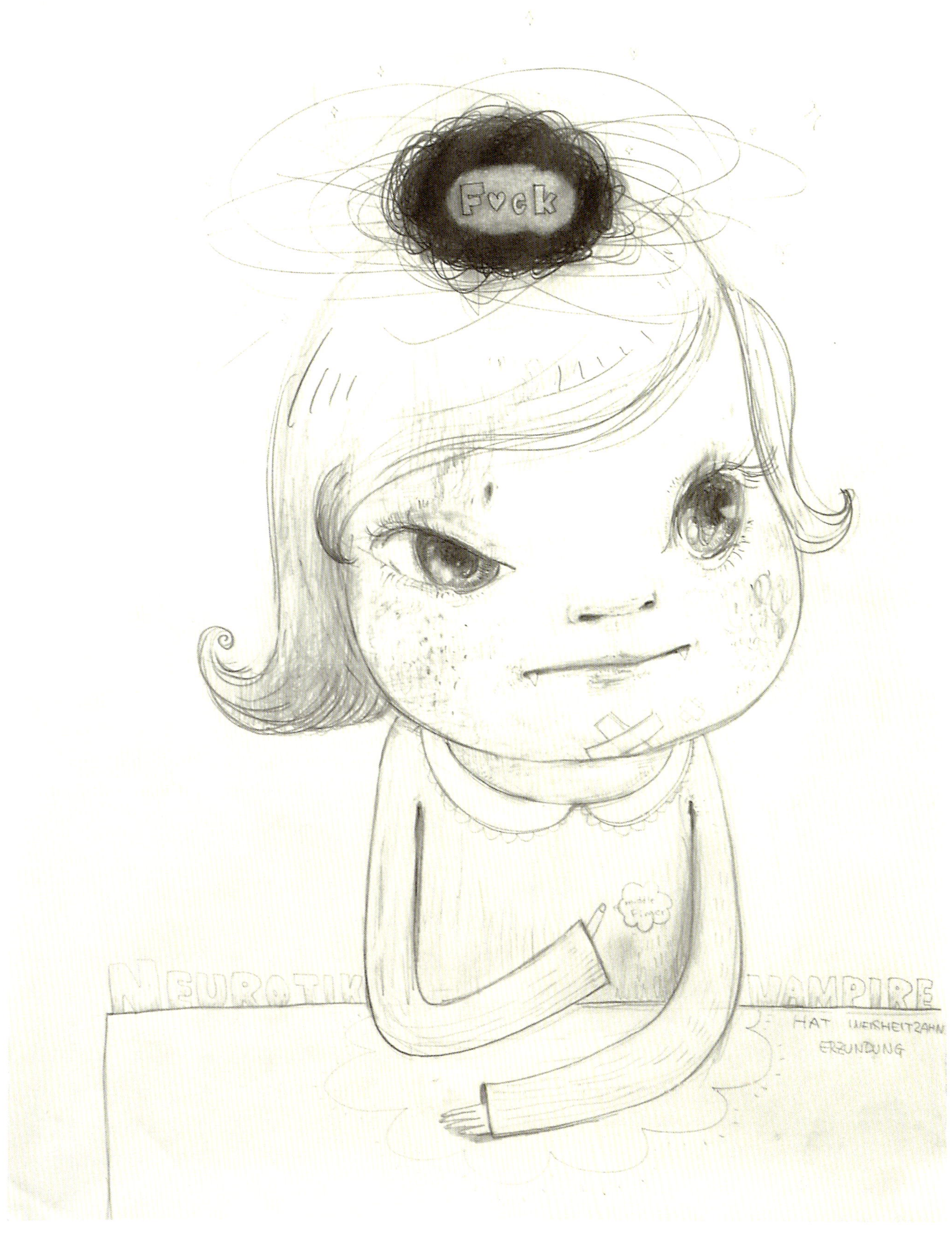
F♥ck
NEUROTIK
VAMPIRE
HAT WEISHEITZAHN
ERZUNDUNG

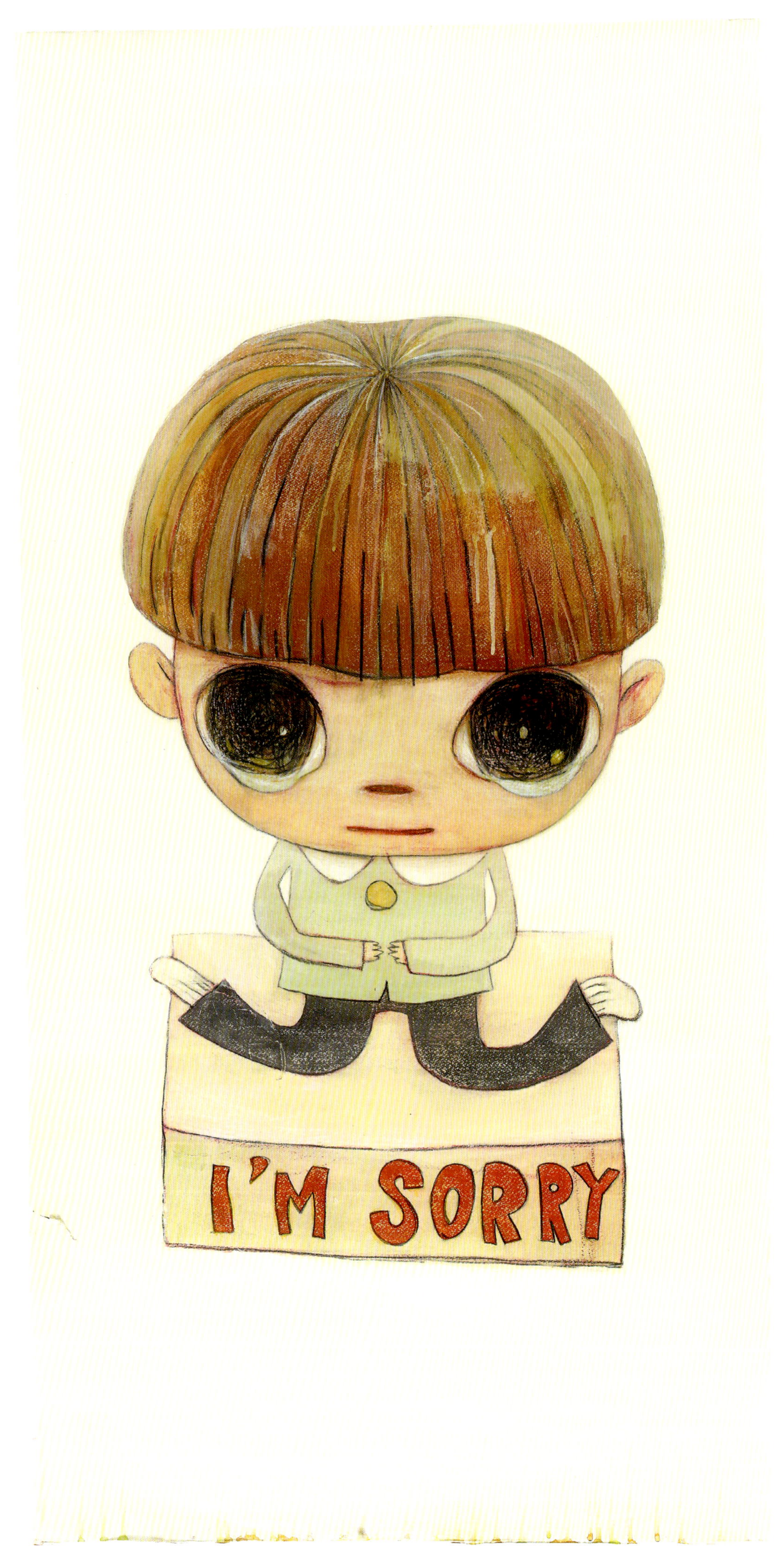
I'M SORRY

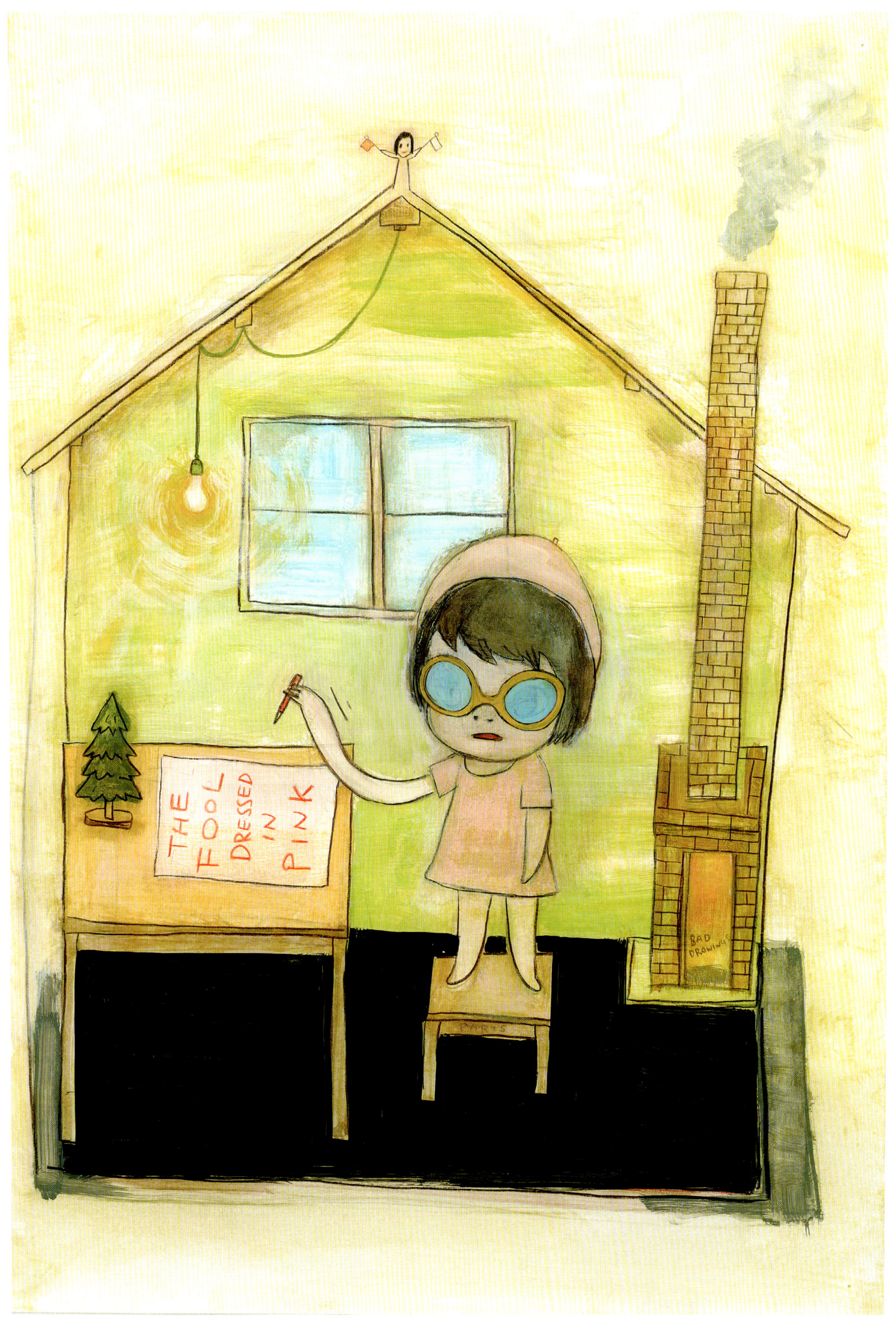
THE FOOL DRESSED IN PINK
BAD DRAWING
PARIS

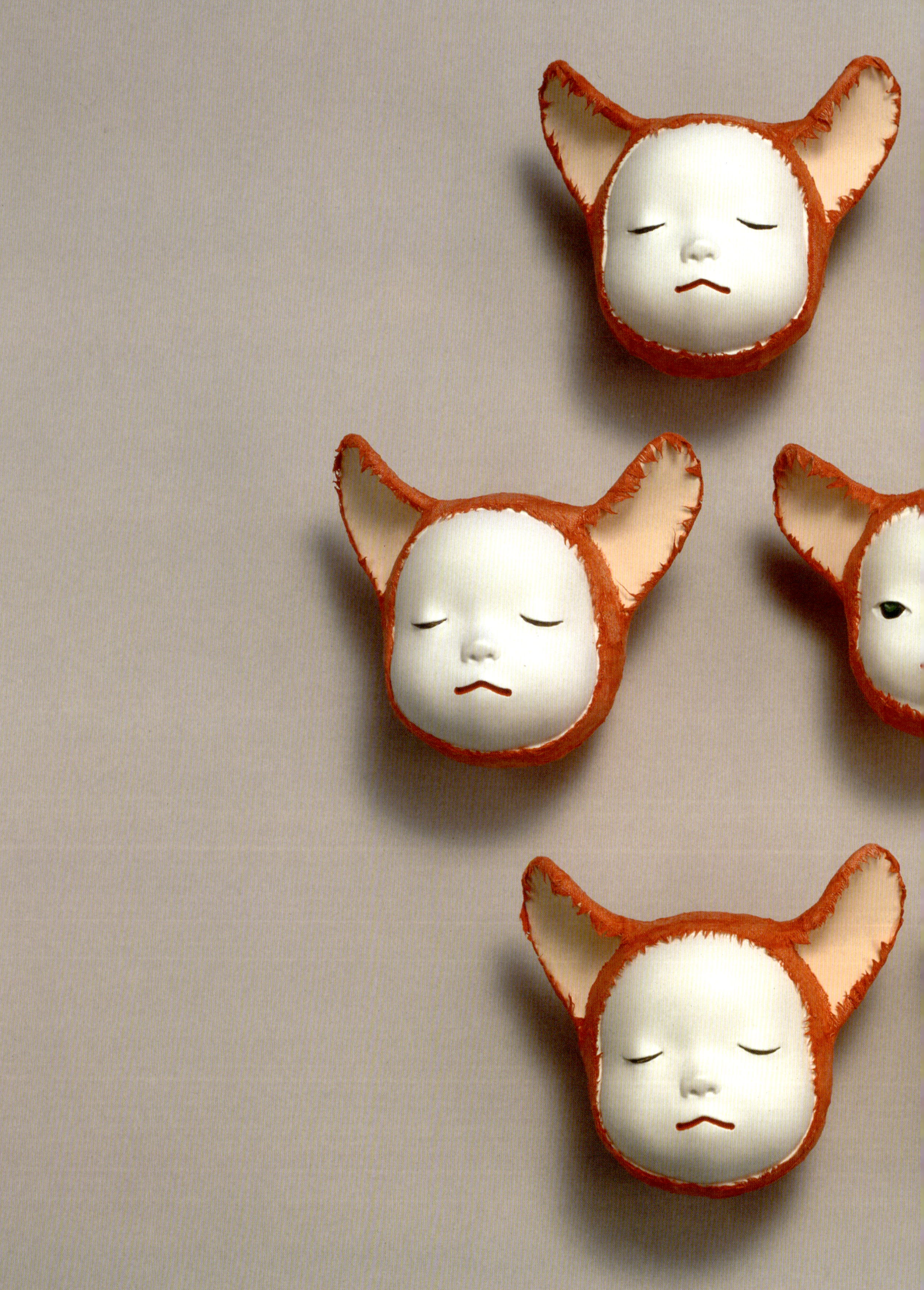

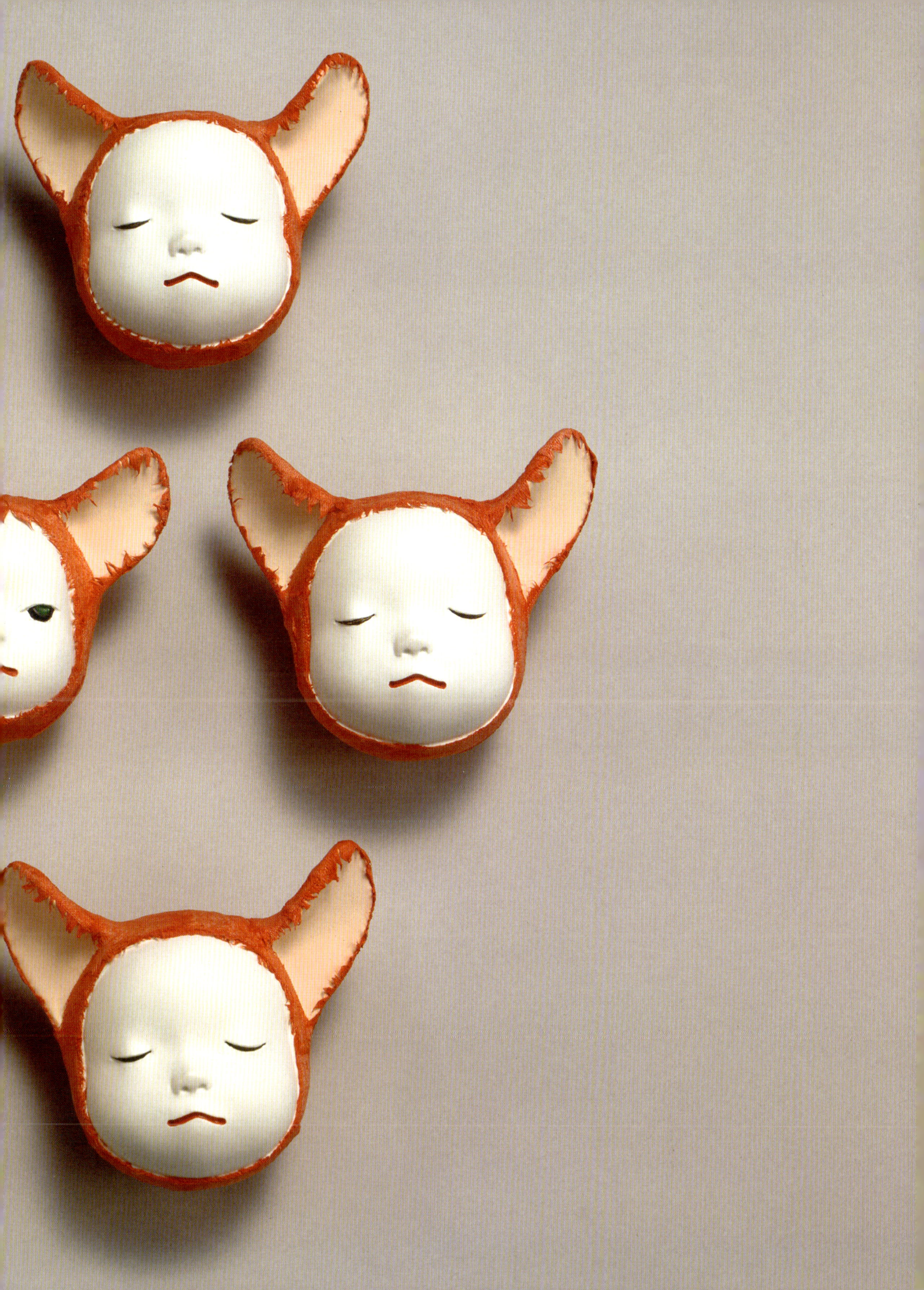

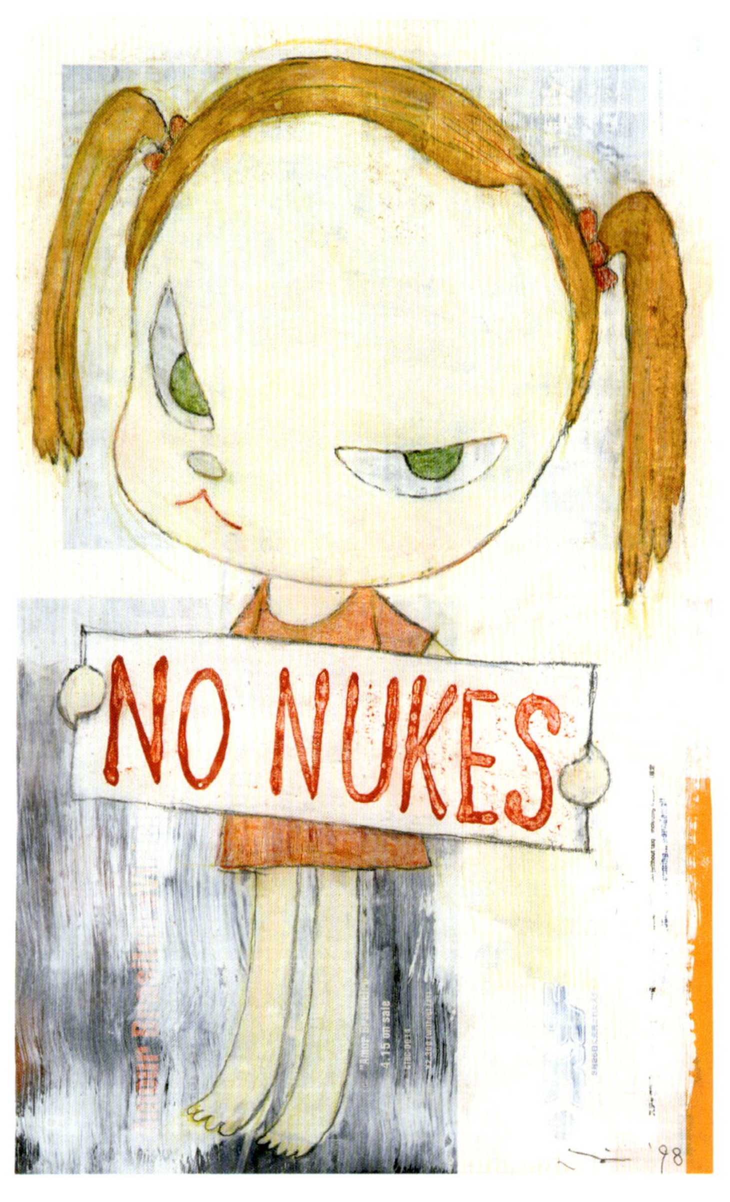
NO NUKES

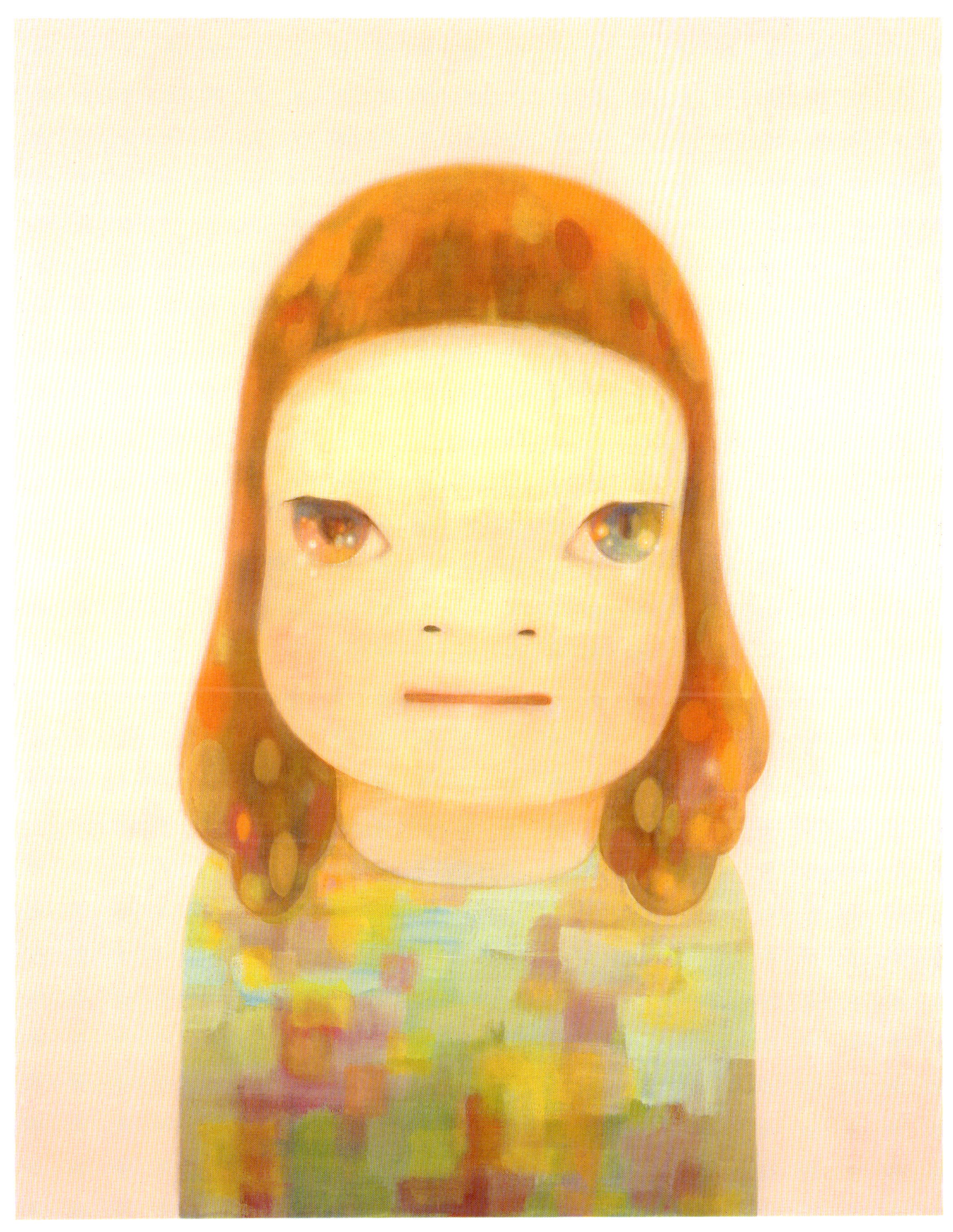

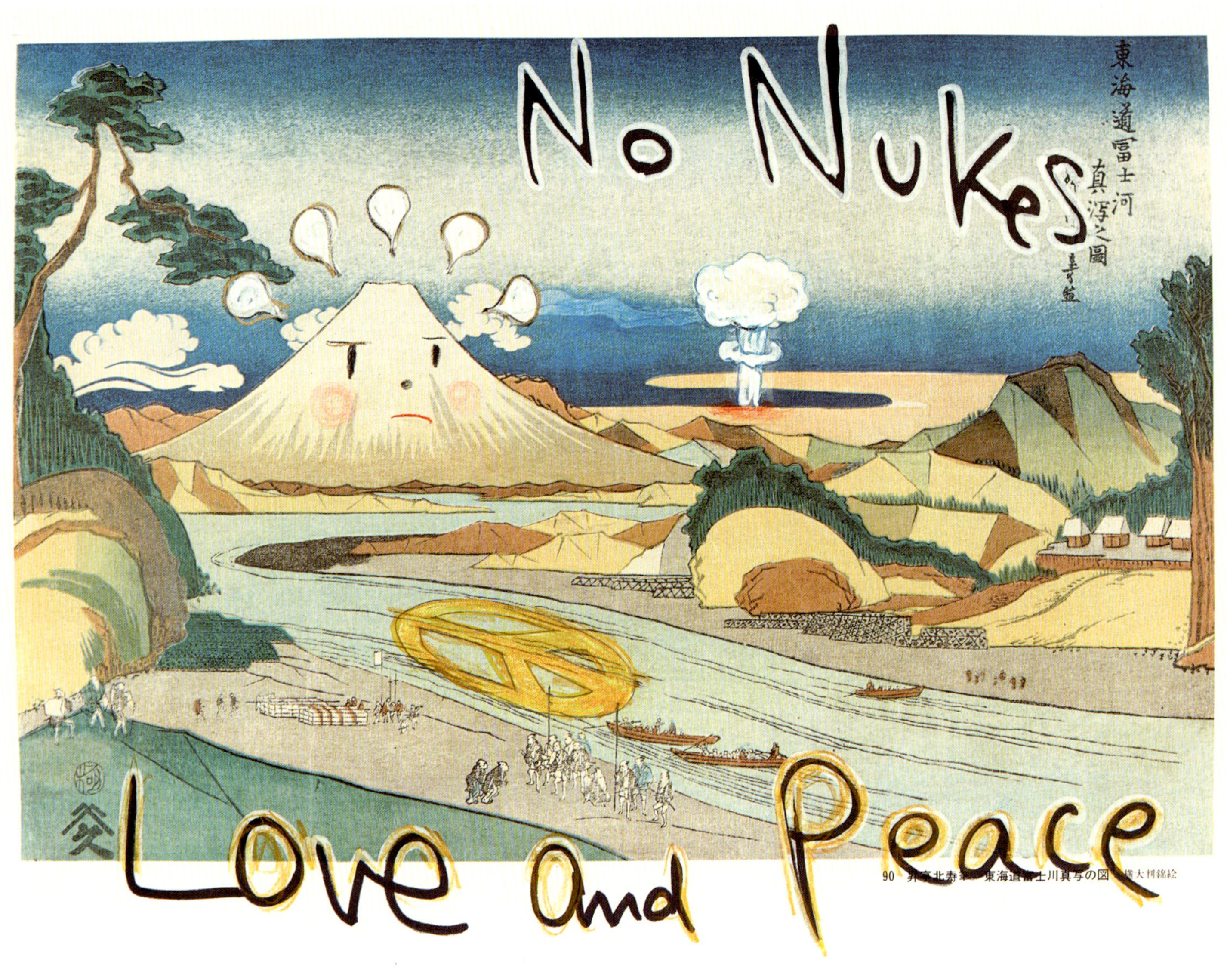

90 昇亭北寿筆 東海道冨士川真写の図 横大判錦絵

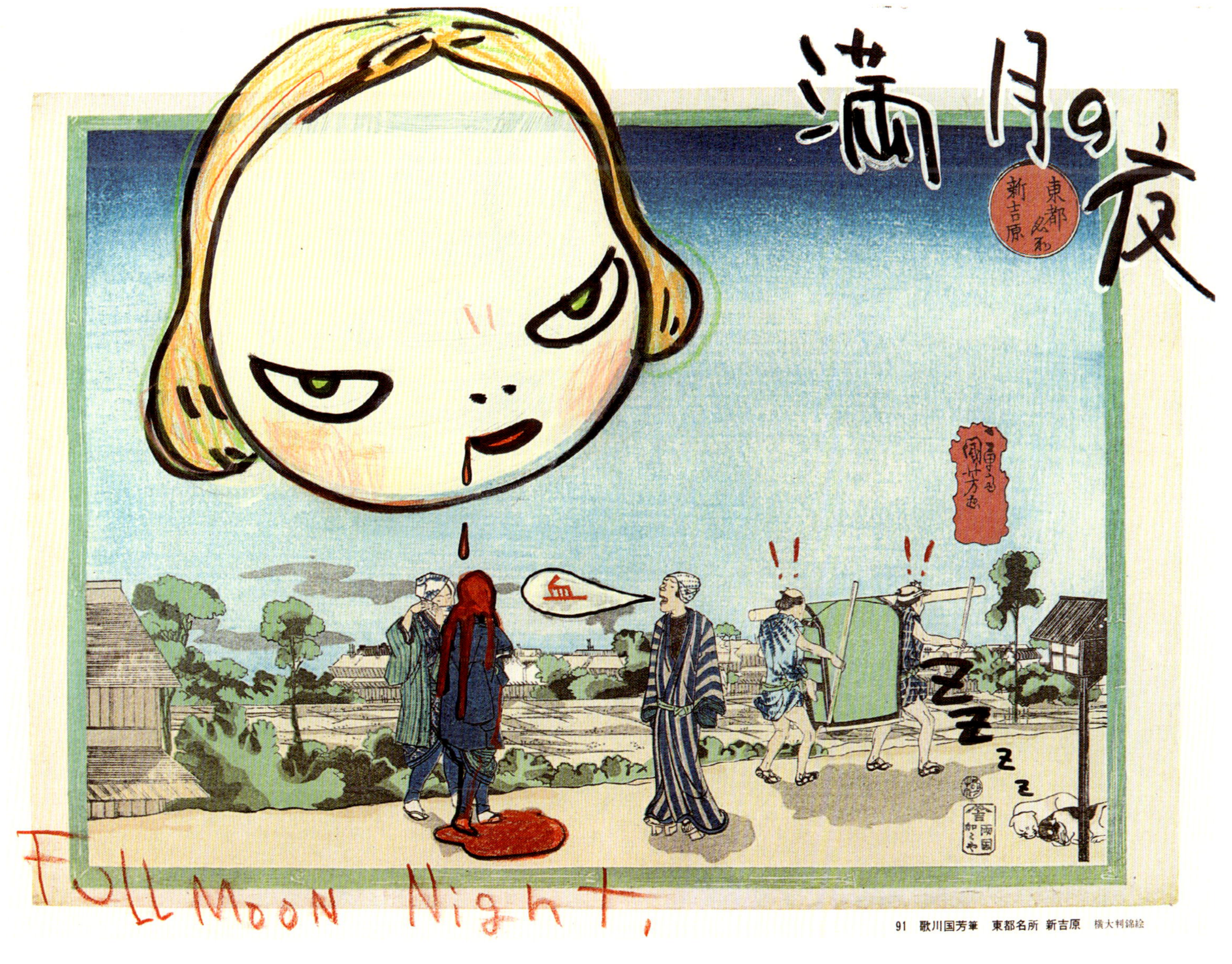

91 歌川国芳筆 東都名所 新吉原 横大判錦絵

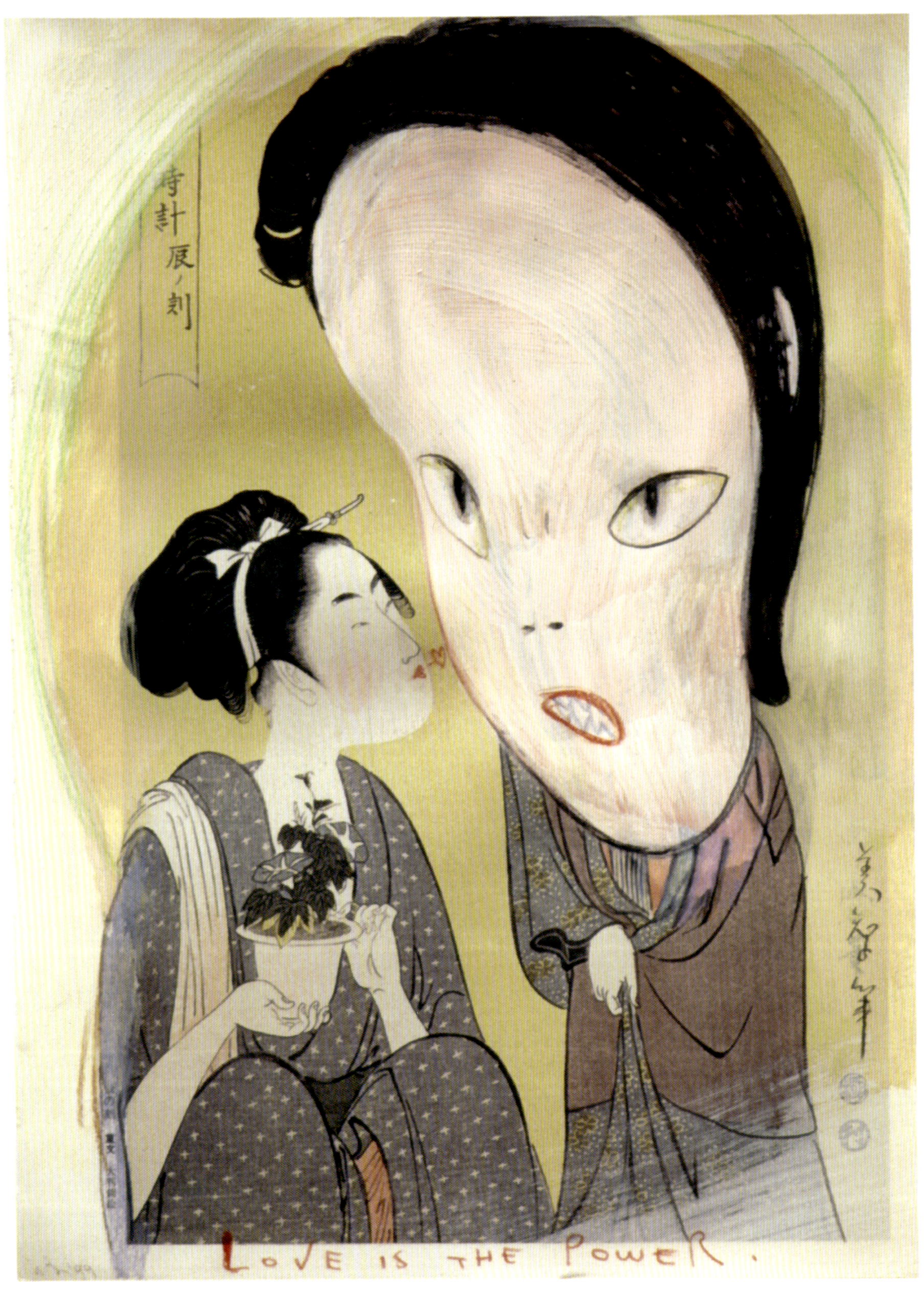
時計辰ノ刻
LOVE IS THE POWER.

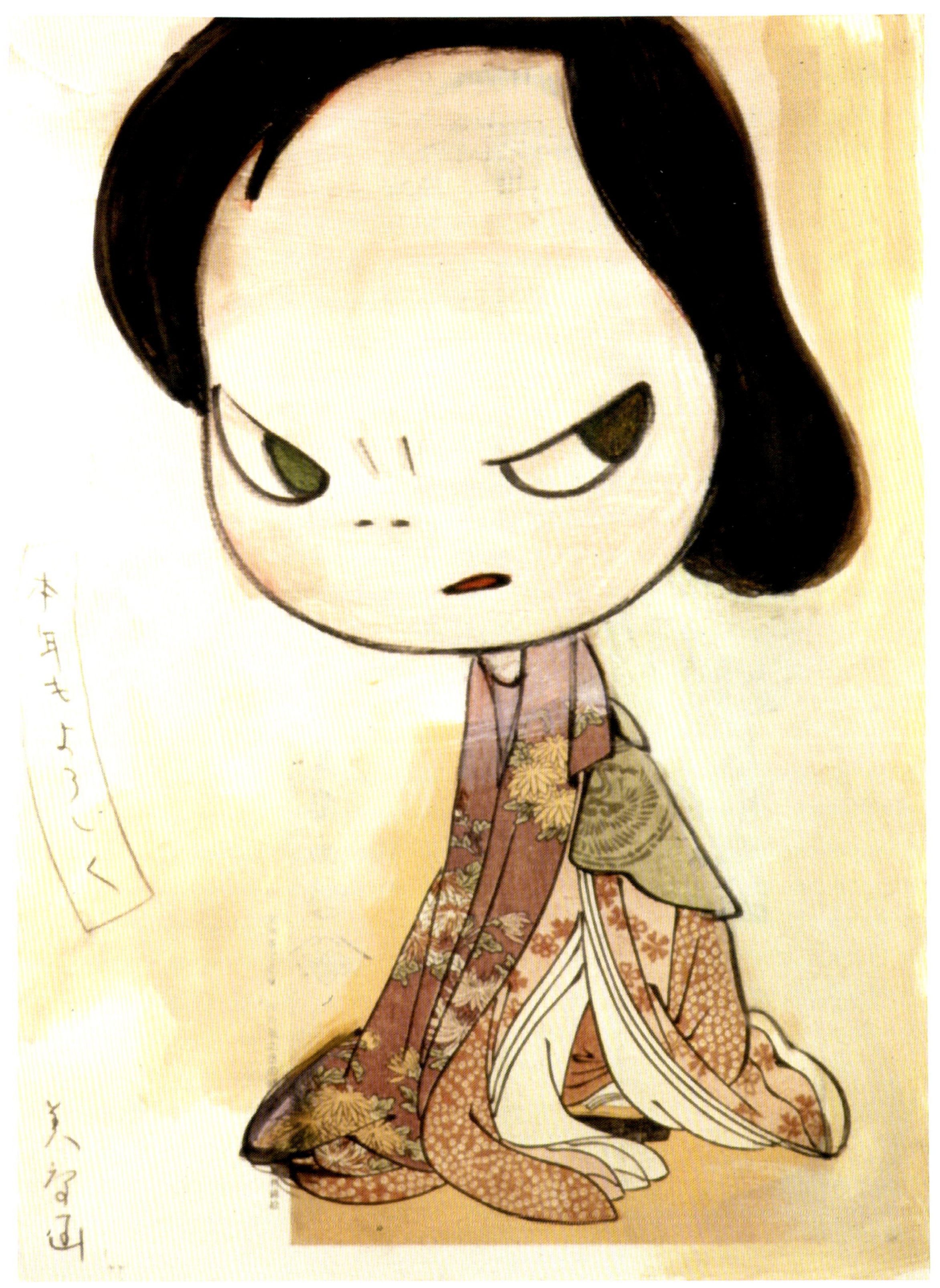
本年もよろしく
美智画

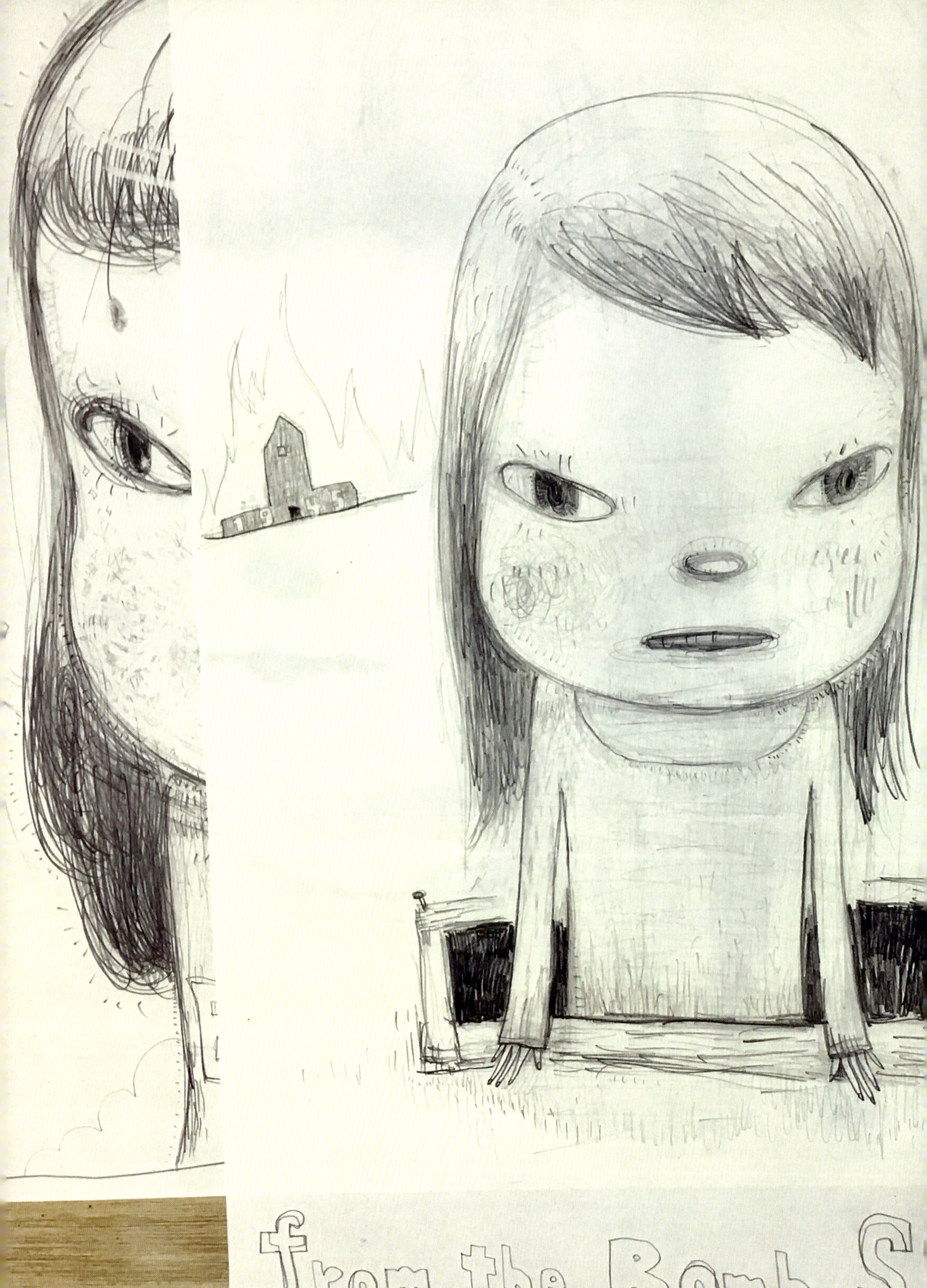
from the Bomb

X

WORK FOR DREAM TO DREAM

Do Not Disturb!, 1996
Untitled, 2003
Untitled, 2003
Untitled, 2003
Untitled, 2003
Untitled, 2003
Untitled, 2003
Untitled, 2003
Untitled, 2003
Untitled, 2003
Untitled, 2003
Untitled, 1985–88
Untitled, 1989
Untitled, 1989
Work for *Dream to Dream*, 2001
Untitled, 1989
Work for *Dream to Dream*, 2001
Untitled, 1990
Untitled, 1993
Untitled, 1993
Searching, 2019
Wounded Cat in the Night, 1993

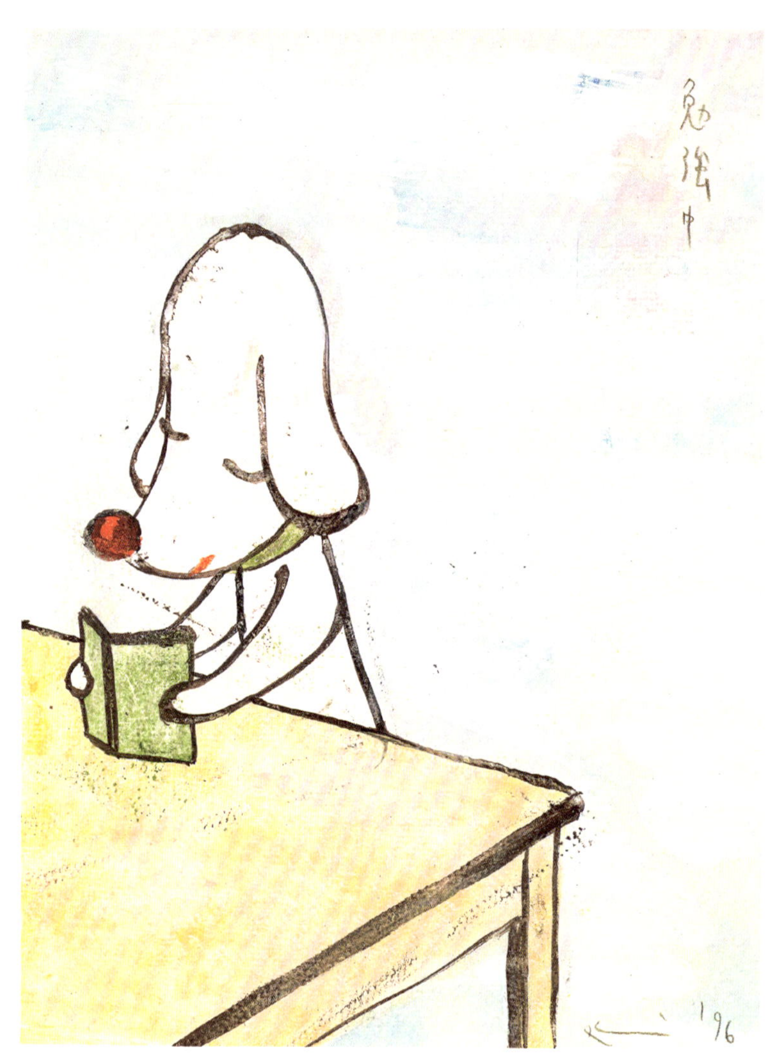
勉強中
'96

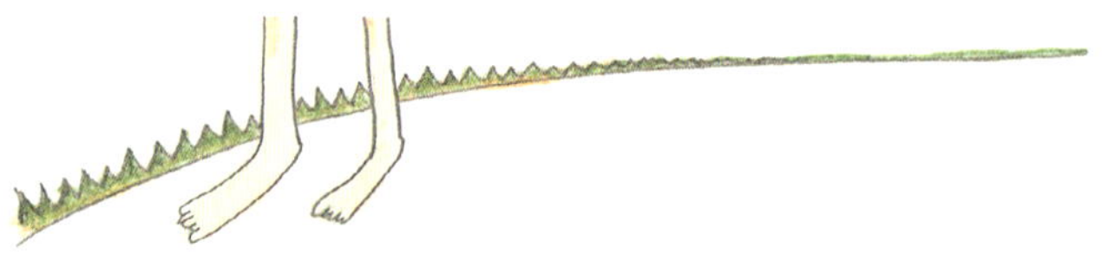

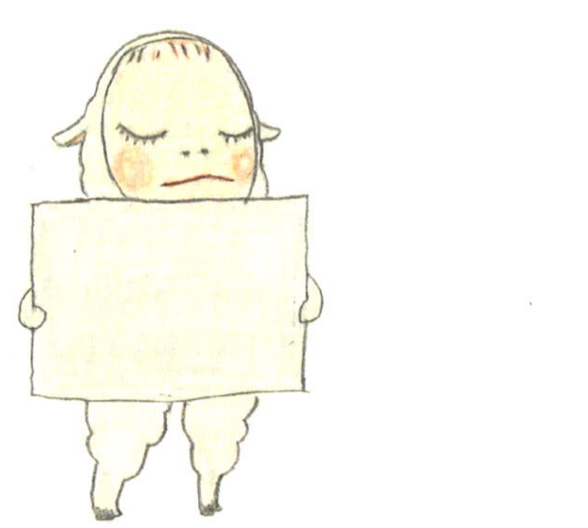

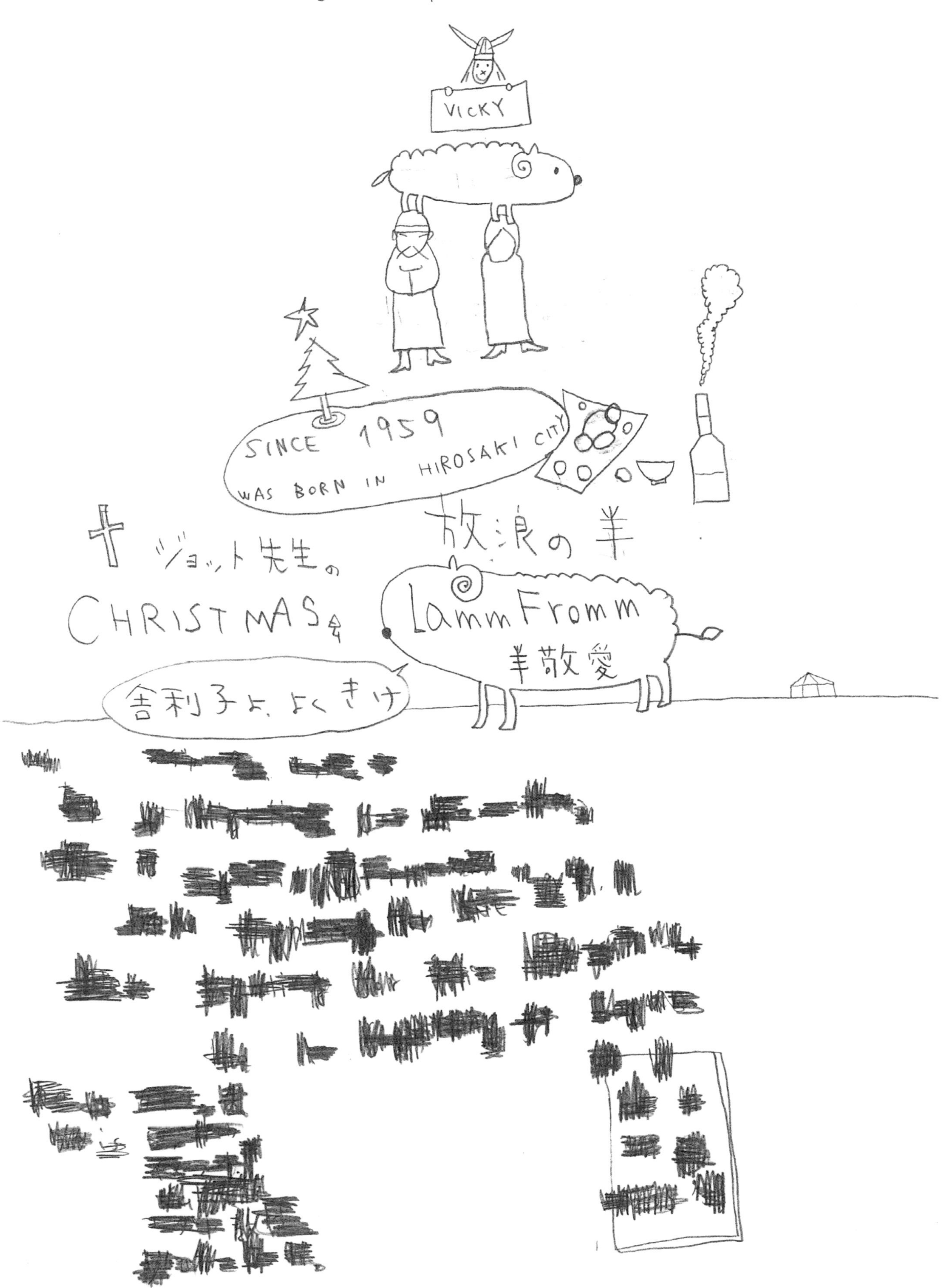
50000 YEARS
VICKY
SINCE 1959
WAS BORN IN HIROSAKI CITY
ジョット先生の
CHRISTMAS会
放浪の羊
Lamm Fromm
羊敬愛
舎利子よ、よくきけ

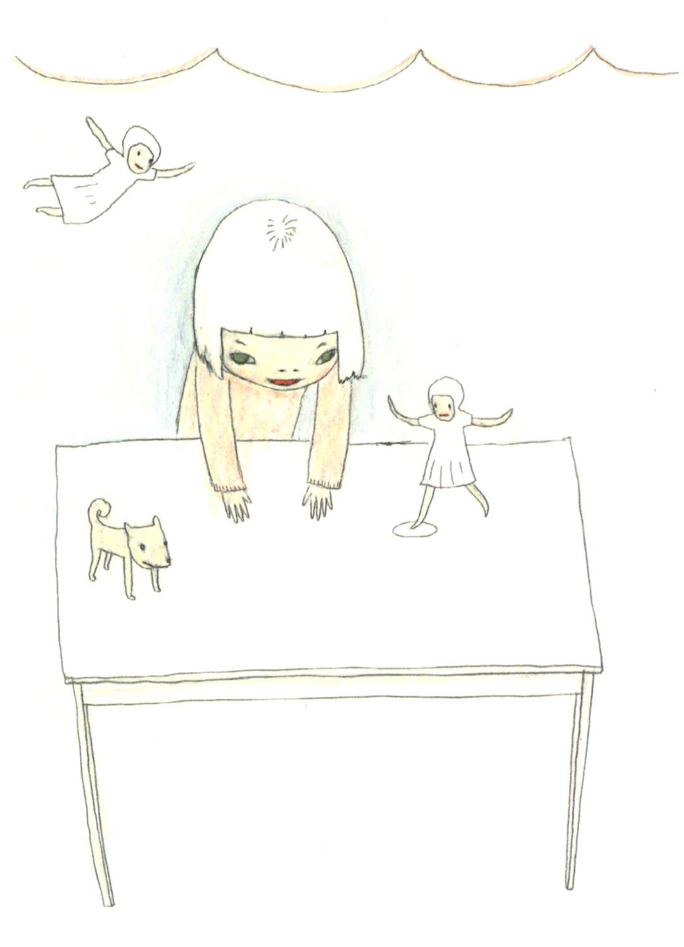

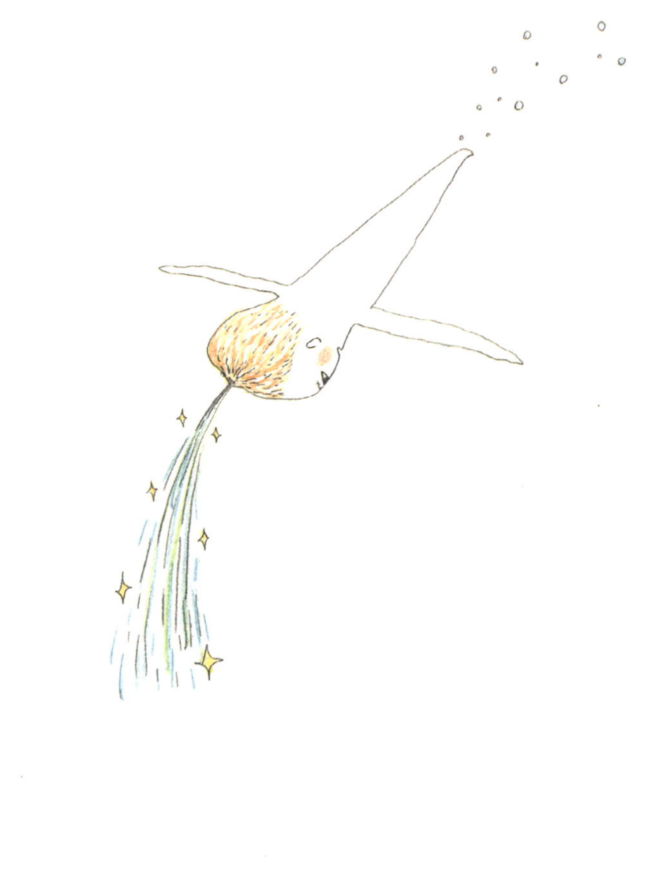

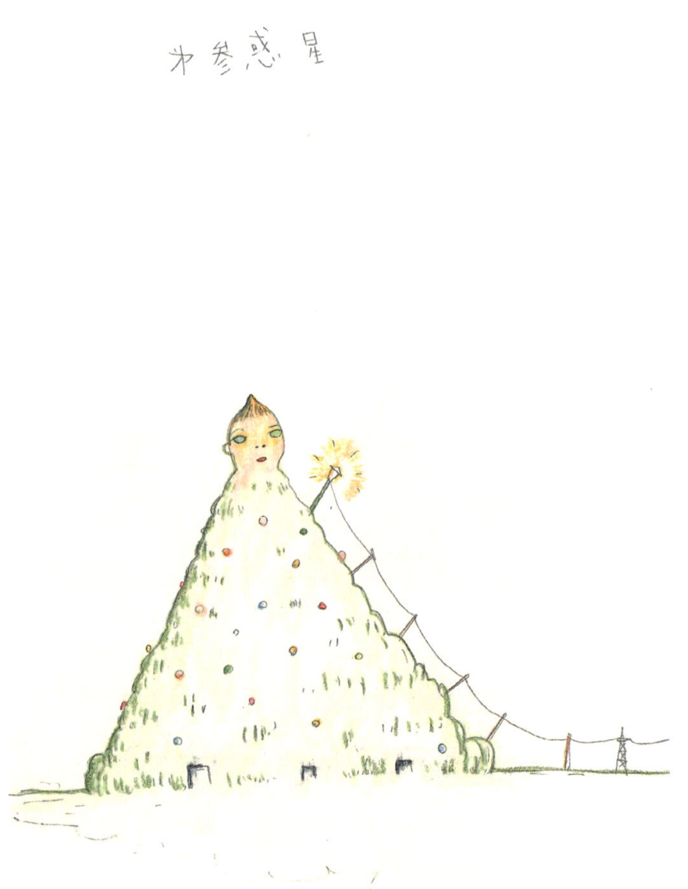
第参惑星

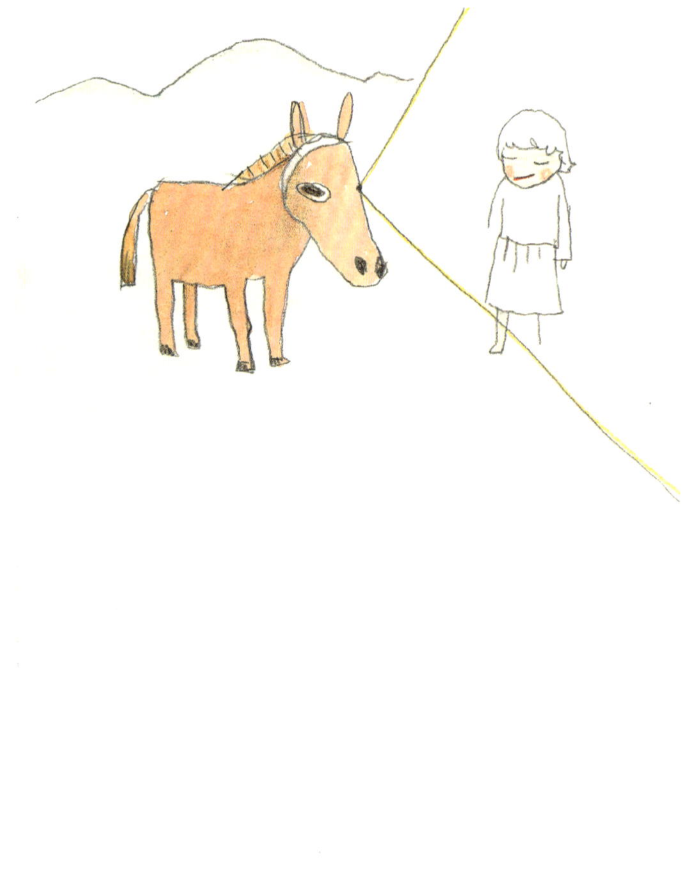

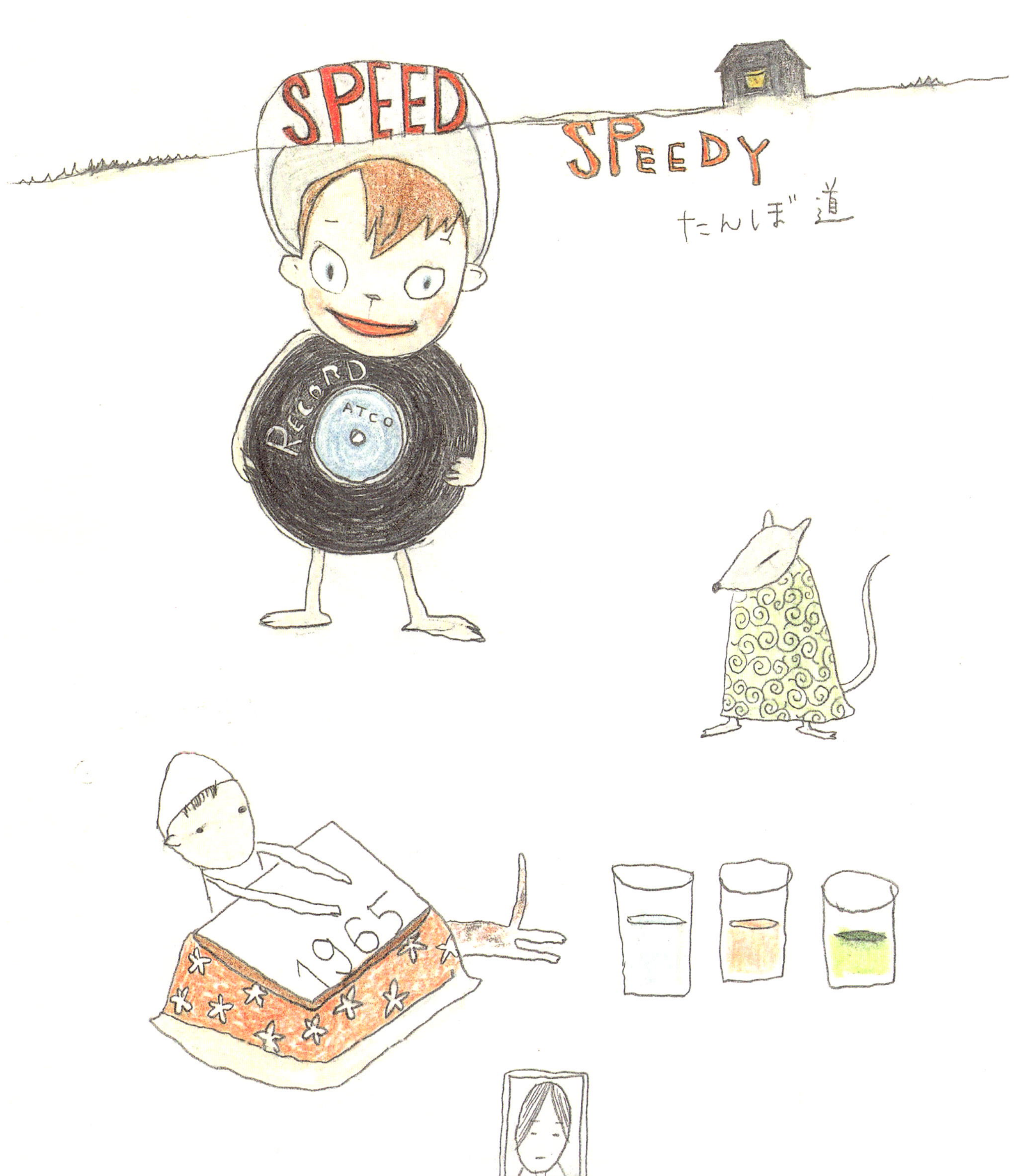
SPEED
SPEEDY
たんぼ道
RECORD
ATCO
1965

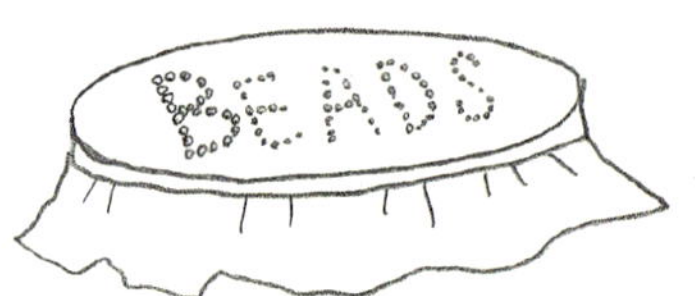
BEADS

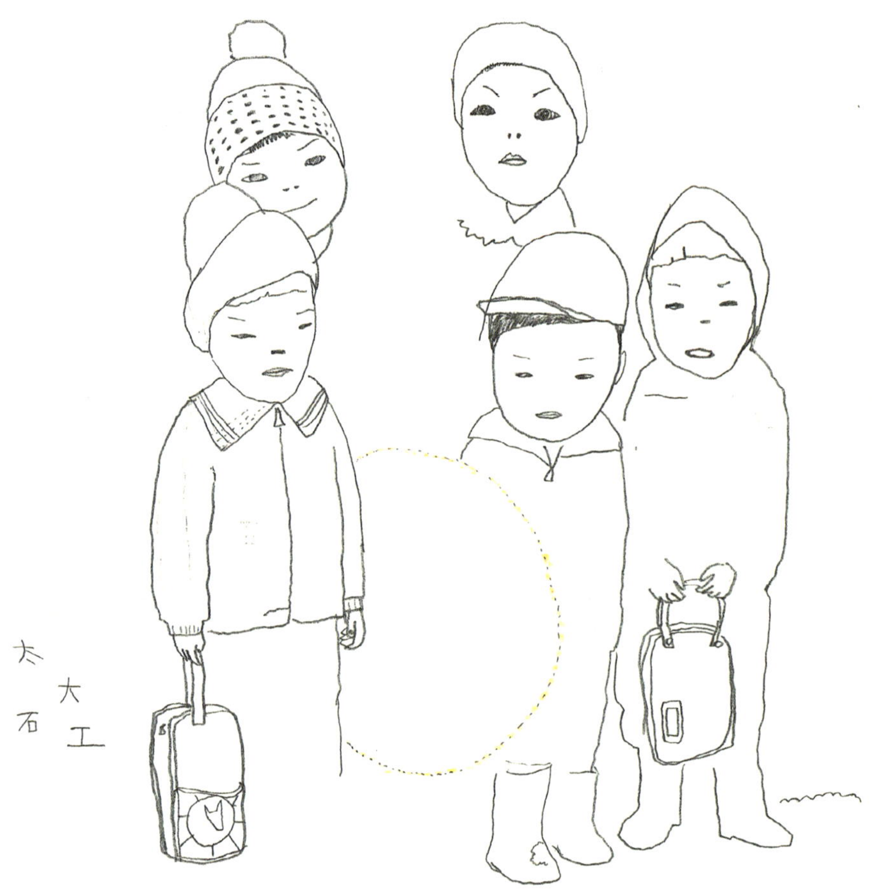
大工
太石

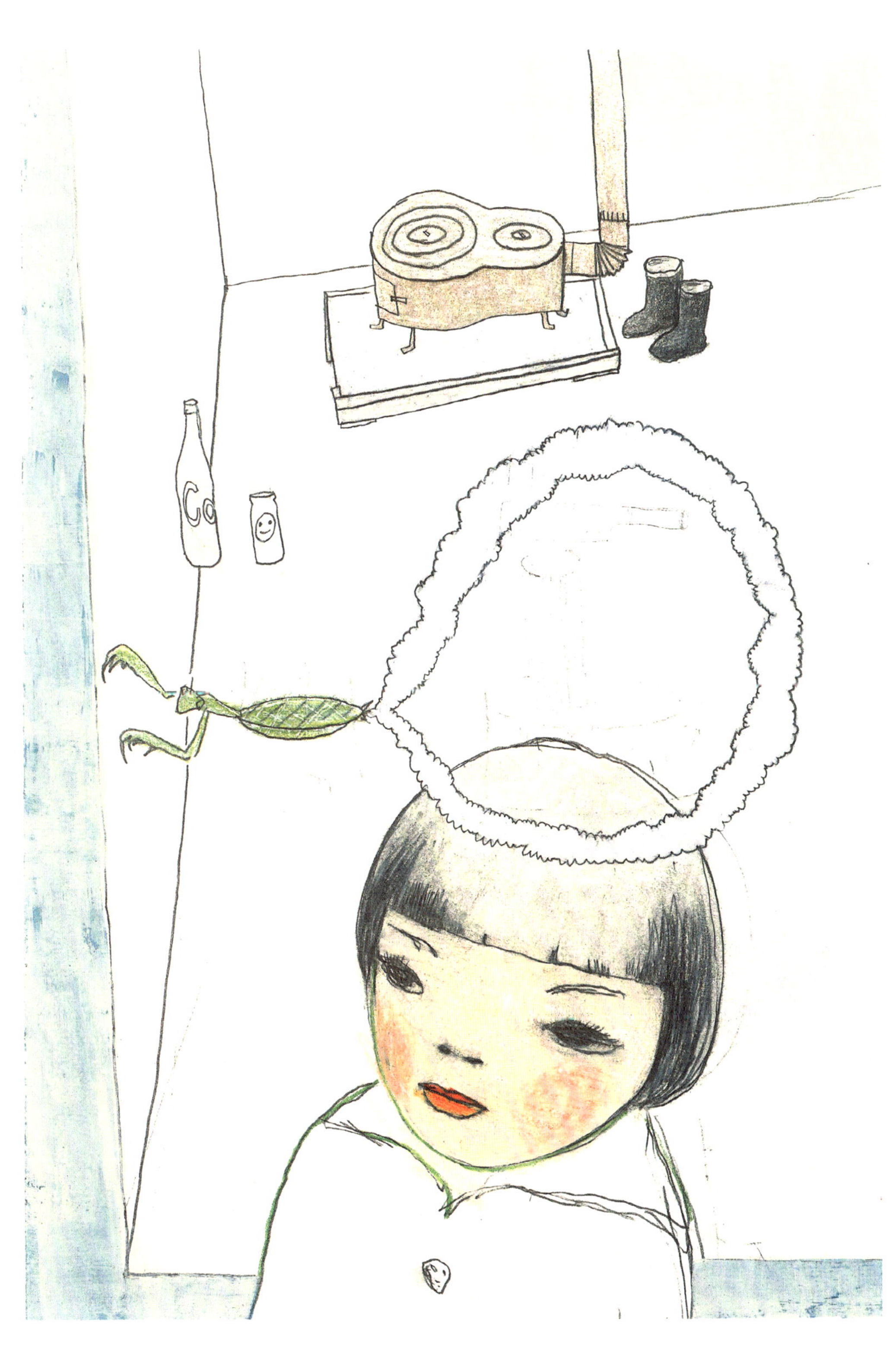

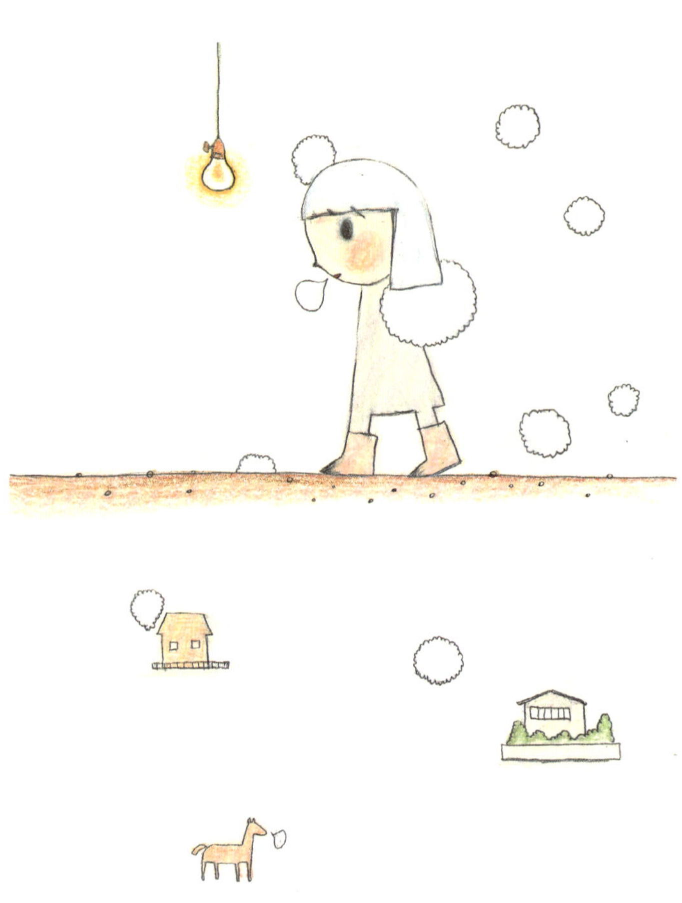

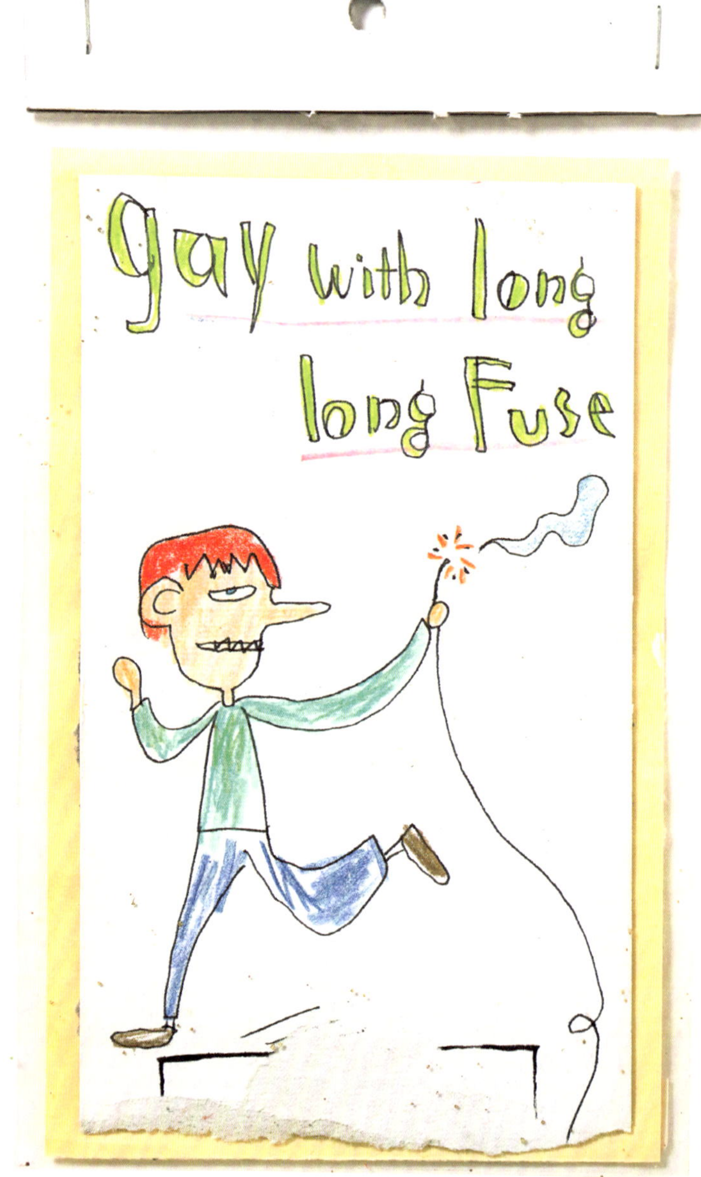
gay with long
long Fuse

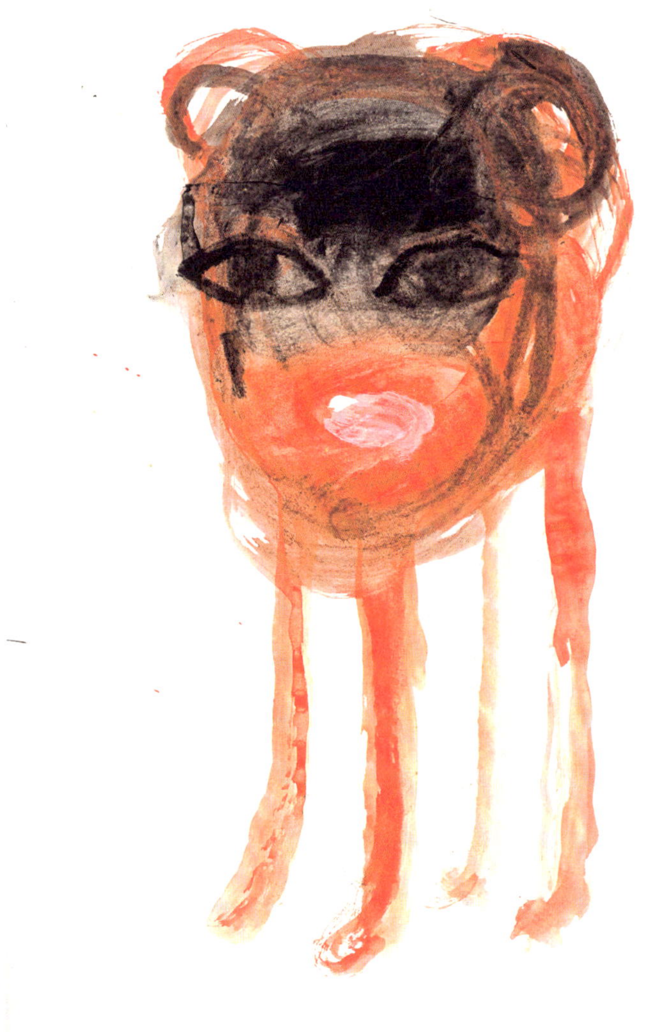

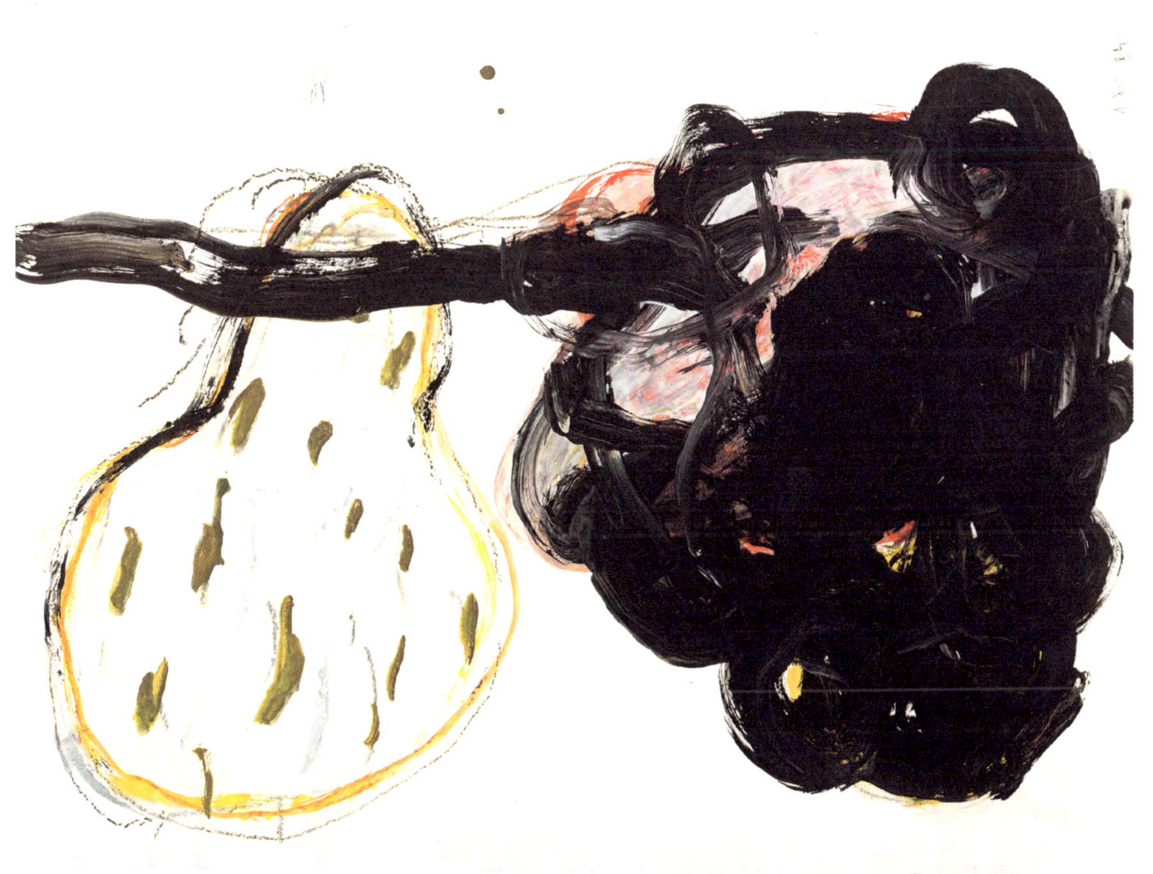

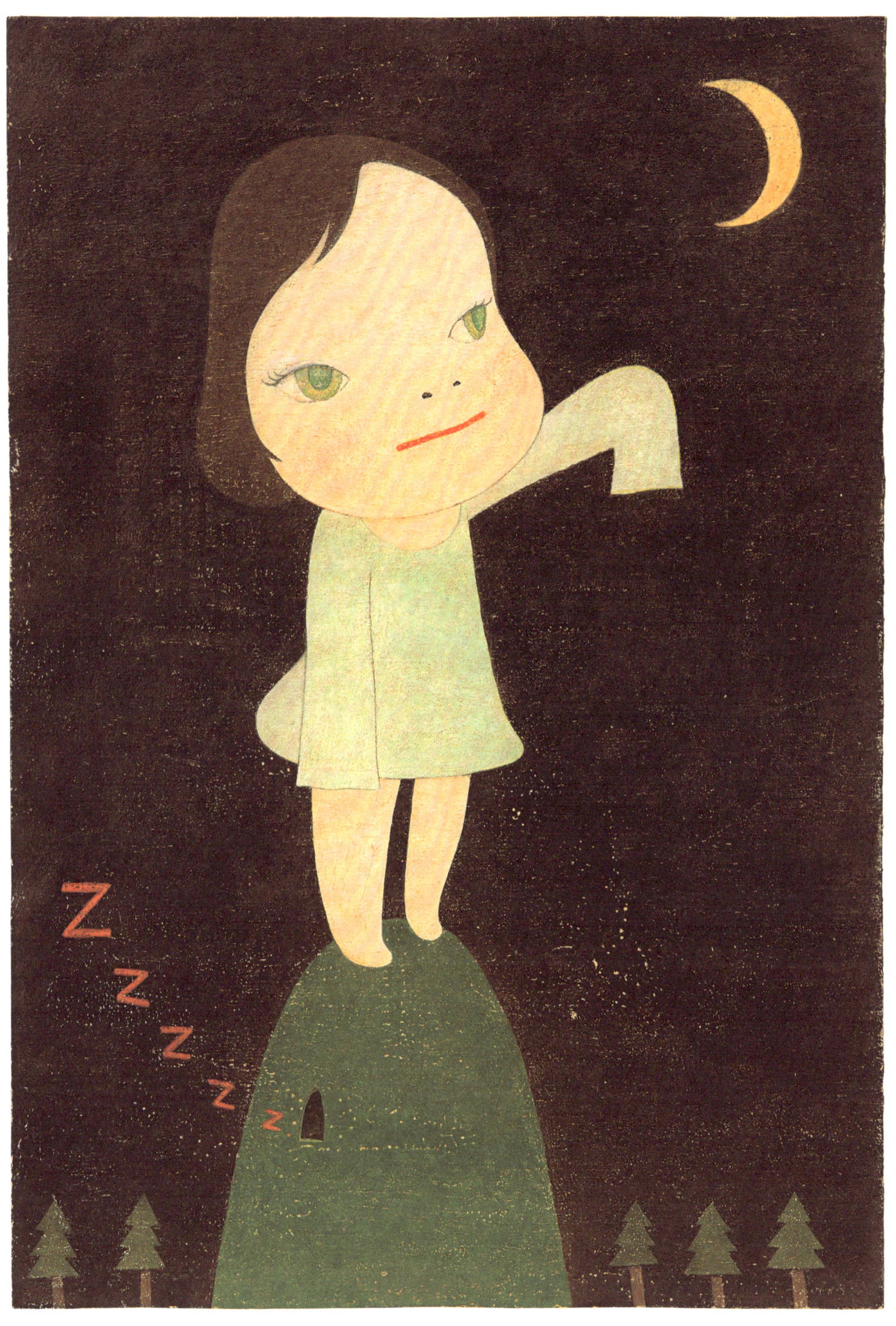

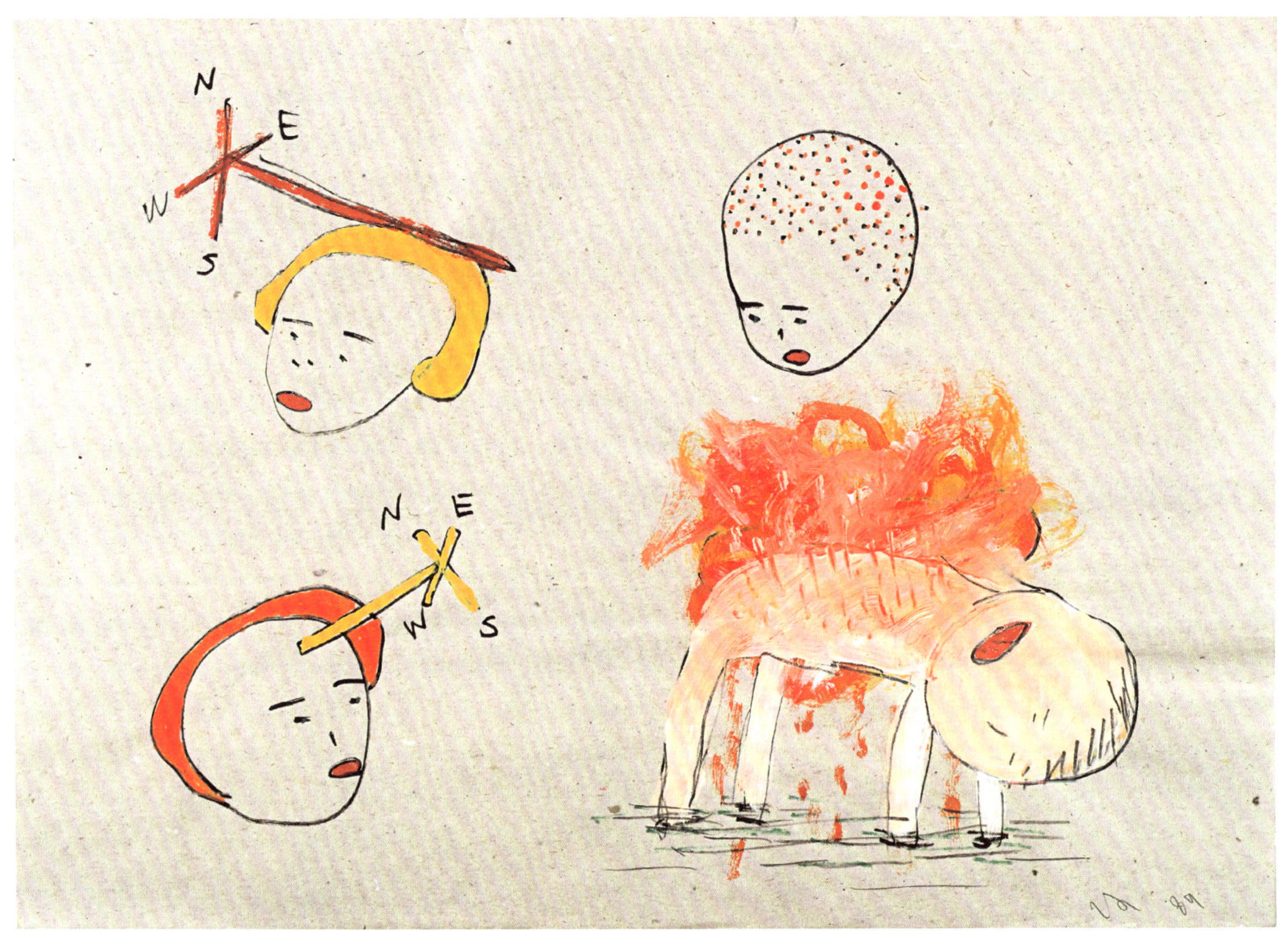
N
E
W
S
N
E
W
S

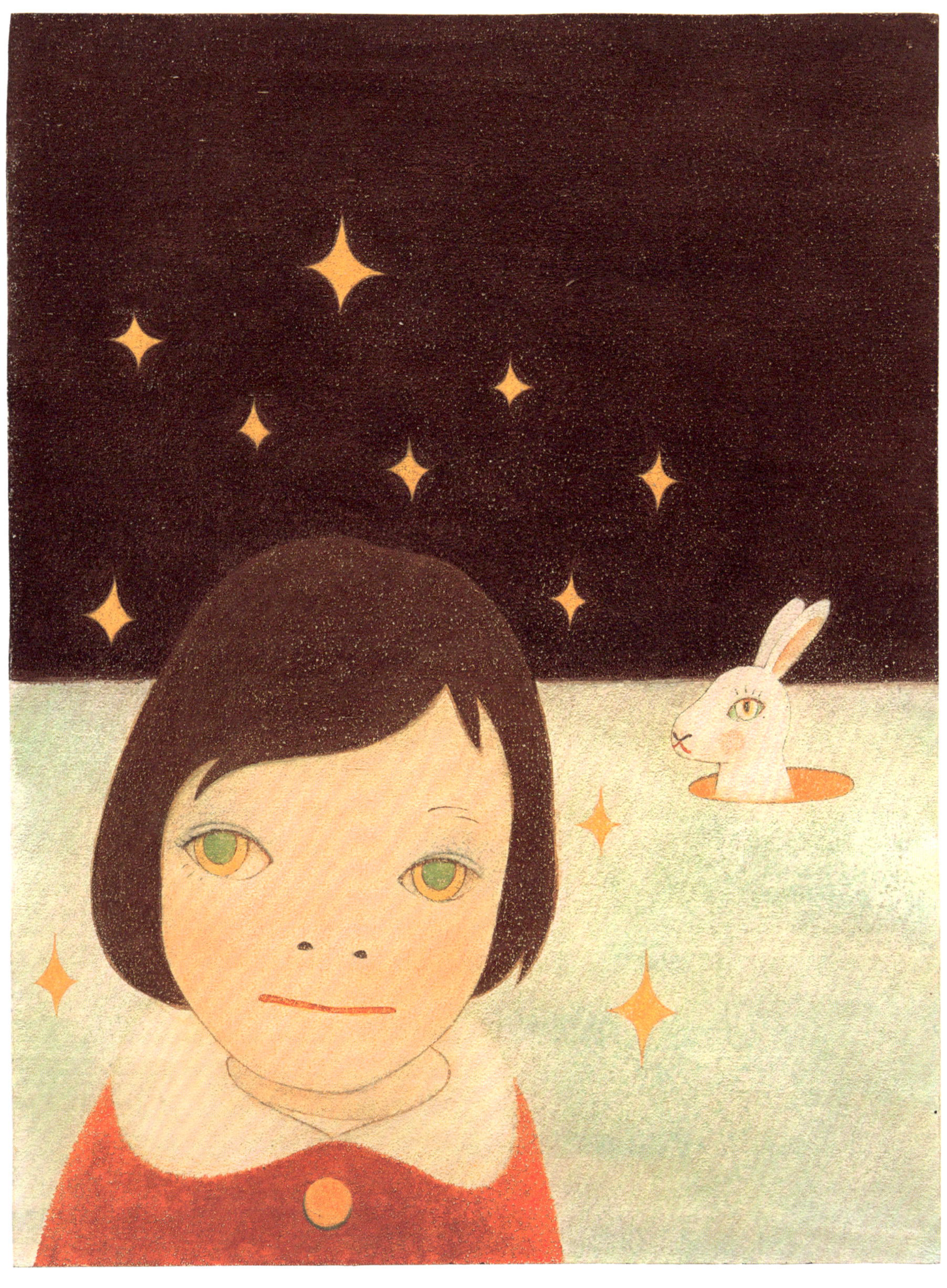

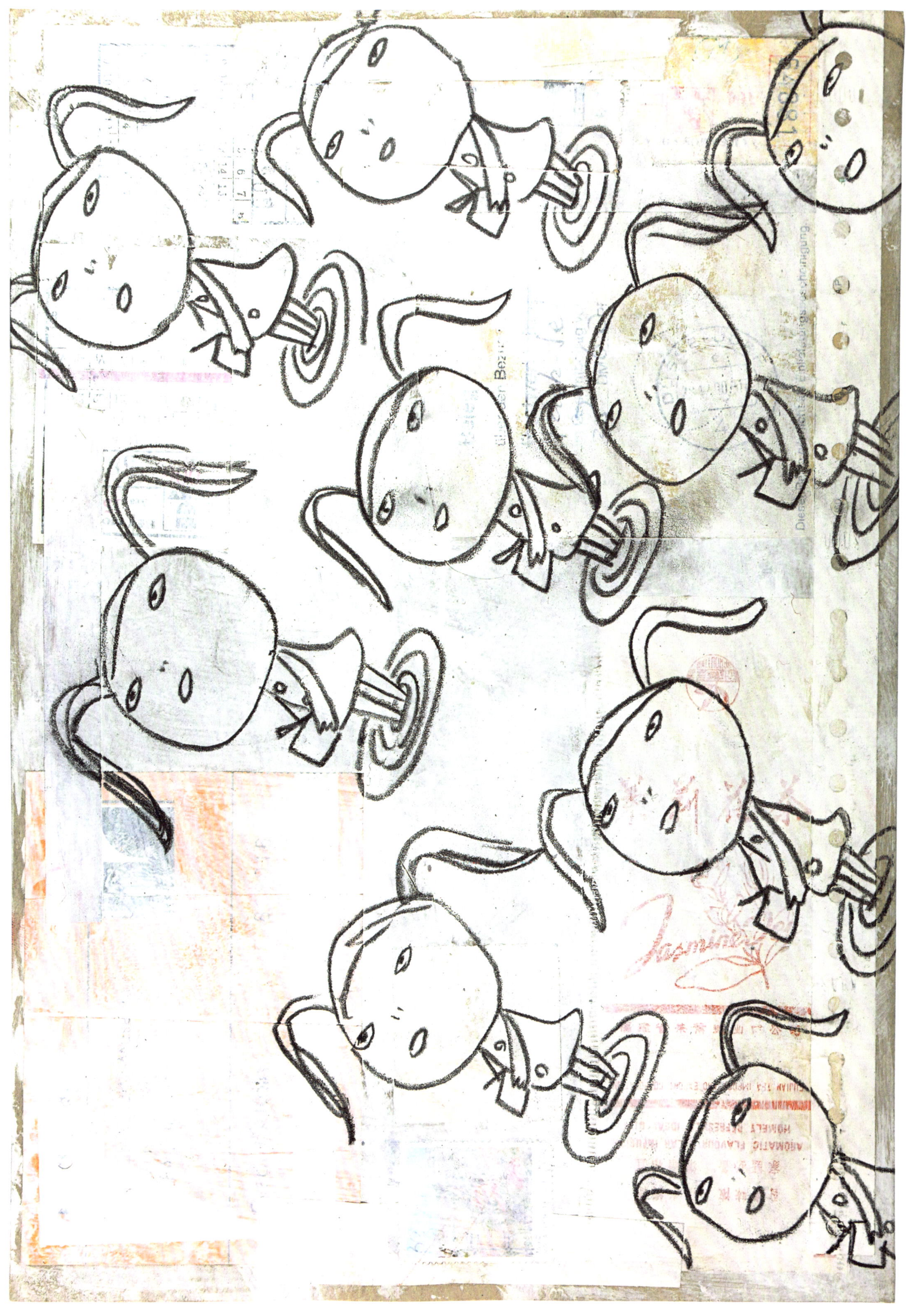

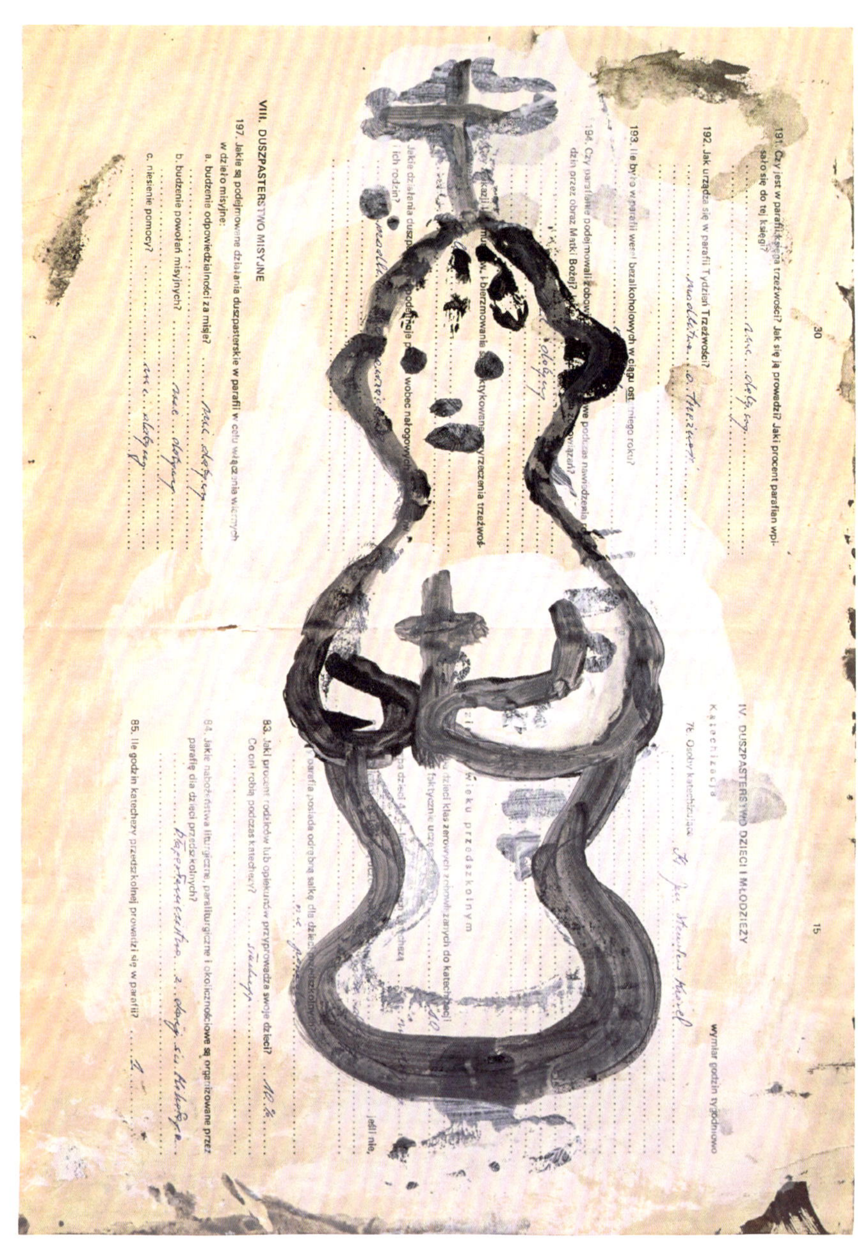

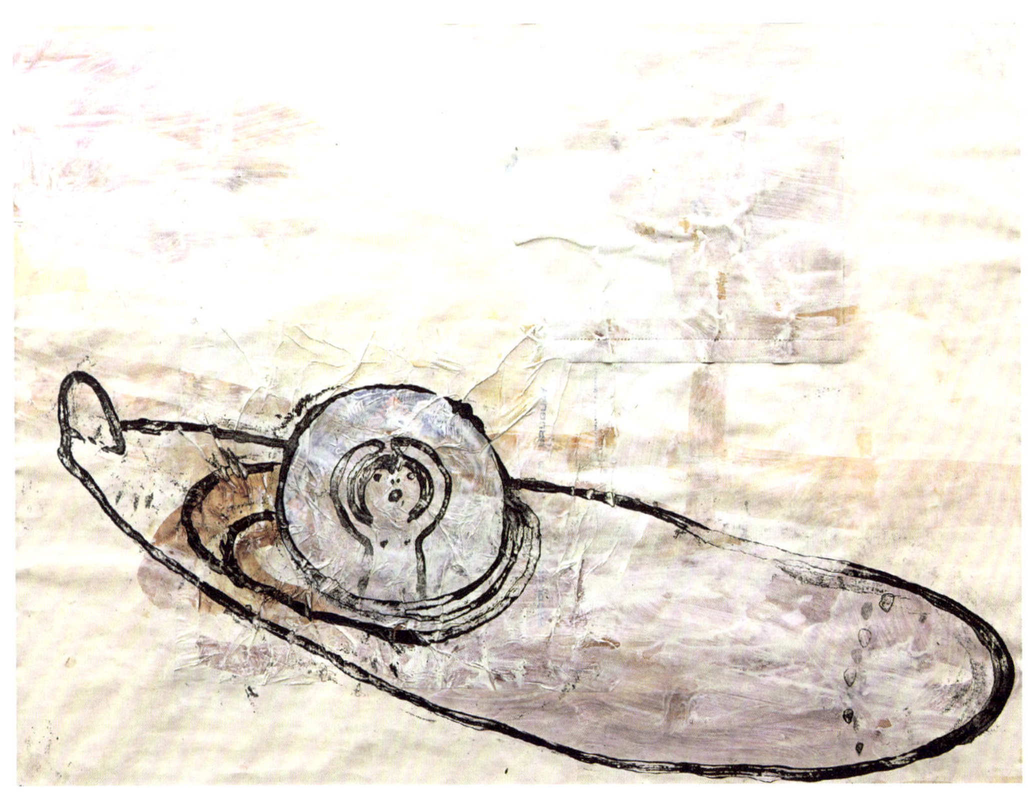

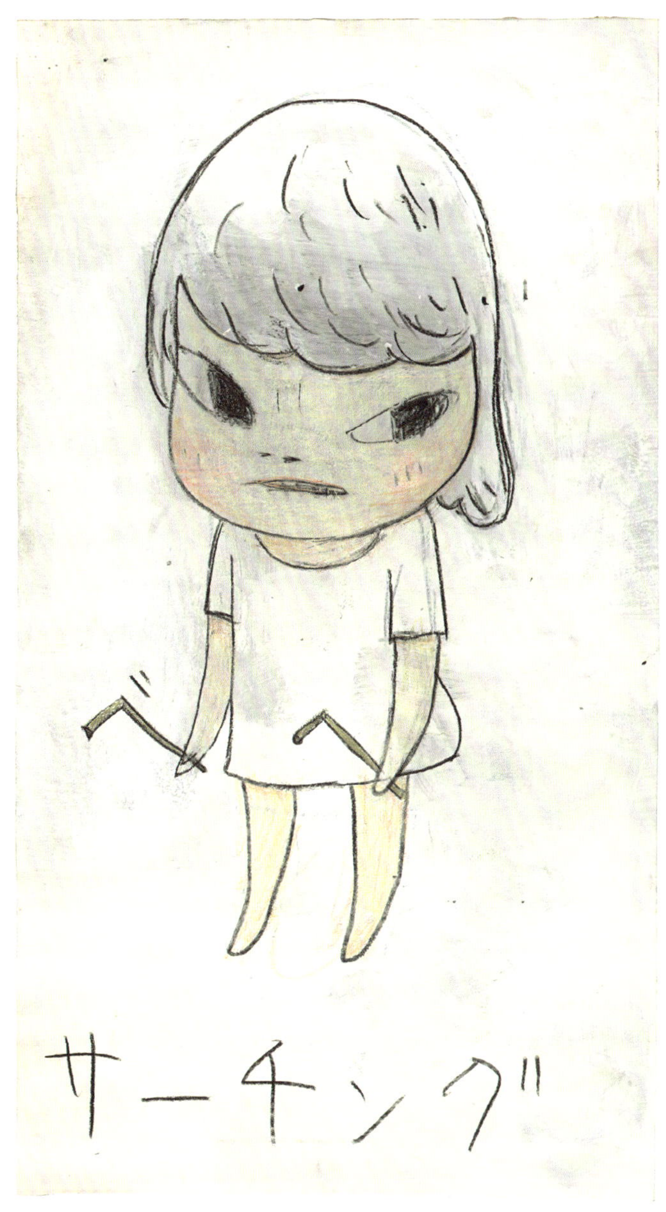
サーチング

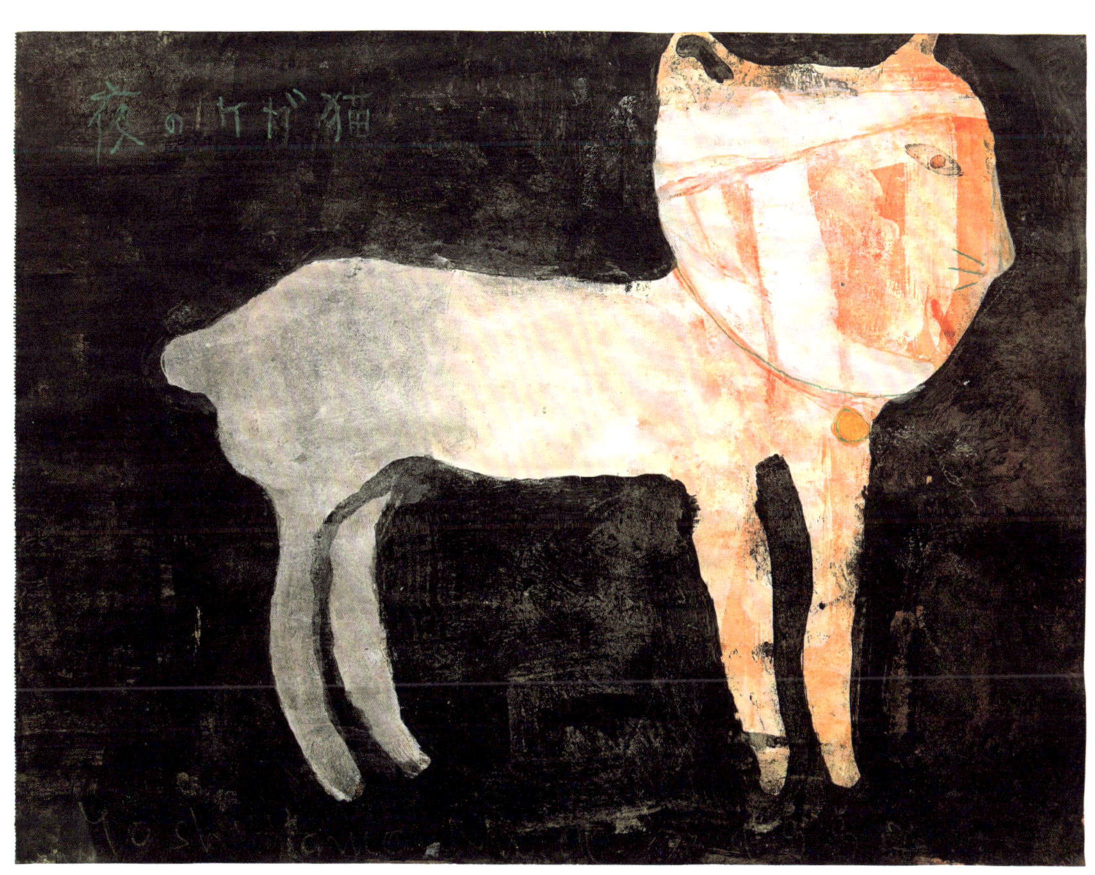
夜のケガ猫

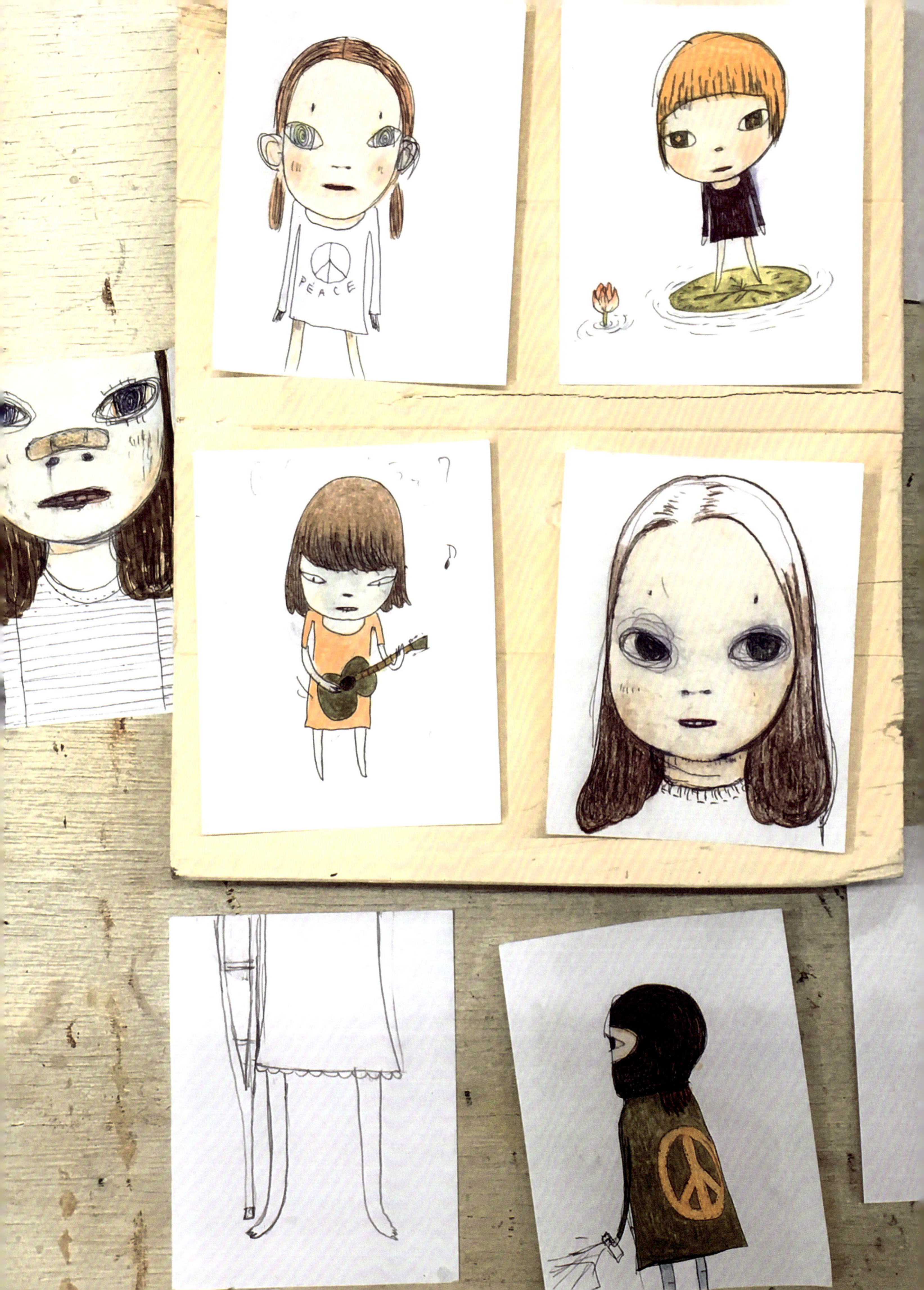
PEACE

XI

DEATH OR GLORY

Untitled, 1999
Untitled, 1998
Untitled, 1998
Ahunrupar, 2018
Death or Glory, 2017
Drawing for *Hard-boiled/Hard Luck*, 1999
Drawing for *Hard-boiled/Hard Luck*, 1999
Work for *Dream to Dream*, 2001
Untitled, 1994
Muñoz's Babies, 1995
Untitled, late 1990s
Nobody's Fool, 2010
Untitled, 2011
Untitled, 2011
I AM Right Wing, I AM Left Wing. Feelings are leaning a little to the right, wavering to the left, 2011
Untitled, 2008
Dead Flower, 1994
Untitled, 2011
Untitled, 2011
Untitled, 2011
Mirror Ball Bon Dance, 2012

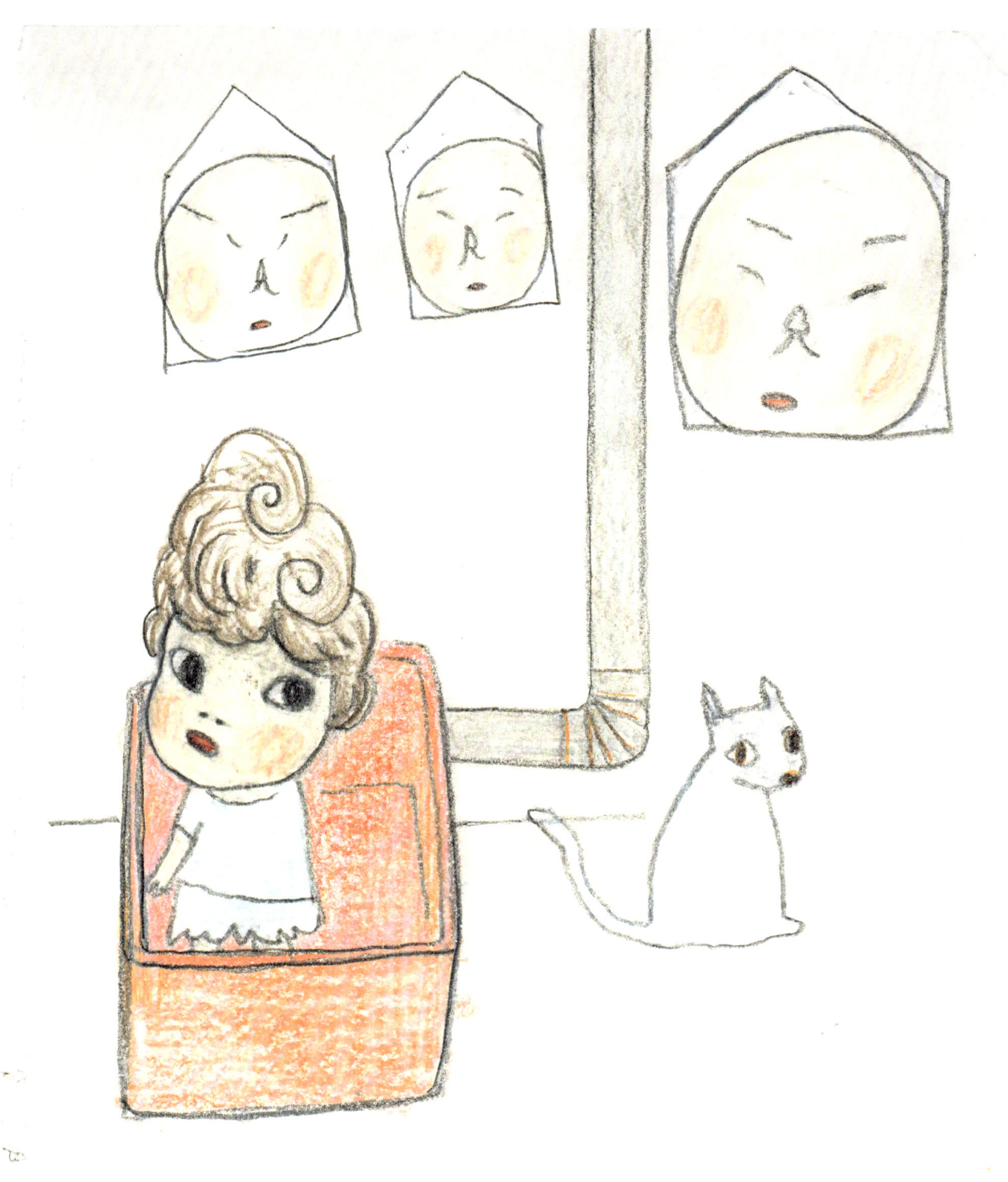

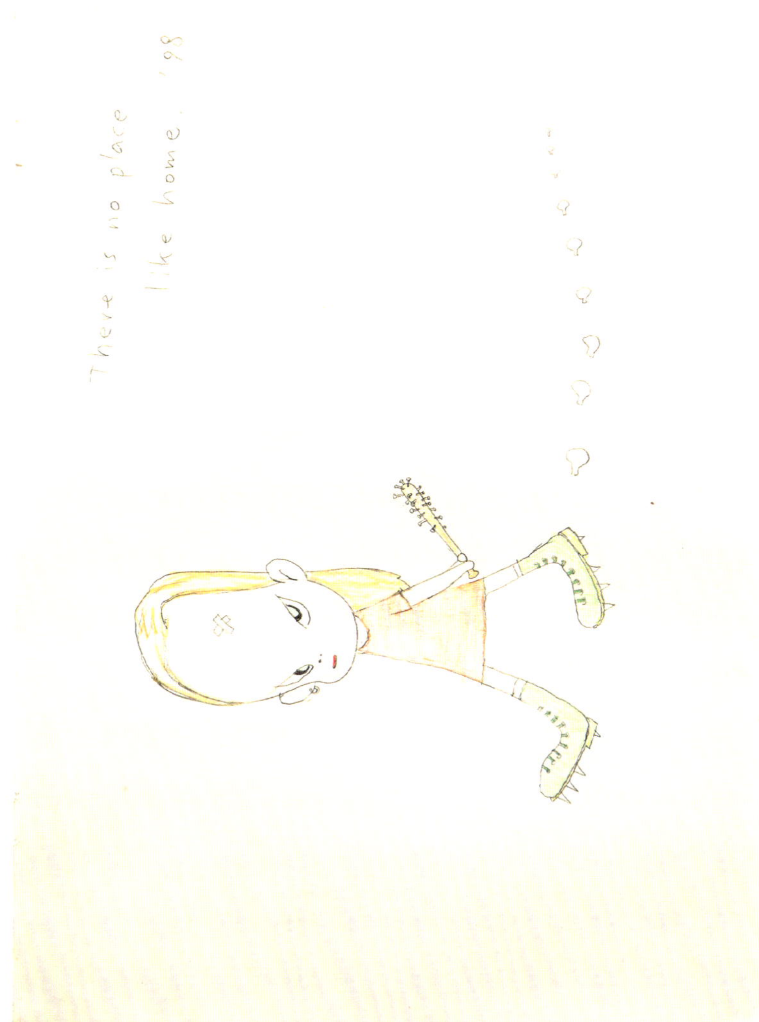
There is no place
like home. '98

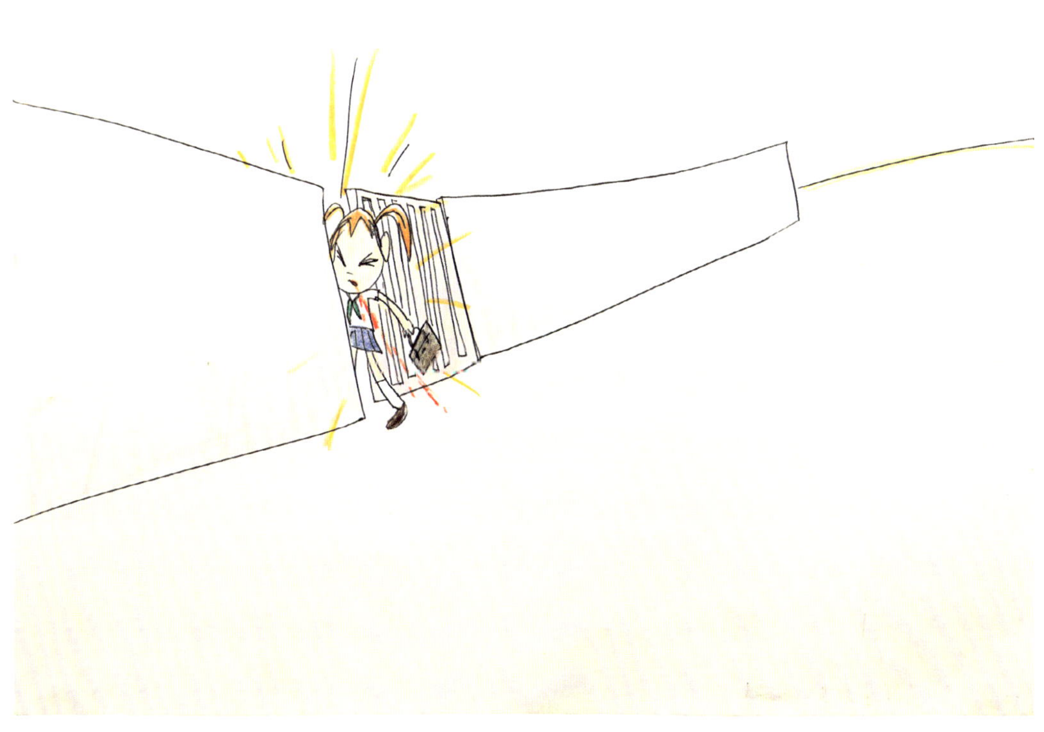

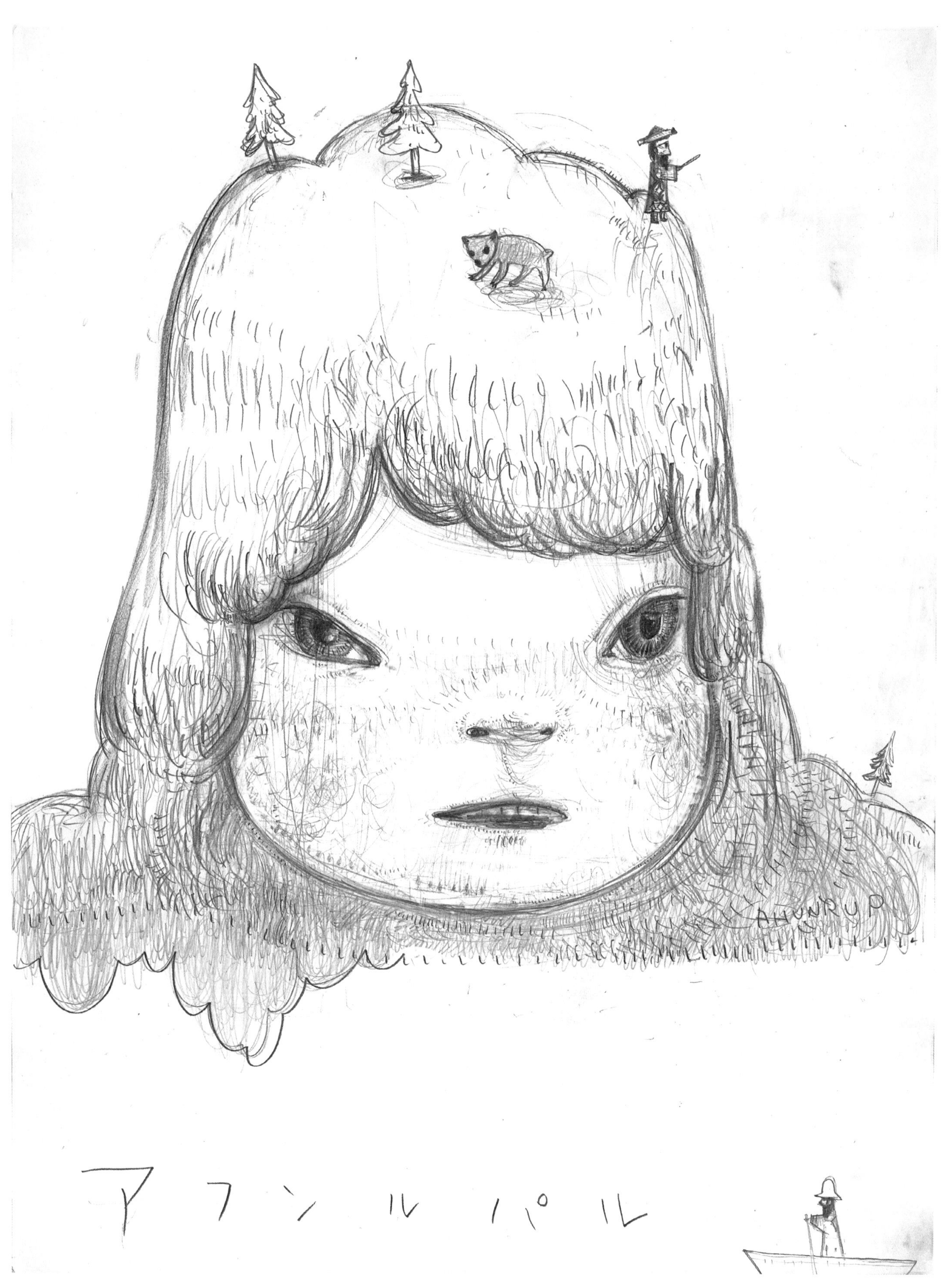
AHUNRUP
アフンルパル

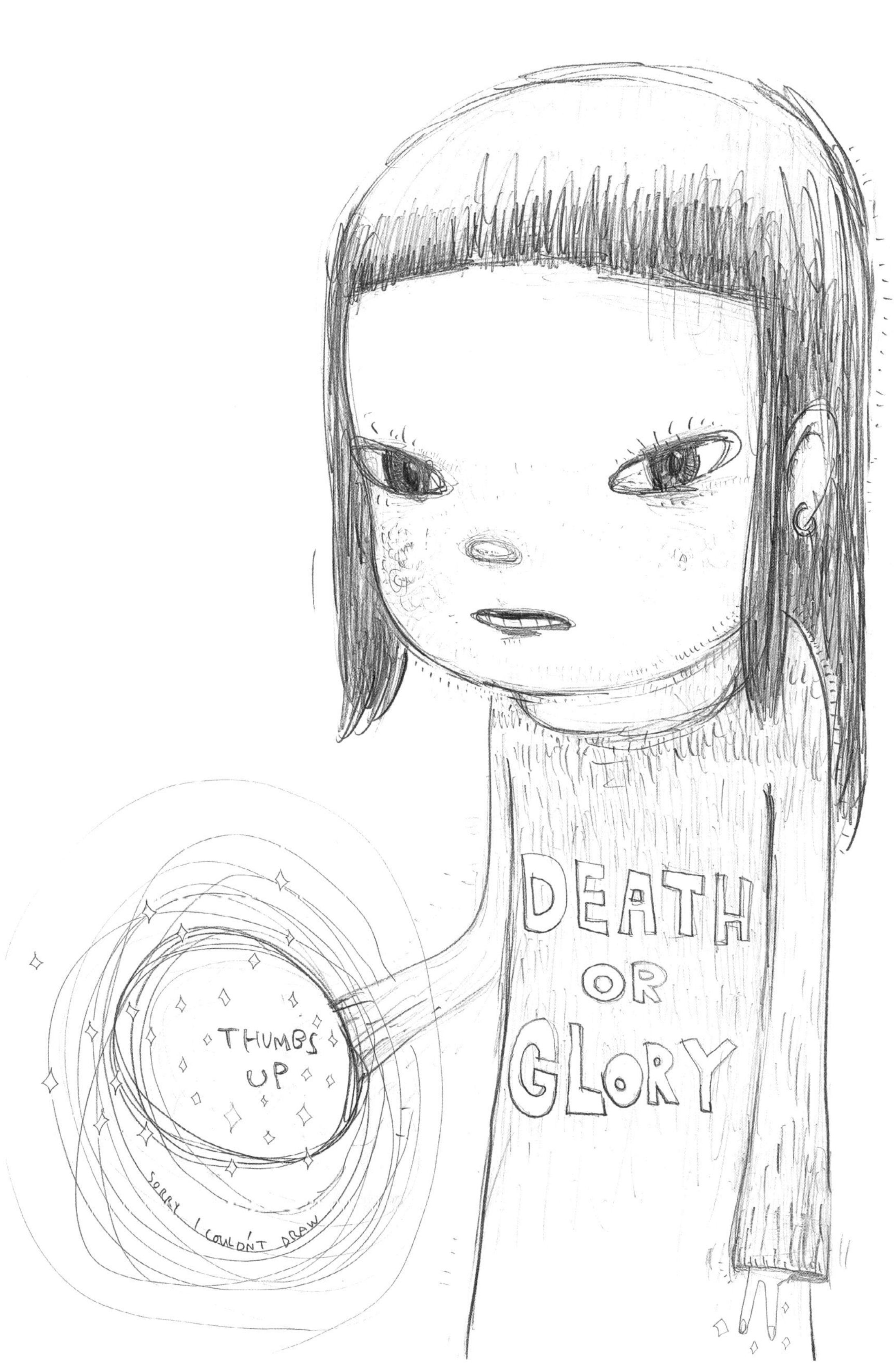
DEATH
OR
GLORY
THUMBS
UP
SORRY I COULDN'T DRAW

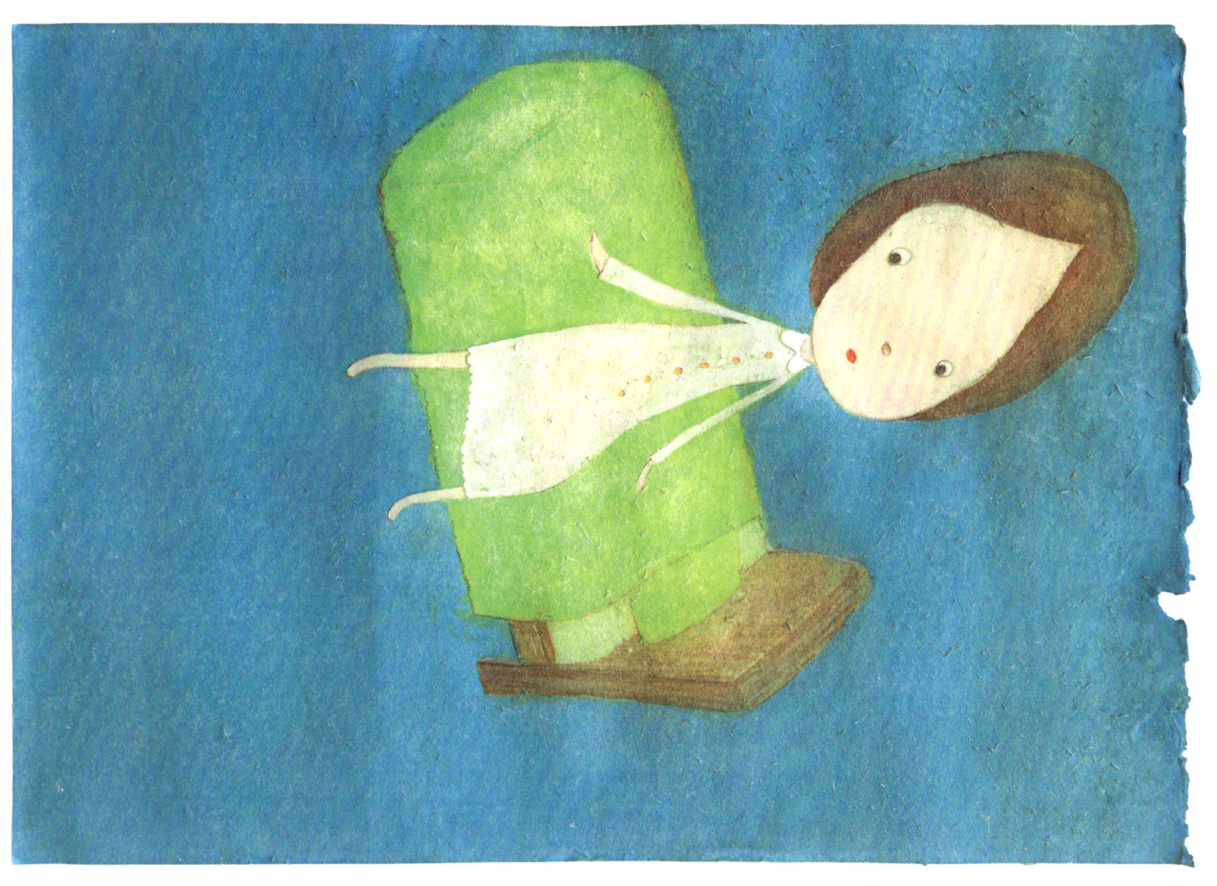

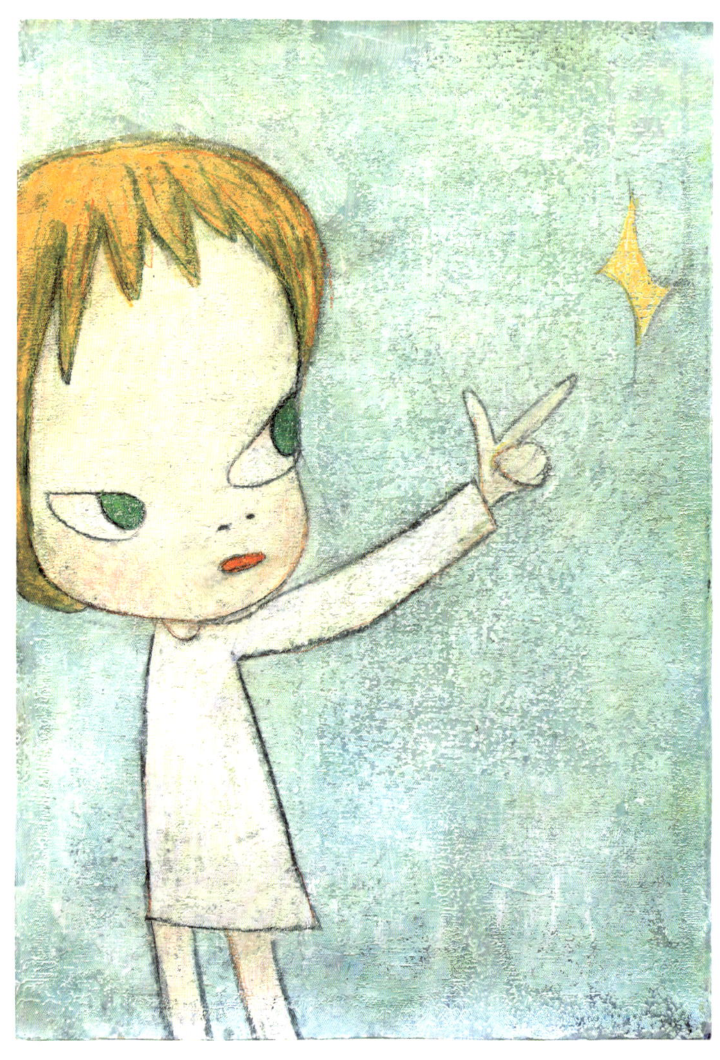

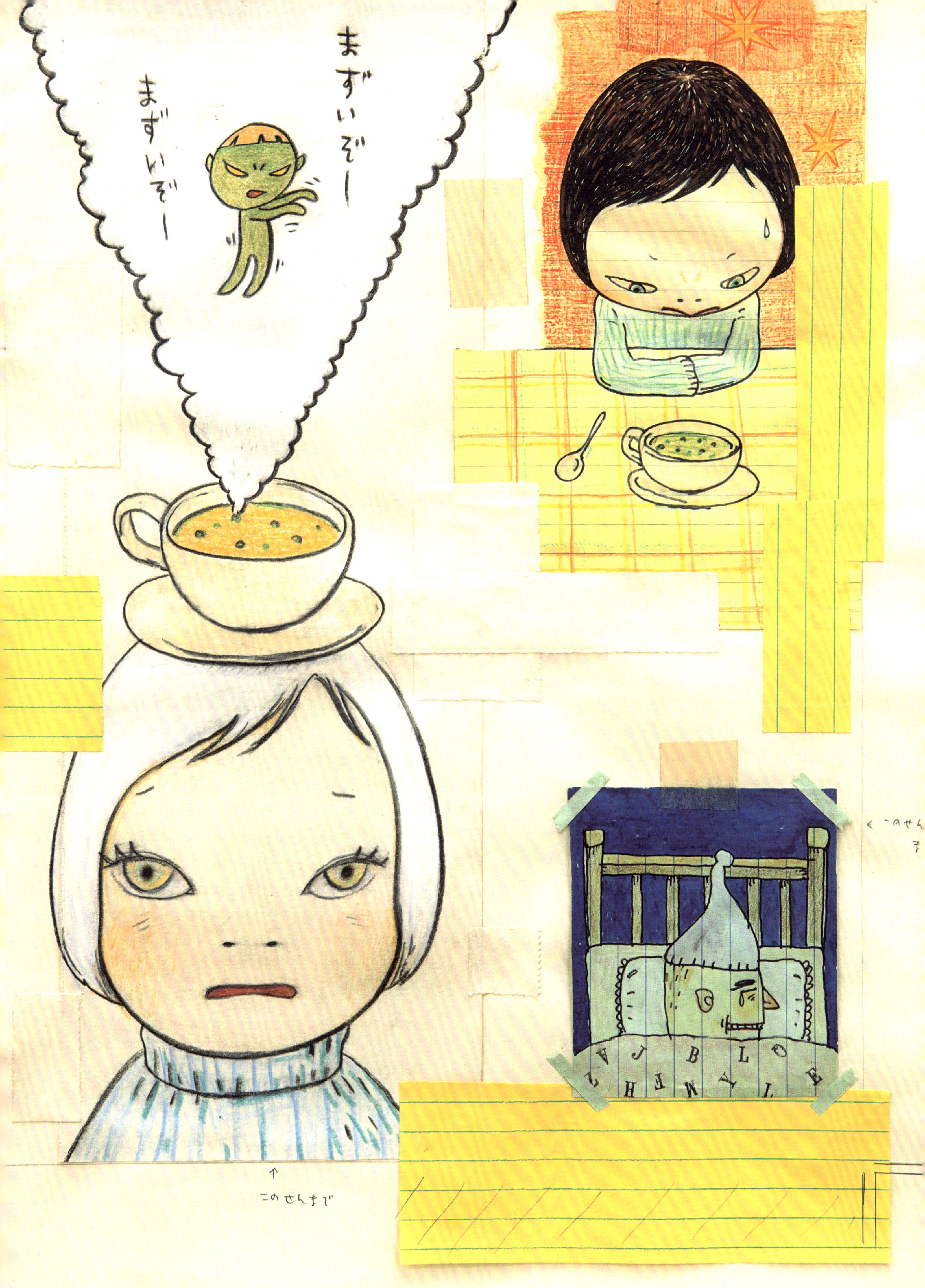
まずいぞー
まずいぞー
このせんまで

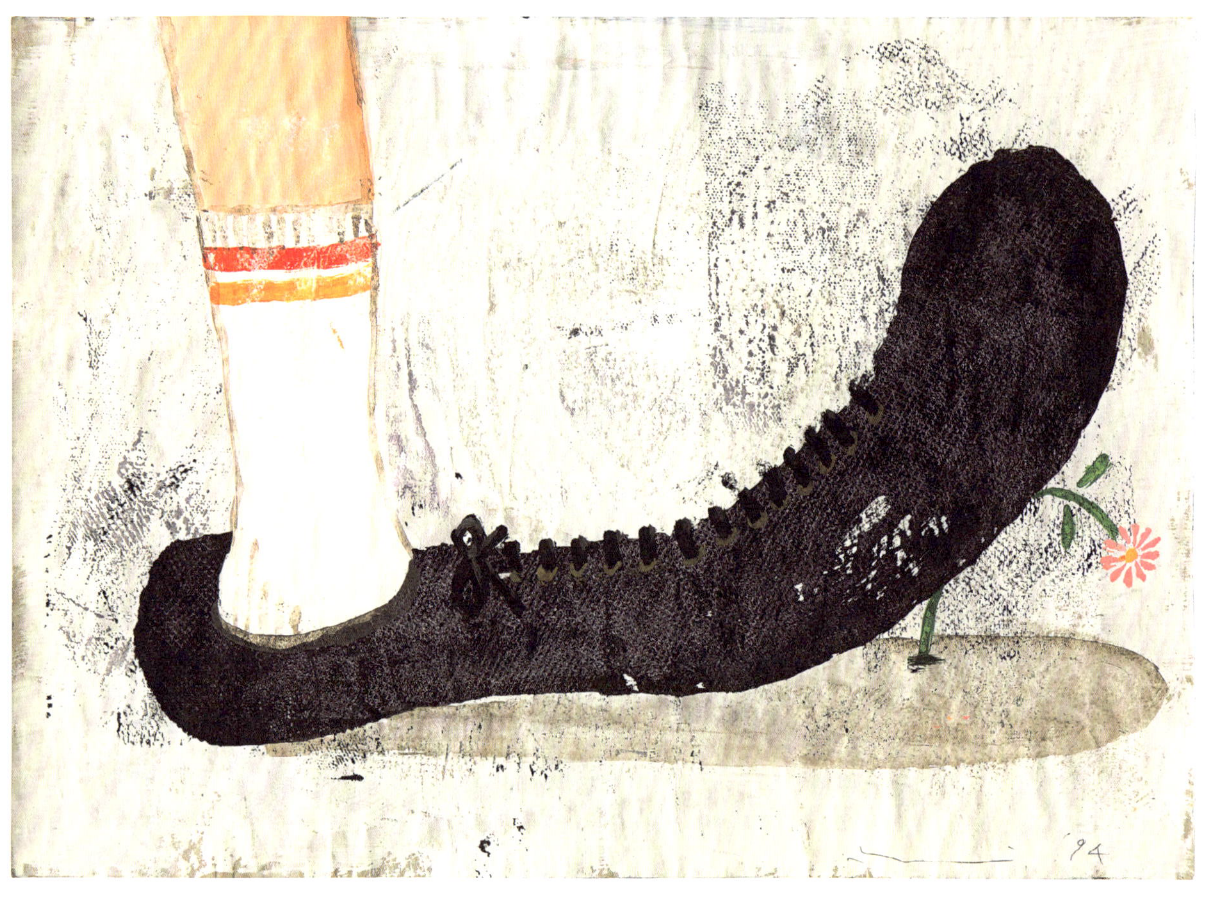

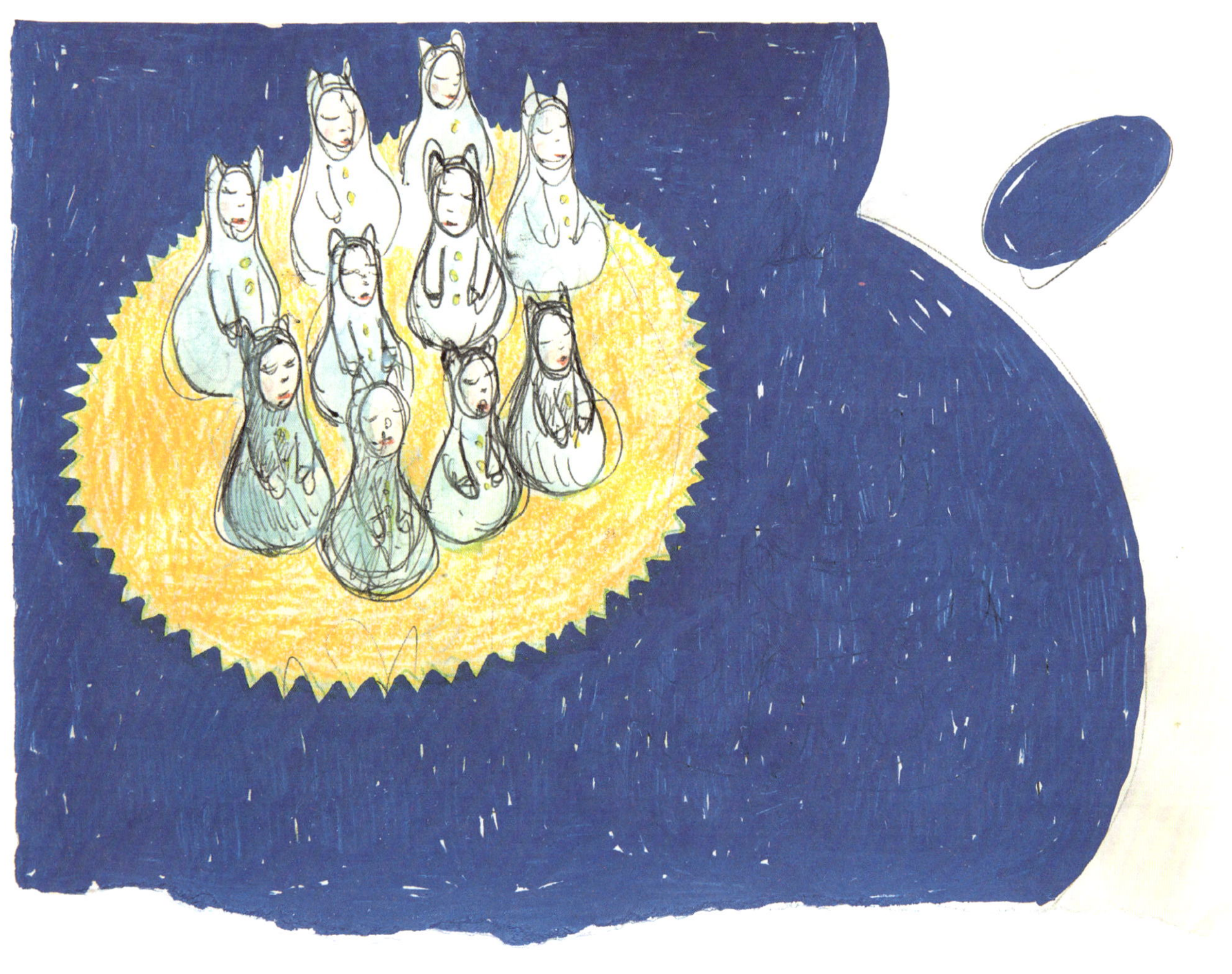

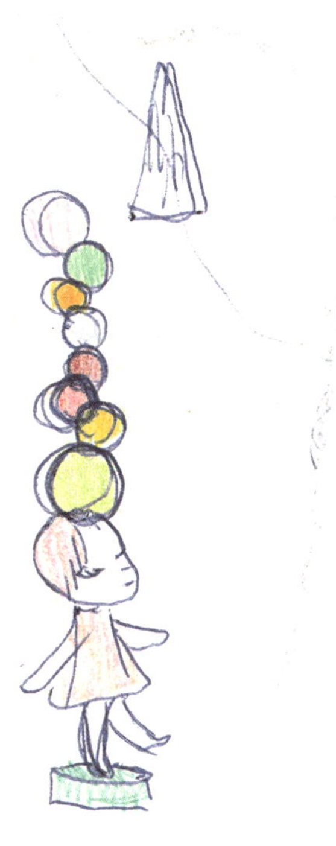

NOBODY'S FOOL

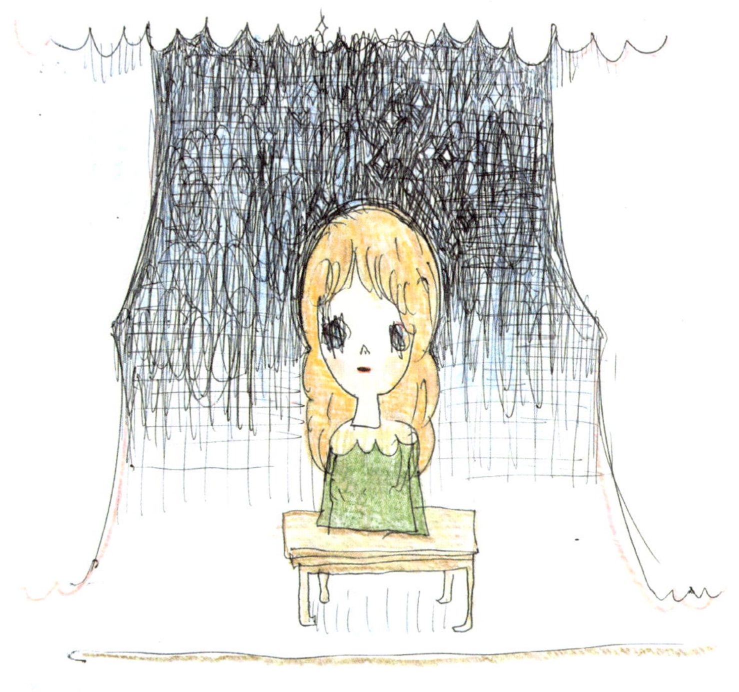

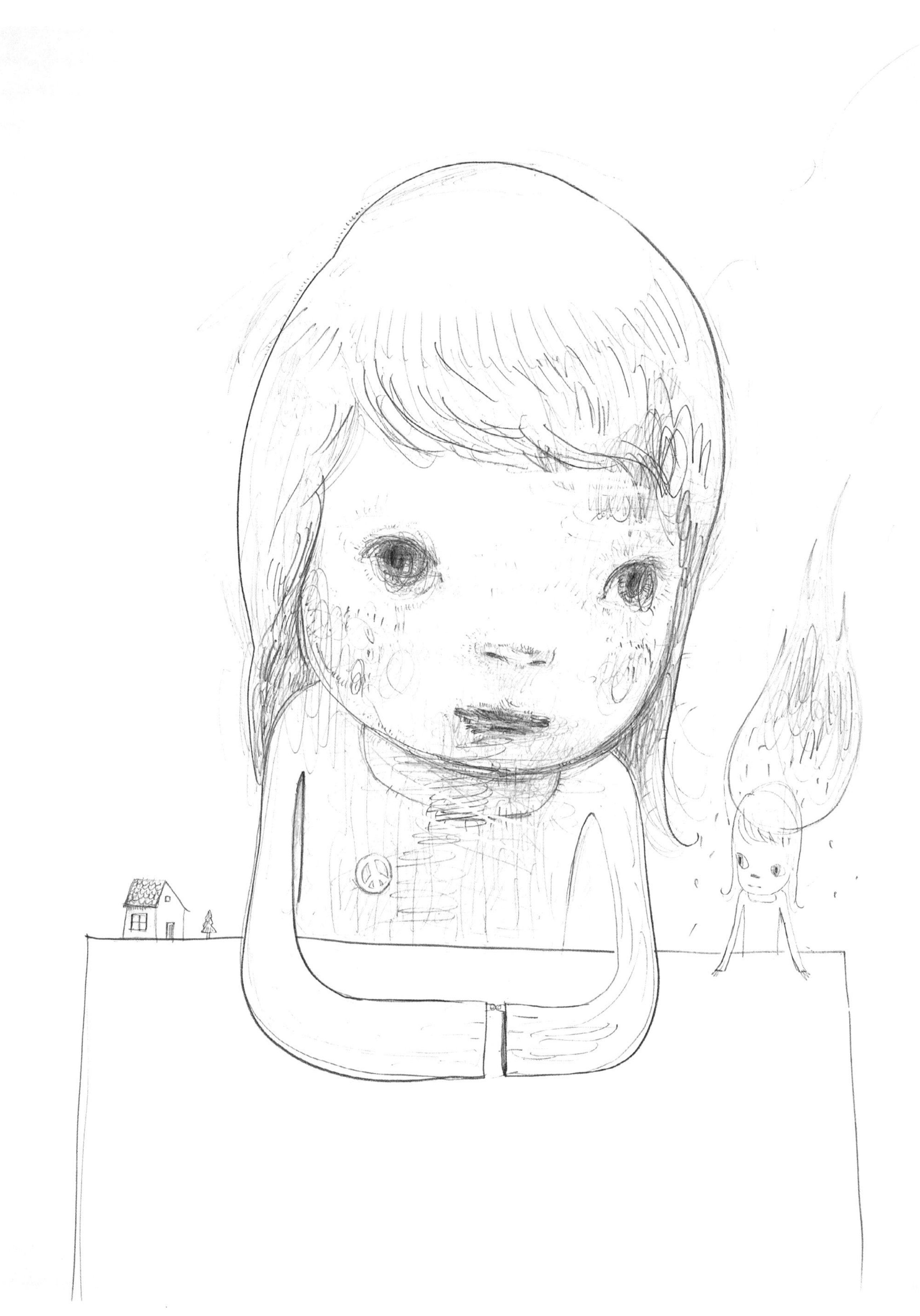

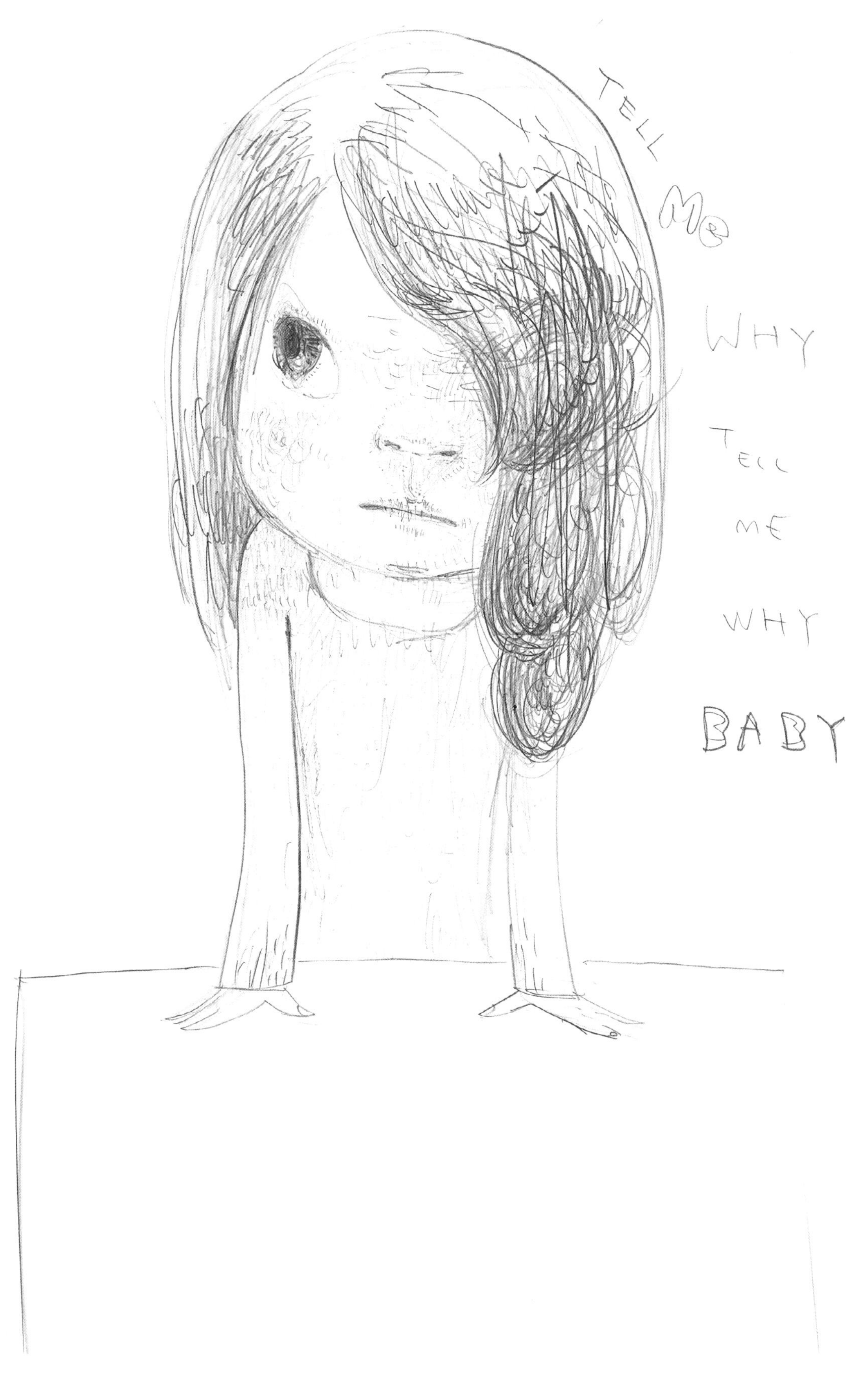
TELL ME
WHY
TELL
ME
WHY
BABY

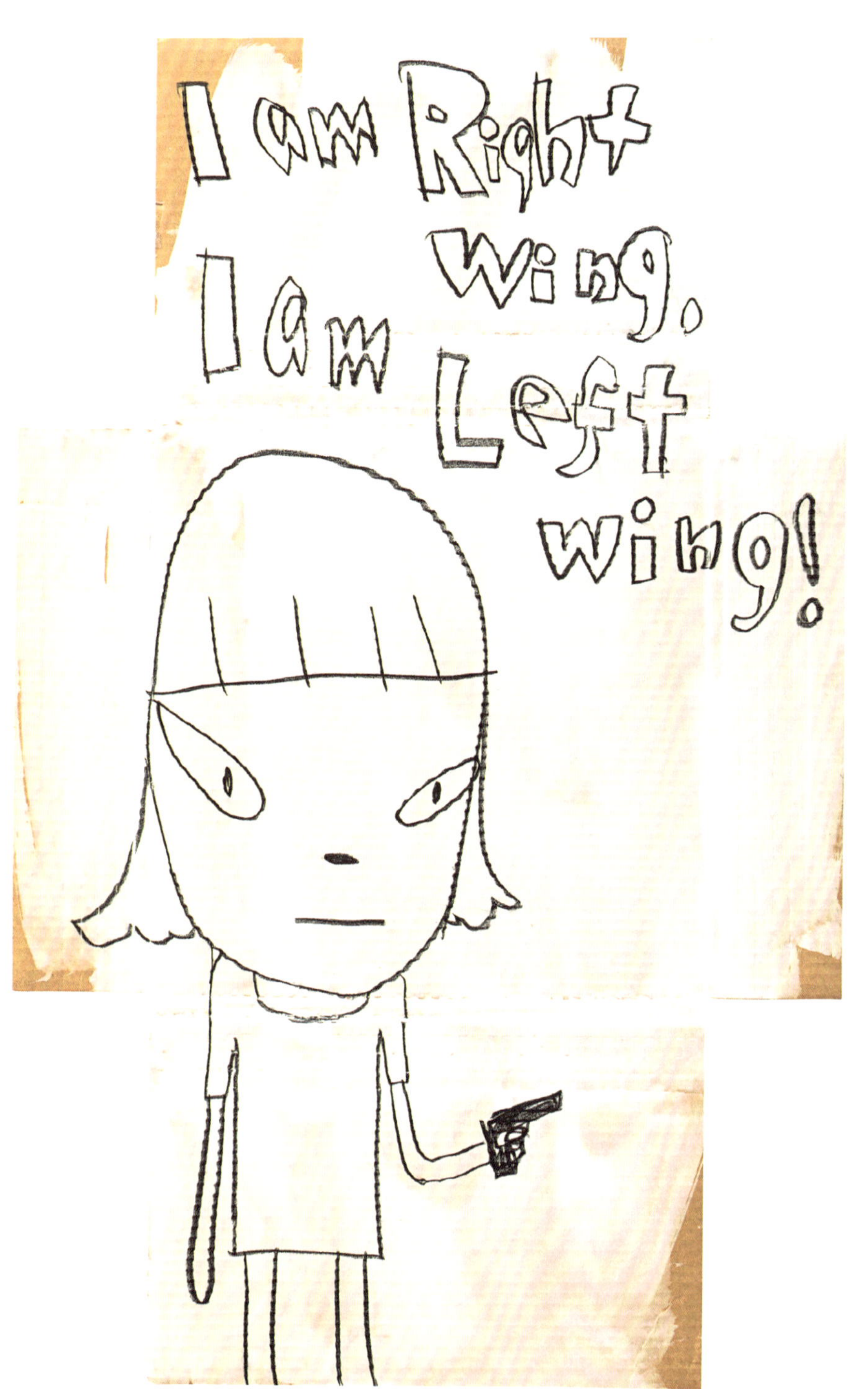
I am Right wing,
I am Left wing!

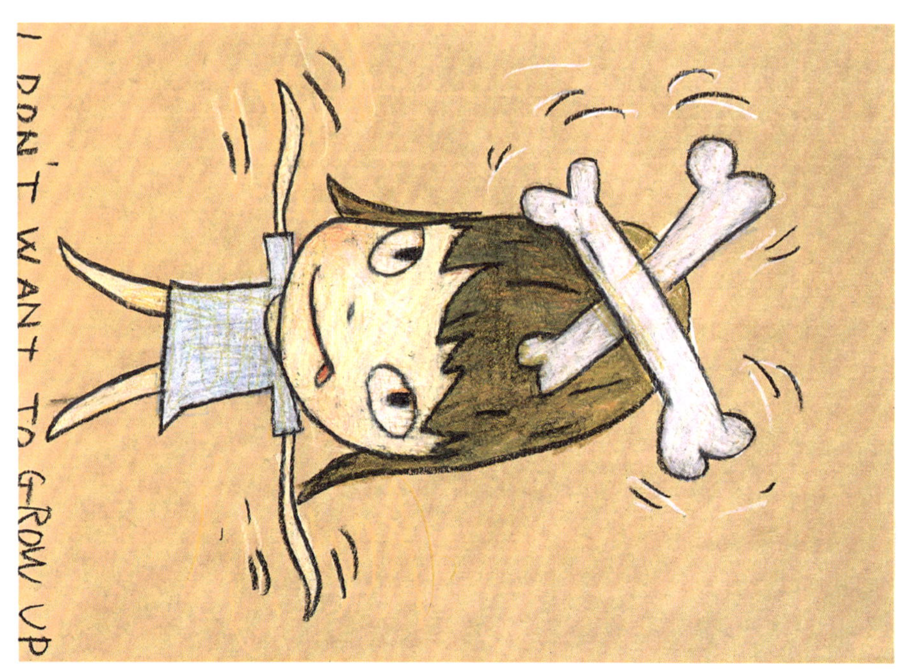
I DON'T WANT TO GROW UP

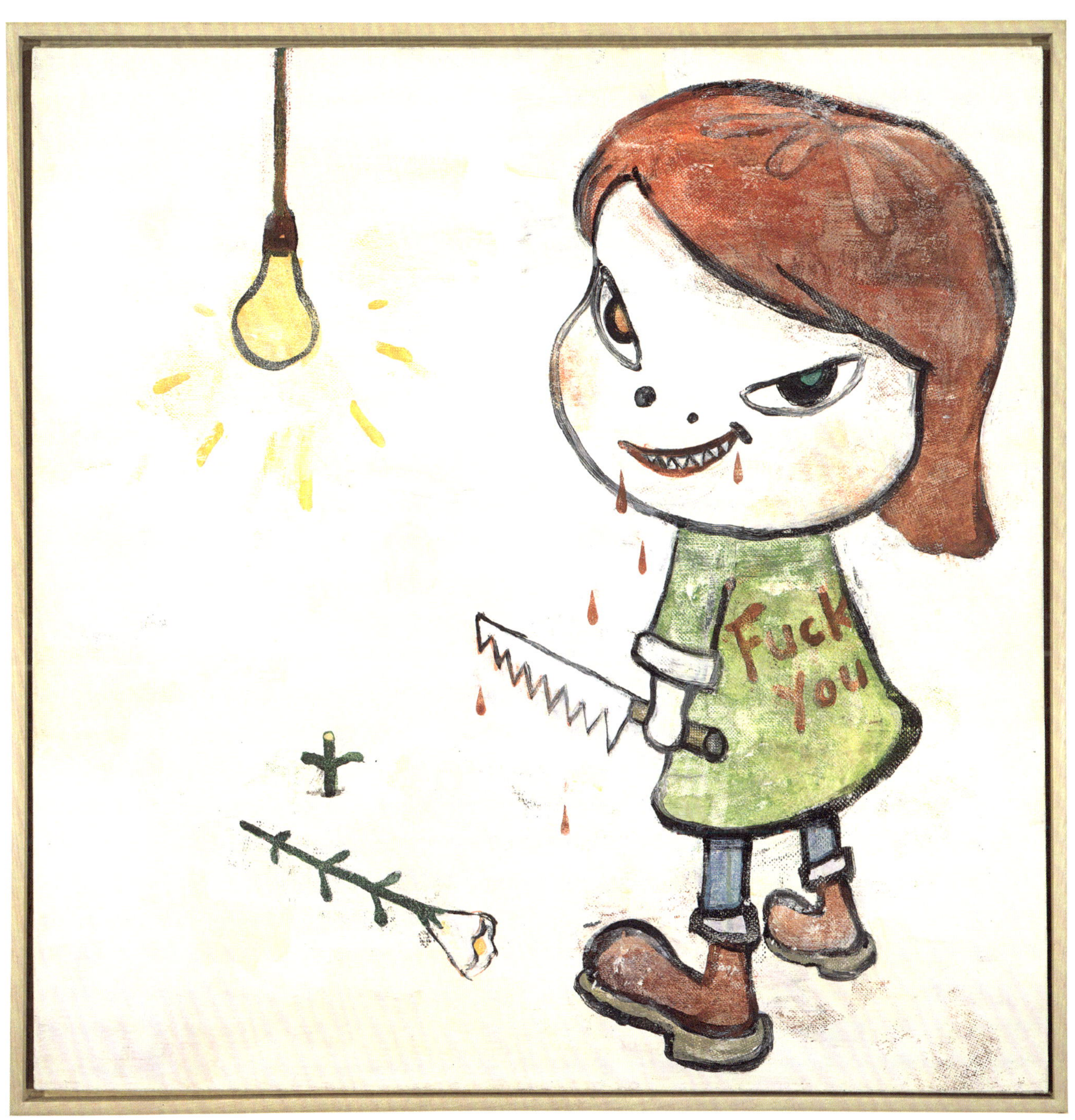
Fuck You

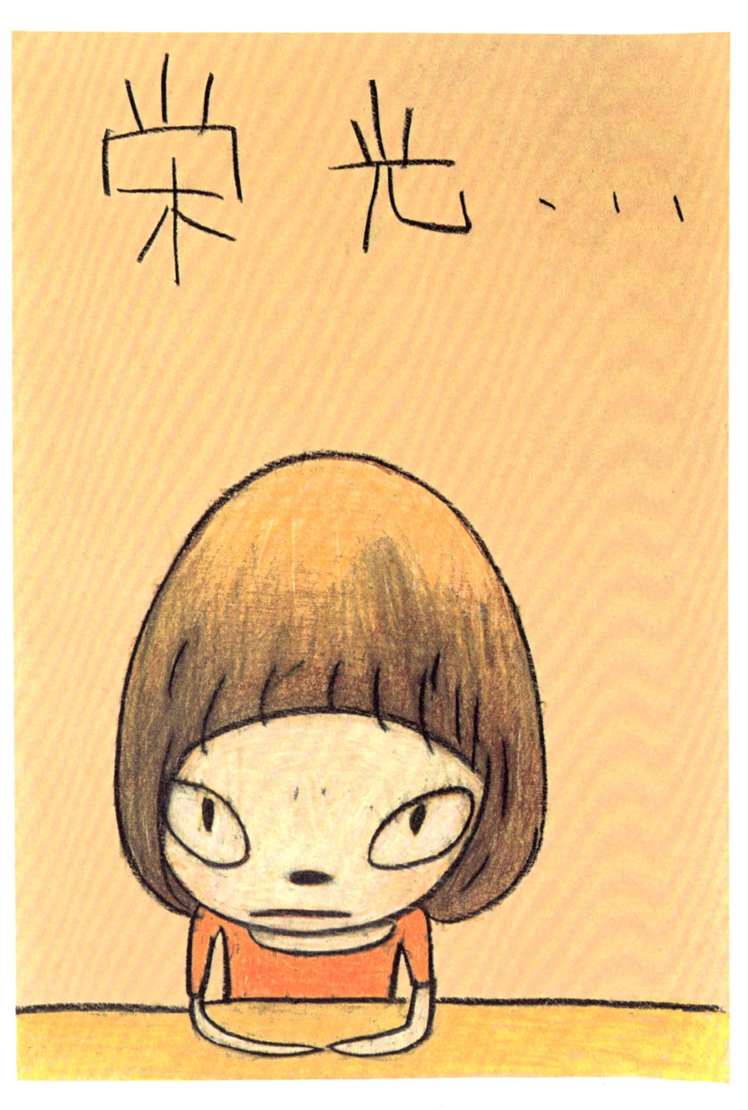
栄光…

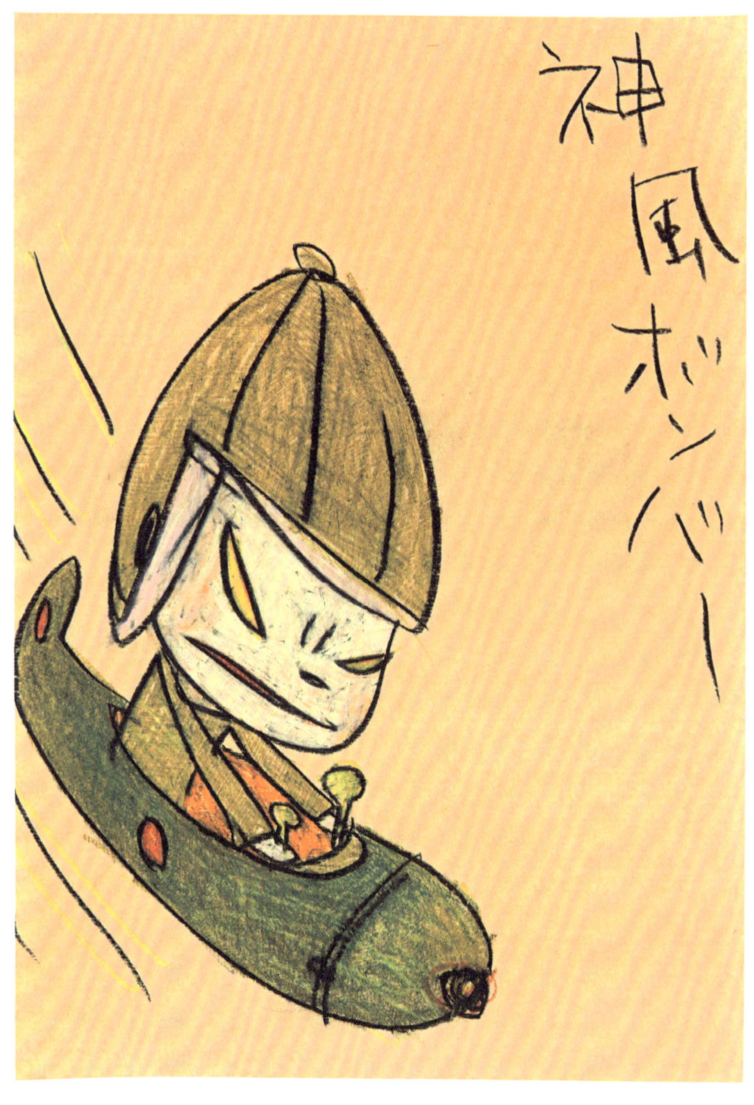
神風ボンバー

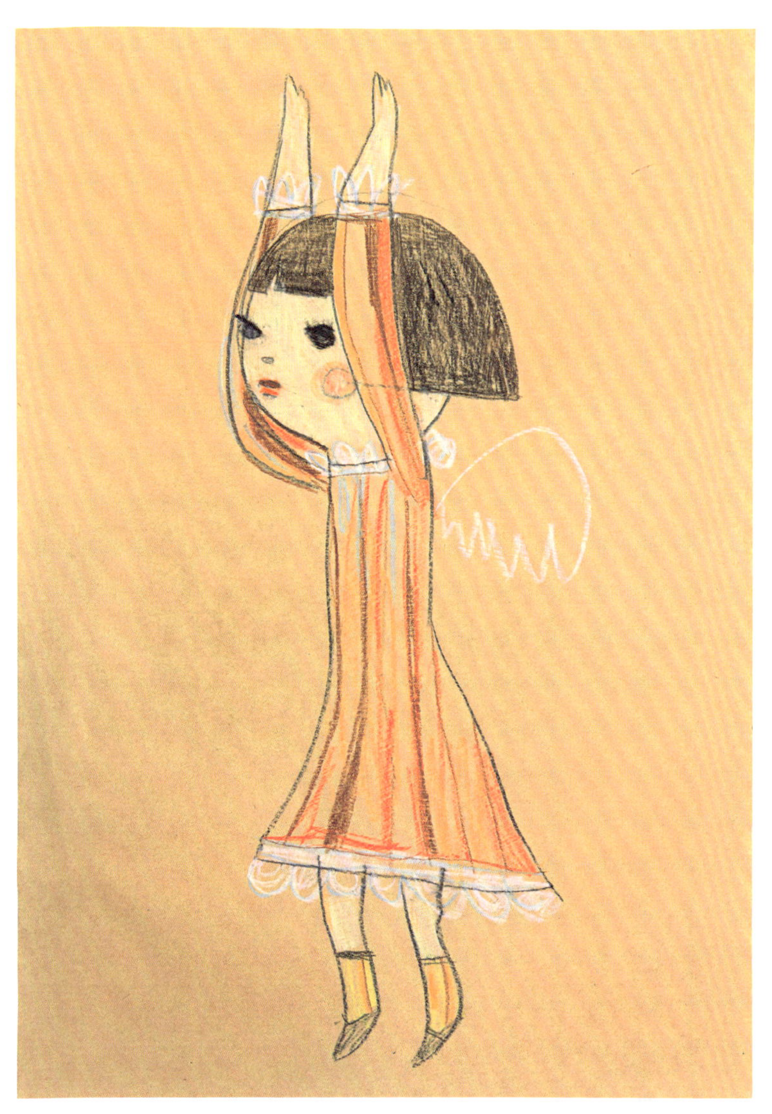

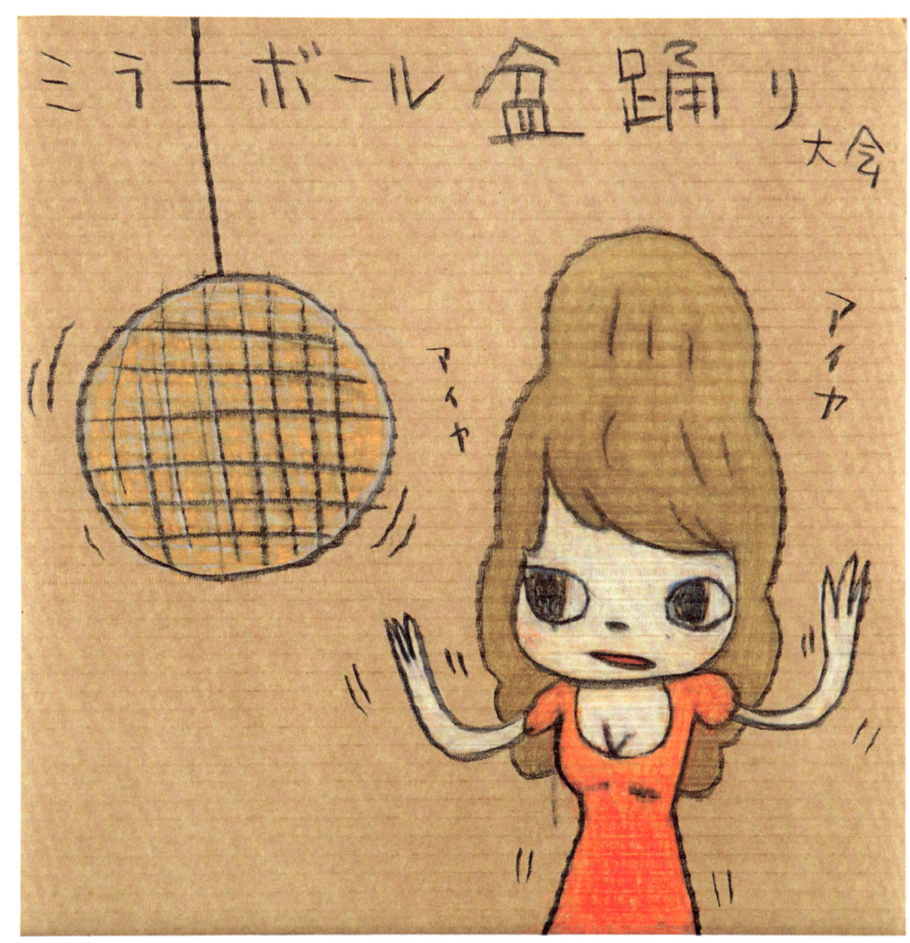
ミラーボール盆踊り
大会
アイヤ
アイヤ

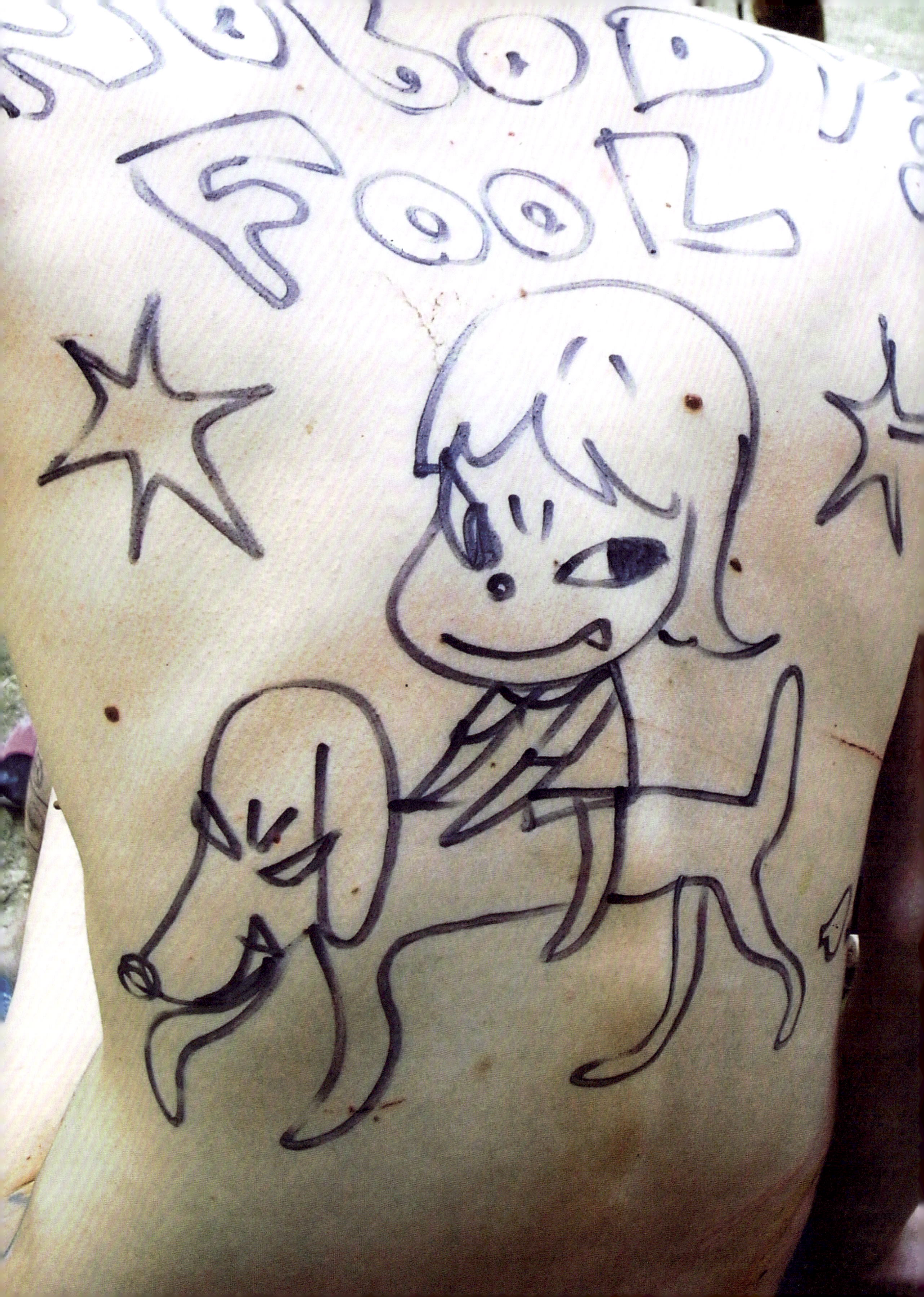
FOOL

XII

MISSING IN ACTION

Untitled, 2010
DON'T FORGET IT., 2012
NOISE, 2010
Untitled, 2010
*FUCK *U*, 2015
E.S.P, 2010
GRIEVOUS ANGEL, 2012
No No No, 2019
I Couldn't Say the Reason Why Tears Fall from the Eyes Now, 1988
Drawing for *Hard-boiled/Hard Luck*, 1999
One Foot in the Groove, 2012
Untitled, 2004
Miss Forest/Creamy Snow, 2016
Hula Hula Dancing, 1998
Missing in Action, 1999
Harmless Kitty, 1994
Daydreamer, 2003
Fountain of Life, 2001/2014

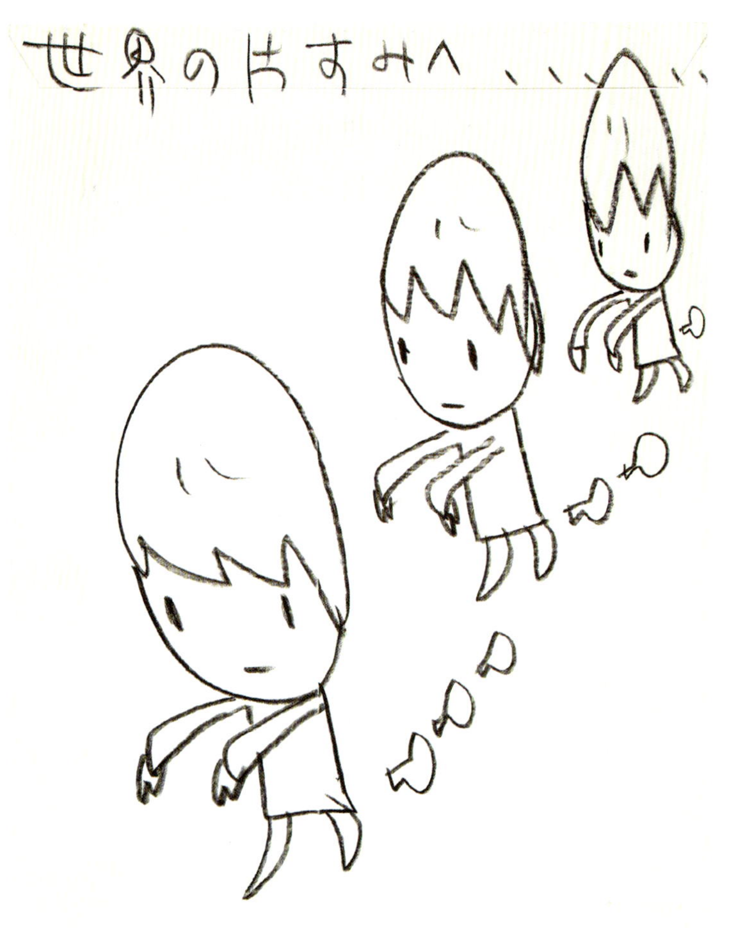
世界の片すみへ、、、、、

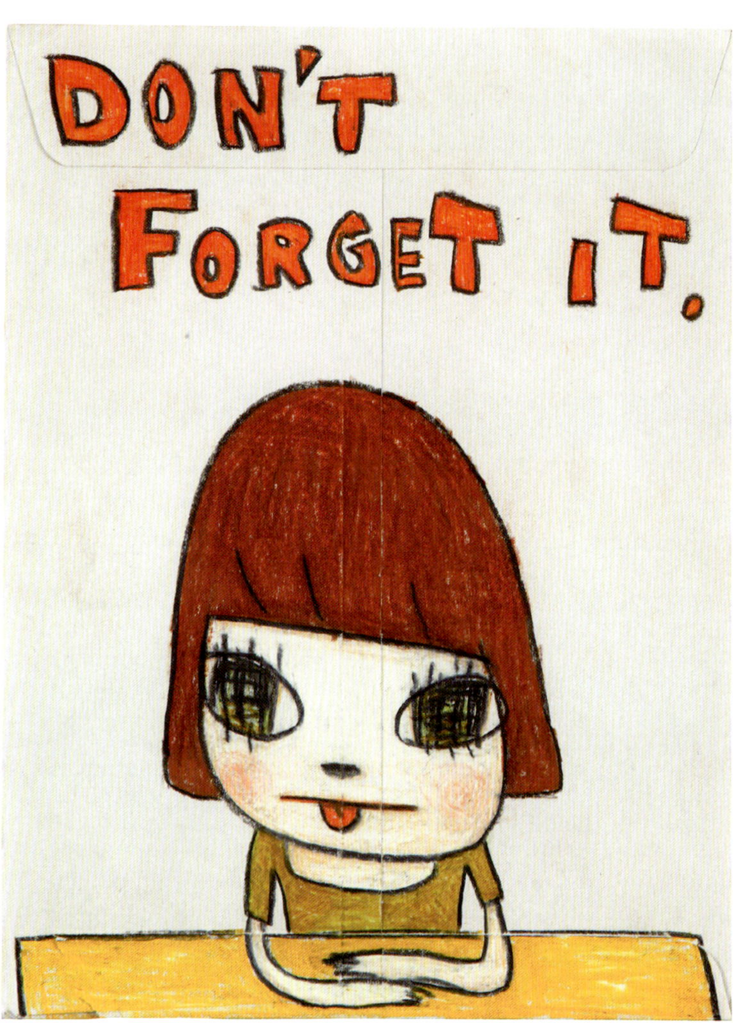
DON'T
FORGET IT.

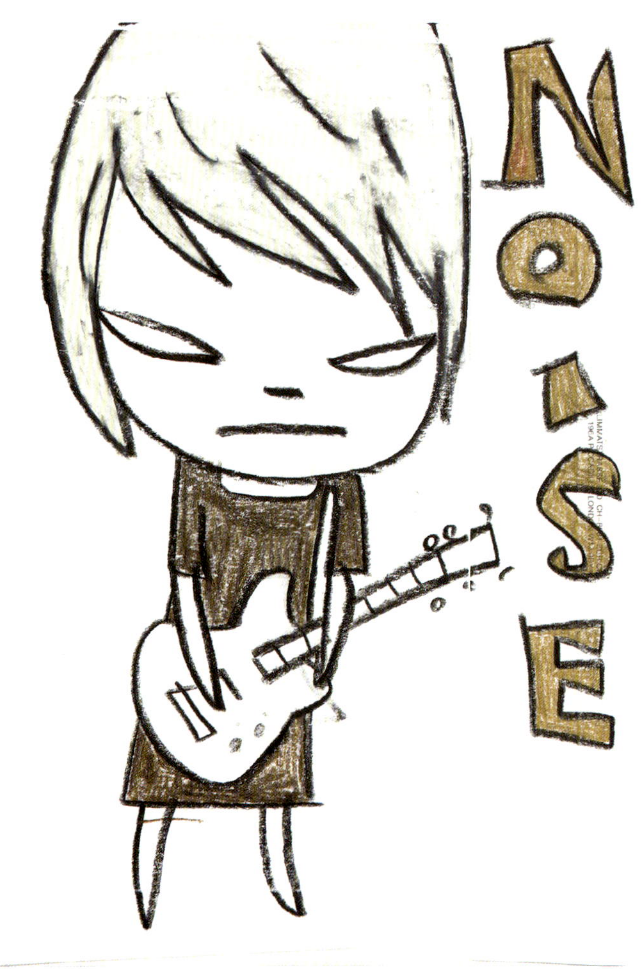
NOISE

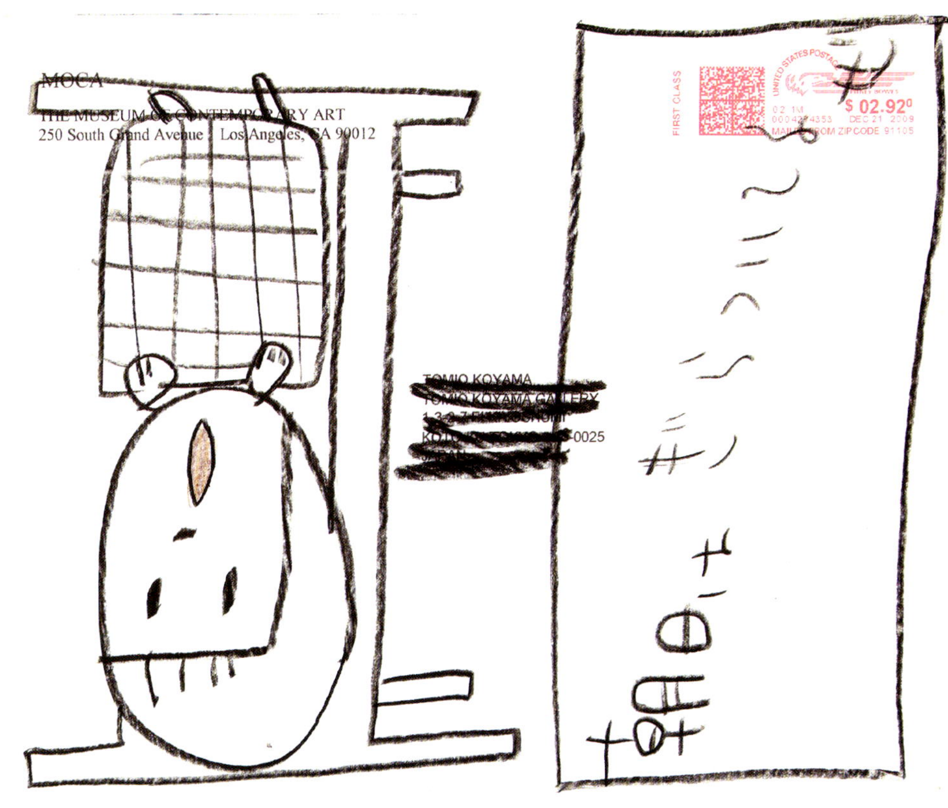
MOCA
THE MUSEUM OF CONTEMPORARY ART
250 South Grand Avenue Los Angeles, CA 90012
FIRST CLASS
$ 02.92⁰
TOMIO KOYAMA
TOMIO KOYAMA GALLERY

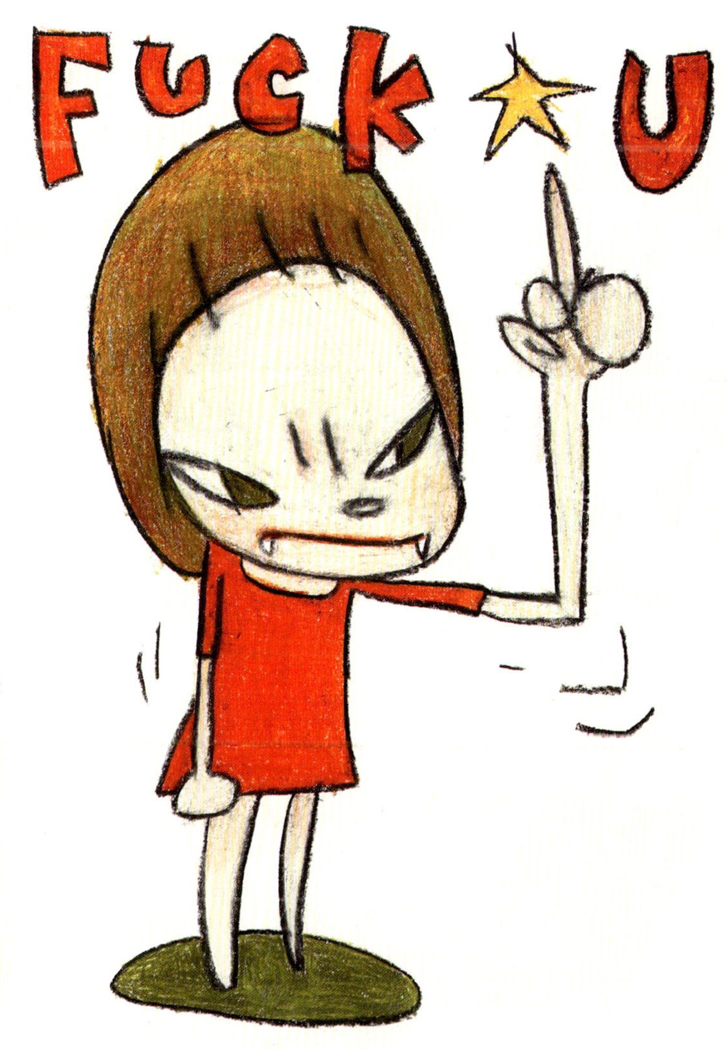
FUCK ★ U

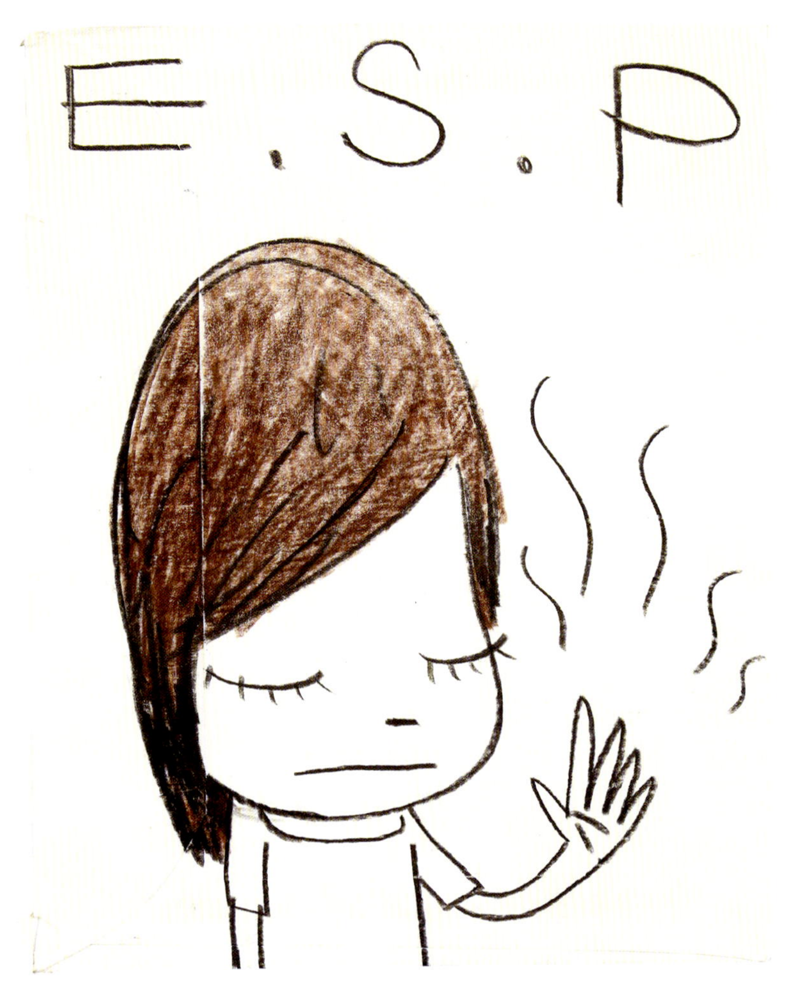

GRIEVOUS ANGEL

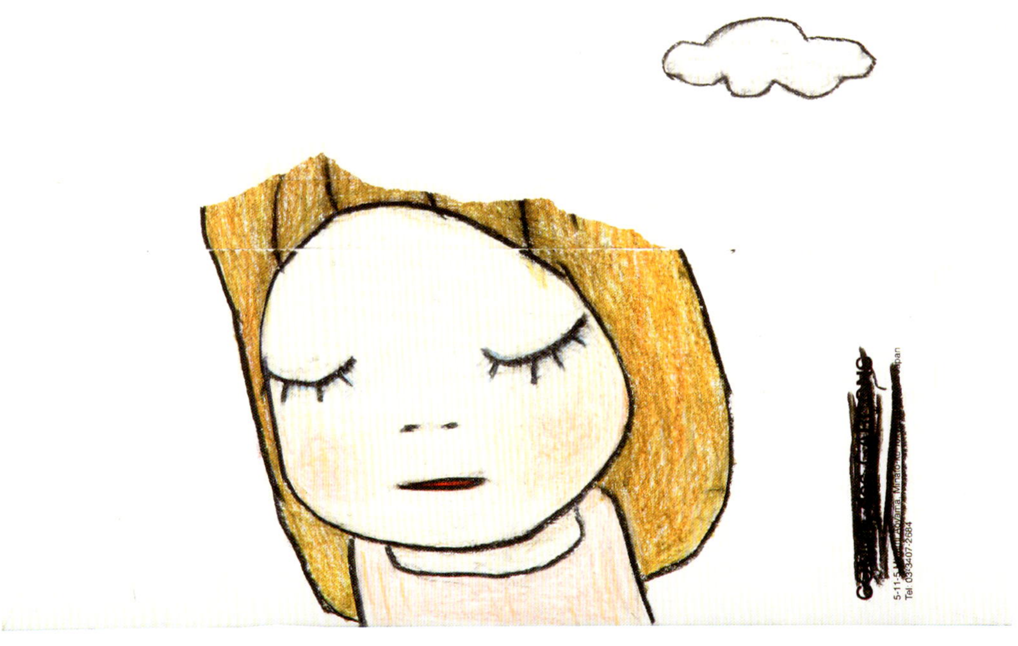

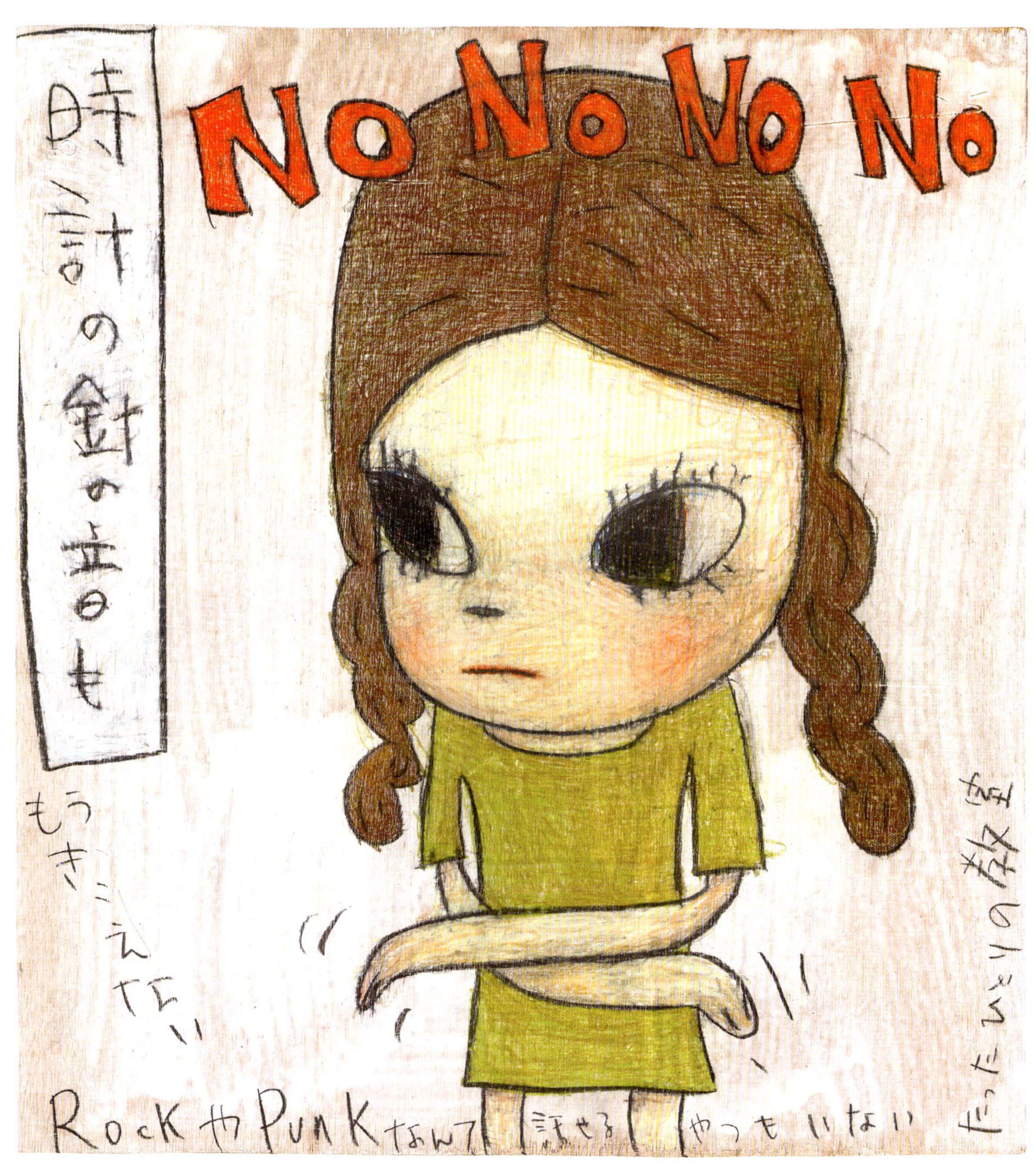
NO NO NO NO
時計の針の音も
もうきこえない
ROCK や PUNK なんて 話せる やつも いない
たったひとりの教室

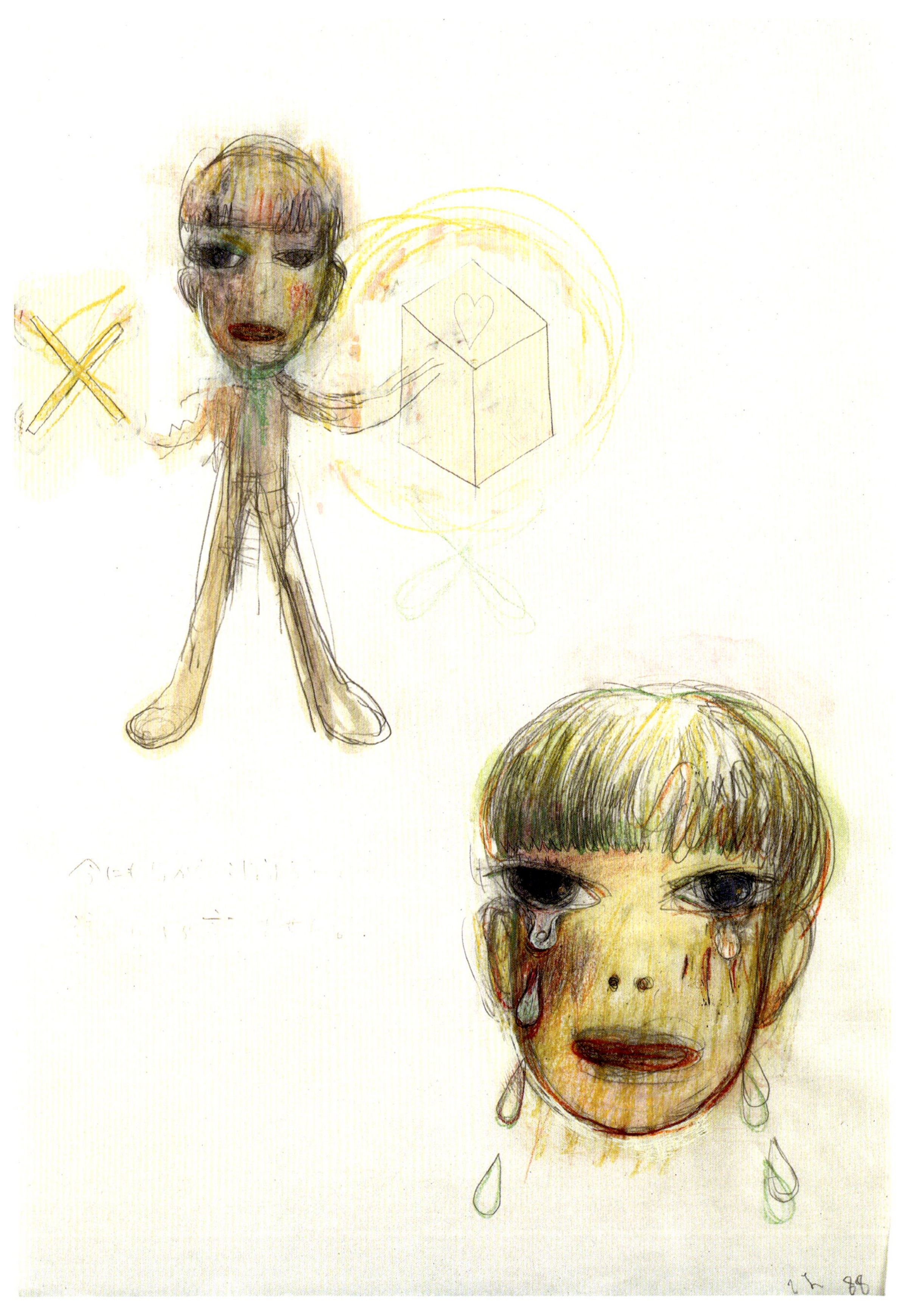

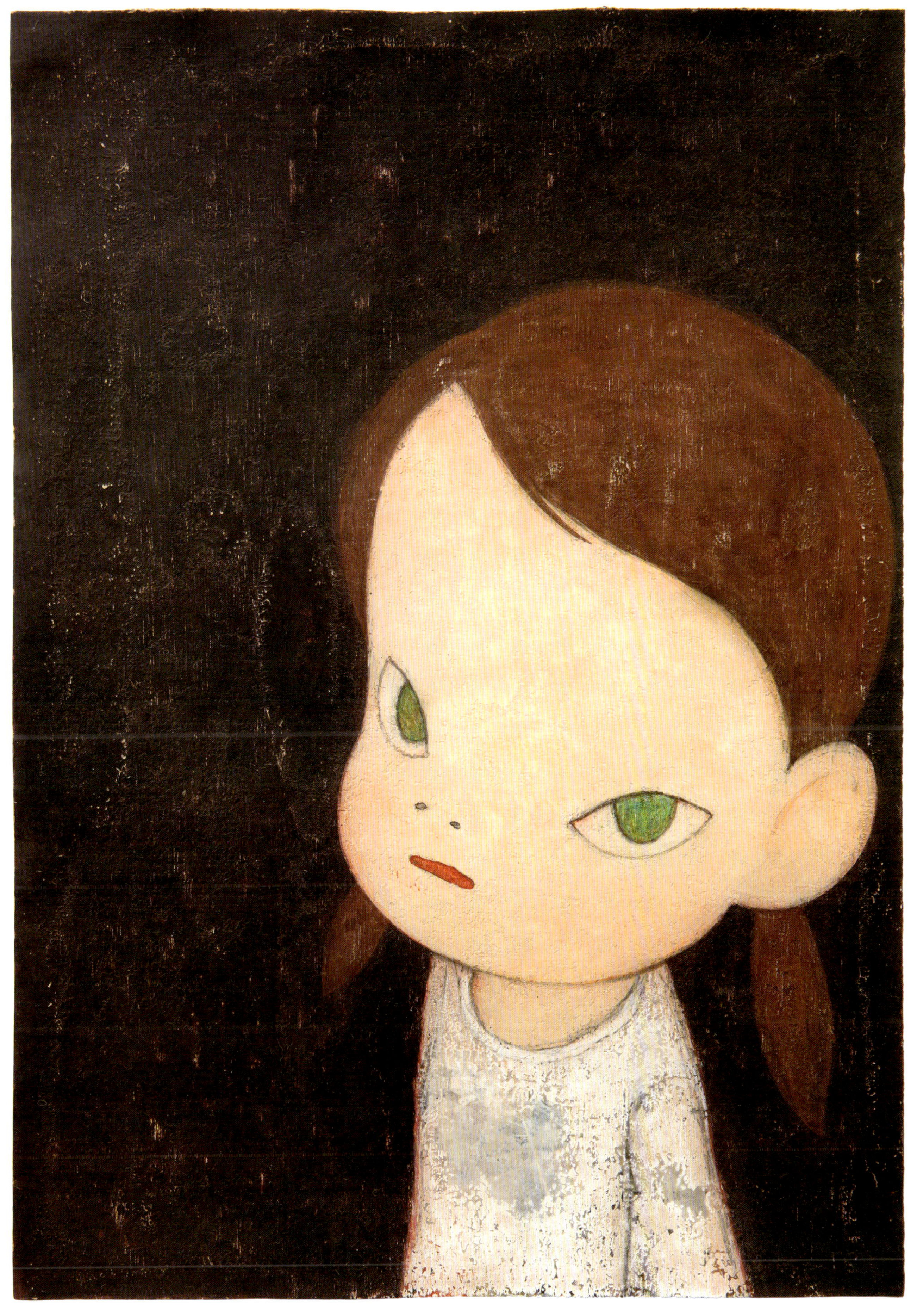

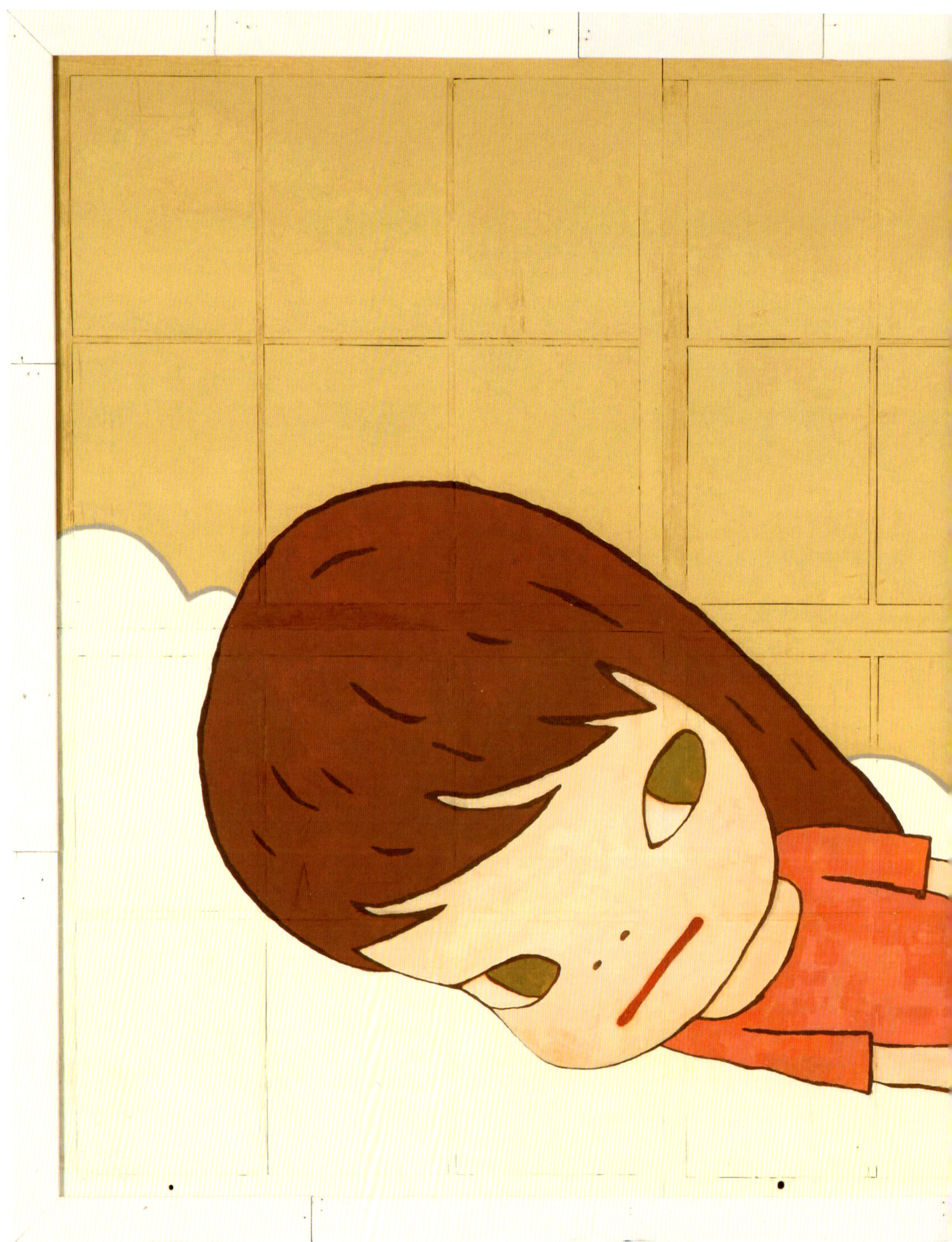

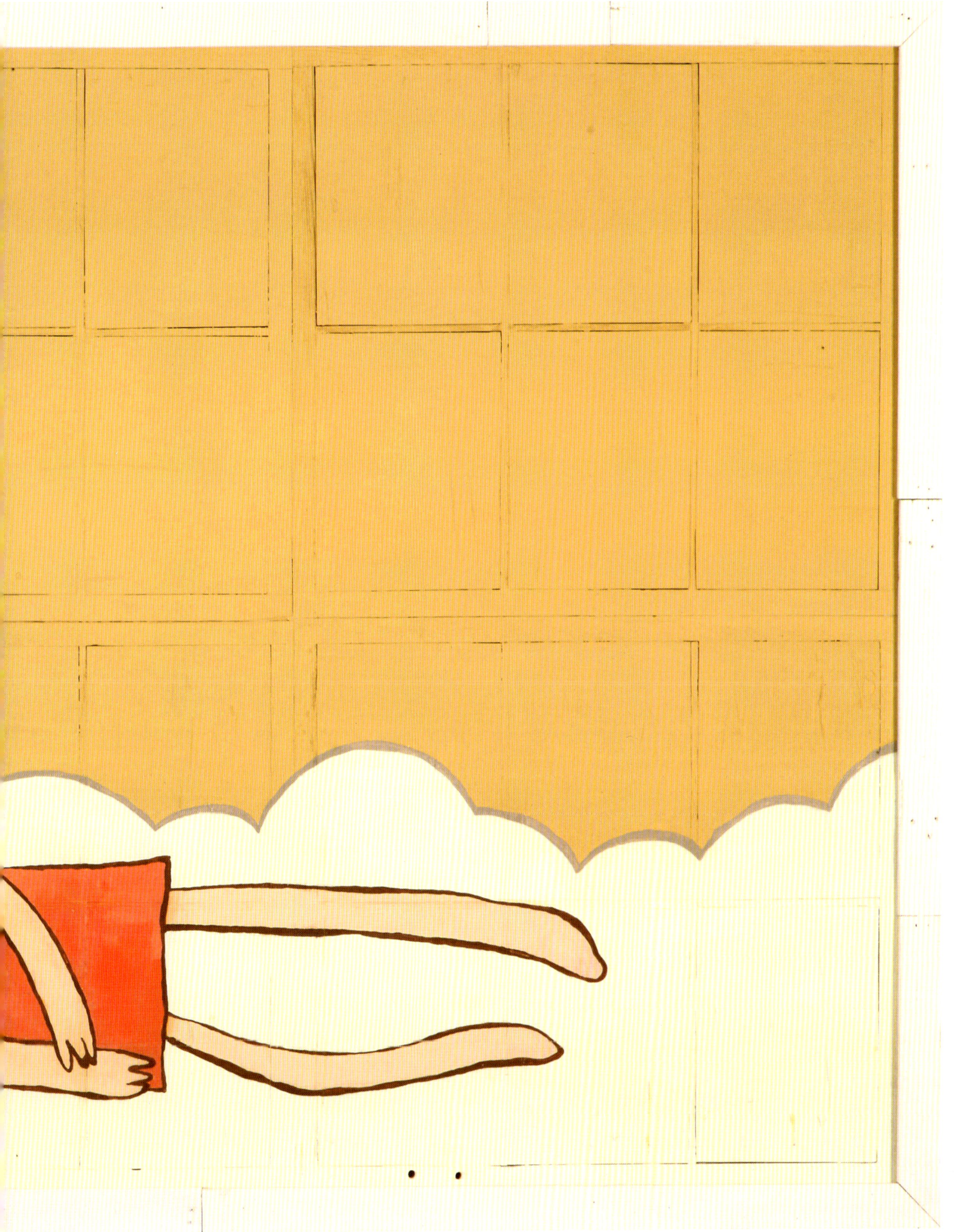

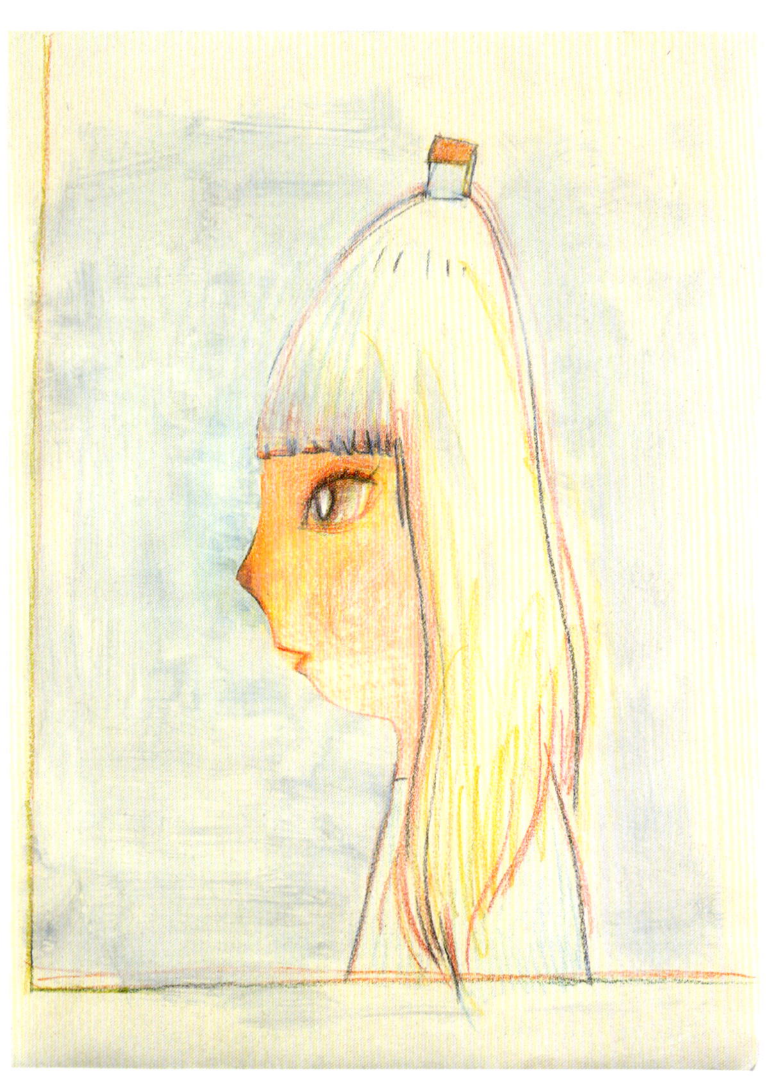

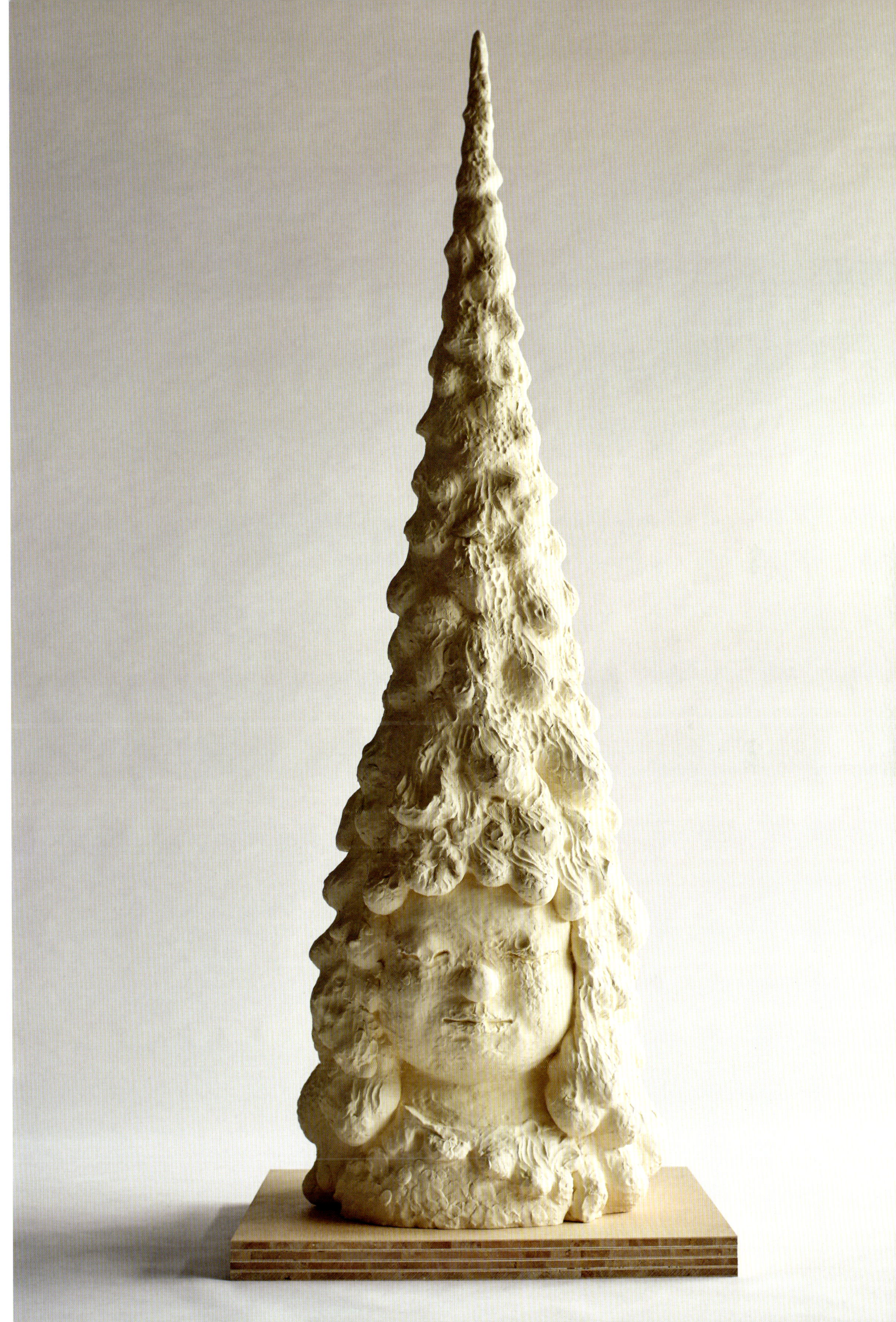

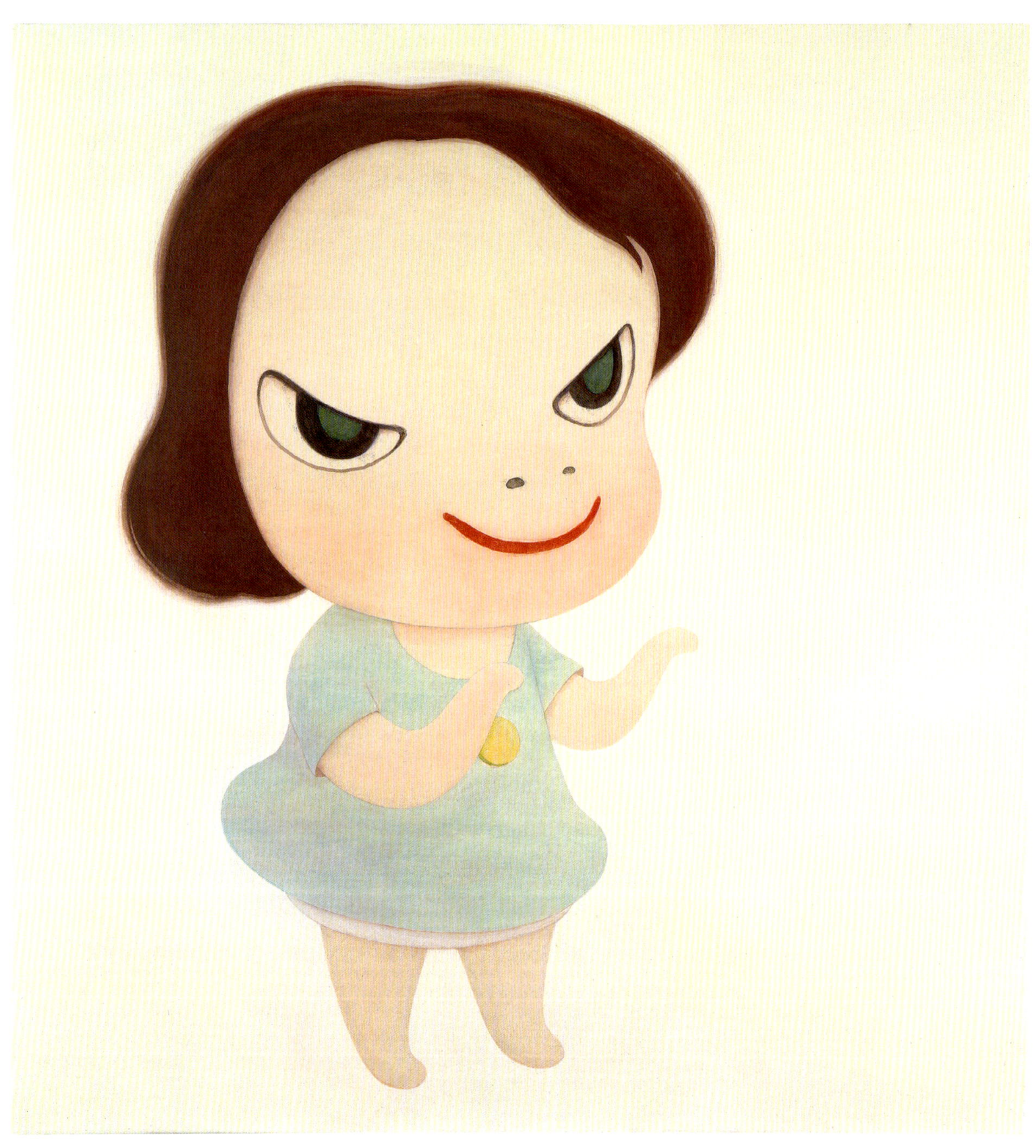

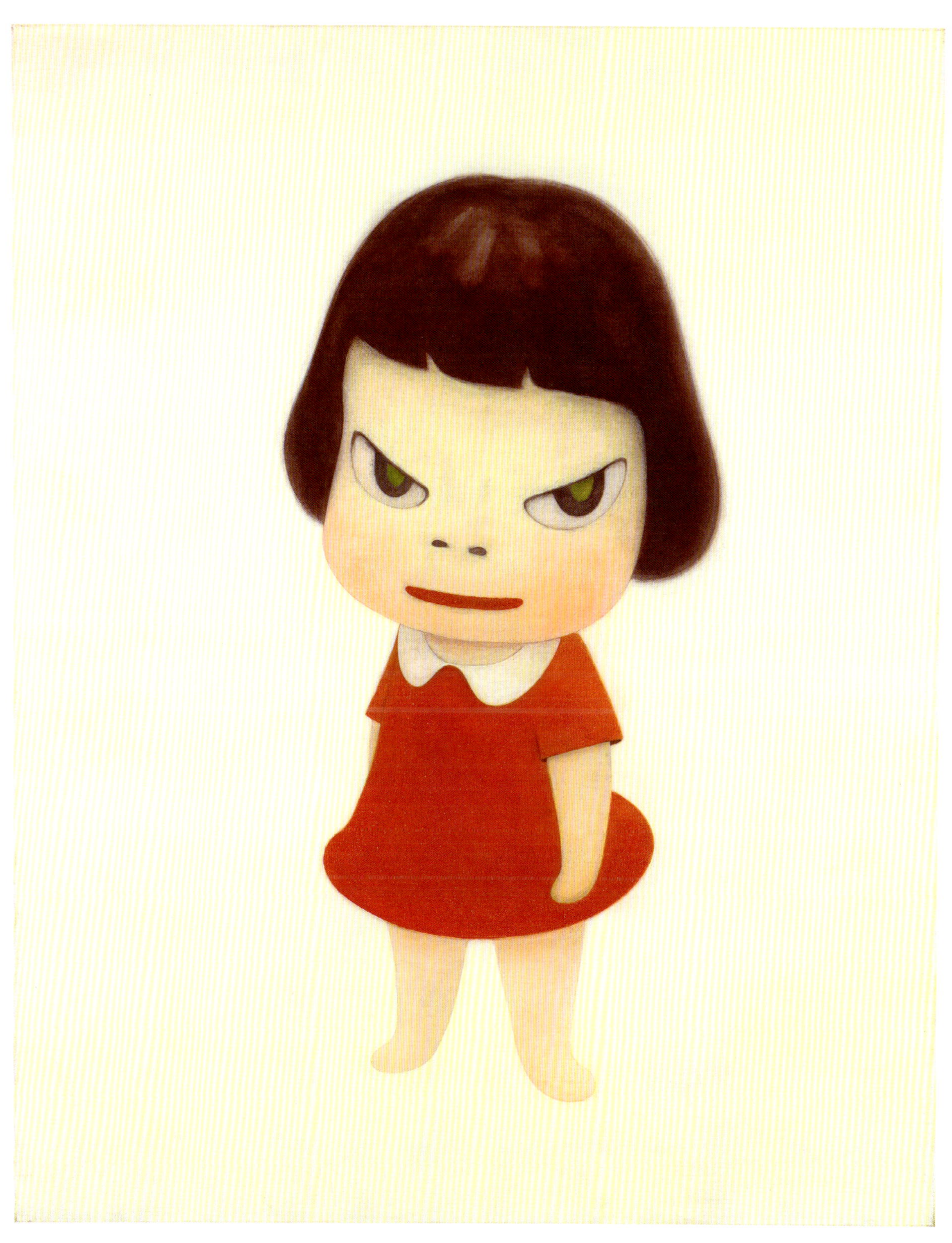

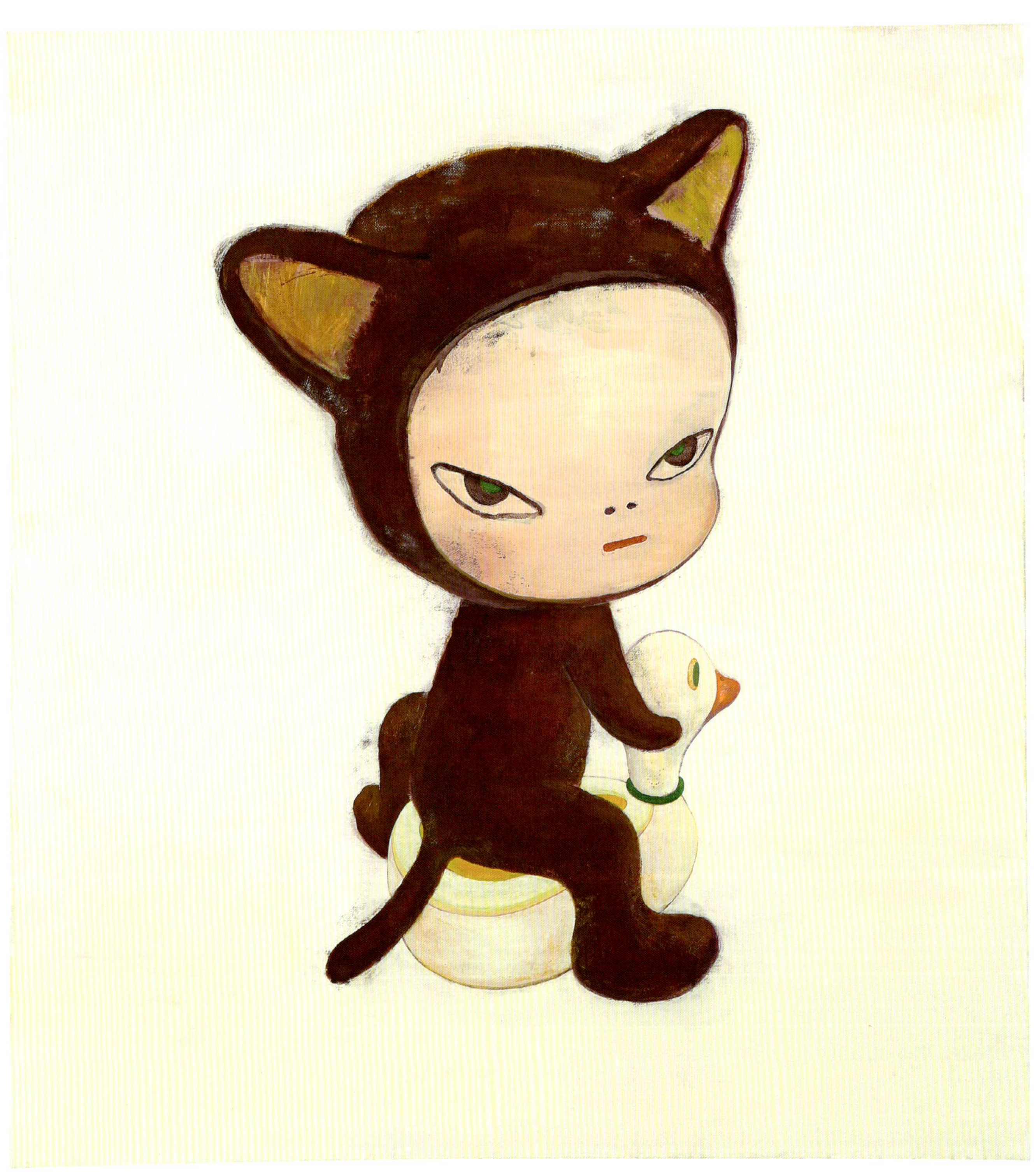

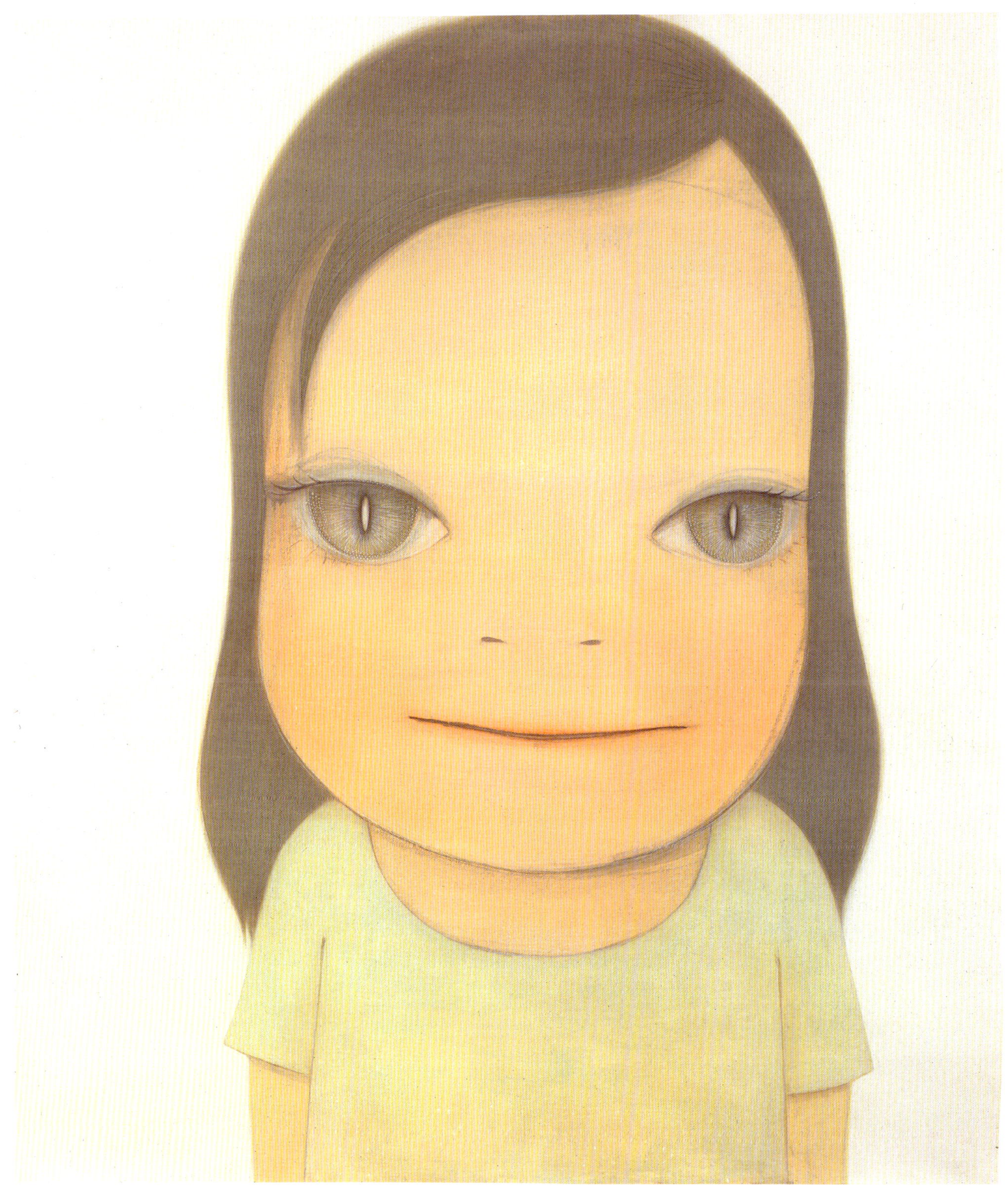

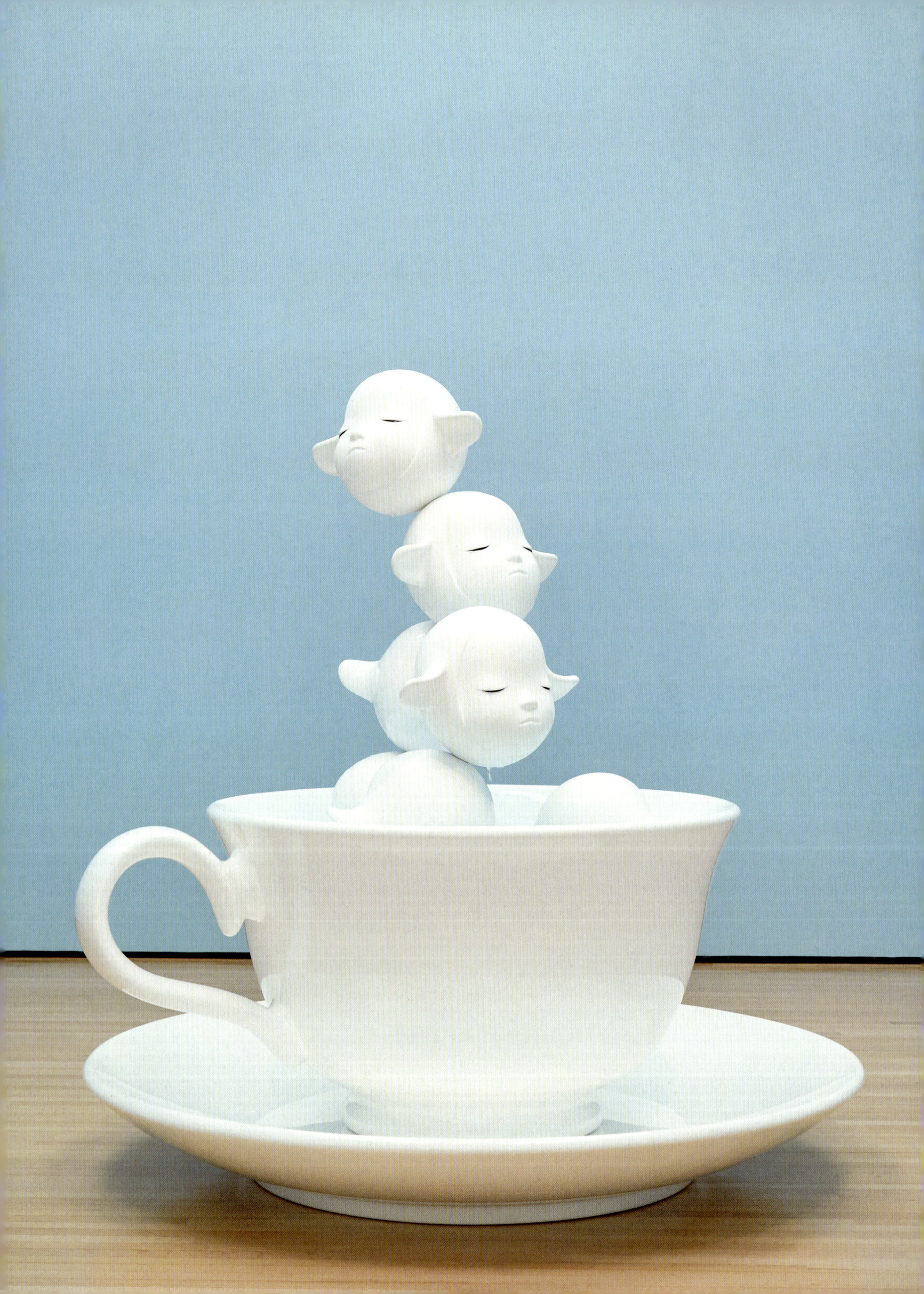

WILLST DU WIRKLICH IMMER HIPPIE BLEIBEN?

Untitled, 2004
Untitled, 2003
Untitled, 2005
Untitled, 2005
Untitled, 2005
Untitled, 2004
Willst du wirklich immer Hippie bleiben?, 2006
Für immer tot möchte ich sein. Leg mich in das Grab hinein., 2006
Untitled, 2006
Untitled, 2006
Untitled, 2005
Dream Time, 2011
Untitled, 2007
Untitled, 2008
Sleepless Night, Sleepless Night, Dream of Teacher, 1989
Untitled, 1988
Untitled, 2002
Untitled, 2002
Untitled, 2002

Do you remember lyin' in bed
with the covers pulled up over you
Radio playin' so no one to see

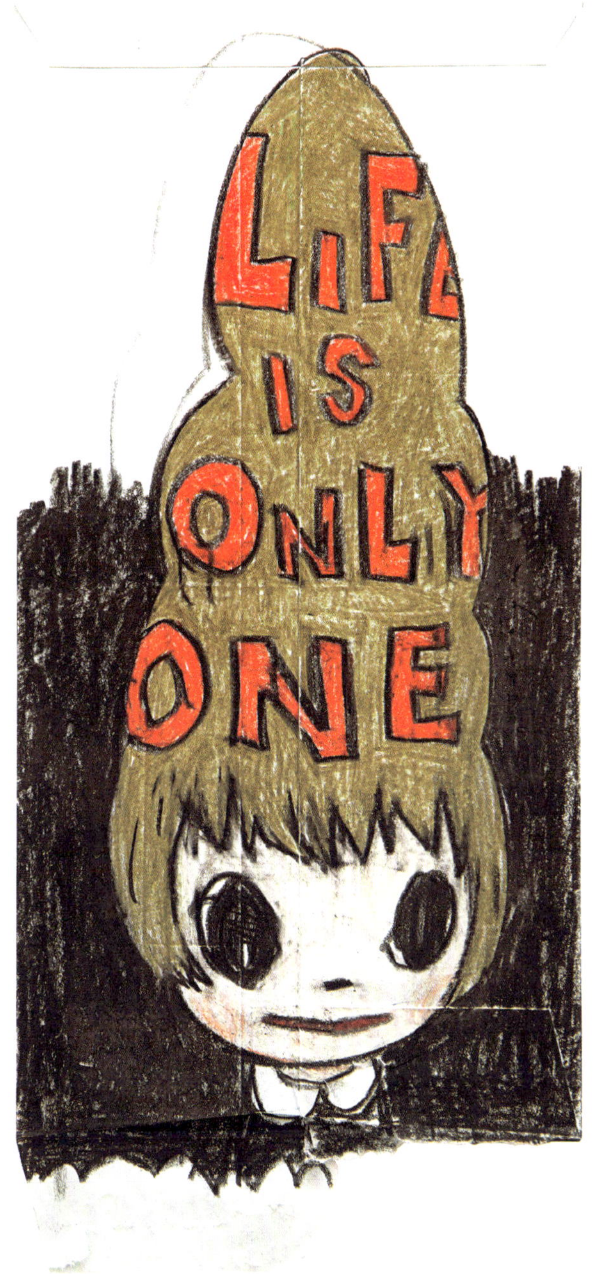
LIFE
IS
ONLY
ONE

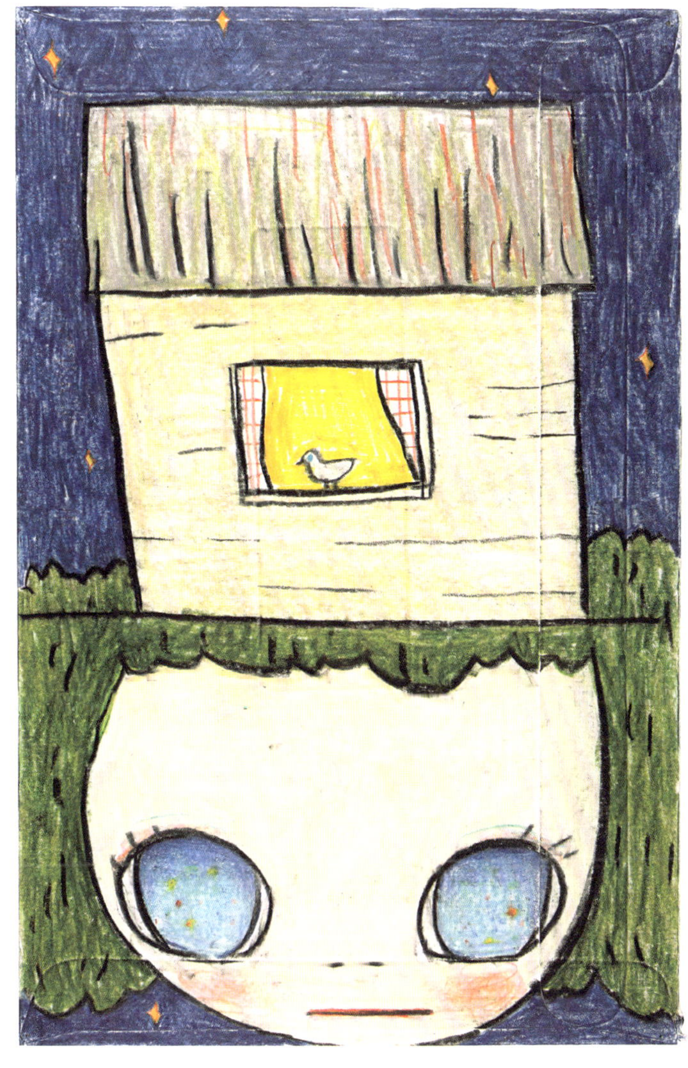

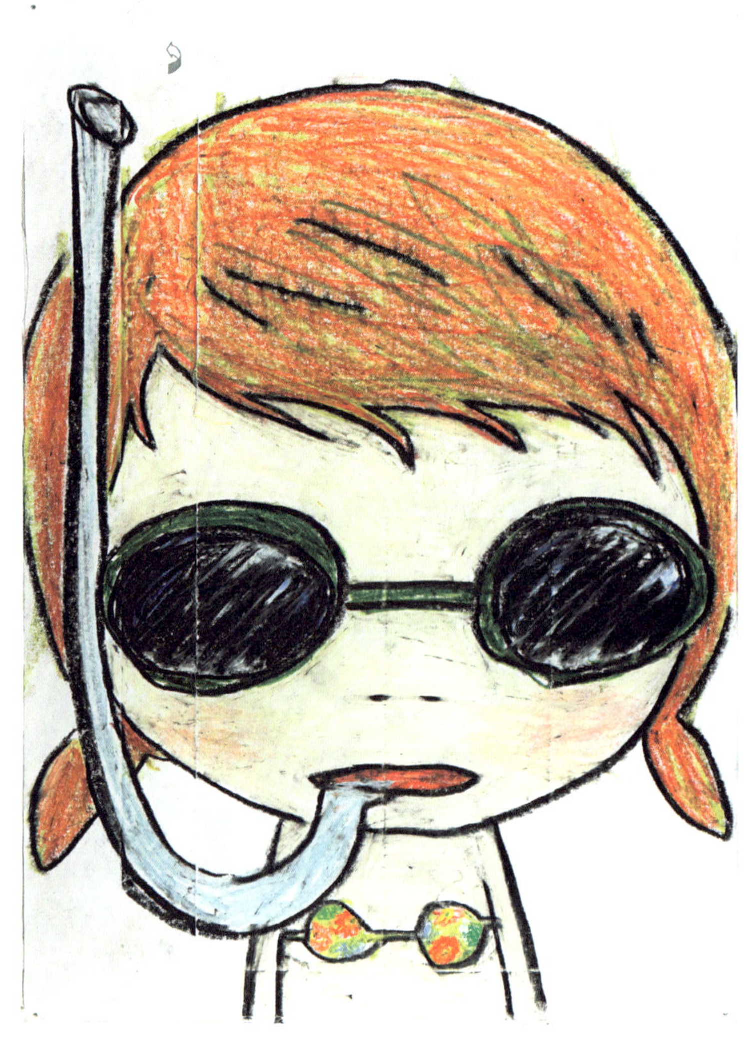

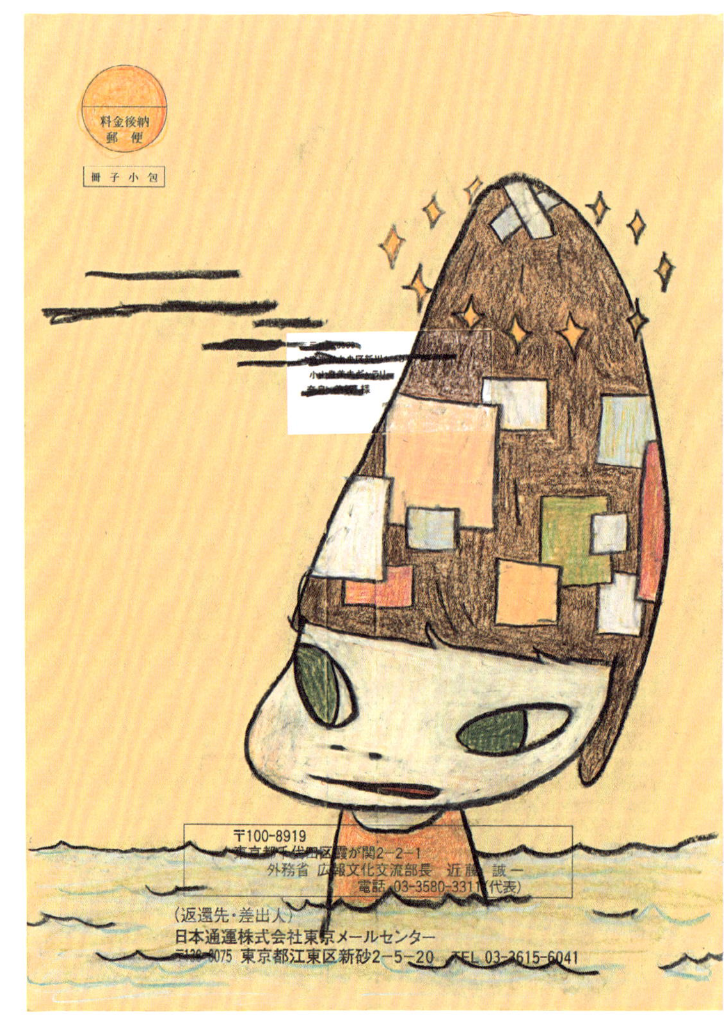
料金後納
郵便
冊子小包
〒100-8919
外務省 広報文化交流部長
(返還先・差出人)
日本通運株式会社東京メールセンター
東京都江東区新砂2-5-20

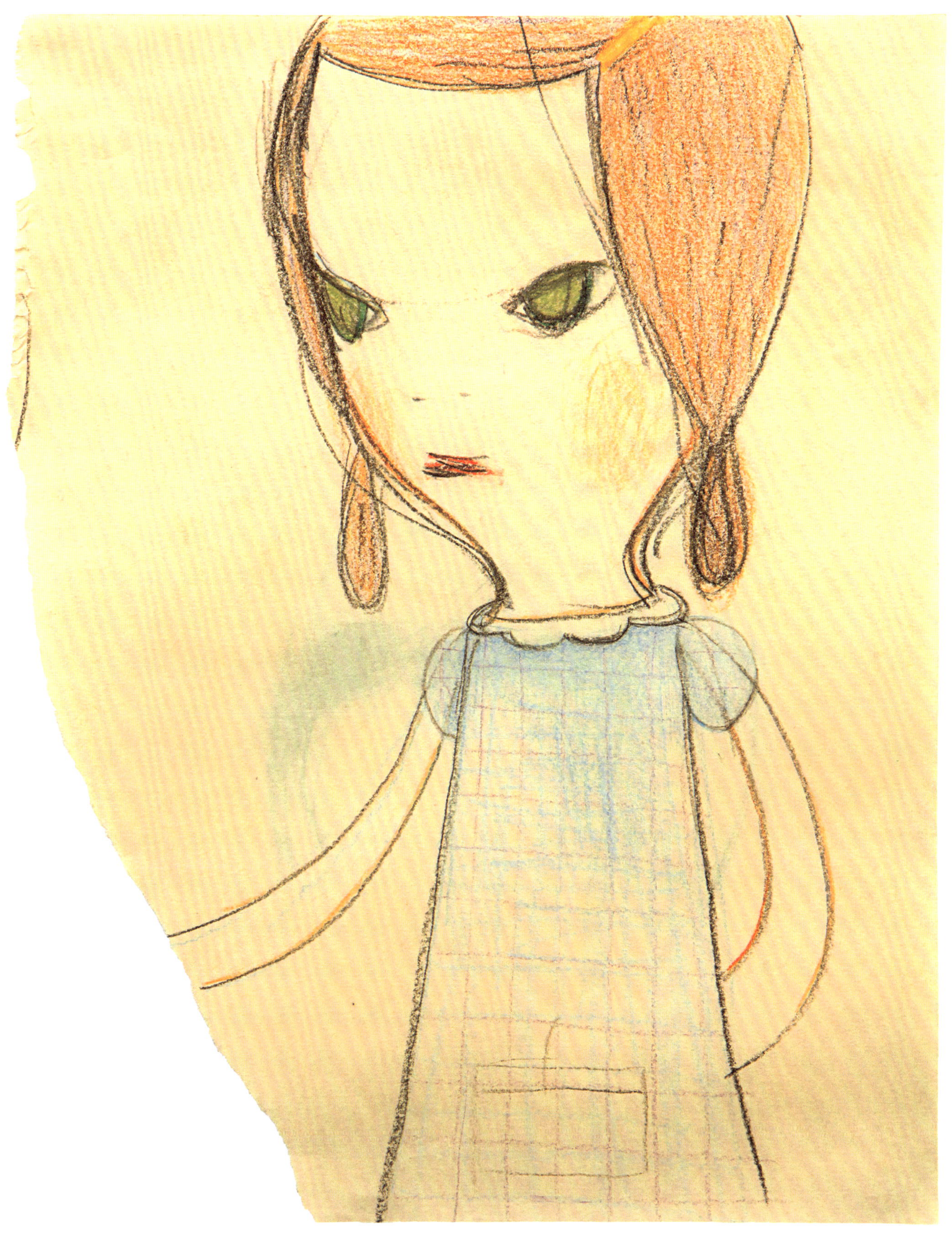

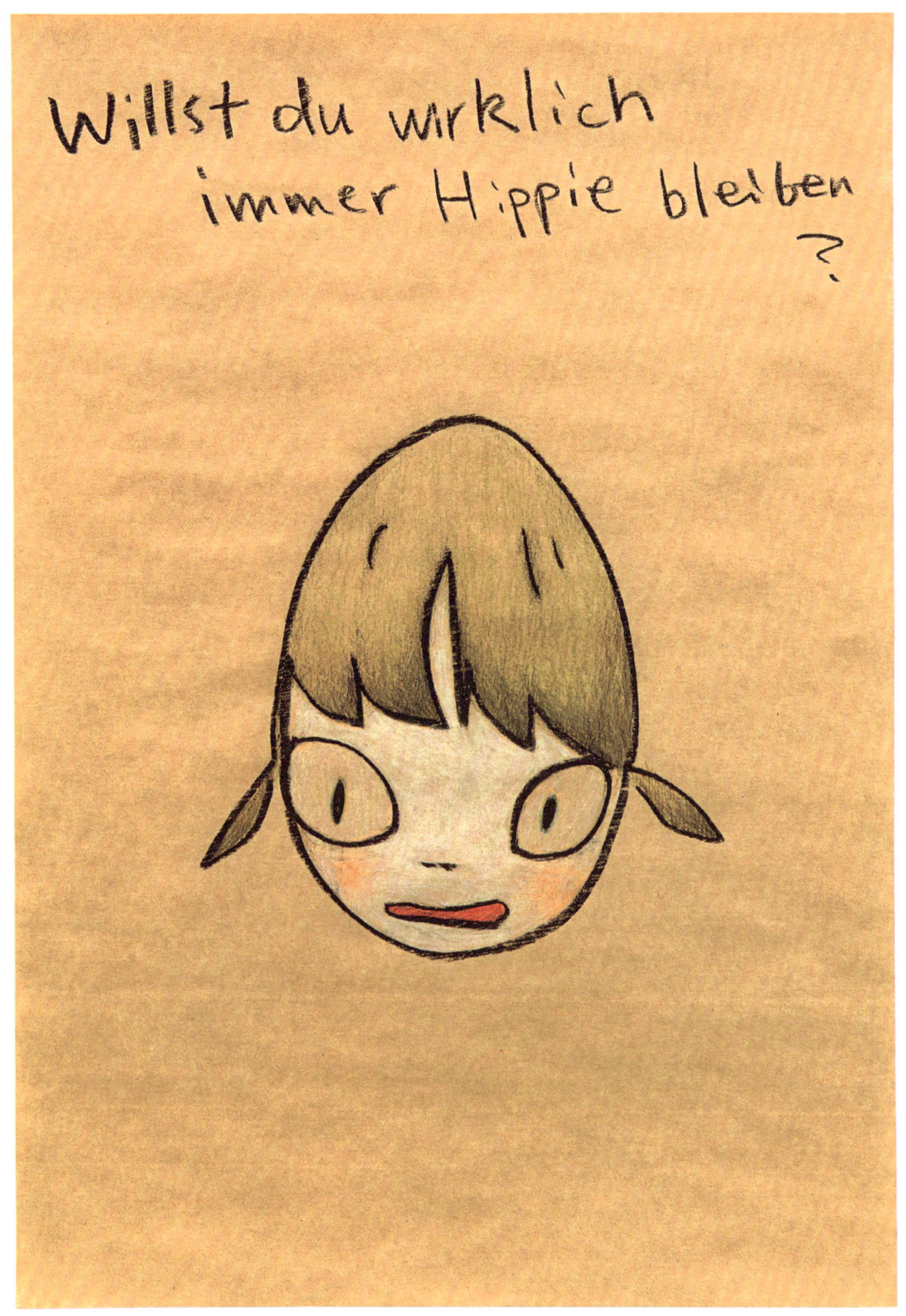
Willst du wirklich
immer Hippie bleiben
?

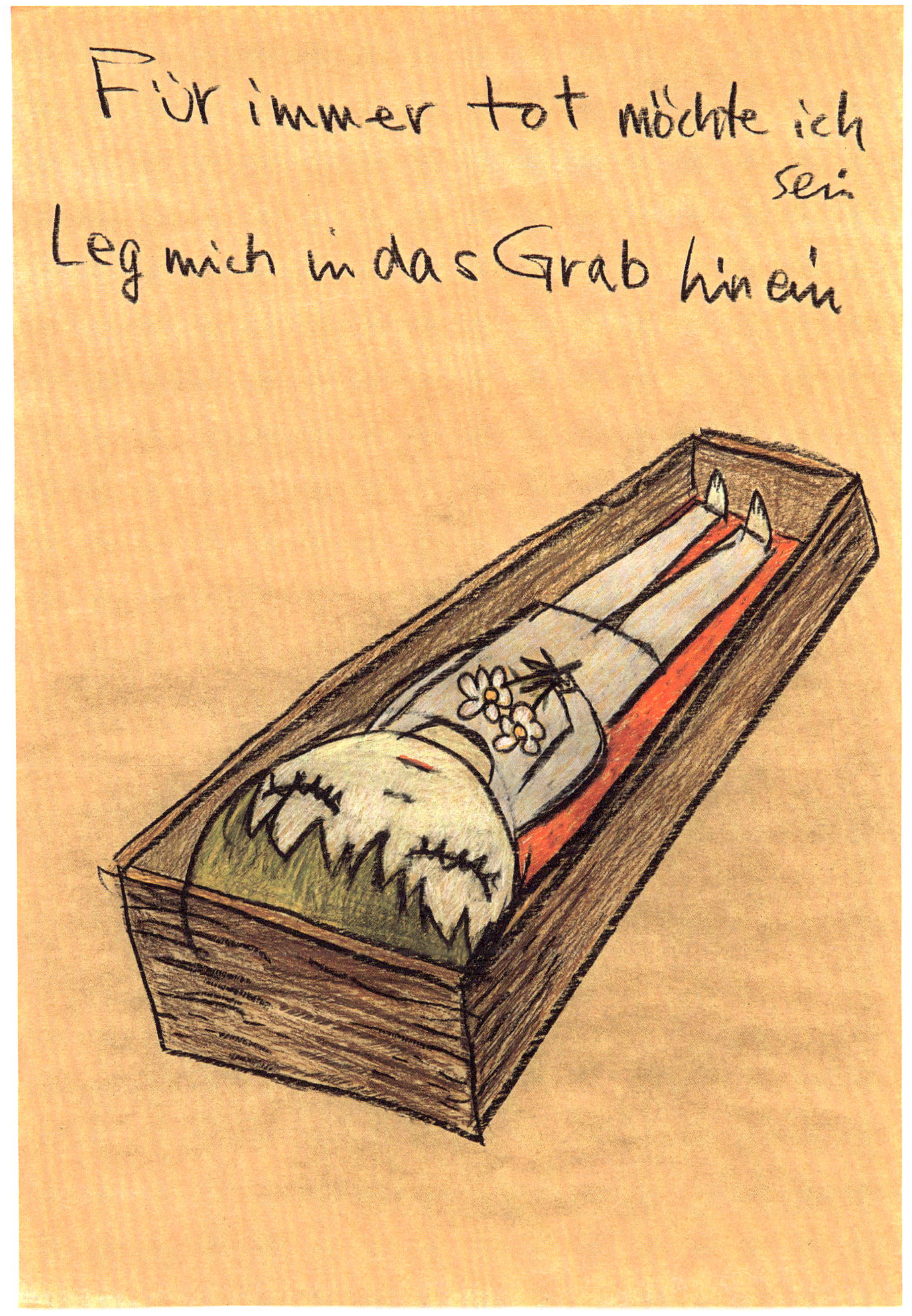
Für immer tot möchte ich
sein
Leg mich in das Grab hinein

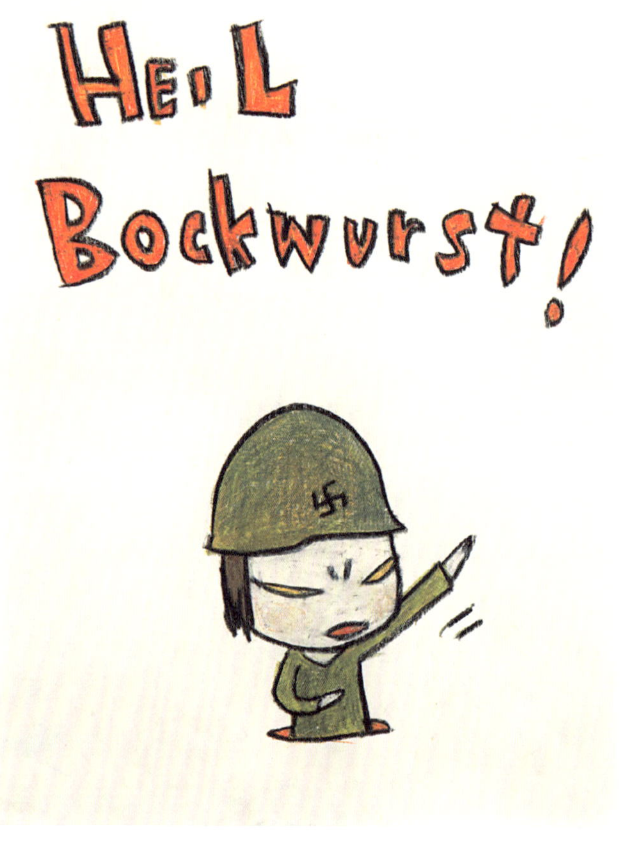
HEIL
Bockwurst!

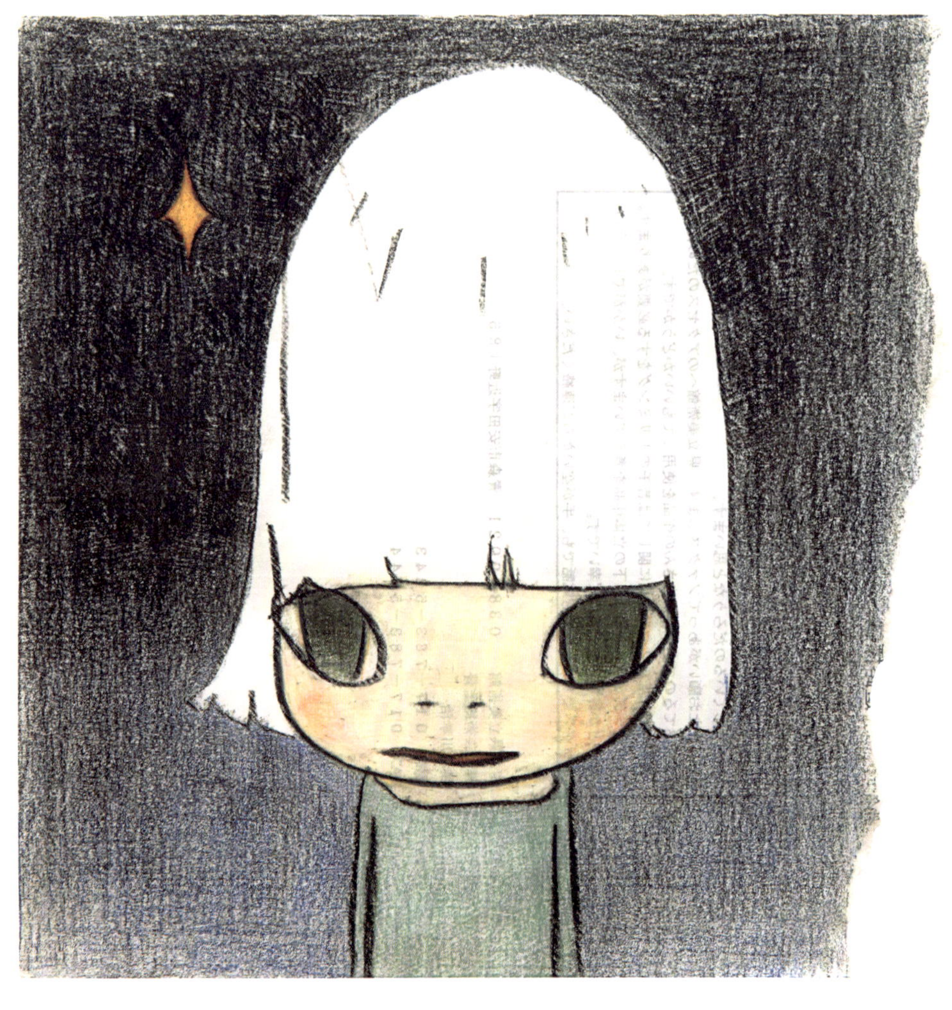

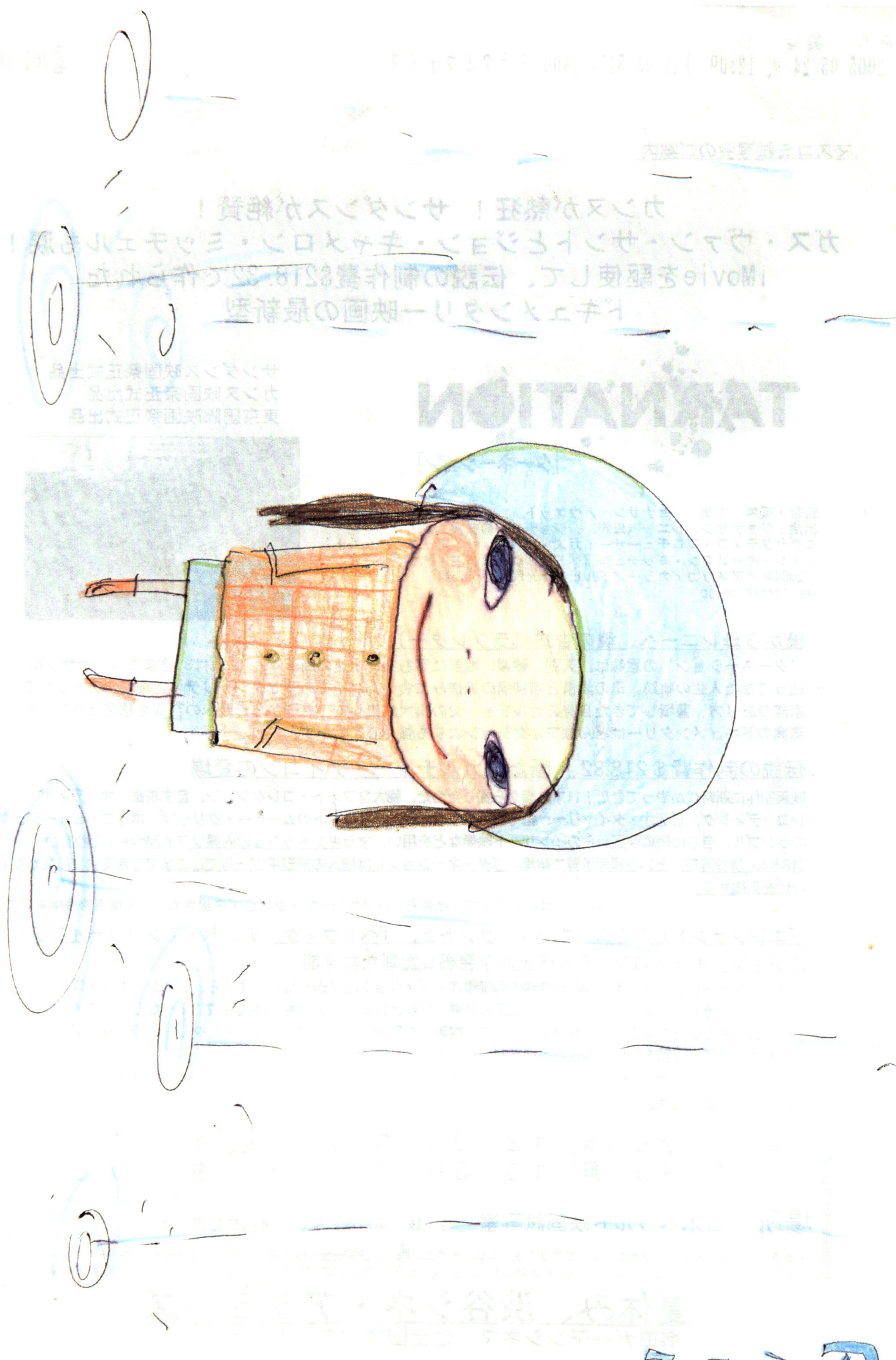

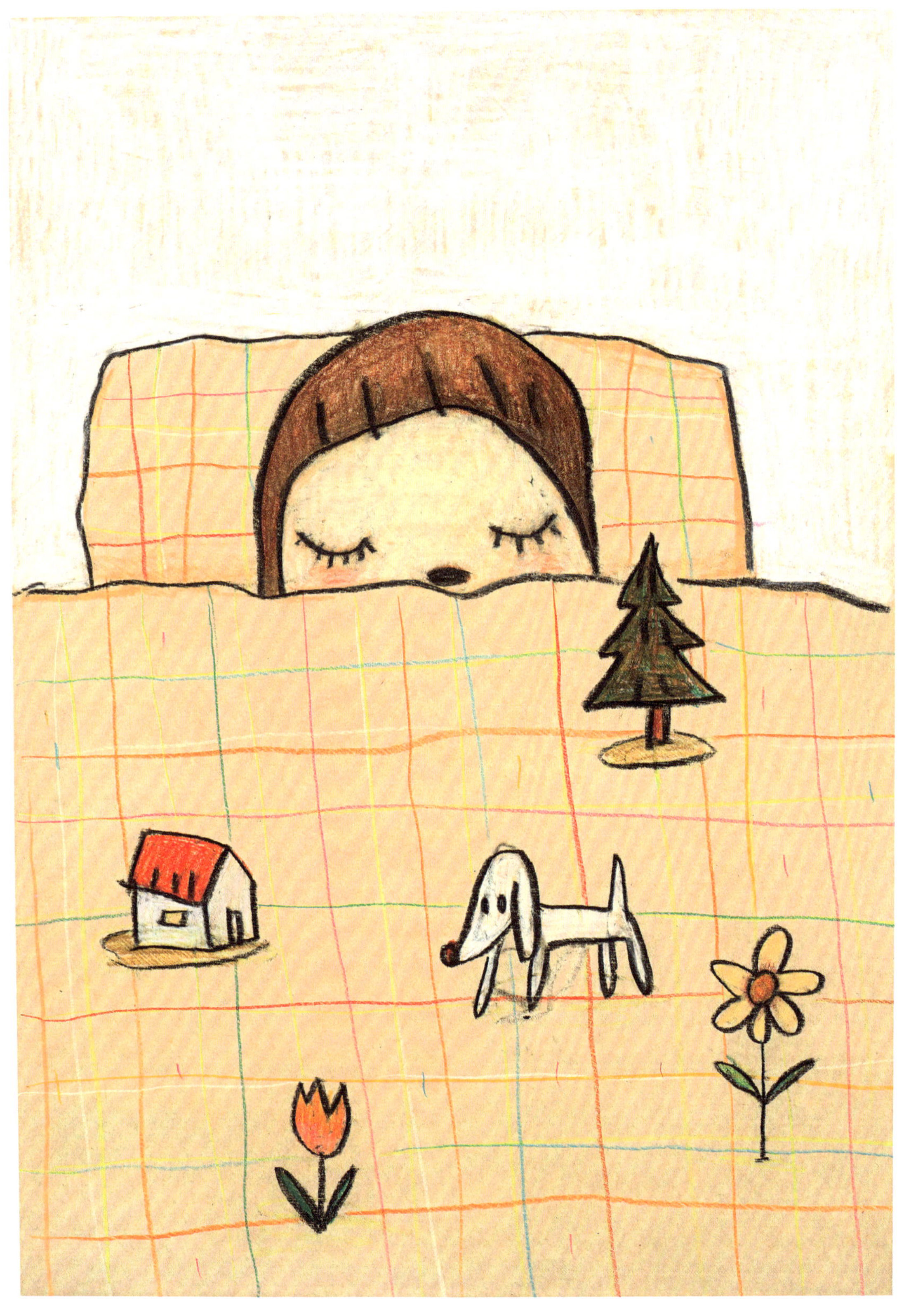

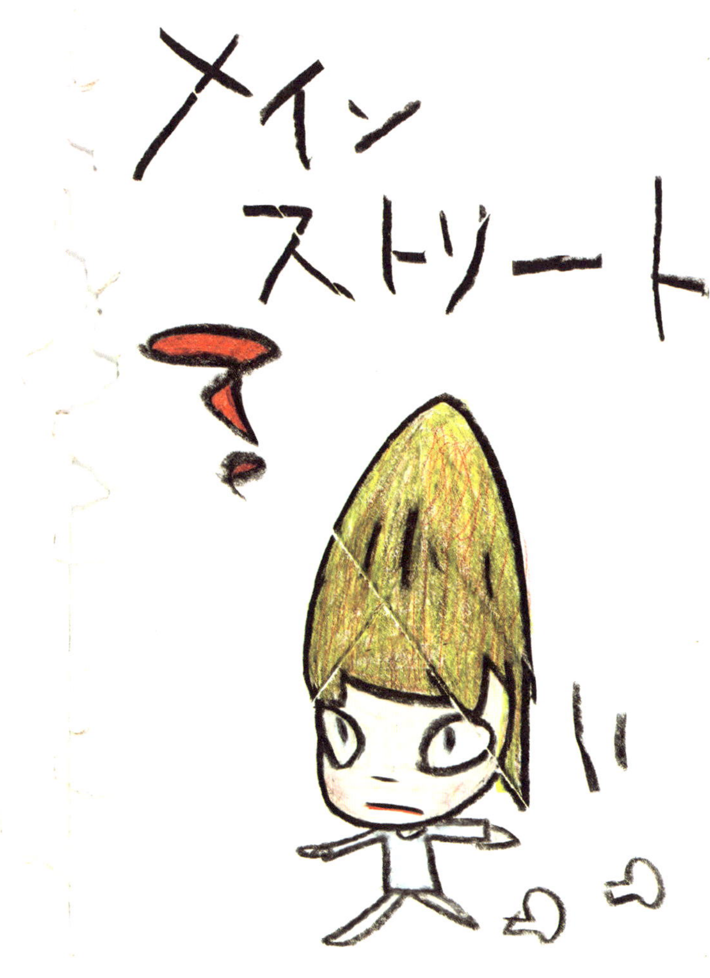
メイン
ストリート
?

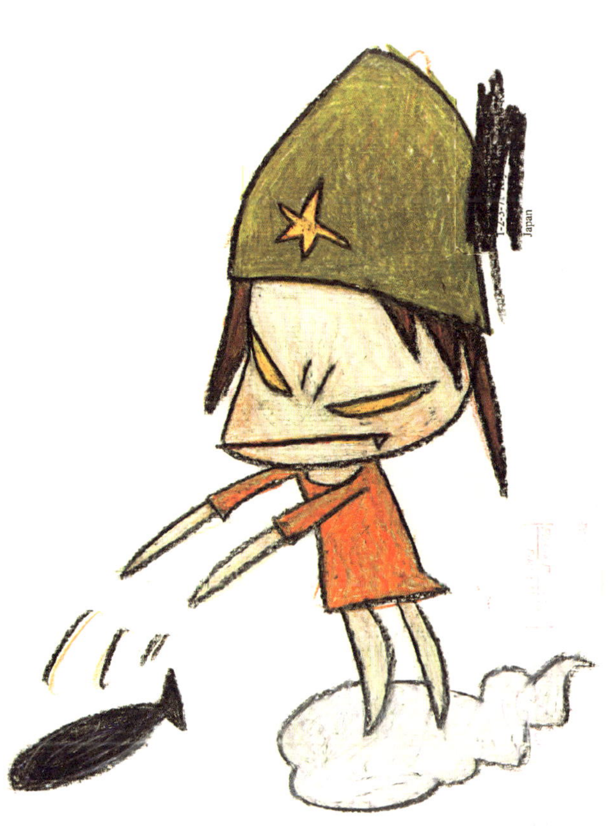

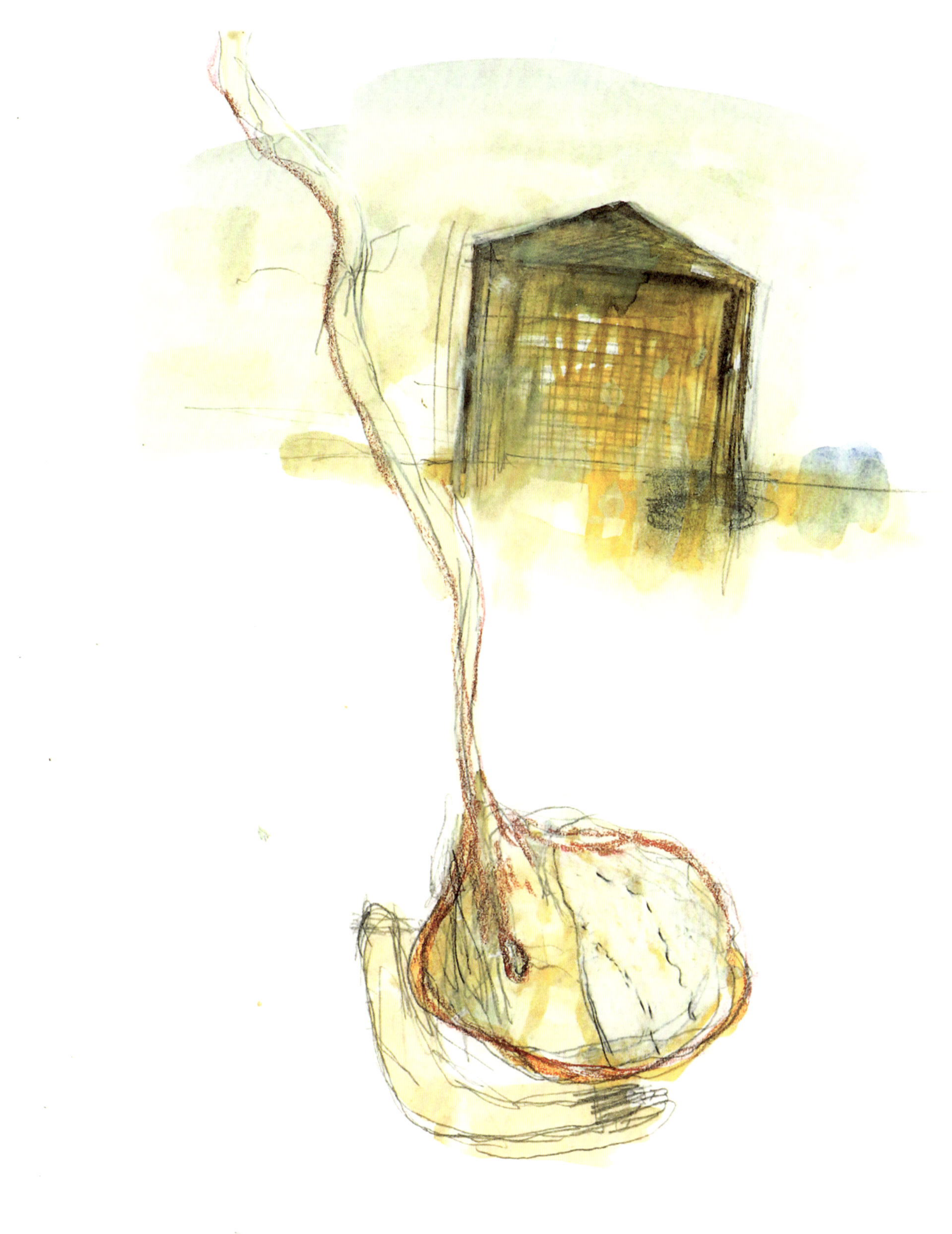
Sleepless night, 先生の夢
NARA '89

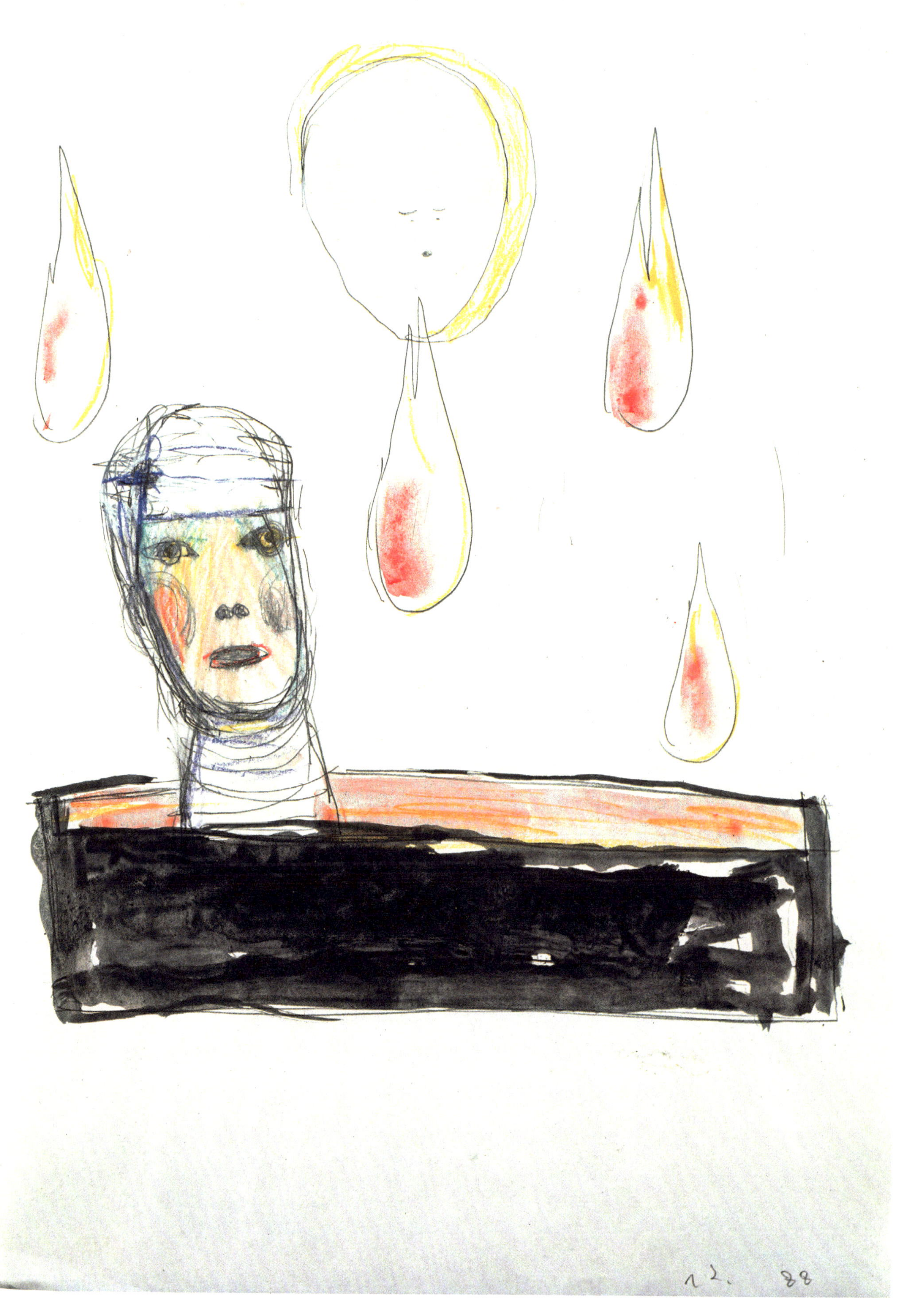

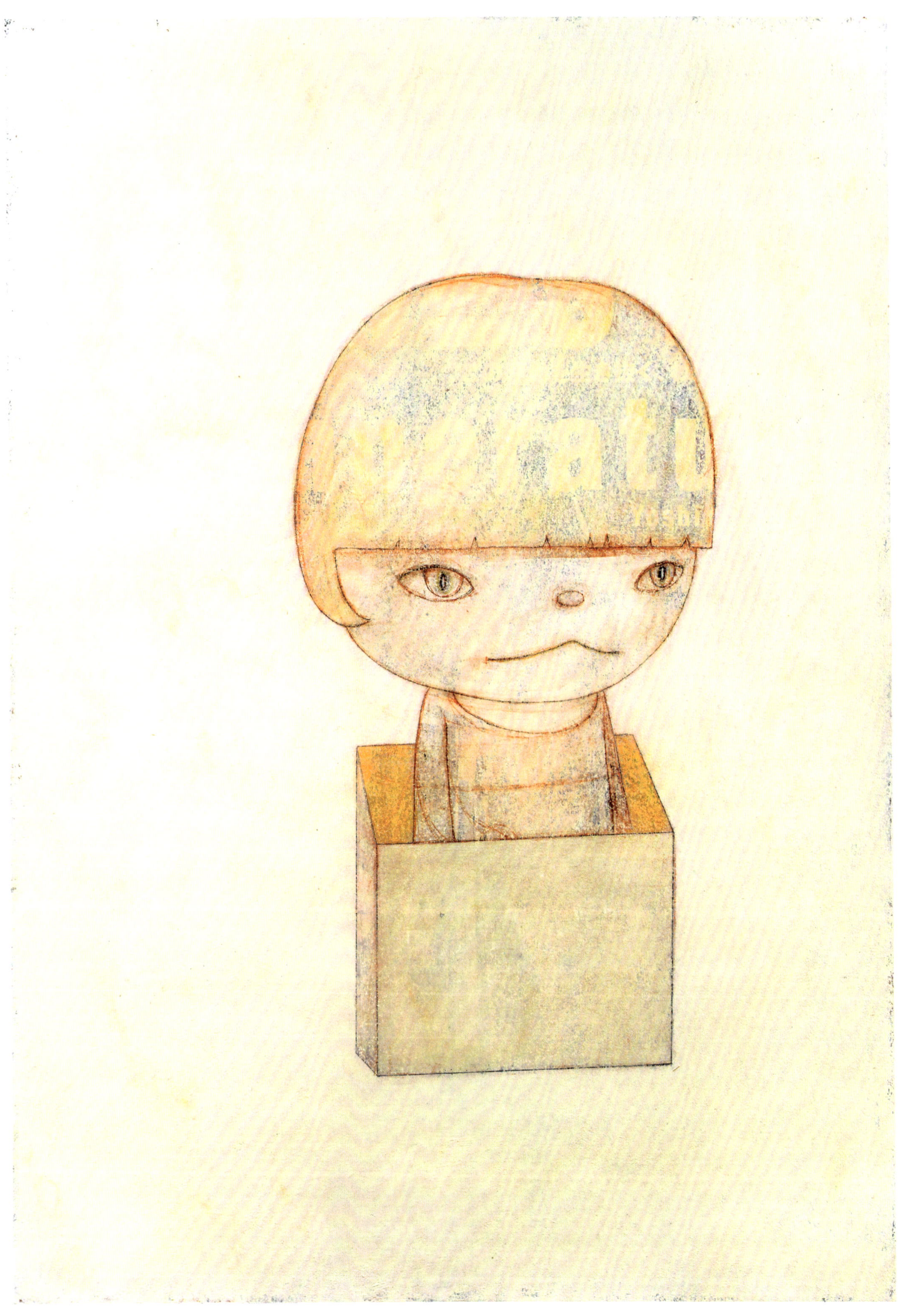

TORKHUM

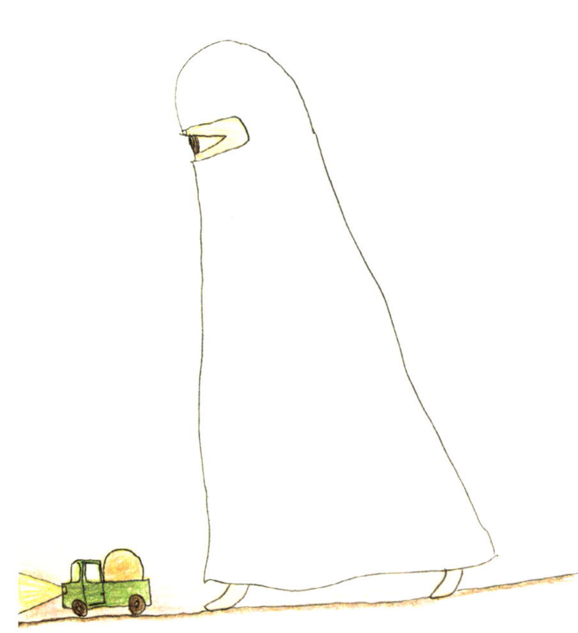

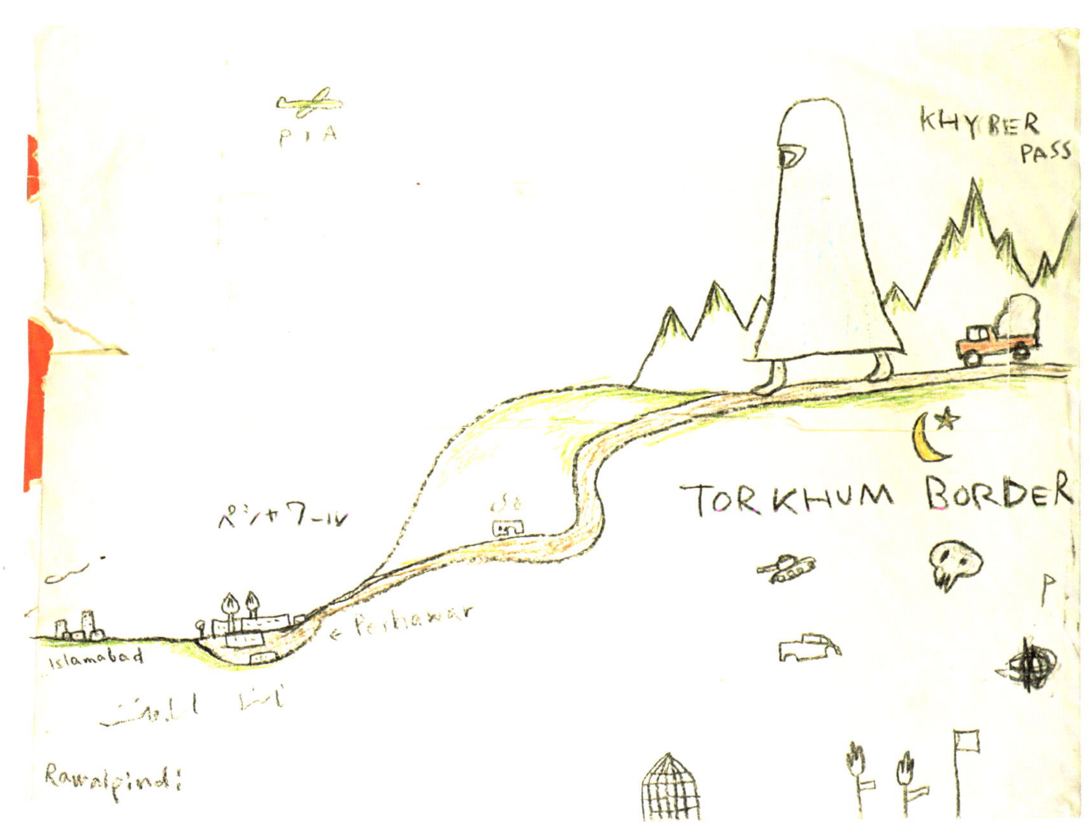

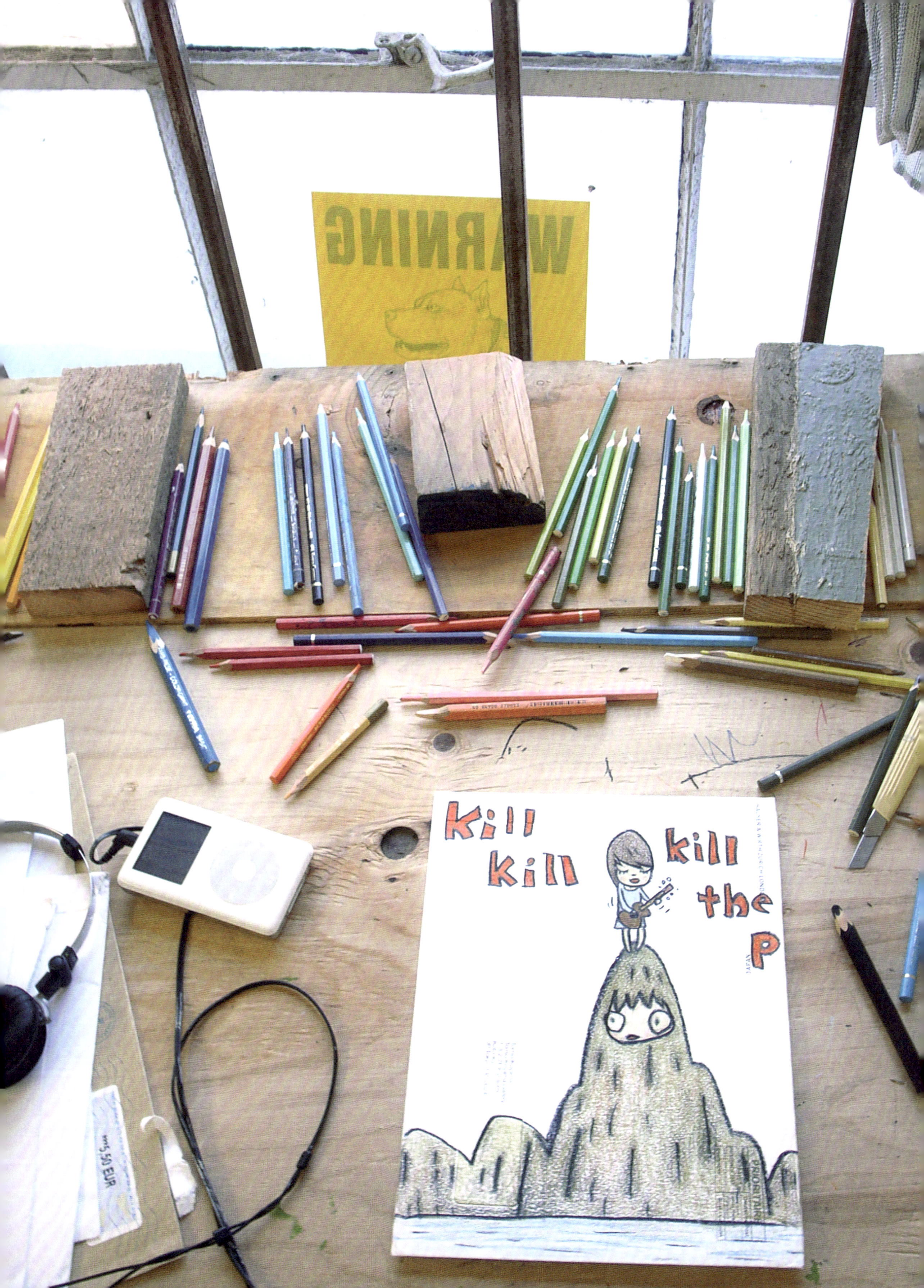

PIA
KHYBER PASS
ペシャワール
TORKHUM BORDER
Islamabad
Peshawar
Rawalpindi

WARNING
kill kill
kill the p

XIV

Index of Works

All works are by Yoshitomo Nara. Dimensions are listed in inches and centimeters. Measurements are given as height by width (by depth). Works that do not appear in the exhibition are marked with asterisks.

All information is current as of November 22, 2019.

Emergency
2013
Acrylic on wood
83⅛ × 73¼ × 3½ in. (211 × 186 × 9 cm)
Collection of the artist
p. 30

E.S.P
2010
Colored pencil on paper
10½ × 8⅞ in. (26.5 × 22.5 cm)
Collection of the artist
p. 180 (top)

Fire
2010
Colored pencil on paper
12¾ × 9 in. (32.3 × 22.8 cm)
Collection of the artist
p. 40 (bottom left)

The Fool Dressed in Pink
2006
Acrylic and colored pencil on paper
31 × 21½ in. (78.8 × 54.6 cm)
Private collection
p. 135*

Fountain of Life
2001/2014
Fiber-reinforced plastic, lacquer, urethane, motor, and water
Edition of 3, artist proof 1/2
68⅞ × 70⅞ × 70⅞ in. (175 × 180 × 180 cm)
Collection of Alaia Chen
p. 192

FROM THE BOMB SHELTER
2017
Acrylic on jute mounted on wood
71 × 63¼ × 1⅞ in. (180.5 × 160.5 × 4.8 cm)
Collection of the artist
p. 105

Fuckin' Street
2013
Colored pencil on paper
12¾ × 9½ in. (32.5 × 24.2 cm)
Collection of the artist
p. 36 (bottom right)

*FUCK *U*
2015
Colored pencil on paper
11⅝ × 8¼ in. (29.7 × 21 cm)
Collection of the artist
p. 179 (bottom)

Full Moon Night
From the series *In the Floating World*
1999
Ink, colored pencil, and acrylic on paper
16⅝ × 13 in. (42.2 × 33 cm)
Private collection
p. 141

Für immer tot möchte ich sein. Leg mich in das Grab hinein.
2006
Colored pencil on paper
16½ × 11⅝ in. (42 × 29.7 cm)
Collection of the artist
p. 199

Girl at the Harbor
1989
Colored pencil, graphite, ink, and watercolor on paper
8 × 5⅝ in. (20.5 × 14.5 cm)
Aomori Museum of Art
p. 92

Girl Left Behind the Night
2019
Acrylic on canvas
86⅝ × 76¾ in. (220 × 195 cm)
Private collection
p. 110

The Girl with the Knife in Her Hand
1991
Acrylic on canvas
59¼ × 55⅛ in. (150.5 × 140 cm)
Vicki and Kent Logan, fractional and promised gift to the San Francisco Museum of Modern Art
p. 22

Give You the Flower
1990
Acrylic on canvas
43⅝ × 36¼ in. (111 × 92 cm)
Private collection
p. 26

GRIEVOUS ANGEL
2012
Colored pencil on paper
8⅞ × 11¾ in. (22.5 × 30 cm)
Collection of the artist
p. 180 (bottom)

Hard Rain
2014
Colored pencil on cardboard
30⅜ × 22 in. (77.3 × 56 cm)
Collection of the artist
Front cover; p. 47 (bottom)

Harmless Kitty
1994
Acrylic on canvas
59 × 55⅛ in. (150 × 140 cm)
The National Museum of Modern Art, Tokyo
p. 190

Headache
2012
Graphite on paper
25⅝ × 19¾ in. (65 × 50 cm)
Collection of the artist
p. 98

Heads
1998
Acrylic, lacquer, and cotton on fiber-reinforced plastic
Each: 4⅜ × 4¾ × 3⅛ in. (11 × 12 × 8 cm)
Aomori Museum of Art
pp. 136–37

HOME
2017
Acrylic on jute mounted on wood
71 × 63¼ × 1⅞ in. (180.5 × 160.5 × 4.8 cm)
Collection of the artist
p. 104

Hula Hula Dancing
1998
Acrylic on canvas
74¾ × 70⅞ in. (190 × 180 cm)
Kadokawa Culture Promotion Foundation, Japan
p. 188

I AM Right Wing, I AM Left Wing. Feelings are leaning a little to the right, wavering to the left
2011
Graphite and gesso on cardboard
29⅞ × 19⅛ in. (76 × 48.5 cm)
Collection of the artist
p. 172 (top)

I Couldn't Say the Reason Why Tears Fall from the Eyes Now
1988
Graphite and colored pencil on paper
11⅝ × 8¼ in. (29.5 × 21 cm)
Hiromichi Nakano, Japan
p. 182

I Don't Care a Fuck about Everything
1989
Ink and acrylic on paper
10¼ × 14⅛ in. (25.9 × 35.9 cm)
Collection of the artist
p. 47 (top left)

I Don't Care a Fuck about Everything
1989
Ink and acrylic on paper
10¼ × 14⅛ in. (25.9 × 35.9 cm)
Collection of the artist
p. 47 (top right)

I'm Sorry
2007
Acrylic and colored pencil on paper
41⅜ × 27½ in. (105 × 70 cm)
Leeum, Samsung Museum of Art
p. 134

In the Deepest Puddle II
1995
Acrylic on cotton mounted on canvas
47¼ × 43⅜ in. (120 × 110 cm)
Takahashi Ryutaro Collection
Front cover; p. 24

In the Milky Lake/Thinking One
2011
Acrylic on canvas
102 × 71⅝ in. (259.2 × 181.8 cm)
Private collection, courtesy of Frahm & Frahm
p. 80

In the White Room
2003
Acrylic and colored pencil on paper
28⅜ × 20¼ in. (72 × 51.5 cm)
Private collection
p. 66

The Last Match
1996
Acrylic on cotton mounted on canvas
47¼ × 43⅜ in. (120 × 110 cm)
Aomori Museum of Art
p. 19

Little Thinker in Garden
2016
Ceramic
20½ × 15 × 13¾ in. (52 × 38 × 35 cm)
Private collection
p. 111

Little Thinker in Silence
2016
Ceramic
29⅛ × 21⅝ × 18⅞ in. (74 × 55 × 48 cm)
Private collection
p. 102

The Longest Night
1995
Acrylic on canvas
47¼ × 43⅜ in. (120 × 110 cm)
Collection of the National Museum of Art, Osaka
p. 20

Love Is the Power
1999
Acrylic and colored pencil on paper
16⅝ × 13 in. (42.2 × 33 cm)
The Museum of Contemporary Art, Los Angeles, purchased with funds provided by Ruth and Jacob Bloom
p. 142

Mädchen mit den Winkerflaggen
1996
Acrylic and colored pencil on paper
12⅝ × 9½ in. (32 × 24 cm)
Private collection
p. 42*

Make the Road, Follow the Road
1990
Acrylic on canvas
39⅜ × 39⅜ in. (100 × 100 cm)
Aomori Museum of Art
p. 27

Midnight Truth
2017
Acrylic on canvas
89½ × 71⅝ in. (227.3 × 181.8 cm)
National Gallery of Art, Washington DC, gift of Lisa and Steve Tananbaum
p. 100

Mirror Ball Bon Dance
2012
Colored pencil on cardboard
12⅝ × 12⅝ in. (32 × 32 cm)
Collection of the artist
p. 175 (bottom)

Miss Forest
2010
Ceramic decorated with platinum, gold, and silver liquid
56⅝ × 40⅛ × 39⅜ in. (144 × 102 × 100 cm)
Leeum, Samsung Museum of Art
p. 99

Miss Forest/Creamy Snow
2016
Urethane on bronze
94⅛ × 29⅜ × 25¼ in. (239 × 74.6 × 64 cm)
Private collection
Front cover; p. 187*

Missing in Action
1999
Acrylic on canvas
70⅞ × 57⅛ in. (180 × 145 cm)
Sally and Ralph Tawil, courtesy of Pace Gallery
p. 189

Missing in Action—Girl Meets Boy—
2005
Acrylic, colored pencil, and watercolor on paper
59 × 54 in. (150 × 137 cm)
Collection of Hiroshima City Museum of Contemporary Art
p. 68

Miss Margaret
2016
Acrylic on canvas
76⅜ × 6⅝ in. (194 × 162 cm)
The Rachofsky Collection
p. 75

Miss Spring
2012
Acrylic on canvas
89⅜ × 71⅝ in. (227 × 182 cm)
Collection of the Yokohama Museum of Art
p. 139

Mumps
1996
Acrylic on cotton mounted on canvas
47¼ × 43⅜ in. (120 × 110 cm)
Aomori Museum of Art
p. 18

Muñoz's Babies
1995
Watercolor pigment marker, colored pencil, and ink on paper
5¼ × 7⅛ in. (13.5 × 18 cm)
Collection of the artist
Front cover; p. 168 (bottom)

My Drawing Room
2008
Mixed media
118¾ × 147⅝ × 149⅝ in. (301.5 × 375 × 380 cm)
Collection of the artist
pp. 50–64

My Skull
2013
Colored pencil on paper
10⅝ × 7¼ in. (27 × 18.5 cm)
Private collection
Front cover; p. 38 (bottom left)*

Nobody's Fool
2010
Ink and colored pencil on paper
11⅝ × 8¼ in. (29.5 × 21 cm)
Collection of the artist
p. 169 (bottom)

No Fun!
From the series *In the Floating World*
1999
Ink, colored pencil, and acrylic on paper
16⅝ × 13 in. (42.2 × 33 cm)
Private collection
p. 130 (top)

NOISE
2010
Colored pencil on paper
10⅝ × 8¼ in. (27 × 21 cm)
Collection of the artist
p. 178 (bottom)

No Means No
2014
Acrylic on canvas
51⅝ × 38⅛ in. (131 × 97 cm)
Private collection, USA, courtesy of Frahm & Frahm
p. 77

No No No
2019
Acrylic and colored pencil on wood
28⅛ × 26⅜ × ⅛ in. (71.5 × 67 × 0.3 cm)
Collection of the artist
p. 181*

No Nukes
1998
Acrylic and colored pencil on paper
14⅛ × 8⅞ in. (36 × 22.5 cm)
Collection of Masayuki Nagase
p. 138

No Nukes!
From the series *In the Floating World*
1999
Ink, colored pencil, and acrylic on paper
13 × 16⅝ in. (33 × 42.2 cm)
Private collection
p. 140

One Foot in the Groove
2012
Acrylic on wood
73⅞ × 122½ × 3⅜ in. (187.5 × 310 × 8.5 cm)
Private collection
pp. 184–85

On the Building
2015
Ink and colored pencil on paper
8¼ × 11⅝ in. (21 × 29.7 cm)
Collection of the artist
p. 95

PEACE GIRL
2017
Acrylic on jute mounted on wood
71 × 63¼ × 1⅞ in. (180.5 × 160.5 × 4.8 cm)
Collection of the artist
p. 107

Peace of Mind
2019
Acrylic on canvas
86⅝ × 76¾ in. (220 × 195 cm)
Collection of Andrew Xue
p. 103

People on the Cloud
1989
Acrylic on canvas
39⅜ × 39⅜ in. (100 × 100 cm)
Private collection, Japan
Front cover; p. 28

Princess of Snooze
2001
Acrylic on canvas
113⅜ × 71⅝ in. (288 × 181.8 cm)
Private collection
Front cover; p. 69

Punk Ebizo
From the series *In the Floating World*
1999
Ink, colored pencil, and acrylic on paper
16⅝ × 13 in. (42.2 × 33 cm)
Private collection
p. 130 (bottom)

Rock You!
2012
Colored pencil on paper
10⅝ × 8¼ in. (27 × 21 cm)
Collection of the artist
p. 38 (bottom right)

Romantic Catastrophe
1988
Acrylic and colored pencil on canvas
45⅞ × 35 ¾ in. (116.7 × 90.9 cm)
Private collection
p. 31

Schallplatten
2012
Colored pencil on cardboard
12¼ × 12¼ in. (31 × 31 cm)
Collection of the artist
p. 36 (top left)

Searching
2011
Graphite on paper
25⅝ × 19¾ in. (65 × 50 cm)
Collection of the artist
p. 93 (top)

Searching
2019
Acrylic and colored pencil on paper
29½ × 16⅞ in. (75.1 × 42.9 cm)
Collection of the artist
p. 159 (top)

Shallow Puddles
2006
Acrylic on cotton mounted on fiber-reinforced plastic
37⅜ × 37⅜ × 5⅞ in. (95 × 95 × 15 cm)
Collection of the artist
p. 73

Ships in Girl
1992
Acrylic and colored pencil on paper
11 × 13⅜ in. (28 × 34 cm)
Collection of the artist
p. 35 (top right)

Slash with a Knife
From the series *In the Floating World*
1999
Acrylic, colored pencil, and graphite on paper
16⅝ × 13 in. (42.2 × 33 cm)
Private collection
p. 131

Sleepless Night (Sitting)
1997
Acrylic on canvas
47¼ × 43⅜ in. (120 × 110 cm)
Rubell Family Collection, Miami
p. 21

Sleepless Night, Sleepless Night, Dream of Teacher
1989
Colored pencil, graphite, ink, and watercolor on paper
8 × 5⅝ in. (20.5 × 14.5 cm)
Aomori Museum of Art
p. 204

Solid Fist
2011
Colored pencil on paper
9½ × 14½ in. (24 × 37 cm)
Collection of the artist
p. 39 (top)

Sprout the Ambassador
2001
Acrylic on canvas
82 × 78 in. (208.3 × 198.1 cm)
Private collection
p. 70

SWEET HOME GATE
2017
Acrylic on jute mounted on wood
71 × 63¼ × 1⅞ in. (180.5 × 160.5 × 4.8 cm)
Collection of the artist
p. 106

Thinking about a Little Star
2014
Colored pencil on cardboard
27⅛ × 17½ in. (68.8 × 44.5 cm)
Collection of the artist
p. 36 (bottom right)

To Hell and Back
2008
Graphite on paper
25⅝ × 19¾ in. (65 × 50 cm)
Collection of Beth Rudin DeWoody
p. 132

UKIYO
1999
Ink, colored pencil, and acrylic on paper
16⅝ × 13 in. (42.2 × 33 cm)
Jack Black
p. 143

Untitled
1985–88
Ink and colored pencil on paper in plastic bag
12⅞ × 4½ in. (32.8 × 11.3 cm)
Collection of the artist
p. 34 (right)

Untitled
1985–88
Ink and colored pencil on paper in plastic bag
10 × 4½ in. (25.5 × 11.5 cm)
Collection of the artist
p. 34 (left)

Untitled
1985–88
Colored pencil and ink on paper in plastic bag
7¼ × 4 in. (18.5 × 10.3 cm)
Collection of the artist
p. 152 (bottom)

Untitled
1988
Acrylic and ink on paper
18¾ × 14¼ in. (47.8 × 35.8 cm)
Collection of the artist
p. 35 (bottom right)

Untitled
1988
Acrylic and ink on paper
18⅞ × 14¼ in. (48 × 35.8 cm)
Collection of the artist
p. 35 (bottom left)

Untitled
1988
Ink, colored pencil, and acrylic on paper
11⅝ × 8⅛ in. (29.5 × 20.7 cm)
Collection of the artist
p. 35 (top left)

Untitled
1988
Acrylic, colored pencil, and graphite on paper
11⅝ × 8¼ in. (29.5 × 21 cm)
Hiromichi Nakano, Japan
p. 205

Untitled
1989
Acrylic and colored pencil on paper
18⅞ × 14⅛ in. (48 × 36 cm)
Collection of the artist
p. 39 (bottom)

Untitled
1989
Acrylic on paper
19½ × 13⅝ in. (49.5 × 34.7 cm)
Collection of the artist
p. 41 (top left)

Untitled
1989
Acrylic on paper
13⅜ × 9½ in. (34 × 24 cm)
Collection of the artist
p. 41 (bottom left)

Untitled
1989
Acrylic on paper
13⅜ × 9½ in. (34 × 24 cm)
Collection of the artist
p. 41 (top right)

Untitled
1989
Acrylic on paper
13⅜ × 9½ in. (34 × 24 cm)
Collection of the artist
p. 41 (bottom right)

Untitled
1989
Acrylic on paper
18¾ × 14⅛ in. (47.8 × 35.9 cm)
Collection of the artist
p. 153 (top)

Untitled
1989
Acrylic and colored pencil on paper
18¾ × 14⅛ in. (47.8 × 35.9 cm)
Collection of the artist
p. 153 (bottom)

Untitled
1989
Acrylic and ink on paper
13⅝ × 19½ in. (34.7 × 49.5 cm)
Collection of the artist
p. 155

Untitled
1990
Acrylic on paper
22 × 23⅞ in. (55.8 × 60.8 cm)
Collection of the artist
p. 43 (top left)

Untitled
1990
Acrylic on paper
22⅜ × 23¼ in. (56.8 × 59 cm)
Collection of the artist
p. 43 (bottom left)

Untitled
1990
Colored pencil and acrylic on paper
8¼ × 11⅝ in. (21 × 29.5 cm)
Collection of the artist
p. 157

Untitled
1991
Acrylic on paper
6⅞ × 9⅝ in. (17.5 × 24.5 cm)
Collection of the artist
p. 43 (top right)

Untitled
1991
Acrylic on cardboard
11 × 5⅞ in. (28 × 15 cm)
Collection of the artist
p. 43 (bottom right)

Untitled
1991
Ink on paper
7⅞ × 4⅛ in. (20 × 10.5 cm)
Collection of the artist
p. 44 (top left)

Untitled
1991
Ink on paper
8 × 4⅞ in. (20.2 × 12.5 cm)
Collection of the artist
p. 44 (bottom right)

Untitled
1991
Ink on paper
8 × 4⅞ in. (20.2 × 12.5 cm)
Collection of the artist
p. 44 (bottom right)

Untitled
1991
Ink and water on paper
9¾ × 7 in. (24.8 × 17.7 cm)
Collection of the artist
p. 46 (bottom right)

Untitled
1991
Ink on paper
7⅞ × 4⅞ in. (20.1 × 12.5 cm)
Collection of the artist
p. 46 (top left)

Untitled
1992
Acrylic and colored pencil on paper
11¼ × 8 in. (28.5 × 20.5 cm)
Collection of the artist
p. 46 (bottom left)

Untitled
1993
Ink and colored pencil on paper
8¼ × 5¾ in. (21 × 14.6 cm)
Collection of the artist
p. 44 (top right)

Untitled
1993
Acrylic on paper
15¾ × 11¾ in. (40 × 30 cm)
Collection of the artist
p. 46 (top right)

Untitled
1993
Acrylic on paper
16½ × 21⅞ in. (42 × 55.7 cm)
Collection of the artist
p. 158 (bottom)

Untitled
1993
Acrylic on paper
16⅛ × 11⅜ in. (41 × 29 cm)
Collection of the artist
p. 158 (top)

Untitled
1994
Acrylic on paper
13⅝ × 19⅛ in. (34.5 × 48.6 cm)
Collection of the artist
p. 168 (top)

Untitled
1998
Ink and colored pencil on paper
7⅞ × 11¼ in. (20 × 28.5 cm)
Collection of the artist
p. 163 (bottom)

Untitled
1998
Graphite and colored pencil on paper
8¼ × 11⅝ in. (20.9 × 29.7 cm)
Collection of the artist
p. 163 (top)

Untitled
1999
Colored pencil on paper
11⅝ × 8½ in. (29.5 × 21.5 cm)
Collection of the artist
p. 162

Untitled
Late 1990s
Ink and colored pencil on paper
4½ × 2⅛ in. (11.5 × 5.5 cm)
Collection of the artist
p. 169 (top)

Untitled
2002
Acrylic and colored pencil on paper
28⅝ × 20¼ in. (72.6 × 51.6 cm)
Collection of the artist
p. 206

Untitled
2002
Colored pencil on paper
9⅜ × 13¼ in. (23.8 × 33.7 cm)
Collection of the artist
p. 207 (bottom)

Untitled
2002
Colored pencil and ink on paper
10¾ × 6¼ in. (27.4 × 15.8 cm)
Collection of the artist
p. 207 (top)

Untitled
2003
Graphite and colored pencil on paper
11¾ × 8¼ in. (30 × 21 cm)
Collection of the artist
p. 146 (bottom)

Untitled
2003
Graphite on paper
11¾ × 8¼ in. (30 × 21 cm)
Collection of the artist
p. 147

Untitled
2003
Acrylic, colored pencil, and graphite on paper
11¾ × 8¼ in. (30 × 21 cm)
Collection of the artist
p. 148 (bottom right)

Untitled
2003
Graphite and colored pencil on paper
11¾ × 8¼ in. (30 × 21 cm)
Collection of the artist
p. 148 (top left)

Untitled
2003
Graphite and colored pencil on paper
11¾ × 8¼ in. (30 × 21 cm)
Collection of the artist
p. 148 (top right)

Untitled
2003
Graphite and colored pencil on paper
11¾ × 8¼ in. (30 × 21 cm)
Collection of the artist
p. 148 (bottom left)

Untitled
2003
Graphite and colored pencil on paper
11¾ × 8¼ in. (30 × 21 cm)
Collection of the artist
p. 149

Untitled
2003
Graphite on paper
11¾ × 8¼ in. (30 × 21 cm)
Collection of the artist
p. 150

Untitled
2003
Acrylic, colored pencil, and graphite on paper
11¾ × 8¼ in. (30 × 21 cm)
Collection of the artist
p. 151

Untitled
2003
Graphite and colored pencil on paper
11¾ × 8¼ in. (30 × 21 cm)
Collection of the artist
p. 152 (top)

Untitled
2003
Colored pencil on paper
10½ × 4¾ in. (26.5 × 12 cm)
Collection of the artist
p. 195 (top)*

Untitled
2004
Colored pencil and acrylic on paper
12½ × 9⅜ in. (31.8 × 23.9 cm)
Private collection
p. 186*

Untitled
2004
Colored pencil on paper
6¼ × 8⅞ in. (16 × 22.5 cm)
Collection of the artist
p. 194

Untitled
2004
Colored pencil on paper
9½ × 7½ in. (24 × 19 cm)
Collection of the artist
p. 197

Untitled
2005
Colored pencil on paper
9 × 6 in. (23 × 15.3 cm)
Collection of the artist
p. 195 (bottom)

Untitled
2005
Colored pencil on paper
13¼ × 9½ in. (33.5 × 24 cm)
Collection of the artist
p. 196 (bottom)

Untitled
2005
Colored pencil on paper
9 × 6⅜ in. (23 × 16.3 cm)
Collection of the artist
p. 196 (top)

Untitled
2005
Ink and colored pencil on paper
8¼ × 11⅝ in. (21 × 29.7 cm)
Collection of the artist
p. 201

Untitled
2006
Colored pencil on paper
12⅜ × 9½ in. (31.5 × 24 cm)
Collection of the artist
p. 200 (top)

Untitled
2006
Colored pencil on paper
8¼ × 8⅜ in. (21 × 21.3 cm)
Collection of the artist
p. 200 (bottom)

Untitled
2007
Colored pencil on paper
7⅝ × 5⅞ in. (19.3 × 15 cm)
Collection of the artist
p. 203 (top)

Untitled
2008
Graphite on paper
25⅝ × 19¾ in. (65 × 50 cm)
Collection of the artist
p. 101 (bottom)

Untitled
2008
Graphite on paper
25⅝ × 19¾ in. (65 × 50 cm)
Collection of the artist
p. 101 (top)

Untitled
2008
Graphite on paper
25½ × 19½ in. (64.8 × 49.5 cm)
Collection of Chong Zhou
p. 133

Untitled
2008
Colored pencil on paper
16½ × 11¾ in. (42 × 29.8 cm)
Private collection, California
p. 172 (bottom)

Untitled
2008
Colored pencil on paper
12¾ × 9 in. (32.5 × 22.9 cm)
Collection of the artist
p. 203 (bottom)

Untitled
2010
Colored pencil on paper
15 × 10⅝ in. (38 × 27 cm)
Collection of the artist
p. 40 (top)

Untitled
2010
Colored pencil on paper
17¾ × 12½ in. (45 × 31.7 cm)
Collection of the artist
p. 40 (bottom right)

Untitled
2010
Graphite on paper
21 × 14¾ in. (53.3 × 37.5 cm)
Collection of the artist
p. 82 (bottom)

Untitled
2010
Graphite on paper
21 × 14¾ in. (53.3 × 37.5 cm)
Collection of the artist
p. 82 (bottom)

Untitled
2010
Graphite on paper
21 × 14¾ in. (53.3 × 37.5 cm)
Collection of the artist
p. 84 (top)

Untitled
2010
Graphite on paper
21 × 14¾ in. (53.3 × 37.5 cm)
Collection of the artist
p. 84 (bottom)

Untitled
2010
Graphite on paper
21 × 14¾ in. (53.3 × 37.5 cm)
Collection of the artist
p. 85

Untitled
2010
Ink, colored pencil, and acrylic on paper
11⅝ × 8¼ in. (29.5 × 21 cm)
Collection of the artist
p. 86

Untitled
2010
Graphite on paper
21 × 14¾ in. (53.3 × 37.5 cm)
Collection of the artist
p. 87

Untitled
2010
Ink on paper
11⅝ × 8¼ in. (29.5 × 21 cm)
Collection of the artist
p. 94

Untitled
2010
Colored pencil on paper
13 × 9½ in. (33 × 24 cm)
Collection of the artist
p. 178 (top left)

Untitled
2010
Colored pencil on paper
12 × 9 in. (30.5 × 23 cm)
Collection of the artist
p. 179 (top)

Untitled
2011
Colored pencil on paper
13 × 9½ in. (33 × 24 cm)
Collection of the artist
p. 38 (top right)

Untitled
2011
Graphite on paper
25⅝ × 19¾ in. (65 × 50 cm)
Collection of the artist
p. 93 (bottom)

Untitled
2011
Graphite on paper
25⅝ × 19¾ in. (65 × 50 cm)
Collection of the artist
p. 170

Untitled
2011
Graphite on paper
25⅝ × 19¾ in. (65 × 50 cm)
Collection of the artist
p. 171

Untitled
2011
Colored pencil on paper
14⅜ × 10¼ in. (36.5 × 26 cm)
Collection of the artist
p. 174 (top)

Untitled
2011
Colored pencil on paper
14⅜ × 10¼ in. (36.5 × 26 cm)
Collection of the artist
p. 174 (bottom)

Untitled
2011
Colored pencil on paper
14⅜ × 10¼ in. (36.5 × 26 cm)
Collection of the artist
p. 175 (top)

Untitled
2012
Colored pencil on paper
14⅜ × 10¼ in. (36.5 × 26 cm)
Collection of the artist
p. 37 (top left)

Untitled
2013
Colored pencil on paper
14⅜ × 10¼ in. (36.5 × 26 cm)
Collection of the artist
p. 36 (top right)

Untitled
2013
Colored pencil on paper
13 × 9½ in. (33 × 24 cm)
Collection of the artist
p. 37 (top right)

Untitled
2013
Colored pencil on paper
12 × 9 in. (30.5 × 22.7 cm)
Collection of the artist
p. 37 (bottom left)

Untitled
2013
Colored pencil on paper
10⅝ × 15 in. (27 × 38 cm)
Collection of the artist
p. 37 (bottom right)

Untitled
2013
Colored pencil on paper
9⅞ × 6⅞ in. (25 × 17.5 cm)
Collection of the artist
p. 38 (top left)

Untitled [after overpainting]
1987–97
Acrylic on paper and wood
35 × 24¾ × 3⅜ in. (89 × 63 × 8.5 cm)
Private collection
p. 29

Walk On I
1993
Acrylic on canvas
39⅜ × 29½ in. (100 × 75 cm)
Private collection
p. 23

West and East, Two Rabbits
1989
Colored pencil and pencil on paper
8 × 5⅝ in. (20.5 × 14.5 cm)
Aomori Museum of Art
p. 109

White Night
2006
Acrylic on canvas
64 × 51¼ in. (162.5 × 130 cm)
Collection of Leo Shih
p. 71

Willst du wirklich immer Hippie bleiben?
2006
Colored pencil on paper
16½ × 11⅝ in. (42 × 29.7 cm)
Collection of the artist
p. 198

Work for *Dream to Dream*
2001
Acrylic and colored pencil on paper
20⅜ × 14⅜ in. (51.7 × 36.5 cm)
Collection of the artist
p. 154

Work for *Dream to Dream*
2001
Acrylic and colored pencil on paper
18¾ × 14⅜ in. (47.7 × 36.6 cm)
Collection of the artist
p. 156

Work for *Dream to Dream*
2001
Colored pencil and ink on paper
15¾ × 11¾ in. (40 × 30 cm)
Collection of the artist
p. 167

Wounded
2014
Acrylic and collage on canvas
47¼ × 43⅜ in. (120 × 110 cm)
Collection of Dan Aloni, Los Angeles
p. 74

Wounded Cat in the Night
1993
Acrylic and colored pencil on paper
16½ × 21⅞ in. (41.8 × 55.6 cm)
Collection of the artist
p. 159 (bottom)

X Company
2010
Ink and colored pencil on paper
11⅝ × 8¼ in. (29.5 × 21 cm)
Collection of the artist
p. 83

Zero Fighter Plane, Dogfight
1989
Colored pencil, graphite, ink, and watercolor on paper
8 × 5⅝ in. (20.5 × 14.5 cm)
Aomori Museum of Art
p. 91

Lenders to the Exhibition

Dan Aloni
Aomori Museum of Art
Jack Black
Alaia Chen
Beth Rudin DeWoody
Frahm Collection
GALLERY MoMo, Japan
Hiroshima City Museum of Contemporary Art
Kadokawa Culture Promotion Foundation, Japan
Leeum, Samsung Museum of Art
Vicki and Kent Logan
The Museum of Contemporary Art, Los Angeles
Masayuki Nagase
Hiromichi Nakano
Yoshitomo Nara
National Gallery of Art, Washington, DC
The National Museum of Art, Osaka
The National Museum of Modern Art, Tokyo
Pace Gallery
Mr. Chen Pao-Ho
The Rachofsky Collection
Rubell Family Collection
Leo Shih
Takahashi Ryutaro Collection
Sally and Ralph Tawil
Yokohama Museum of Art
Andrew Xue
Chong Zhou

And those who wish to remain anonymous

Los Angeles County Museum of Art Board of Trustees, 2020

Rights Information

 Unless otherwise noted, all photos are provided courtesy of the artist. Works and photographs are reproduced courtesy of the creators and lenders of the materials depicted; the following images, keyed to page number, are those for which additional or separate credits are due.

Cover, clockwise from top left: photo by Yuki Morishima (D-CORD); photo by Keizo Kioku; photo courtesy of the artist; photo by Yoshitaka Uchida; photo by Keizo Kioku; photo by Keizo Kioku; photo by Norihiro Ueno; photo by Norihiro Ueno

Pp. 18, 19, 24, 30, 36 top left, 36 bottom left, 36 bottom right, 38 bottom left, 38 bottom right, 39 top left, 47 bottom, 73, 74, 75, 76, 77, 78, 79, 80, 98, 99, 100, 102, 103, 104, 105, 106, 107, 110, 111, 139, 164, 165, 175 bottom, 178 top right, 178 bottom, 179, 180 bottom, 184–85, 189, 190: photos by Keizo Kioku; pp. 20, 23, 25, 28, 42, 138, 146 top left, 159 bottom, 173: photos by Norihiro Ueno; pp. 21, 34 left, 35 top left, 39 bottom right, 41 top right, 41 bottom left, 41 bottom right, 44 top left, 46 bottom left, 47 top left, 47 top right, 67, 68, 71, 72, 153, 154, 155, 157, 158 top right, 166, 167, 168 bottom, 169 top left, 182, 183, 188, 205, 206: photos by Yoshitaka Uchida; pp. 22, 35 bottom left, 35 bottom right, 41 top left, 101, 132, 186, 195 bottom right, 196, 198, 199, 200 top right, 207: photos by Ikuhiro Watanabe; pp. 27, 90, 91, 92, 108, 109, 136–37, 204: photos courtesy of The Aomori Museum of Art; p. 29: photo by Nobuhiko Nuka; pp. 34 right, 40, 43 top right, 43 bottom right, 44 top right, 46 top right, 82, 83, 84, 85, 86, 87, 94, 152 bottom right, 162, 163 top left, 169 bottom right, 172 bottom right, 178 top left, 180 top, 194, 195 top left, 197, 200 bottom, 201, 202, 203: photos by Kei Okano; pp. 35 top right, 36 top right, 37, 38 top left, 38 top right, 133, 142: photos courtesy of the artist and Blum & Poe, Los Angeles/New York/Tokyo; pp. 43 top left, 43 bottom left, 44 bottom left, 44 bottom right, 46 top left, 46 bottom right, 156, 158 bottom left, 168 top, 174, 175 top: photos by Sam Kahn, courtesy of the artist and Blum & Poe, Los Angeles/New York/Tokyo; pp. 50–51, 52–53, 54–55, 56–57, 58–59, 60–61, 62–63, 64, 192: photos by Mie Morimoto; pp. 116 top, 117 top: artwork by Sarah Burnett, photos courtesy of *Bijutsu Techō*; pp. 116 upper middle, 116 lower middle, 117 upper middle, 117 lower middle: artwork by Joni Mitchell, photos courtesy of *Bijutsu Techō*; pp. 116 bottom, 117 bottom: photos by Jim Bogin, cover design by Milton Glaser, courtesy of *Bijutsu Techō*; pp. 118 top, 118 middle, 119 top: photos by Greg Gorman, cover design by John & Barbara Casado, courtesy of *Bijutsu Techō*; p. 118 bottom: artwork by Bob Cato, photo courtesy of *Bijutsu Techō*; p. 119 bottom: artwork by Milton Glaser, photo courtesy of *Bijutsu Techō*; pp. 120 top, 120 upper middle: artwork by Michael Hurley, photos courtesy of *Bijutsu Techō*; pp. 120 lower middle, 121 top: artwork by Phil Travers, photos courtesy of *Bijutsu Techō*; pp. 120 bottom, 121 bottom: artwork by Michael Trevithick, photos courtesy of *Bijutsu Techō*; pp. 122 top, 122 upper middle, 123 top, 123 upper middle: photos by Sanders Nicholson, courtesy of *Bijutsu Techō*; pp. 122 lower middle, 123 bottom: artwork by Annie, photos courtesy of *Bijutsu Techō*; p. 122 bottom: artwork by Shusei Nagaoka, photo courtesy of *Bijutsu Techō*; pp. 124 top, 125 top: photos by Marcus Keef, courtesy of Bijutsu Techō; pp. 124 bottom, 125 bottom: artwork by Abdul Mati Klarwein, photos courtesy of *Bijutsu Techō*; pp. 126, 127: artwork by Seiichi Hayashi, title lettering by Genpei Akasegawa, photos courtesy of *Bijutsu Techō*; pp. 130, 131, 140, 141, 143: photos by Heather Rasmussen, courtesy of the artist and Blum & Poe, Los Angeles/New York/Tokyo; p. 135: photo courtesy of Stephen Friedman Gallery, London; pp. 146 bottom right, 147, 148, 149, 150, 151, 152 top left: photos by Heather Rasmussen, courtesy of Pace Gallery and Blum & Poe, Los Angeles/New York/Tokyo; p. 172 top left: photo by Nobutada Omote, courtesy of the artist and Hyogo Prefectural Museum of Art; p. 187: photo by Yuki Morishima (D-CORD).

All text pp. 114–27 originally appeared in Japanese in *BT*. Yoshitomo Nara, "Jūdai no koro, boku wa rekōdo jaketto de bijutsu o mananda" [In My Teens, I Studied Art through Record Jackets], *BT*, January 2013–June 2015. Translations by Chisato Uno.

Acknowledgments

Yoshitomo Nara has been an absolute feat. Comprising one hundred major works made since 1984 and over seven hundred works on paper and pieces of ephemera, this is Nara's first major international retrospective and the largest exhibition dedicated to a single living Asian artist in LACMA's history. Nara's signature portraits possess the unique ability to capture a complexity of emotions that reflects the cultural psyche of his generation. The artist's inspiration from the world of 1960s and 70s folk and rock music filters throughout his practice. This show reconsiders Nara's practice within a global contemporary context.

It has been an honor to work with Yoshitomo Nara, who has guided the process with care and conviction. The exhibition has benefitted tremendously from the oversight and precision of Nara's assistant, Satoko Hamada. I am deeply indebted to Satoko, along with Nara's galleries, which were integral to the exhibition. At Blum & Poe, I thank Tim Blum and Jeff Poe, who have grown alongside Nara over the past twenty-five years, as well as Sam Kahn for his deft and detailed coordination, Marie Imai for translation and loan assistance in Japan, and Yusuke Nishimura for preparing models and manuals, and for installation assistance. At Pace, I thank Arne and Marc Glimcher, and especially Joseph Baptista and his assistant Hansi Liao for their critical support and guidance throughout. I am incredibly grateful to Melanie Lum for her vital support and enthusiasm from the earliest stages of the project.

At LACMA and on behalf of the artist, I thank Director and CEO Michael Govan for inviting me to curate this show, and for bringing the artist's practice into a global conversation within the context of LACMA's encyclopedic collection. I am utterly grateful to Rita Gonzalez and Christine Kim, curators of Contemporary Art, for their moral support throughout this process, and to Curatorial Assistant Meghan Doherty for her organizational expertise in managing the show's massive checklist with diligence and an affirmative spirit. From the beginning, I worked closely with Deputy Director for Curatorial and Planning Zoe Kahr and Exhibitions Manager Carolyn Oakes, who, together with Senior Assistant Registrar Elspeth Patient, handled the complex exhibition budget, worked out logistics, and coordinated the checklist with tour venues in Asia and Europe. I am indebted to their professionalism and guidance. I also thank Head Registrar Erika Franek and Maia November and Delfin Magpantay in Insurance and Risk Management for their tireless work during the indemnification process. Nara was intimately involved with the exhibition layout and I am grateful to Martin Sztyk and Victoria Behner in Exhibition Programs, who gracefully helped execute his vision. Thank you to Managing Editor Erica Wrightson for editing the exhibition texts. Head of Art Preparation and Installation Julia Latane was instrumental in working with engineers to install Nara's monumental twenty-six-foot outdoor sculpture, *Miss Forest*, on Wilshire Boulevard. During installation, on behalf of the artist, I also thank Kazumasa Aoki and Hiroshi Tachibana.

I had the wonderful pleasure of working with Publisher Lisa Gabrielle Mark on our third book together. This was the first time either of us had produced a record as part of a catalogue, and the album would not have been possible without Lisa's ability to navigate this new terrain with extreme foresight and a generous spirit. The album grew out of a longtime friendship between Nara and the members of Yo La Tengo—Ira Kaplan, Georgia Hubley, and James McNew—who recorded exquisite cover songs as well as a beautiful new song written for this album. In addition, they oversaw the mastering of the record; no one else could have captured the soul of Nara's practice in sound. Both the deluxe and trade editions of the catalogue were expertly designed by Brian Roettinger, whose intuitive talent in producing exceptional album and catalogue designs Nara trusted from the start. Editor Claire Crighton refined the texts with great precision as well as care for the artist's rich biographical information. Many thanks to the Rights and Reproductions team, especially Mike Tran, for his tireless work on image permissions and captions, and his diligent contact with record companies to obtain copyright licenses for the album. I am also grateful to the team at Abeism—Nagayuki Higuma, Hideto Yoshioka, and Misaki Funahashi—who worked closely with Nara's studio in Japan to compile image files to Nara's specifications. Deep gratitude to translator Chisato Uno for bringing Nara's voice to light.

Communications Manager Jessica Youn and Editor Chi-Young Kim promoted Nara's work with great strategy and enthusiasm, and Vice President of Education and Public Programs Naima Keith and Assistant Vice President of Education Consuelo Montoya worked to develop programming for a diverse audience. I thank LACMA's exceptional Development team for deftly managing exhibition supporters. Thanks to Tomas Garcia and Agnes Stauber in Web and Digital Media for creative innovative multimedia content, and to Grant Breding and Zandra Van Batenburg of the LACMA Store for dreaming up imaginative products. Many thanks to Director of Music Programs Mitch

Glickman for coordinating a spectacular opening event for the exhibition.

The exhibition benefitted greatly from the generous financial support of Zoltan and Tamara Varga, Andrew Xue, Blum & Poe, and Pace Gallery, as well as Sally and Ralph Tawil and the Japan Foundation. Numerous institutions, public collections, and private lenders lent their important works to the exhibition. I am particularly grateful to Shigemi Takahashi at the Aomori Museum of Art; Naoko Sumi at the Hiroshima City Museum of Contemporary Art; Jinyoung Oh at the Leeum, Samsung Museum of Art; Ayako Ogawa at the National Museum of Art, Osaka; Kenjirō Hosaka at the National Museum of Modern Art, Tokyo; Toshiharu Suzuki at the Toyota Municipal Museum of Art; and Kyoko Sakamoto at the Yokohama Museum of Art. Special thanks to Vicki and Kent Logan, Neal Benezra, and Gary Garrels at the San Francisco Museum of Modern Art for their enormous support in making a keystone work available for LACMA. Thanks also to GALLERY MoMo, Japan; the Kadokawa Culture Promotion Foundation, Japan; the National Gallery of Art, Washington, DC; the Museum of Contemporary Art, Los Angeles; Pace Gallery; and all the individual lenders who made this exhibition a reality, including Dan Aloni, Jack Black, Alaia Chen, Beth Rudin DeWoody, the Frahm Collection, Masayuki Nagase, Hiromichi Nakano, Mr. Chen Pao-Ho, the Rachofsky Collection, the Rubell Family Collection, Leo Shih, the Takahashi Ryutaro Collection, Sally and Ralph Tawil, Andrew Xue, Chong Zhou, and numerous private collections.

Finally, I wish to acknowledge our tour partners for the presentation of *Yoshitomo Nara* across the United States, Asia, and Europe: Budi Tek, who has been a vital partner for LACMA, and Wen Shi of the Yuz Museum Shanghai; Daniel Vega, Carolina Erdocia, and Lekha Hileman Waitoller of the Guggenheim Museum Bilbao; and Nathanja van Dijk and Eva van Diggelen of Kunsthal Rotterdam.

Mika Yoshitake
Exhibition curator

Published in conjunction with the exhibition *Yoshitomo Nara* at the Los Angeles County Museum of Art, Los Angeles, California (April 5, 2020–January 2, 2022)

This exhibition is organized by the Los Angeles County Museum of Art.

Major support is provided by Mr. Zoltan & Mrs. Tamara Varga, London; Andrew Xue, Singapore; Blum & Poe; and Pace Gallery.

Generous support is provided by Sally and Ralph Tawil and

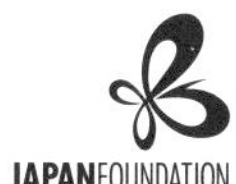

Exhibition Itinerary
LOS ANGELES COUNTY MUSEUM OF ART
April 5, 2020–January 2, 2022

NATIONAL TAIWAN MUSEUM OF ART
March–August 2022

YUZ MUSEUM SHANGHAI
September 2022–March 2023

Originally copublished in 2020 by
LOS ANGELES COUNTY MUSEUM OF ART
and
DELMONICO BOOKS • PRESTEL

Second edition published by
LOS ANGELES COUNTY MUSEUM OF ART
5905 Wilshire Boulevard
Los Angeles, California 90036
(323) 857-6000
lacma.org

Distributed by DELMONICO BOOKS
Available through ARTBOOK | D.A.P.
75 Broad Street, Suite 630
New York, NY 10004
delmonicobooks.com
artbook.com

Publisher: Lisa Gabrielle Mark
Editor: Claire Crighton
Rights and Reproductions: Mike Tran
Designer: Brian Roettinger (WP&A)

This book is typeset using Founders Grotesk and Korinna.

ISBN 978-1-63681-029-4

Library of Congress Control Number: 2021939011

Printed and bound in China

Front cover, clockwise from top left:
Miss Forest/Creamy Snow (detail), 2016
My Skull (detail), 2013
Princess of Snooze (detail), 2001
Muñoz's Babies (detail), 1995
In the Deepest Puddle II (detail), 1995
Hard Rain (detail), 2014
Do Not Disturb! (detail), 1996
People on the Cloud (detail), 1989

LOS ANGELES COUNTY MUSEUM OF ART